Peru's Indian Peoples and the Challenge of Spanish Conquest

Huamanga to 1640

STEVE J. STERN

The University of Wisconsin Press

Published 1982

The University of Wisconsin Press
114 North Murray Street
Madison, Wisconsin 53715

The University of Wisconsin Press, Ltd.
1 Gower Street
London WC1E 6HA, England

First printing

Printed in the United States of America

For LC CIP information see the colophon

ISBN 0-299-08900-2

Portions of chapter 2 appeared in altered form in
Hispanic American Historical Review, 61:3 (1981).

Publication of this book was made possible in part
by a grant from the Andrew W. Mellon foundation.

Dedicated

to the memory of my grandparents Israel and Judy Weisz,

and their children Nosenlipe, Leah, Moritz,
Ester, Joseph, Abraham,
Bordehay, and Rachel.

Contents

Illustrations

Figures and Maps

FIGURES

MAPS

Tables

Acknowledgments

Individual efforts are often best understood as parts of a broader, socially created product. This book is no exception, and it would be impossible to record completely the intellectual and personal networks of support and influence which contributed to the manuscript. For gracious access to rich archival materials, I am grateful to Srta. Graciela Sánchez Cerro, Dr. Guillermo Durand Flores, Sr. Mario Cárdenas, Srta. María Mendo Muñoz, Sr. Alfredo R. Alberdi Vallejo, and Sr. Juan Clímaco Zorrilla Aramburú. For hospitality, friendship, and shared experiences, I thank Don Moisés Ortega, Doña Emilia Contreras de Ortega, Sr. Juan Mateo, Sra. América Ortega de Mateo, Srtas. Paula and Claudia Mateo Ortega, Sra. Yolanda Kronberger, Sr. Carlos Límaco Barnett, Sra. Amanda Córdova Miranda, and Sra. Marcia Koth de Paredes. During the course of my research in Peru, I was fortunate to enjoy the social companionship and intellectual stimulus of Olinda Celestino, Marisol de la Cadena, Carlos DeGregori, Alberto Flores Galindo, Modesto Gálvez, Enrique González Carré, Patrique Husson, José Ignacio López Soria, Helen O'Brien, Juan O'Brien, Scarlett O'Phelan, Cristina Rossel, Ernesto Yepes, and Madeleine Zúñiga. Dr. Lorenzo Huertas Vallejos generously shared his commitment, experience, and intellectual curiosity. His example and friendship are unforgettable, and can never be thanked adequately.

Andean specialists owe an enormous intellectual debt to John V. Murra. I am grateful also for personal encouragement. Adel Stern and Egon Stern, my parents, had a special hand in shaping my view of the world and the questions I ask. My thanks to them, and to my wife's parents, Ignacia Mallon and Richard Mallon, are great indeed. This book originated in graduate school, where bonds of intellectual exchange and personal friendship sometimes intertwine themselves delightfully. I was fortunate to experience this with Steven Hahn, Rachel Klein, Rosario Pérez, and Barbara Weinstein. Each of them taught me a great deal. I benefitted, too, from an outstanding committee of critics and advisors. Richard Morse and Peter Winn have graciously encouraged my work, and have helped me to place it in historical perspective. Karen Spalding has been truly inspiring. She is not only an intellectual pioneer who has set challenging standards, but also a generous teacher, critic, and friend. Emília Viotti da Costa's insights, criticisms, and dedication to teaching have improved my work at every stage of its development. One cannot thank enough a teacher-scholar brimming with intellectual curiosity and excitement, and exceptionally giving of her time and energy. I owe heartfelt thanks to Florencia E. Mallon. Her honest criticism, formidable intellectual power, and generosity of spirit are a rare combination of qualities which I have been fortunate enough to experience firsthand. It is too bad, however, that she could not transmit by osmosis her literary flair.

My colleagues at Wisconsin, Thomas E. Skidmore and Peter H. Smith (now at M.I.T.), have been a source of personal encouragement and intellectual stimulation since we first met. My work also benefitted from interchanges with Heraclio Bonilla, John French, Brooke Larson, Rolando Mellafe, Franklin Pease, and Ann Wightman. Elizabeth Steinberg and Peter Givler of the University of Wisconsin Press, and my copy editor, Pericles Georges, have by their praise, criticism, and suggestions coaxed and cajoled me to sharpen the manuscript and bring it to completion. I thank them and two reviewers of the manuscript for their comments.

The manuscript could not have been completed without the material support of a number of people and institutions. I am grateful to the Danforth Foundation, Social Science Research Council and American Council of Learned Societies, and the Fulbright-Hays Training Fellowship Program for awards which made possible graduate study and dissertation research. I thank the staff of the Department of History of the University of Wisconsin-Madison, especially Betty Jo Newton and Katy Spohn, for typing the manuscript with skill and care. Gail Richman and Karyn Rotker helped me compile the lists of cited manuscripts and publications for the bibliography.

This book is dedicated to ten people, most of whom lost their lives at the hands of the Nazis. I never met them directly, yet they have touched my life deeply. Their memory is a reminder that to ignore the past experience of humankind is to engage in a form of amnesia that misunderstands the inheritance of the present, and harms the prospects of building a more just future.

Introduction

This book tells how conquest transformed vigorous native peoples of the Andean sierra into an inferior caste of "Indians" subordinated to Spanish colonizers and Europe's creation of a world market. Despite some pioneering work by historians and anthropologists, this story has not yet been told — least of all from the point of view of the experiences, achievements, and failures of the colonized Andean peoples.

In short, this book studies the creation of a new society — a colonial society — in the Andes during the century which followed Spanish conquest of the Inca Empire in 1532. To understand this process better, I have chosen to give it a regional focus, but one which keeps in mind the wider setting that conditions every region's history. Research on a regional level allowed me to view people, institutions, and trends in a much more concrete way. Just as important, a regional approach reflects a fundamental dynamic of Spanish colonization. The conquerors established a series of major cities as spearheads of control and expansion over their respective hinterlands. It was on regional and local levels that the confrontation of Europeans and Indians created a new kind of society in the Americas.

The region I selected in order to study this process was that controlled by the city of Huamanga (today Ayacucho), founded in 1539. All the classic socioeconomic trends — native population decline, the rise of commercial agriculture and cloth manufactures, the mining boom, etc. — conditioned the colonial development of Huamanga. The discovery of important mining centers (Huancavelica and Castrovirreyna) within the region facilitates a close look at relationships between mining and agricultural economies, and between urban commercial centers and rural hinterlands. Outbreaks of anti-European heresies among Huamanga's Indians left behind data which draws us closer to the thoughts of the Indians themselves. Because Huamanga was not the capital of the Inca Empire, its history speaks clearly about the experiences of local Andean societies — the peasantry — without distortions imposed by the special case of Cuzco's Inca elite. Finally, Huamanga spans a large enough geographical area (Map 1) to allow us to take

Note: Parinacochas and Andahuaylas formally belonged to the hinterland of the city of Cuzco, but were in certain respects oriented to Huamanga. Andahuaylas belonged to the Bishopric of Huamanga in the seventeenth century, and Parinacochas to the Intendancy of Huamanga in the eighteenth century. I will cite data or patterns from these peripheral provinces only when they accord with evidence from the core districts of Huamanga.

Map 1. The Huamanga region in greater Peru, c. 1600

into account significant local variations in colonial trends. For these reasons and others, Huamanga serves well as a region in which to study the principal dynamics behind the foundation of colonial Andean society.

Moreover, the Huamanga region enjoyed great importance throughout the period under study. In its first colonial years, it had strategic value as an area whose consolidation by Spanish colonizers could neutralize the military threat posed by Inca rebels northwest of Cuzco. Soon thereafter, Huamanga acquired vital economic importance. The region lay directly along the highland route linking Lima, Jauja, Cuzco, and Potosí (in Charcas, or modern Bolivia). Huamanga thus served as a zone of commercial passage between the two most important markets in Spanish South America: Lima, the capital city on the Pacific coast which controlled commercial connections to Europe, and Potosí, the fabulously wealthy city which sprang up following the discovery of an enormous silver vein in 1545, and whose population numbered some 150,000 by the year 1600. Furthermore, Huamanga was an important mining region in its own right. It included mercury and silver mines which gave rise to two urban centers, Huancavelica (1564) and Castrovirreyna (1591) respectively, in addition to the city of Huamanga. Mercury, in particular, was indispensable for the amalgamation of Potosí's silver ore from the 1570s on, and Spanish viceroys justifiably considered Huancavelica and Potosí to be the twin economic pillars sustaining the Peruvian viceroyalty. Huamanga's strategic commercial location, mercury and silver mines, and large Indian populations all constituted good reason to attract the attentions of colonizers, merchants, and officials.

By relating a history of oppression, I do not wish to limit myself to repeating a well-known story—namely, that Spanish colonizers abused and exploited the Indians. Nor do I pretend to write a definitive or "complete" history, in my view an impossible and ill-conceived undertaking, of the native peoples of Huamanga during the years 1532–1640. And although Spanish colonizers figure prominently in my discussion, I make even less claim to having written their history, a complicated and vast subject which merits, and has received, much attention in its own right.

Instead, I wish to focus more specifically on how the Indian peoples of Huamanga met the challenge of European conquest, and with what consequences for themselves, their colonizers, and the society that was created. By telling this story, I hope to achieve three interrelated purposes. First, I wish to document and to understand the struggles and achievements of Andean peoples in the face of their colonization. Second, I wish to demonstrate how their actions conditioned the evolution of colonial society and limited the options of the European ruling class. Even though the native peoples proved incapable of abolishing the oppressive structure as a whole, their resistance and creative adaptations challenged the colonials, forcing them to work out new modes of exploitation or else slide into decadence. Finally, I hope to use the colonial experience in Huamanga as a case study which can address key issues in the history of class societies. The European ruling class, despite moments of crisis and near-failure, succeeded in establishing an exploitative society which lasted for centuries. Studying their success in overcoming the many obstacles which recalcitrant natives threw in their path — and which "friendly" Indians helped them to remove — can help us to understand the forces which support or undermine a ruling class's attempt to consolidate its hegemony over society. Such an understanding may even deepen our insight into the manifold character of exploitation itself.

A guide to the chapters which follow may assist the reader. Chapter 1 introduces indigenous life in Huamanga before the Spanish conquest, within the context of a broader discussion reconstructing characteristically Andean institutions and relationships found in many highland cultures of central-south Peru and Bolivia. Chapter 2 explores the first cycle of Spanish-Indian relations in Huamanga; it focuses upon the conditions favoring alliances — or at least cooperation — between the region's native peoples and Spanish conquistadores, and upon the dynamics which led inexorably to a breakdown of Indian-white alliances. Chapter 3 documents the crisis of early colonial relationships, as manifested by the anti-Christian millenarian movement which swept Huamanga in the 1560s. The chapter culminates with Spanish responses to a general crisis of the Peruvian viceroyalty, including wholesale reforms implemented by Viceroy Francisco de Toledo in the 1570s.

Chapters 4–7 explore various social, economic, and political consequences of the reformed regime, and of Indian resistance and adaptation. On one level, these chapters may be viewed as different dimensions of a single process defining the entire 1570–1640 period. On another level, the chapter sequence corresponds to a chronological evolution. Chapter 4 explores the political economy of the colonial regime restructured during the 1570s. Chapter 5 documents a strategy of Indian resistance which assumed increasing importance by the 1600s: the adroit use of Spanish juridical institutions and devices to undermine exploitative practices. Chapter 6 discusses the changing character of colonial political economy, and of the labor system in particular, which sustained the seventeenth-century colonial regime. My argument, in part, is that new patterns of labor represented a European adaptation to crises and problems imposed by the Indian resistance described in Chapter 5. Chapter 7 analyzes the rise of a minority of "successful Indians," increasingly prominent by 1640, and studies the ways in which their achievements affected the changing internal structure and culture of native society, and provoked new forms of strife and conflict among Indians.

The sketches reproduced in Chapters 1–7 are taken from an extraordinary "letter," 1,200 pages in length, written to the King of Spain by a dissatisfied and acculturated Indian from southern Huamanga, Felipe Guaman Poma de Ayala. Poma de Ayala's description of pre-Columbian and colonial life, and his proposed reforms, constitute one of the most valuable indigenous sources available from colonial Peru. His revealing sketches are available in the published facsimile of his letter listed in the Bibliography. An important critical edition of his letter was published (by Siglo Veintiuno Editores) in Mexico in December 1980, too late to be consulted in the preparation of this book.

The concluding chapter of this book assesses the historical significance of a century of colonization in Huamanga. It identifies enduring legacies which, with modification, continue to shape life in "Indian" highland regions today. It proceeds to analyze the forces which sustained the hegemony of a colonial ruling class, and thereby rendered a wholesale assault by the native peasantry against the exploitative structure unrealistic by the seventeenth century. Finally, Chapter 8 examines the evolution of Huamanga's labor system as a product of ongoing social struggle and conflict. The specific patterns of labor exploitation used by colonials changed — under pressure, and in response to Indian adaptations and resistance. From this perspective, the native peoples of Huamanga were agents of their own history, even though they could not shape society according to their own dreams.

Peru's Indian Peoples and the
Challenge of Spanish Conquest

1

Pre-Columbian Landscapes

FROM HUAMANGA, the tapestry of reds and purples coloring the mountains to the north looks magnificent and inviting — as if someone had etched a spectacular sunset in rock.

Up close, however, to someone assigned the task of carving out a life or growing food, the jagged landscape of the high Andean sierra can turn cold and forbidding. Fifty-seven peaks climb over 5,400 meters (17,500 feet), and many mountain passes hang some three kilometers, or two miles, above sea level.[1] In Huamanga and other parts of the southern sierra, the rainy season (December to March) is short, and irrigation capacity limited. The rough, broken-up features of the landscape — the changing kaleidoscope of slopes and grades, the narrow river valleys and deep canyons cut by mountain streams, the hard rockiness of the earth itself — dominate almost everywhere except in some high *punas,* the cold plains where stretches of bunch grass (*ichu*) serve as pasturage. A patchwork of high and low intermontane valleys punctuates these high lands, gathering the headwaters for coastal streams rushing west and south, and for the Amazonian river system to the north and east. Towards the west of Castrovirreyna and Lucanas (see Map 1) one descends into the hot desert lands and river valleys of the Pacific coast; on the eastern slopes of Huanta, one heads down to the *montaña* region, the relatively warm and wet transition areas to tropical Amazonian rain forests.

This "vertical" landscape often incorporates a stunning variety of ecological microenvironments within a relatively small area. In almost any subregion of Huamanga, for example, one can walk from temperate agricultural fields up to cold puna pastures, or down to warm valleys or montaña, within a few days. Throughout the Andes, the traveller who climbs or descends

3

several hundred meters feels the change in temperature and climate, sees changing fauna and vegetation. Headed down, one will feel the chill in the air disappear, see the spread of cactus, or encounter an irrigated vegetable garden announcing entry into drier, hotter lands. On the way up, one returns to an undercurrent of chill, walks past potato fields, finally climbs to lonely springs and pastures, which are welcome homelands for tall, woolly llamas. Even at the same altitude a number of variables — angle of slope; degree of erosion; quality of soil cover; amount of sunshine, rainfall, and water run-off; irrigation possibilities; wind direction and intensity; frost frequency — create various environmental pockets, each with its own particular ecological configuration.[2]

Agriculture is risky. Half the time a disappointing rainy season threatens crops in all but the highly prized irrigated lands.[3] In high zones, the dry season brings violent daily fluctuations in temperature, which menace even the hardiest tubers and cereals with nightly frosts and daily thaws.[4]

Forbidding or bewildering as such an ecology may seem, Andean communities nevertheless worked out highly effective methods of exploiting their environment. Indeed, over the centuries, large economic surpluses produced by such methods sustained several great sierra civilizations. Let us see the relationships which indigenous peoples created amongst themselves and with nature to produce abundance and a characteristically Andean way of life.

THE ORGANIZATION OF MATERIAL LIFE

Self-sufficiency and community served as twin principles of material life. The first principle demanded that people scatter into dispersed patterns of settlement adapted to the ecological rigor and plurality of their environment. Economically, dispersal limited the effect of crop failures in particular environmental pockets, and provided access to a variety of ecological zones suited to producing different resources. Even small-scale social groups settled a series of economic "islands" designed to turn the variety of microenvironments to their advantage.[5] In addition to growing major foods such as potatoes and maize in its agricultural nucleus or core area (between the altitudes often of about 2,800 to 3,400 meters), a community normally sought to establish itself in (1) higher puna zones (about 3,700 to 4,600 meters) to pasture llamas and alpacas, and perhaps to hunt game or to extract salt, and (2) lower valleys and hot lands to produce coca leaf, *ají* (hot peppers), fruit, cotton, wood, perhaps more maize, and so forth. By sending out colonizers (*mitmaq*) from the core areas, or by conquering preexisting peoples in strategic ecological zones, communities incorporated into their domain a series of "outliers" whose natural conditions enabled them to cultivate coca, herd animals, mine salt, and so forth. Even in the core areas, agricultural and herding practices scattered communities into noncontiguous patterns of settlement.

Because households and communities defined economic viability — and beyond that, wealth — in terms of self-sufficiency, they went to great lengths to create such "archipelagos" of dispersed producers who exploited complementary ecological zones. The Yauyos and Chocorvos peoples, for example, who were settled in the high punas of Castrovirreyna, cultivated cotton fields in warmer valleys descending to the Pacific coast. Ethnic groups situated in the Río Pampas region of Vilcashuamán competed with other communities for warm coca lands in the northern reaches of Lucanas. The Soras people of eastern Lucanas reached out well over 100 kilometers to mine salt near Huamanga to the northwest, and to cultivate ají in hot coastal lands to the southwest.[6] By working as many different microenvironments as possible, these and other peoples limited their dependence upon barter with other communities or ethnic groups.

Within this context, households and kin groups tried to place within their reach the requisites for producing all the agricultural, animal, mineral, and manufactured products they needed. By combining agricultural, herding, and weaving activity within the household or more extended kindred, people minimized dependence upon specialized groups of laborers outside the kin group. True, some households, kin groups, or communities developed special skills as pot-makers and cup-makers, silversmiths, wool shearers, or herders. But at least in the small-scale societies scattered throughout Huamanga, the ongoing self-sufficiency of households held in check the development of a full-scale division of labor based upon such specialization. Artisans continued to work lands and herd animals; special herders charged with caring for the community's animals exercised claims to household fields and animals; laborers sent away to work in the coca fields later returned to look after their interests in the core area.[7] Despite a degree of stratification and specialization, households retained the right and the obligation to produce their subsistence foods, weave their own clothing, and the like.[8]

The impulse toward self-sufficiency implied direct control of scattered microenvironments. But how, in practical terms, could households mobilize access to dispersed lands and resources, and to the labor necessary to work them? Access to labor assistance from other households was, after all, the key to economic wellbeing in the labor-intensive Andean agricultural system. Without teamwork, how many rocky slopes could be cleared or terraced? How many potato and grain fields planted and harvested? Special ecological zones exploited? Without cooperative relationships, who would build and maintain the irrigation ditches? How reliably could one guard against unfair raids upon dispersed holdings?

Here is where the principle of community made self-sufficiency more practical. Kinship bonds defined people's identity in terms of larger "families" who were themselves component parts of a community or ethnic "family." These bonds of community among relatives tied together dispersed producers into a pattern of cooperation which provided self-sufficiency to everyone in the collective family. On the most intimate, household level, one addressed a large group of relatives as "brothers" and "sisters" (up to third cousins descended from a common great-great-grandfather, and living in various domestic units). The extended web of "household" relatives joined together with other such groups to make up a larger *ayllu,* the basic kin unit of Andean social structure. Formally, the ayllu was an endogamous lineage which claimed (for social purposes) descent from the same ancestor. Well into the seventeenth century, native peoples still viewed marriage outside their ayllu lineages as a special, exceptional event.[9] Nevertheless, the ayllu grouping was much more flexible in practice than in theory—simultaneously denoting larger and smaller kindreds (ayllus within ayllus), allowing for strategic exogamous marriages which might create new ayllus, and so forth.[10]

By depicting themselves as "brothers" descended from a mythical ancestor-god, ayllus extended the boundaries of the kin group to include a larger whole.[11] By uniting households into ayllus, incorporating these primary ayllus into more extended ayllu lineages, and forging the more extended ayllus into still more inclusive groupings of related peoples, kinship served as an idiom which defined the boundaries of a community, tribe, or ethnic group. (I shall use these words interchangeably, though "community" will usually imply a smaller-scale population, which may form part of a larger ethnic or tribal family.)

Within this overlapping network of kin relationships stretching back to include several ancestral generations, individuals and families found their identity and the means for survival.[12] The dispersed fields, pastures, waters, and animals at the disposal of Andean families belonged not to them as alienated property, but rather to the collective domain of their ayllus, communities, and ethnic groups. True, each household and ayllu within the community sought self-sufficiency and direct access to various microenvironments. But these units existed as dependencies of larger networks rather than as free, independent entities. It was by virtue of membership in a larger ayllu that a household exercised rights to lands, animals, and labor. Work for local and state authorities tended to be organized as communal tasks assigned to ayllus. Social mobility had a collective rather than individualized flavor.[13] The various kin groups, gods, and authorities who composed the larger society shared overlapping rights to a communal domain which none could truly expropriate. In 1578, when the Indian community of Motoy, in Huanta, was awarded 330 pesos as compensation for lost lands,

The importance of ancestors in Andean cultures. The deceased is washed and dressed in fine clothes, honored with a procession and feast, then deposited in a resting place such as a tomb or a cave. The annual calendar included further celebrations and offerings to the ancestors.

every single household or individual—down to orphans—held a right to the property. The community distributed the money to everyone according to a calculation of the unequal and overlapping rights enjoyed by all households and members to community property.[14]

Within this context, households and ayllus activated and reinforced community or ethnic bonds by engaging in reciprocal exchanges of labor among "relatives." Such exchanges provided energy to work resources, and knitted together dispersed producers into cooperative relationships. Wealth in Andean society came from access to labor based on building such a web of kinship and mutual obligation. The reciprocal exchange of services mobilized by kin groups *within* their ayllus became the ideal model extended outward to ties *between* ayllus of the larger community or ethnic group. Such an extension of cooperation allowed groups to reach farther outward for distant resources, and to engage in collective works such as irrigation, bridge-building, or terracing—in short, to increase the productive forces at their disposal. Equal exchange was the core principle governing local reciprocity. The "gifts" and exchanges which defined such relations were carefully calculated, with increasing precision and formality as labor claims moved from closer to more distant groups of relatives.[15] The term *ayni,* which serves as a root word for measured reciprocity in both Quechua and Aymara languages, captured the spirit behind labor relationships in community settings. In Quechua, *aynillmanta llamkakuni* meant "to work the same for another, as him for me."[16]

As a preferred labor relationship defining interchange among a community of relatives, ayni reciprocity encouraged a particular understanding of rights and obligations, of justice and vengeance. Native vocabulary shows that Andean peoples conceived of ideas such as justice, retribution, and wrongdoing in terms of balances or imbalances in the moral quality of one's relationships—judged by standards of reciprocal rights and obligations—with households, ayllus, authorities, supernatural powers, and so forth. An avenger, or *ayniycamayok,* was literally the caretaker of an ayni reciprocity relationship,[17] one who followed the principles of ayni by repaying harm in kind. The concept of *tincu* ("that which is just, that which is faultless, finished and complete")[18] tied justice to a concept of encounter between ideally equal, reciprocally paired entities. In sixteenth century Quechua, a tincu was the "junction or meeting of two things." One aspect of a tincu encounter was competition, an attempt to gain an edge on the other party. *Tincuni* signified joining together to fight; a *tincucmasiy* was "my opponent in festivals, in sport, in quarrels." The other aspect of tincu "meeting points," however, was that of cooperation, equality, adjustment. The modifier *tincuska* described "a thing suitably fitted, correct." *Tinqui* described "a pair of equal things, such as gloves, socks, shoes, ears, eyes." Items paired for a purpose were known as *tinquipura tinquintin*. The modifying particle *pura* indicated the ideal form of reciprocal pairing: "among one another, one with another, one and another, mutually."[19] The tincu concept of the "just" or "perfect" referred to the necessary pairing of distinct entities in ideally equivalent, but often conflictual, relationships to achieve a larger unity. As in the case of African societies organized on tribal "family" principles, Andean peoples conceived of justice in terms of the moral quality of relationships of mutual obligation, in terms of restoring "balance" or reconciling enemies.[20]

Andean communities, then, invoked reciprocity relations not only as a basic labor relationship allowing "relatives" to extend their economic reach, but also as a cultural value which shaped much of the community's social life. What we call "charity," for example, often took on the coloring of a reciprocal exchange. The community planted fields assigned to old and crippled people, but they in turn provided essential services as diviners, sorcerers, and curers.[21] Such practices, like the multiple references of Andean root words, expressed an ideal of reciprocally balanced interchange among co-proprietors of the communal domain.

STRATIFICATION, RIVALRY, CONFLICT

Reality, however, did not always conform to such ideals. As we shall see, the impulse towards self-sufficiency, the "tribal family" character of identity and property, and the reciprocal interchanges which governed cooperative work were all inseparable from dynamics of social stratification, rivalry, and power.

Reciprocity relations, for example, functioned not as an idyllic expression of unruffled harmony, but rather as a cultural institution manipulated by various groups in their social relations. The ayllu with fewer households, or with fewer kin ties which it could effectively translate into labor assistance, had to work longer and harder to complete its share of community labors.[22] Equal exchanges or contributions of labor-time did not imply that the parties involved were in fact equals. On the contrary, the dynamics of carefully measured reciprocity hinged on alliances between competitive and often unequal households and lineages who all aspired to self-sufficiency, wealth, and power. Competition and inequality imparted an onerous, "double-edged" character to reciprocity relations *within* stratified regional or local "families." Among the Huarochirí peoples northeast of Lima, for example, the Checa group was considered "younger brothers of the Quintes, and therefore hated the Quintes very much." Why did hostility plague relations between older and younger lineage "brothers"? Because the younger "sons" of the ancestor-gods Pariacaca and Tutayquiri were "sons hardly taken into account, and thus they gave them very little lands and few clothes."[23]

The extension of kinship and reciprocity networks which made possible a larger society, then, also generated structural conflicts between loyalty to one's ayllu or to one's closer "household" relatives, and the need for cooperation with competitive kindreds in wider community or ethnic settings capable of exploiting a broader range of resources.[24] Large and even small ayllus of the Lucanas and Soras peoples in the south of Huamanga preserved such a strong sense of separate identity and interest that they spoke differentiated local languages or dialects.[25] The very impulse towards autonomy and self-sufficiency, which made equal interchange among relatives the preferred means of economic cooperation, also gave birth to rivalries which marred relations among unequal households or ayllu "brothers." Small wonder that the Aymara verb for reciprocal labor exchange ("to work for others so that later they will work for him") also signified "to contradict, or argue among one another."[26]

Even the most primitive societies have leaders or authorities who look after the collective norms and interests of the group. In Andean society, from the division of the larger community or ethnic group into two related halves, to further subdivision into four or more large lineages or peoples, down to the proliferation of smaller, more intimate ayllus — at each level of social organization, and for the community as a whole, a *kuraka* lord symbolized the unity of identity and interest of "his" people. A kuraka — almost invariably a male — inherited his position by virtue of a close kin relationship to the previous lord.[27] Just as important, the local reciprocity relationships that governed interchange among the community's households and ayllus set cultural standards for judging the legitimate privileges and responsibilities of kuraka authority. Among other duties, the kuraka lord was expected to represent the group, defend its domain against intrusions by other ayllus or communities, redistribute rights to lands and enforce legitimate claims to resources, tend to the circulation and storage of goods in the core and outlying areas of the group's economic archipelago, organize work and ritual, and generously distribute a stream of "gifts." In turn, a high-level kuraka acquired special rights to labor services. In exchange for his stewardship of community norms and interests, "his" people (organized by ayllu) worked his fields, herded his animals, wove his cloth, and tended to household necessities such as water and wood.[28]

The exchange between chiefs and their "kin" had to appear more or less equivalent to enjoy legitimacy. The rituals of reciprocity expressed a calculated social transaction rather than an automatic institution — the chief had to "request" services from the ayllus in his domain.[29] A successful ethnic lord bound people to him through a "generous" style which redistributed surplus goods in the forms of "gifts" from personal and community stores. By consolidating successful bonds of mutual obligation with the ayllus in his domain, a major kuraka could expect not only seasonal help, in agriculture, by the community as a whole, but also rotations of *mit'a* workers for limited periods of duty, and perhaps even full-time *yana* retainers for lifelong duty.[30]

In the relationship between kuraka elite and laboring household or ayllu, we find a dynamic potentially at odds with the general absence of a division of labor or interest capable of splitting society into opposing classes. On the one hand, the ethnic lord symbolized the communitarian unity of his people. His prestige derived from his position as a caretaker or steward — not as owner or creator — of the community's property and norms. Through management of community activity and "generous" redistribution of accumulated surpluses, the chieftain earned legitimacy as the representative who embodied the collectivity and its interests. On the other hand, the "reciprocal" exchange between a major kuraka and his people no longer represented a truly measurable interchange of equal labor-time in production — the standard which governed reciprocity relations among households and ayllus. The beneficiary of a work party — whether a newlywed couple hosting a house-building project, or a kuraka sponsoring a communal harvest of the fields assigned him — sought to create a holiday mood, a larger sense of unity and celebration, by feasting the laborers with food and beer. Unlike the newlyweds, however, the kuraka could not be expected to reciprocate with productive labor in a similar setting later. A certain irony or "double edge" colors a relationship in which a chief who repeatedly demands labor does so in a context of "generosity," and those who serve him do so joyfully, amidst singing, dancing and feasting. The successful chief offered his people good management and a stream of "gifts" and hospitalities; they in turn reciprocated with their labors, and freed him from productive work in the fields.[31]

An astute lord of a large group could create a network of dependencies and mutual obligations which reinforced his privileged position as leader of the community. In Lucanas Andamarcas, some elites wore special headcloths to symbolize their differentiation as exceptional figures of the community.[32] The contradictory position of major elites as embodiments of the collective unity, who enjoyed privileged relationships to people and resources, created an incipient possibility of class division or exploitation based upon differentiated relationships to society's property or means of production. To the extent that native elites, or their primary household or ayllu relatives, acquired the capacity to stretch or convert principles of community kinship and reciprocity into a dominion based upon their organization of military, political, economic, and (as we shall see) religious power, social relationships took on a more seigneurial or authoritarian quality.[33] As the exchange of mutual services between elites and common households moved to the level of large-scale regional kingdoms and finally to the Inca State, "reciprocity" became less intimate, freer of kin ties, more directly hierarchical, and more vulnerable to sabotage or rebellion.[34]

But in the local and regional societies of Huamanga, such dynamics existed more as an incipient tendency than an accomplished pattern, as a seed whose flowering depended upon historical circumstances. A stronger tendency toward class relationships may have spread through Huamanga when expansive states or large-scale polities, such as the Wari Empire (c. 800) or the Chanka Confederacy (c. 1430), arose in the region.[35] But the Inca conquest (c. 1460?) limited the autonomy of local elites and converted independent communities or ethnic groups into subordinate peasantries whose surplus labors sustained the Inca Empire. Moreover, by transferring a series of foreign ethnic populations to the Río Pampas, Huanta, Angaraes, and other zones, the Incas furthered the division of local society into opposing communities rather than large-scale polities.[36]

In addition, fierce local attachments to closer household and ayllu relatives, and to formal reciprocities between ayllus, tended to fragment authority. Decentralization among competitive and self-sufficient kindreds further limited the development of class relations within local or regional society. Labor contracts between ethnic groups and Europeans in the first decades after the Spanish conquest required the joint approval of the heads of various ayllus to secure the cooperation of the community or ethnic groups. In such contracts, the overarching unity of the community was represented not in the will of one or two lords, but rather in the reciprocal relationships and agreements of a confederacy of lineages, each represented by its own chief(s).[37] On the lower levels of ayllu organization (and in a few areas for the community as a whole), the kuraka elites were merely working members of the community charged with special duties. Their obligation to represent and manage the larger interests of the kin group did not relieve them from cultivating crops or herding animals.[38]

In the local societies of Huamanga of the early 1500s, then, local and imperial (Inca) dynamics stifled the development of class contradictions between community elite and laboring household or ayllu. Exploitative dynamics centered upon the relationship between the Inca elite and bureaucracy on the one hand, and conquered communities on the other. Within the local setting, the heads of ayllus and larger communities continued to represent the communitarian unity of their peoples. Kuraka lords enhanced their status by improving the collective welfare of kin or ethnic groups in the face of rivalry with competing groups. Within local society, class dynamics reached at most an embryonic or primitive form.

As a result, conflict within local or regional society tended to express the contradictions of competing ethnic or kin groups rather than of opposed social classes. As we have seen, even within the bounds of a community or ethnic group, competition for self-sufficiency, wealth, and power created tension and disunity, divided ethnic families into richer and poorer households and ayllus. To such internal contradictions we must add the fierce conflicts of rival communities and ethnic groups for precious resources.[39] Throughout Huamanga, neighboring peoples preserved their ethnic differentiation, or separateness, from others by wearing uniquely patterned clothing, especially headdresses, and by speaking their own languages or dialects.[40] The quest of each group for an archipelago of productive pockets encouraged conflict by interspersing land holdings and settlements of different communities amongst one another. Moreover, in coveted outlying pockets where mitmaq colonizers mined salt, grew coca or ají, gathered fruit, and so forth, communities and ethnic groups confronted one another in a multiethnic setting where all groups maneuvered continually to improve their share of the ecological zone's resources. Here coexistence was precarious; sharing arrangements broke down into open confrontation.[41] Archaeological remains scattered throughout Lucanas and Andahuaylas confirm a history of local wars and struggles between rival communities and ethnic groups.[42]

The local mode of production, then, tended to divide producers into competing, self-sufficient groups with localized or decentralized senses of identity. Social contradiction and conflict tended to manifest itself in ethnic rather than class terms. Even when the global organization of society created class relationships, as in the case of the Inca Empire, class contradictions took on an ethnic overtone. An expansive foreign people, the Incas, converted previously independent peoples into an exploited peasantry. Conquest by foreign invaders, however, gave economic exploitation an ethnic cast — all the more so since the Incas transferred colonies of foreign peoples (mitmaq) to the region to secure their control. The object of liberation — a return to independent status, expulsion of the foreigners — reinforced communal or ethnic consciousness.

RELIGION AND SOCIETY

Andean households and ayllus enjoyed an especially rich religious and ritual life. The ancestral deities worshipped by Andean peoples permeated all aspects of life. Religious ideologies and relationships lent an external objectivity to the kin relationships of the community, in part because they endowed gods with the very dynamics of ethnic rivalry and reciprocal exchange which governed material life. We shall see, too, that the socioeconomic functions of religion went beyond its capacity to confirm the "natural," objective quality of local political economy. The power of the gods over material life was also an important source of social control which reinforced the privileges and authority of the community's political and religious elites. Finally, the performance of "religious" obligations by ayllu "brothers" created settings of cooperation which, by holding in check the destructive aspects of local rivalries, facilitated the productive tasks of the entire community.

Religious mythology and institutions provided an explanatory vision, an internally coherent world view capable of interpreting experience. When the larger collectivity of ayllu lineages came together each year to ask for rains, they knew that water was the gift bestowed upon them in exchange for their services to the appropriate god. If the rains did not come in spite of rituals and hopeful expectations, the disaster did not create a crisis of world view, or imply that the Andean knowledge system failed to explain the weather. Instead, the prolonged dry season signified that the community had failed to render proper homage to the thunder god, who was angry. And when the rains did come to rid the air of choking dust—such joy! Now the thunder god would shower life upon the earth cracked by drought; now ayllus could sow fields and plant crops! Whatever the meteorological episodes of the year, they were perfectly intelligible within the system of logical relationships known to local society.[43]

The Andean peoples' image of the cosmos seemed plausible, however, not simply because of its internal logic and explanatory power, but also on account of its consistency with known social relationships. The kin groups within a hierarchy of households and ayllus paid homage to parallel networks of *huacas,* sacred beings or powers materialized in hills, waters, caves, stones, ancestor mummies (*malquis*), and so forth.[44] As mythological founder-creators, huacas were ancestors in a social rather than strictly genealogical sense. The entire community or ethnic group worshipped a group of powerful major huacas, including the *pacarina* hills or waters venerated as mythological places of origin.[45] Among the major huacas were several whose prestige transcended the bounds of particular peoples, but the majority were specifically identified with local or regional families of peoples. Of the various lineages within the group, "every faction or ayllu has its principal huaca, and other less important ones." At every level of authority, ayllus and households preserved and worshipped the mummies of their ancestors, "whom they call children of the huacas." Households worshipped *conopa* objects, commonly stones. These household gods served as guardians of the family, its crops, and so forth.[46]

Andean peoples thereby projected their network of kin groups and lineages into a cosmological space which gave each kindred, and the larger community, a more external, multi-generational objectivity.[47] "Worship of the [huacas] is public and common to the entire province, pueblo, or ayllu, depending on the huaca, but the worship of the conopas is secret and particular to each household." The experience of Spanish *extirpadores* (Catholic priests charged with "extirpating" native religion) hints that the internal contradictions which marred community life also conditioned religious loyalties. Despite the greater prestige of major regional huacas, loyalties seemed to intensify as one descended to deities associated with the more intimate, lower-level kin groups. Extirpadores had erred, advised a veteran priest, by not burning the mummies of deceased ancestors, "whom [the Indians] esteem more than their huacas." Household conopas presented formidable problems, "for it has proven much easier to discover the celebrated huacas than the private ones that everybody has."[48]

Andean peoples not only created a network of ancestry relationships parallel to their own kinship relations, but also endowed supernatural relations with the dynamics of material life. Mythology expressed the realities of local struggle between rival ethnic groups striving for self-sufficiency and "vertical" expansion. According to the Huarochirí peoples, their ancestor-god Pariacaca had to throw out peoples from all parts of the region to clear the area for his "sons." One of Pariacaca's sons, also a local god, later defeated the peoples of the lower, hotter lands to augment the resources available to his seven ayllu "sons." Military struggle pitted against one another not only rival peoples, but also the huacas associated with them. Like other Andean peoples, the Incas offered sacrifices to their deities before engaging in military ventures, asking that the huacas of their enemies be weakened.[49]

Local mythologies projected the expectations and tensions of reciprocity exchange into relations with the gods. Consider, for example, a Huarochirí tale about Topa Inca Yupanqui, who led the Incas in the bulk of their conquests between 1463 and 1493. Topa Yupanqui, after much fighting, could not defeat one of his enemies. Asking himself why he served so many huacas with gold, silver, cloth, and food, he called the huacas to a meeting in the Cuzco plaza. There, the Inca sought to cash in on past generosity and services to the gods by formally requesting the huacas' assistance in a war which had consumed thousands of lives. Hearing only silence, he added a threat to burn all the possessions of the huacas he had once served unless they helped him. Finally, Macahuisa (son of Pariacaca) replied with a vow to go wherever Topa Yupanqui wished. Consummating their alliance, Macahuisa sent torrential rains in a campaign which finally destroyed the opposition. "From that time, they say, the Inca revered Pariacaca even more. He gave him fifty of his men of service and said: 'Father Macahuisa, what can I offer you?'"[50]

In ritual, the extension of reciprocity relationships into a supernatural realm of ancestor-deities found its living expression.[51] In major celebrations tied to harvests, fertility rites, and the like, the chief priest of the wider community supervised preparations. He gave notice to the kurakas and others to prepare *chicha* (corn beer), and collected the various offerings to the gods. On the appropriate day, priests and their helpers offered food, beer, cloth, and other gifts to a hierarchy of huacas and malquis. The gods' "children" sought material well-being—"life, health, and good fields"—in return. Nightfall brought the celebration of the *pacaricuc,* an all-night vigil of singing, dancing, storytelling, and fasting (abstention from sexual relations, and from eating salt and pepper).[52] A critical event of the festival — confession of misdeeds such as stealing, mistreatment, adultery, or neglect of deities — exposed its deeper meaning. The confessor, reported a Spanish extirpador, "tells them to reform, etc. They put the offering powders on a flat stone, and the Indian blows them. With a small rock that they call pasca, meaning pardon, . . . the confessor rubs the Indian's head and washes it with white corn meal and water in some arroyo, or where two rivers meet, which they call tincuna."[53] The meeting point of two streams, called *tincuna,* was the symbolic high point of the ceremony. The meaning of Andean ritual purification lay in the tincu concept of an encounter or "meeting point" which achieves unity, harmony, and justice through balancing or equalizing reciprocal relationships.[54] Ideally, ritual celebration restored equilibrium to reciprocal relations with gods perceived as ancestor relatives.

Reciprocity bonds thus not only energized social and economic relationships on the ground; they also powered a system of mutual rights and obligations which defined relationships with the ancestor-deities. These gods lived as personalities of the ethnic group's more comprehensive, cosmological community. As guardians or custodians of the community's welfare, major huacas joined the kurakas as claimants of special rights to land, animals, and labor. Local ayllus worked lands assigned to community shrines before sowing their own lands toward the end of the dry season.[55] Like the Inca Topa Yupanqui, households and ayllus who served and feasted the huacas expected to receive concrete services in return — abundant crops, good health, fertile herds, reliable rains, etc.[56] As in all reciprocity relations, loyalties depended upon the expectation of services from the other partner in the exchange. An entity unwilling or unable to fulfill such expectations faced the possibility of reprisal, or malign neglect. A shrewd Spanish observer urged extirpadores to burn or destroy huacas publicly to show up their impotence, "because the community pays little respect to a huaca once it is defeated."[57] From the other side, the huacas would neglect or take vengeance upon those who ignored their obligations to the gods. In general, Andean peoples interpreted disasters such as epidemics, poor crops, devastating storms or wars, as the work of offended or neglected deities.[58] Indians invoked confession to end illness, since "they think that they fall sick because their malquis, and the huacas, are angry."[59] In a fundamental sense, ill health warned of poorly functioning social relationships, whether with deities or with human contemporaries. "Your wife is an adulteress," related a Huarochirí myth. "And by her being so you have fallen sick."[60]

In view of the gods' impact on material welfare, religious institutions provided potent tools for privilege and social control in local society. Only fools would scoff at the need to maintain "balanced," "reciprocal" relationships with the gods. The authority of priests could not be dismissed lightly, for their specialized knowledge enabled them to control relations with supernatural powers. Customarily, people went to the priest-confessors of their ayllus to achieve a tincu purification before embarking on a long trip, or when suffering from illness.[61] As the "broker" for a major huaca, a *huacacamayoc* directed ritual required to enjoy the deity's good favor, and managed the considerable animal, land, and labor rights claimed by the god. Such priests enjoyed sufficient authority to "reprimand those who are neglectful in the worship and veneration of the huacas." "Consulted for everything" were a group of curers who directed sacrifices to the huacas or conopas of their clients.[62]

Relations of a group with high-level priests embodied a potential contradiction similar to the reciprocal exchange between major kuraka and household or ayllu. The priest, like the chief, offered and controlled essential management services needed by households or ayllus; they in turn labored the fields assigned to the priest on behalf of the deity, feasted the shrine with gifts and sacrifices, and so forth. In a deep sense, political and religious relationships interpenetrated one another in style and concept. The same Aymara word, *angu caura,* denoted a young llama offered to the gods or one cooked for visiting ethnic chiefs. Indians used the same blowing-kiss motion to express their reverence for political and supernatural lords.[63] In effect, the community priesthood sanctified local institutions by committing lineages to obligations and relationships with ancestor-gods comparable to those which prevailed in the "civil" social structure.[64]

As one might expect, historical evidence suggests strong ties between political and religious elites who together supervised society's relationships. A religious inspection of southern Huamanga several decades after Spanish conquest organized lists of huacas by kurakas and lesser lords.[65] Recruitment of priests generally proceeded within the limits set by preexisting relationships and authority. Priests, like the kurakas, inherited positions from parents or close relatives. But "when the inheritance method fails or whenever they choose, the other ministers, counseled by the kurakas . . . , pick someone whom they judge most fitting."[66] True, a person might acquire a priestly position — especially minor divining and curing offices — on his or her own initiative. But even in these cases, success in claiming rights as a priest depended upon one's acceptance by kinfolk or prestigious authorities.[67]

Aside from buttressing the authority of priests and local chiefs, religious practice played an important unifying role in local society. As we have seen, even within community or ethnic "families," the local mode of production tended to divide people into rival kindreds competing for resources. Nevertheless, cooperation among competitive rivals was necessary to protect and extend the economic reach of local society. A Huarochirí tale clearly states the problem. When the ancestor-god Pariacaca widened an irrigation ditch, the animals had to organize themselves to sweep the ditch. But all of them wanted to go first and supervise the project. The fox finally "won" and declared himself kuraka, but his tenure did not escape defiance from the fractious animals.[68] Ritual practice in the service of major gods forced households to submerge such antagonisms in cooperation for the larger tasks at hand. Otherwise, failure to perform obligations would endanger everyone by angering the neglected deity. Anthropological studies of African peoples have shown that one form of controlling antagonisms among conflictual partners is to ritualize hostility in the form of "friendly" teasing or taunts. In effect, certain rituals allow internal hostilities to express themselves, but in a format which affirms a higher, unifying principle. In Andean societies, ritual served such a function. It allowed lineage brothers to unleash their antagonisms, but imposed "friendly" or at least controlled formats such as taunting exchanges or sport-like competitions. In this way, and by directing necessary cooperation in the service of the gods, ritual practice tended to tame internal hostilities, to place competition in the service of the larger unity of the community. By masking hostilities in friendly, funny, or teasing guises, ritual practice ideally controlled internal contradictions in deference to a higher principle—that of cooperative fulfillment of mutual rights and obligations.[69]

The cooperative efforts demanded in ritual had economic importance because Andean societies, like many pre-capitalist societies, intertwined "economic" and "religious" activities. Many productive efforts (sowing fields, harvesting crops, cleaning irrigation ditches, etc.) which required cooperative labor among competitive or hostile kindreds took place within a ritual rubric.[70] Ritual cooperation in the fulfillment of common "religious" obligations simultaneously mobilized the community's network of "relatives" for the fulfillment of common productive efforts. Ritual, cooperative labor, wealth—these three went together in Andean society. The belief that relations with the gods affected material welfare, though it strengthened the authority of the community's elites, was nonetheless rooted in practical experience. As one folk comment put it, the *waranqa* (a group of about 1,000 units) which worked hard on the fields of the ancestor-god Macahuisa grew very rich and enjoyed numerous products.[71] By drawing together ayllu relatives in the adoration of common ancestors, by emphasizing the importance of "balanced" reciprocal relationships in all dimensions of life, and by mobilizing collective work efforts within a holiday context supervised by the community's lords, ritual practice performed indispensable services for the community's mode of production.

Planting maize fields in August. Note the complementarity of the sexes. Men and women worked as units breaking the earth and planting the seed. The sun and the moon, male and female deities respectively, both influenced agricultural welfare. The planting took place in a holiday atmosphere, as depicted by the dress of the men and by the woman on the right bringing *chicha* (beer).

INCA RULE

The analysis sketched until now may be thought of as a model of the dynamics of independent local or regional societies. We know, however, that the Incas conquered Huamanga around 1460 and converted communities and ethnic groups into a peasantry whose surplus labors sustained an expansive state. (By "peasantry," I mean subsistence-oriented agricultural producers or communities whose integration into a wider political structure subjects them to the authority and economic demands of the state, or of a landed class of overlords.) We must consider, therefore, to what extent the Incas distorted or transformed the internal dynamics of local production and social organization.

Inca conquest did not come easily. After Pachacuti Inca Yupanqui (1438–1471) managed to defeat the Chancas in Andahuaylas, he encountered fierce resistance among ethnic groups to the west. In the south of Huamanga, the Soras and Lucanas peoples were well organized, wealthy, and proudly independent. They held out in a regional fortress for more than two years against an Inca siege, until food warehouses emptied out. In the north of Huamanga, the Angaraes peoples fought just as desperately. "They were among the bravest and most stubborn peoples . . . , and thus they always embarrassed the Incas in continuous wars."[72]

To secure the Huamanga region, the Incas had to organize an impressive state apparatus. They peopled Huanta, Angaraes, and the Río Pampas with a series of foreign ethnic settlements, including groups of "Incas by privilege." Some mitmaq colonies settled to secure imperial hegemony received special privileges, such as access to prized coca fields, to enhance their loyalty and prestige. In addition to intensifying preexisting ethnic rivalry and fragmentation in these areas, the Incas established political and administrative control centers in Quinua and Huamanguilla. To the south, in Vilcashuamán, they headquartered the state's military, economic, and religious might. There, Inca rulers built a huge palace and sun temple, housed military garrisons, and constructed state warehouses to store coca, wool, dried meat, and other goods. The urban center and warehouses, laboring retainer populations, and nearby lands and herds dedicated to the state and its gods could support an urban population of at least 10,000.[73]

As shrewd statesmen, Pachacuti and his son Topa Inca Yupanqui (1471–1493) tried to operate within cultural idioms appreciated by all Andean peoples. The state, like major kurakas, used "generosity" to extend and reinforce obligations and loyalties. Ritual "gifts," especially cloth, created dependencies by obligating beneficiaries to reciprocate. Rather than destroy powerful regional huacas, the Incas tried to assimilate their prestige to the state. The Incas showered herds, lands, servants, and gifts upon pacarina and other pre-Incaic shrines, and had major ethnic gods carried to Cuzco in

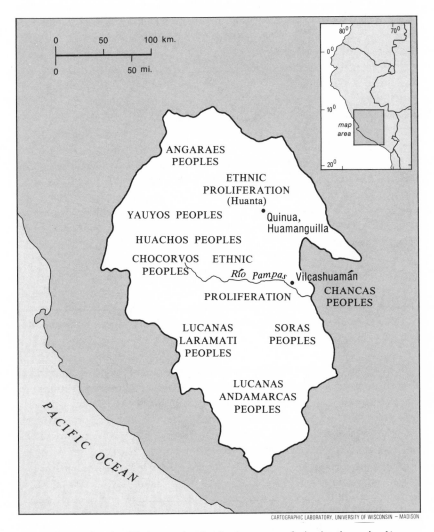

Note: This map is a simplified approximation for the purpose of orienting the reader. No zone was ethnically homogeneous, and the land claims of various groups were scattered and interspersed.

Map 2. Ethnic sketch map, centers of Inca control, c. 1500

litters as honored guests in royal festivals. By elevating the resources and prestige of selected gods under Inca auspices, the state hoped to place local gods in their service, to extend a network of loyalties and mutual obligations which would give imperial dominance a less forced character. In the final analysis, the state sought to present new relations as mere extensions of old ones. The state diligently followed the generosity rules of local reciprocity labor by feasting its work parties with food and beer, and by supplying the necessary raw materials and tools.[74]

And in truth, the state generally allowed pre-Incaic self-sufficiency and local modes of organizing social relations and production to continue in exchange for loyalty and labor services. Local ayllus and communities engaged in a long-run "exchange" of two major sets of rights and obligations defined by John V. Murra. For agricultural duty on lands assigned to the state and to its shrines, peasants retained rights to produce crops on their own ayllu lands for local use. The state could not demand a tribute in goods from community harvests or warehouses. In exchange for weaving cloth supplied from state herds and stores, ayllus reserved exclusive rights to the wool and cotton from their own herds and warehouses. Traditional relations of reciprocity among ayllu "brothers" continued to define the dynamics of local life and production. As a "redistributive" state, the Inca Empire absorbed surplus labor from a self-sufficient peasantry and dispensed the fruits of this labor to the royal population and its retainers, the army, peasants on corvée duty, strategic beneficiaries, and so forth, but without in general transforming local modes of production.[75]

Despite such continuities, however, conquest by the Incas represented a radical departure for many local societies. Lands carved out for the state, its shrines, and mitmaq colonies had once formed part of the domain of local groups, "who held them and hold them as resources of their own since their beginnings."[76] State policy worsened ethnic fragmentation, and simultaneously undercut communal or ethnic automony in the face of new competition. The state took over key management functions, such as protecting or expanding local resources against possible intrusions by other groups. Economic improvement or deterioration became linked to service for the state. Yauyos peoples situated north of Huamanga received pasture lands in the punas once dominated by the Chocorvos peoples of Castrovirreyna; rebellious Indians in Huancavelica lost coca fields to mitmaq sent by the Incas.[77] Obligations to work for the state and its gods cut the labor-time available to households and ayllus for their own use, thereby robbing them of potential energy and accumulation of surpluses. In addition, the state created a servant class of full-time retainers alienated from local ayllus and communities. (As late as 1532, however, the state still extracted the bulk of its revenues from the self-sufficient ayllus converted into peasantries rather than from the growing class of dependent retainers.)[78]

In short, the state left intact the community's internal relations of production, but harnessed them to a wider, exploitative economic formation. Local peoples proudly retained oral traditions of resistance against the invading Incas.[79] Despite the considerable skills of Inca statecraft, sources from Huamanga confirm that rebellion and social banditry marred imperial political stability.[80] Maintaining control over an expanding empire became costly. Repression of local groups required that the state feed armies, that it generously carve out new resources for loyal mitmaq colonies. Conciliatory strategies to avoid repression could be just as costly, if the state made concessions which limited the surplus it could extract. The fiercely proud Lucanas and Soras peoples, for example, were converted into "honored" carriers of Inca litters and communications exempted from the other labor services normally demanded of peasants.[81] The fragile loyalties enjoyed by the Incas, and the costs of maintaining them, indicated the limits of Inca attempts to mask prestations of labor as mere extensions of local relationships. In the final analysis, such prestations were based not on the intimate web of reciprocities among relatives which continued to govern communal production, but on the lordship of a conqueror who organized an imposing apparatus of state power.[82]

THE PRE-COLUMBIAN LEGACY

Inca domination left Huamanga a legacy of intensified ethnic fragmentation, anti-Inca politics and attitudes, and usurpation of resources and labor, but it did not really change the internal organization of local production. The decapitation of the Inca Empire in 1532 brought a panoramic resurgence of small-scale community and ethnic economies whose vitality drew on centuries of local tradition and experience. In a region whose total population was less than 200,000 it is doubtful that the largest ethnic groups exceeded a population of some 30,000 individuals, or 5,000–6,000 domestic units.[83]

Property, work, and identity all grew out of a subsoil of community and kinship. Though the household economy combined the agricultural, herding, and craft capacities needed to produce food, shelter, and clothing, no household could live unto itself. In the vertical Andean environment, households achieved self-sufficiency through efficient production in scattered ecological pockets, and this required cooperation within a wider framework. Indeed, a multigenerational landscape of ayllus and ancestor-gods, along with the mountains, waters, and property tied to them, preceded and presupposed the very existence of those born into this world. By belonging to this communal landscape of people, gods, and nature, one acquired an identity, an attachment to natural resources, a right to call upon the labor assistance of relatives, and a series of responsibilities. When the community assigned a household lands to work for its subsistence, the family did not have the option of letting the lands lie fallow. By planting the designated fields, the households fulfilled an obligation to the community.[84] An overlapping hierarchy of large and small ayllu lineages and major and minor chiefs made up a larger unity whose parts "treated and spoke with one another as brothers in meals and exchange."[85]

Reciprocity relationships in work and exchange went hand in hand with a pattern of community kinship within which all kindreds sought self-sufficiency. The principle of equal exchange or contributions of labor allowed the community's rival households and lineages to cooperate and to extend their economic reach despite competition, inequality, and friction. Historically, it has been theorized, in societies where autonomous tribes or producers complement their output by trading for certain goods, the original basis of barter has been the exchange of equivalent amounts of labor-time embodied in the commodities traded.[86] In local Andean society, kin groups aspiring to complete self-sufficiency tended to exchange labor-time itself, in production, rather than goods in a commercial transaction. As coproprietors of a collective domain, households and ayllus built a cooperative network of reciprocal exchange which committed them all to collective tasks, to production of diverse necessities in scattered ecological zones, and to effective circulation or redistribution of products among all contributing members of the community. Reciprocity among a community of producer-relatives constituted the central institution or relationship governing the production of material life in local society.

A society's fundamental relations of production tend to generate a particular kind of ethos, world view, and set of values.[87] In Andean society, the mutual obligations of reciprocally related "brothers" of the community pervaded local values and lifeways. As we have seen, Andean notions of justice or vengeance were closely related to a concept of "balanced" exchange among those paired together for a purpose, whatever the latent conflicts between them. Andean peoples understood and judged their relationships with themselves, their chiefs, and their ancestor-gods in these terms. Andean ideas of morality and wrongdoing expressed judgments about the quality of reciprocal relationships of mutual obligation, rather than adherence to abstract rules of behavior.

Community, self-sufficiency, and reciprocity did not create an idyllic life free of divisive dynamics or internal contradictions. On the contrary, the local mode of production tended to divide peoples into warring ayllus, communities, and ethnic groups. The division of local and regional landscapes

into autarkic communities of producers with distinctive ethnic identifications generated endemic struggles over lands and important outlier resources such as coca or salt. Even within the bounds of a community or ethnic group, distinct kindreds competed for self-sufficiency, prestige, and
wealth. Each lineage, though dependent for its existence and rights upon
membership in the larger tribal family, nevertheless retained a separate
sense of identity, interest, and aspiration. In effect, a decentralized social
structure of overlapping and competitive ayllu lineages — each with its own
political and religious authorities — imbued the larger communal unity with
dynamics of internal rivalry and friction. The dynamics of material life
within and between communities of related lineages and ayllus thus
spawned stratification, competition, and keen resentments.

In addition, relations between political and religious elites and their peoples created incipient possibilities of contradictions along class lines. Local
chiefs embodied and managed the communitarian unity and interest of
their ayllus and communities. Their authority, prestige, and access to resources rested in part upon kinfolk's perceptions of their worthiness as
protectors of local norms and interests. In exchange for such management
services, however, major lords built networks of economic privilege and obligation. Whatever the ideology of community and reciprocity which sanctioned such relationships, they nevertheless differentiated elites from the
mass of laboring households, ayllus, and minor lords. By dominating essential services and "generously" redistributing prized goods and necessities,
major kurakas and priests emancipated themselves from labor in production
and held distinctive relationships to people, labor, and resources. What is
important for our purposes, however, is that in Huamanga's small-scale societies, ayllu bonds confined class contradictions to an incipient, or latent
level. Decentralization, self-sufficiency, the presence of brothers, sons, or
cousins eager to replace discredited incumbent kurakas[88] — all made it difficult for elites to emancipate themselves from communal norms and sanc-
tions. Indeed, community decisions tended to take the form of a consensus
reached among a family of lineages, each represented by a lord whose authority rested upon his ability to look after his people's interests. Except under more favorable historical conjunctures, the seed of class dynamics could
not develop beyond a most primitive state.

Religious life and institutions served multiple functions in Andean society. Native religion transformed dynamics particular to Andean history and
culture into "natural" relationships inherent to the universe. A chain of
ancestor-gods related to the community's ayllus and households gave contemporary kin relationships and lineage structures a more time-honored objectivity. By filling their mythologies of ancestor-gods with the dynamics of
ethnic rivalry and reciprocal exchange of services, Andean peoples gave the

relationships which characterized their lives on earth more cosmic proportions. The ideological function of religion was related to a political one. Andean peoples believed that their gods affected the material fortunes of the
living, and conceived of their relationships with huacas as a necessary exchange of reciprocal services. In practice, such ideologies and institutions
offered elites a means of social control and sanctioned political relationships
by committing ayllus and households to analogous relationships with the
ancestor-gods.

Finally, religious practices performed a vital economic function which
lent a measure of truth to the idea that relations with gods affected the everyday welfare of their peoples. The performance of "religious" obligations by
ayllu "brothers" often drew them together for cooperative productive tasks
in a holiday atmosphere. By mobilizing such productive gatherings and
holding in check rivalries and disunities, religious institutions revitalized relations of kinship and reciprocity which sustained the community's economy. Small wonder the Andean belief, then, that "if they skip [ceremonial
obligations], . . . they become sterile."[89]

2

Rise and Demise
of the Post-Incaic Alliances

EASY CONQUESTS create false mystiques. Many of our contemporaries, for example, will recall the Nazi Blitzkrieg of Europe; the lightning attacks shocked the world with a terrifying vision of Fascist invincibility. Reality usually sets in, however, and the mystique begins to crumble. When the Nazis floundered on the Russian front, they lost their superhuman proportions. Four and a half centuries ago, in 1532, the 168 conquistadores who swiftly defeated and captured the Inca Emperor Atahualpa surely impressed the Andean peoples with their power and good fortune. We need not assume ingenuous interpretations of foreigners as gods to appreciate the aura of invincibility that accrued to a band of outsiders who had outmaneuvered the head of an empire stretching across thousands of miles — and the Andean peoples' willingness to accommodate them. But the aura could fade, particularly if the Spaniards tried to make the transition from simple plunder to territorial occupation and, finally, to imperial rule. Having captured the Inca Empire, the Europeans would have to learn how to govern it.

The Europeans, riding the crest of Spain's explosive search for gold, territory, and Catholic salvation, wanted riches and lordship. After the distribution of the precious metals brought to Cajamarca to ransom the Inca Atahualpa, Francisco Pizarro and his fellow conquistadores set out towards the south to subjugate, plunder, and rule over an Andean colony. The looting of prestigious shrines and the European thirst for precious metals created the folk legend that Spaniards ate gold and silver instead of food![1] Pizarro distributed *encomiendas* of Indian peoples to his conquistador allies. The *encomendero* lord was charged with serving the Crown's military and political needs in the colony, and with tending to the material and spiritual wellbeing of the Indian pagans "entrusted" to his care. In exchange, he was free to

27

command tribute and labor from his wards. As the personal representative of the Crown in the field, the encomendero could use lordship over "his" people to enrich himself, but he also carried the burden of forging colonial relationships with the new Indian subjects.[2]

Military security quickly became a top priority. The puppet Inca emperor, Manco Inca, soured on his European friends and escaped to the montaña northwest of Cuzco in 1536. From his hidden jungle fortress, Manco Inca organized raids that disrupted European commercial routes and harassed Indian societies allied to the Europeans. The resistance of the "Neo-Inca State" became so troublesome that Pizarro resolved to consolidate European control and expansion on the highland route between Lima and Cuzco. The few Europeans who had set up a frontier town in the Huamanga area, at Quinua (see Map 2), held out precariously against Manco Inca and the local groups who supported the Inca cause. Pizarro sent Vasco de Guevara, a veteran of Nicaragua and Chile, and twenty-five Spaniards to the area in 1539, hoping to establish the Europeans more firmly in the region of Huamanga.[3]

For the more than twenty encomenderos centered in the area, the problem of military security was ever present in the early years. Several were veterans of Manco Inca's terrifying assault and siege of Cuzco in 1536–37. Under Vasco de Guevara, the Spaniards decided in 1540 to move south from Quinua to a more defensible site. This was to become the colonial city of Huamanga (whose official title, "City of San Juan de la Frontera de Huamanga," and status as a city were finally issued in 1544).[4] Huamanga overlooked a strategic area west of the neo-Incas, and the conquistadores repeatedly sought to stabilize a European population in the new city to counter the threat of neo-Inca raids and local rebellions.[5] Those who settled in Huamanga saw the local Indian societies they hoped to rule as a source of labor and plunder. Spanish society demanded Indian labor and tribute for the most basic necessities: food; transport of water, wood, and merchandise; construction of houses and public works such as churches, roads, and bridges.[6] Just as important as these exactions, however, was the Spaniards' need to cultivate the loyalty of local Indian societies to defend the European presence against Inca encroachments. The *cabildo,* a municipal council controlled by the European encomendero elite, sought to curb abuses of the natives in 1541 because it "would give the Indians reason to turn against us, killing Spaniards as they used to do."[7]

THE RISE OF UNEASY ALLIANCES

Fortunately for the conquistadores, local Andean societies had good reason to ally themselves with European conquest. The military prowess of the Spaniards, skilled masters of horse and sword, impressed the kurakas who

A presumed meeting of Indian and Spaniard in Cuzco. The native asks what Spaniards eat;
the answer, Poma de Ayala states, is gold and silver. Despite the ominous implications, the
initial encounter is amicable.

accompanied Atahualpa in Cajamarca in 1532. Peasant societies, to survive, are notoriously sensitive to changes in power balances, and the Lucanas peoples of Andamarcas and Laramati quickly recognized the Spaniards as new masters. The kurakas of the Lucanas Laramati peoples proclaimed themselves "friends of the Spaniards" when the victorious entourage passed through Vilcashuamán en route to its historic entry into Cuzco. Once the Spaniards defeated local rebel forces and the Inca siege of Cuzco, such proclamations acquired additional credibility.[8] Besides having a healthy respect for Spanish military skills, local societies of Huamanga saw positive benefits in an alliance with the Europeans. They could finally break the yoke of Inca rule, and advance ethnic interests in a new, post-Incaic era. Some of the mitmaq populations settled in northern Huamanga by the Incas returned to their home communities, and left behind a life as foreigners amidst resentful local populations. The Europeans were not the only people who plundered the Andean sierra in the early years. Local communities sacked warehouses once dedicated to the discredited Incas and major huacas associated with the state. A mushrooming population of *yanaconas,* individuals who left ayllu society to become dependent retainers of the Europeans, joined their masters in the hunt for precious metals.[9]

Within these circumstances, and despite tenuous loyalties and occasional conflicts between Europeans and their native allies, the conquistadores got the help they needed. Early in 1541, Indians from northeast Huanta, who had suffered the brunt of Manco Inca's assaults, came to Huamanga to warn of the Inca's plans to overrun the new Spanish city. The cabildo sent Francisco de Cárdenas to lead an expedition of twenty Spaniards and "two thousand Indian friends" to stop the attack and "to protect the natives."[10] Through the early 1550s, the continual turbulence of civil war among the Spaniards[11] and fights with the neo-Incas put local societies and their kurakas on the spot. Amidst the claims all sides were making for logistic and military support, native peoples could not choose neutrality. They had to decide what kind of alliance — given the balance of forces in their area — would most benefit their own ethnic or communal interests. Robbed of the option of neutrality, local societies participated heavily in the early wars, which "[left] the Indians destroyed." While some Indians of Huamanga joined forces with the neo-Incas, most groups — even Incas settled in Huamanga — fought for the Spanish Crown. The strategic highway connecting Lima, Jauja, Huamanga, and Cuzco threw the burden of fighting upon the societies of the northern districts through which it passed: Huanta, Vilcashuamán, and Andahuaylas. In addition, Huanta and Andahuaylas bordered on the area controlled by the neo-Incas. A kuraka "guarding a pass out of fear of the Inca" sent urgent notice in 1544 that Manco Inca, with the help of dissident Spaniards, was planning an attack that threatened the encomienda Indians of Pedro Díaz de Rojas. Even societies far to the south did not escape involvement. When Francisco Hernández Girón rebelled against the Crown in the early 1550s, he raided the rich herds of the Soras and Lucanas people for supplies. The raids provoked Indian elites into supporting the royal campaign.[12]

The encomenderos knew that they needed favorable working relationships with "their" kurakas; the shrewdest sought to cement alliances with favors and gifts. Encomenderos and other Spaniards frequently came before the cabildo in Huamanga's first decade to ask for land grants (*mercedes*) for ranches (*estancias*) or farms. Intelligent encomenderos got the cabildo to grant mercedes to their kurakas as well. The kurakas of Juan de Berrio received ten *fanegadas* (about twenty-nine hectares) in the fertile valley of Viñaca west of Huamanga; one kuraka sponsored by Berrio received title to twenty fanegadas. Francisco de Balboa asked the cabildo to grant sixteen fanegadas to his chief kuraka (*kuraka principal*) in the rich Chupas plains south of Huamanga.[13] These lands were fertile plums near the city of Huamanga. Some had once been claimed by the Inca State, its shrines, or by Inca mitmaq. Now they were targets of European claims, but astute encomenderos saved or carved out a share for their kurakas. Diego Gavilán claimed twenty fanegadas for himself in the Chigua Valley, and then had the cabildo grant the rest of the valley to his kuraka.[14] One of the most successful encomenderos, Diego Maldonado, showered gifts upon the kurakas of his Andahuaylas encomienda. The native elite received a black slave, mules, horses, livestock, and fine Inca and Spanish cloths. In a later dispute, a kuraka pointed out that such gifts were given "because [Maldonado] owed it to them for the services they would render him."[15]

Communities and ethnic groups hoped that alliance with Europeans would help them gain the upper hand in their own native rivalries. As we have seen, the local mode of production tended to divide native peoples into self-sufficient groups who competed with rival ayllus, communities, and ethnic groups for prized resources. Unfettered by Inca control, native societies now sought to use relations with powerful Europeans to protect or advance ethnic interests. In 1557, for example, the Lucanas Laramati peoples complained that neighboring groups were intruding upon valuable hunting lands. With the help of their encomendero, Pedro de Avendaño, secretary of the viceroy and a resident of Lima, they obtained a viceregal ban on hunting directed against the Lucanas Andamarcas, Yauyos, Huancas, Parinacochas, and coastal peoples who surrounded the core settlement area of the Lucanas Laramati.[16] The Chancas of Andahuaylas, traditionally bitter rivals of the Incas, used European power against their enemies. When the neo-Incas kidnapped the Chanca guardians of coca fields in Mayomarca (between Huanta and Andahuaylas), ethnic groups from Huamanga

Soras and Lucanas Indians fight for the Spanish Crown against the rebel Francisco Hernández Girón.

threatened to take over this rich outlier. The Chancas solved their difficulty by persuading their encomendero to lead an expedition to Mayomarca which secured their control.[17] Collaboration with Europeans, despite the tolls of war, tribute, and labor, brought its advantages.

A closer look at the Chancas of Andahuaylas shows how intelligent encomenderos cultivated working relationships with native elites and societies. Diego Maldonado, one of the richest and most successful encomenderos, preferred to negotiate agreements with the kurakas rather than resort to brute force. Through one such agreement, Maldonado got some natives who had lived in distant valleys and punas to resettle in a valley nearer the royal highway of Cuzco. Maldonado avoided usurping treasured Chanca resources. Instead he carved out lands and herds for his *hacienda,* or rural estate, from the vast holdings once dedicated to the Inca state and its cults. In the beginning, at least, Maldonado settled personal yanaconas on his lands rather than demand encomienda labor. When Indians complained that his expansive herds damaged their crops, he (or his administrator) inspected the claims and distributed corn, potatoes, ají, and other products as compensation. Maldonado negotiated agreements with the kurakas specifying the tribute obligations of his encomienda; he preferred agreements to unsystematized plunder, and in a sense integrated himself into native society as a generous, "redistributive" patron. Maldonado's son later exaggerated that his father's gifts were responsible for the kurakas' impressive wealth. Maldonado customarily set aside a third of the tribute in foodstuffs for redistribution, and in lean agricultural years donated food and relieved his encomienda of various tribute obligations. He contributed the labor of slaves and yanaconas to the construction of an *obraje* (primitive textile factory) jointly owned by his Indians and a Spanish entrepreneur, and gave away European novelties such as scissors and glass cups. In his will, Maldonado donated thousands of cattle to his Indians. During his lifetime, the conquistador sometimes acted as if he were a shrewd ethnographer applying Andean rules of "generosity" to create dependencies and "reciprocal" exchange obligations. Indian workers on his fields received, besides the customary payments, "gifts" of corn, coca, salt, ají, meat, sheep, and wool. During the twenty-two day harvest of coca leaves, Maldonado would regale workers with eight baskets of coca.[18]

Alliance did not, of course, imply that life was free of conflict or abuse. Behind the negotiations, often, lay violence and a struggle for power. At one point Indians killed an African slave of Maldonado, and the encomendero sometimes jailed the Chanca elites. In 1542, a group of Angaraes Indians rose up and killed their first encomendero, Martín de Escarcena. A record of fines collected by Huamanga officials from 1559 on documents the violent episodes which marred many relationships. In 1561, Gonzalo Pérez stormed into an Indian crowd on horseback and trampled a woman. The incident was only one example of the personal abuses which subjected Indians to whipping, looting, and rape by Spaniards, blacks, *mestizos* (descendants of mixed Indian-white parentage), and mulattoes.[19] In addition, labor conditions could be crude and harsh. Construction of Huamanga at its original site cost the lives of Indian workers. As conquering lords who aspired to commandeer the labor-power of their subjects, encomenderos and masters of yanaconas tended, where possible, to treat their wards as personal property.[20] For the native workers they controlled, such a relationship imposed harsh demands. A lively business flourished around the rental of Indian workers, or sale of Indian subjects.[21] Rental of Indian labor-power encouraged its exploiters, like some conquistadores bent upon returning to Spain after a few years of plunder, to ignore the long-run survival of workers. The buyer of Indians who sought to squeeze out the most work in a short time period, as one observer put it, "enters like a hungry wolf."[22]

These abuses should not blind us, however, to facts that were obvious to the native peoples themselves. The disparate, often rival groups had to come to grips with the Spanish presence in some way, particularly if they lived near the city of Huamanga, in militarily strategic zones, or along the commercial route which connected Lima, Huamanga, and Cuzco. Cooperation or alliance with the conquerors of the Incas offered at least the possibility of protection against extreme violence. Significantly, the majority of fines collected for personal abuse of Indians came not from members of Huamanga's small circle of elite families, but from lesser Spanish, mixed-blood, and native residents. If alliance did not create an idyllic era, it nonetheless offered the advantages sketched above: continued freedom from Inca (or neo-Inca) rule and labor demands, special privileges for the kuraka friends of the conquistadores, and valuable help in the endemic rivalries or fights among local communities and ethnic groups.

Early relations, then, between the Andean native peoples and the Europeans displayed an uneasy mixture of force, negotiation, and alliance. The parties to the post-Incaic alliances probed one another for weaknesses or vulnerabilities, testing the limits of the new relationships. In the early years, each encomendero — accompanied by soldiers if necessary — "asked his cacique [kuraka] for what he thought necessary, and [the chief] bargained about what he could give." Ill treatment and extortion varied "according to the care and greed of each [encomendero], and the skill which he had with his Indians."[23] Sheer ignorance of the resources available to local societies handicapped the conquistadores. The first inspection of the Huamanga region, in 1549, turned up only 12,179 native males between the ages of fifteen and fifty; several years later, when population should have declined, Damián de la Bandera counted 21,771 tributaries. Despite his considerable skills and knowledge, Bandera had little choice but to rely on kurakas for much of his information.[24] Felipe Guaman Poma de Ayala wrote a scathing indictment of the European colonials around 1600; but, significantly, this bitter Indian critic from Huamanga praised the first generation of encomenderos. The conquistadores, he wrote, "used to sit down to eat and gave all the clothes and textiles the [Indian] notables wanted, and if the crops froze or were lost they pardoned the poor Indians [of their tribute]." Francisco de Cárdenas, who had led 2,000 Indians against the neo-Incas in 1541, left his Indians thousands of sheep on their punas in Chocorvos (Castrovirreyna) and Vilcashuamán. Don Pedro de Córdova, said Poma de Ayala, helped protect his Lucanas Laramati peoples from abusive priests and officials.[25] The Lucanas Laramati, who had always sought to be "friends of the Spaniards," granted Córdova a huge ranching estate "for the many releases of taxes and tributes which, as encomendero, he made and pardoned them."[26] The parties of the post-Incaic alliances understood very well that, in a real sense, they needed one another.

THE EARLY COMMERCIAL ECONOMY

By securing cooperative relations with native elites and societies, an aspiring ruling class of encomenderos laid the foundation for a colonial economy and society in Huamanga. By the 1550s, a *corregidor* (chief magistrate of a district) and other appointed officials began to assume responsibility for many judicial and administrative tasks. The colonial state, centered in Lima, thereby began to intervene in a restricted way to limit the regional autonomy of Huamanga's leading families. Colonial officials, however, tended to enter into alliances with powerful local figures, and in the early years, the cabildo, dominated by encomenderos, had moved quickly to establish rules and guidelines for a colonial society. In the central plaza, officials set up a public whipping stock for the ritualized performance of justice. The municipal council limited the price of corn, contracted bread supplies for the new city, regulated weights and measures, and tried to cut down on cheating in bread and coca leaf sales. The cabildo oversaw public works, including road repair. As the political organ of Huamanga's elite, the cabildo interested itself in stopping abuses which might harm the city's future. Deforestation by Spaniards, blacks, yanaconas, and encomienda Indians threatened to strip Huamanga's landscape. In 1543, the cabildo banned the cutting of certain trees within two or three kilometers (a half league) of the city.[27]

Perhaps most important, the cabildo took on the task of assigning *solares* (town lots) for homes, shops, gardens, and small farms,[28] and of granting mercedes for farm and pasture lands. Between 1540 and 1543, the cabildo granted forty-two mercedes for estancias (grazing sites) and farm lands to twenty residents.[29] In 1546 the city appropriated common lands "that are around this town that are neither worked nor populated by Indians." Some eighteen notables of Huamanga received an average of eighty hectares (nearly twenty-eight fanegadas) each.[30] Twelve years later, the cabildo distributed thousands of hectares in the irrigated Chaquibamba plains to over sixty "citizens" (*vecinos,* usually encomenderos) and other residents.[31]

Leading citizens wanted lands and pastures to make a profit from commercial opportunities. Encomienda tributes already supplied the cities with food, cloth, artisan products, and precious metals.[32] An encomendero who owned a fine home in the city and lorded over a rural encomienda had little reason to yearn for a huge estate to satisfy status pretensions. Commercial agriculture, however, offered lucrative possibilities. The capital city of Lima, the former Inca capital of Cuzco, and the booming silver mines of Potosí (in Charcas) created markets for foodstuffs, cloth, wine, sugar, coca, tallow, hides, and craft items. Huamanga itself served as an economic pole attracting rural products. Corn and potatoes doubled in price, for example, when sold in Huamanga rather than in faraway rural Lucanas.[33] Through mercedes, sales by kurakas, negotiations, or force, encomenderos and lesser European residents began to claim lands. Rather than consolidate a single large estate, the Europeans commonly carved out multiple holdings — often small or middle-sized — on lands whose fertility, suitability for prized goods such as coca or wine, or location near the city or commercial routes promised material reward. Herds of cows, sheep, and goats; irrigated patches of wheat, corn, vegetables, and alfalfa; water-powered flour mills; groves of fruit trees and carefully kept vineyards began to dot the valleys of Huatata, Yucay, and Viñaca near the city of Huamanga. Encomenderos carved out haciendas and estancias amidst the "core" areas of their native societies. They, along with other colonials, also sought fertile farmlands or pastures near the main highway in Huanta and Vilcashuamán. Along the eastern edges of Huanta, aggressive entrepreneurs set up coca plantations.[34]

Commercial capital, then, structured economic enterprise and development. True, in a society where most Indians could produce their own necessities on ayllu lands, capitalist production was impossible. Capitalist production bases itself upon the sale of labor-power for a wage, induced primarily not by political, social or cultural coercions but rather by economic necessity. Separated from the lands and resources needed to produce their subsistence, or items which can be exchanged for subsistence goods, workers freely sell their labor-power to earn a living wage. Capitalist *production* based on wage labor relationships (industrial capital, as distinguished from commercial capital) was simply beyond the social and economic horizons of the conquistadores. Nevertheless, the colonial ventures of Spain and Portugal created a genuine world market and commercial system which unleashed the key drive—profit, in "money" or easily exchangeable commodities — which motivates capitalist production. An insatiable thirst for the money-commodities (i.e., precious metals), and the hope to make money "work" or grow now captivated a spreading entrepreneurial imagination. Through mining and commerce, the sixteenth-century colonials of Peru could hope to realize such dreams despite the scarcity of free wage labor. Commercial capital, understood as buying (or producing) cheap to sell dear, became the lifeblood of the colonial economy.[35] Even the Bishop of Cuzco could not resist the temptation to sell thousands of baskets of coca—officially frowned upon by the Church—in the high-priced markets of Potosí.[36]

The Europeans therefore looked for opportunities in commercial agriculture, mining, manufactures, and trade to enrich themselves. As we have seen, Huamanga's colonizers cast their entrepreneurial eyes toward emerging markets in agriculture. Even before the discovery of Potosí in 1545, coca became a prized commercial crop.[37] Already in 1541, Pedro Díaz de Rojas had uncovered rich gold mines in the coca montaña of Mayomarca (eastern Huanta). The gold mines attracted fortune-seekers fired with passion and dreams of glory; in 1545, the cabildo sent a leading citizen to restore order and authority to the violent, rough-and-tumble life style which always plagued mining centers.[38] The discovery of major gold and silver deposits in Atunsulla (Angaraes) in 1560, and mercury mines in Huancavelica in 1564, made Huamanga a major mining region in its own right. The royal accountant in Huamanga joined encomenderos rushing to Atunsulla to extract minerals worth tens of thousands of pesos. Several years later, on 1 January 1564, the encomendero Amador de Cabrera registered the fabulous mercury mines of Huancavelica. Mercury, valuable for amalgamating the silver ore mined in Huamanga and Potosí, soon circulated as a regional medium of exchange like gold or silver.[39] With the discovery of major mines in the 1560s, Huamanga's entrepreneurs began to build textile workshops and obrajes. Within fifteen years of Cabrera's discovery, encomenderos had established at least three major rural obrajes to supply the growing mining and commercial centers of Huamanga. In neighboring Andahuaylas, another obraje had been supplying the Cuzco textile market since the 1550s.[40] Huamanga's encomenderos had established trading networks with Lima very early, and the Vilcashuamán *tambo* (lodging site for travellers) on the Inca highway from Huamanga to Cuzco rapidly emerged as a major trading center.[41]

As usual, the Indians, rather than isolate themselves from these economic developments, sought to take advantage of new trends and opportunities. Individually and collectively, Indians incorporated the search for money and commercial advantage into their daily existence, and for their own benefit. To be sure, native societies had to find ways to earn money if they were

to pay the money tributes owed to the encomenderos. The early documentation, however, offers evidence which belies the conclusion that native societies participated reluctantly in the commercial economy just to gather
monies needed for tribute. On the contrary, communities displayed an
open, aggressive — even enthusiastic — attitude which rivaled the boldness of
Diego Maldonado's amateur ethnography in Andahuaylas. Long before the
Spaniards gained control of Atunsulla around 1560, communities well over
a hundred kilometers away had sent mitmaq to mine "the hill of gold" abandoned by the Incas. The Lucanas Indians worked local gold and silver
mines for their own benefit, but later complained bitterly about demands
that they work Spanish mines in faraway sites. Kurakas in Andahuaylas
sent natives to set up ethnic outposts in the distant mines of Potosí.[42] Un-
hampered by Inca claims on coca fields, local societies expanded coca production and sales. One group used coca to pay "the tribute [they owed] and
with what remained after paying tribute they sustained themselves." Another group used the coca left after tribute to buy sheep and pigs.[43] By the
1550s, the Chancas and Adrián de Vargas, a Spanish entrepreneur, agreed
to build an obraje half-owned by the Indians, who sold some of the finished
textiles to their encomendero in Cuzco.[44]

Individually, too, natives reacted innovatively to the new colonial economy. By 1547, Indian workers and traders had captured an impressive share
of the Mayomarca gold dust in exchange for their services and products.
With money, a European could "rent" Indian workers in transport and
coca.[45] Native merchants flocked to supply the dynamic mines and commercial centers of Huamanga,[46] and artisans left ayllus to find opportunities
elsewhere. Silverworkers joined encomenderos in Huamanga, where their
skills yielded handsome rewards. Stonecutters earned money in colonial
construction, and skilled native artisans became indispensable specialists in
the Huancavelica mines.[47] Earlier, we saw that ethnic "families" were
plagued by internal tension and stratification; now, colonial society offered
new possibilities to dissatisfied individuals willing to abandon or loosen ties
with ayllu society. Some looked for alternatives in the city of Huamanga. In
the mines, the loyalties of mitmaq to the communities which had sent them
to work distant ore deposits sometimes slipped.[48] The brisk commerce in
coca led Indian entrepreneurs, especially the kurakas, to join Spaniards in
setting up private coca plantations.[49]

The kurakas, in fact, were best equipped to take advantage of new opportunities. The Europeans needed their cooperation to stabilize the early colony and to extract tribute and labor from ayllu society. The native elite,
moreover, enjoyed special privileges precisely because their "kinfolk" recognized them as guardians of the collective welfare of their ayllus and communities. The long-run "reciprocal" exchange between peasant households and

kurakas gave elites, as privileged leaders, the means to initiate rewarding activities in the colonial economy. One knowledgable observer called the privately owned coca farms "their particular trade." The kurakas' power, complained the corregidor of Huamanga, allowed them "to rent [the natives] like beasts and to pocket the money themselves."[50] True, a kuraka who consistently violated his kinfolk's sense of a fair reciprocal exchange ran the risk of encouraging emigration or disloyalty. In extreme cases, Indians even turned to colonial authorities or patrons to denounce a kuraka or challenge his authority. In 1559, Huamanga's officials fined one such chief 250 pesos for "certain torments and deaths of Indians."[51] In less extreme cases, however, or when native societies found alliance with the European colonials beneficial to their interests, the kurakas' economic initiatives did not necessarily erode their traditional prestige or "influence" among ethnic "relatives."

Culturally, too, a wide spectrum of native society belied images of reluctant participation in colonial society. Indians displayed an "open" attitude towards European culture and religion. The yanaconas who became personal retainers of European masters, of course, easily learned European styles of dress, religion, and habit. In ayllu society, kurakas led the trend towards the adoption of Hispanic symbols. The native elite grew fond of mules and horses, to which they fed surplus corn stocks. The Lucanas Laramati peoples, who forged amicable relations with encomenderos if not with Andean neighbors, seemed "inclined to learn to read and to write and to know the things of the Spaniards."[52]

Given the impact of a people's ancestor-gods on the fortunes of the living, an alliance with victorious Spaniards dictated an alliance with their deities as well. Such a choice conformed to an age-old pattern of Andean politics; even in the case of enemies, one often tried to control, obligate, or appease rather than destroy the supernatural powers of their gods.[53] Andean peoples therefore proved receptive to Catholic religion, though they interpreted its significance within the terms of their own culture. They established working relationships with Catholic priests in the countryside, and in the city of Huamanga, Lucanas Andamarcas natives built the impressive Indian church of Santa Ana.[54] The shrine symbolized a willingness to ally with the Christian pantheon of religious personalities (including saints), a policy which — from the Indians' point of view — did not require abandoning the traditional huacas of native society.

Thus the Indians joined in the creation of a colonial society impelled by the hunt for money and commercial profit. The native-white alliances of the new, post-Incaic era not only enhanced the ability of Huamanga's colonials to create an impressive array of commercial enterprises and relationships; they also reinforced "open" strategies among the natives: i.e., a willingness to take advantage of new opportunities, rather than withdraw sullenly from contact. The goals of Indians and Spaniards, as we shall see, were different and ultimately contradictory, but Andean participation in the commercial economy was nevertheless quite real. The Indians embraced the entry of commercial capital onto the Andean stage; only later would they discover that the embrace was deadly. The encomenderos saw that alliance with local elites and societies could lay a foundation for colonial exploitation; only later would they discover that the foundation was unstable, and could crumble under pressure.

LABOR AND TRIBUTE, ANDEAN STYLE

The problem was that, under the terms of the early alliances, the colonial economy continued to depend for goods and labor almost wholly upon an Andean social system, managed and controlled by Andean social actors, relationships, and traditions. A colonial state apparatus had rooted itself only partially, if at all, in Huamanga. Despite the presence of outside colonial officials and formal tribute lists by the 1550s, the colonials could not rely on the state to organize a new economic system that would funnel them native goods and labor. On the contrary, the natives went "over the heads" of local colonials to appeal for favorable rulings from metropolitan-oriented officials in Lima and Spain. Essentially, the "state" in Huamanga remained the personal responsibility of some twenty-five encomenderos[55] and a handful of cooperating officials who, as the King's representatives, sought to rule over the area. Under such conditions, it was difficult to reorder the native economy.

Instead, it seemed more feasible to the colonials to base their extraction upon long-standing Andean traditions. As we have seen, encomenderos and kurakas negotiated agreements on tributes. The more formal lists by officials in the 1550s and 1560s tended to include an astounding variety of items, far more impressive than the contents of short tribute lists after 1570. Aside from the gold and silver, food, animals, and cloth of the post-1570 lists, the early tributes included items such as wooden plates, vases, washtubs, chairs, footwear, horse and saddle gear, large sacks, ropes, cushions, rugs, and whips.[56] This diversity not only testifies to the capacity of native societies to incorporate new products and skills into their organization of economic life; it also dramatizes the dependence of Europeans upon indigenous communities, governed by Andean-style labor relations, for items that would later be supplied by a more Hispanized artisan and handicrafts economy.

The documents hint also that, in order to get their tributes, early encomenderos had to respect at least some of the traditional rules governing Andean labor and "taxes." Households continued to retain exclusive rights to crops produced on ayllu lands for local use; to pay tribute, households and ayllus contributed labor time on other lands specifically designated to satisfy outside claimants.[57] Traditionally, such practices protected ayllus and households from having to pay a tribute in goods from subsistence crops or food in storage in years of poor harvests. A shrewd observer of Andean life commented that Indians would rather go as a community to work fifteen days on other fields than give up for tribute a few potatoes grown by the family for its own use.[58] Poma de Ayala's praise of Huamanga's early encomenderos for lightening the Indians' tribute burdens in bad years probably reflected the encomenderos' inability or unwillingness to overturn such cherished rules. In Andahuaylas, Diego Maldonado supplied the wool needed to make textiles the Indians "owed" him.[59] Such practices—by no means exceptional in early colonial Peru[60]—respected the rule that peasants supplied to claimants labor-time rather than raw materials or local subsistence products. Ethnic groups and communities distributed tribute obligations—including money tributes—among themselves by ayllu, in accordance with traditional practices.[61]

To extract labor for public works, transport, and agriculture, the colonials had to pursue a similar policy. To replace worn fibrous cable bridges the cabildo ordered "that all the caciques [kurakas] and Indians of this province come together [to say] which are obligated to make bridges . . . from old times, and their [European] masters are ordered to donate the Indians [thereby designated]."[62] The kurakas, in their role as guardians and leaders, became the indispensable mediators of labor relationships. To "rent" Indians to transport wares or work lands, a European often had to make the arrangement with kurakas rather than hire the laborers directly. A contract from as late as 1577 shows that the prominent Cárdenas family could not hire independently the workers they needed on their estancia in Chocorvos (Castrovirreyna). Instead, a kuraka loaned twenty-seven kinsmen to the family and received the 162 pesos owed them after six months of labor. (Presumably the chief would then distribute six pesos to each worker.)[63]

We should not exaggerate, of course, the dependence of the Europeans. They had alternatives and used them. Aside from an impressive population of yanaconas, they could draw on the services of slaves or mestizos and other mixed-blood dependents, or exploit individual natives directly by extortion or agreement. But for ambitious enterprises these alternatives could only supplement rather than replace the labor of ayllu-based encomienda Indians. In the case of the Cárdenas estancia, the twenty-seven encomienda herders far outnumbered the "five yanaconas and four Indian cowboys" on the ranching complex.[64] Furthermore, even if an encomendero wished to deal directly with individual natives to work various farms and estates, his ability to do so stemmed from a general spirit of cooperation with native societies as a whole, led by their chiefs. The capable Maldonados of Andahuaylas, for example, were able to secure individual workers to tend to various herds, grow wheat and barley, harvest coca leaf, and so forth. Such relations sometimes carried the flavor of a direct interchange with native individuals who earned food and money for their labors. But often the Indians worked not to receive money, but to discharge collective tribute accounts settled upon with the kurakas. Even in the cases where encomienda Indians received individual payments in money or in kind, Diego Maldonado's access to their labors was facilitated by the kurakas' early approval, as spokesmen for communities and ethnic groups, of such relations. In the first year, they had given Maldonado llamas and Indian workers to transport items to Potosí and Lima. A tribute list in 1552 probably systematized earlier rules on the numbers of workers kurakas could spare to work on Maldonado's farms, orchards, ranches, and for domestic service.[65] As we saw earlier, Maldonado's success was related directly to a shrewd amateur ethnography. He rewarded cooperation with "gifts" and favors, negotiated agreements with the kurakas, and tended to respect traditional Andean prerogatives.

Perhaps it is not surprising that the majority of the agricultural and artisanal surplus, and a considerable amount of the tributes in precious metals funnelled to the Europeans rested heavily on the kurakas' ability to mobilize the labor of kinfolk in accordance with traditional Andean norms and expectations. More striking, however, is that even in the most dynamic sectors of the colonial economy — mining and textile manufactures — the Europeans could not transcend their reliance upon the kurakas. The mines and obrajes were strategic nerve centers crucial for the growth of a thriving commercial economy. Yet the voluntary flow of individuals or families to work the mines was not enough to assure an adequate and regular labor force. In 1562 a special commission struggled unsuccessfully to reform Huamanga's mines and stabilize a labor force. Still, as late as 1569, Amador de Cabrera had to negotiate with the kurakas of his encomienda to contract Indians he needed to work the mines of Huancavelica. The corregidor complained that Huamanga's rich mine deposits were languishing "because of a lack of Indian workers."[66]

Well into the 1570s — a transitional decade — European entrepreneurs depended upon the kurakas to supply workers for obrajes. In 1567, Hernán Guillén de Mendoza reached an agreement with the Tanquihuas Indians of his encomienda to rotate a force of sixty Indians for his obraje "Cacamarca" in Vilcashuamán. Ten years later, in Castrovirreyna, the kurakas of the Cárdenas family agreed to provide forty adults and fifty children to run a new obraje. Contracts which depended upon Andean relationships to mobilize a labor force would be conditioned by traditional norms governing work in local societies. In such cases, neither an encomendero, nor a colonial state, nor one or two chief kurakas could command the labor of the ayllu Indians who made up a community or ethnic group. Only an agreement among the chiefs of the various lineages — tied to one another and to their people by the long-standing expectations and interchanges of local kinship and reciprocity—could commit ayllu Indians to labor in the obraje. One Huamanga contract recorded the formal approval of seven different chiefs; a similar contract from another region recorded the unanimous agreement of sixteen kurakas and notables (*principales*). Significantly, the kurakas of Cárdenas sent a minor chief to oversee productivity in the new obraje. In the 1570s, unlike later years, Antonio de Oré had to appoint prominent encomienda Indians instead of Europeans or mestizos to manage his obraje in Canaria (Vilcashuamán). The native elites oversaw labor relations within the obraje and adapted traditional Andean techniques to the manufacture of textiles.[67]

Closed out of the traditional web of reciprocities among "kinfolk" which mobilized labor and circulated goods in Andean ethnic "families," and unable to reorganize the native economy or control directly the basic elements of production, the colonials had little choice but to rely upon their alliance with the kurakas. Even if Europeans aspired to take on the precarious task of reordering internally the native economy, the limits of their position would force them to rely upon the kurakas' ability to convince their kin. By cultivating working relationships with the managers of autonomous native economies, Huamanga's colonials could receive a portion of the wealth and labor-power available in dynamic local economies without having to organize an impressive state apparatus or reorder local society. Whether the alliance was more voluntary or forced in character, the chiefs would use their traditional prestige to mobilize a flow of labor and tribute to the colonial economy. Combined with an impressive show of Spanish military skill in Cajamarca and elsewhere, and some willingness to help local societies promote ethnic interests, such a strategy seemed sensible at the time. It is no accident that the early decades produced figures like Juan Polo de Ondegardo and Domingo de Santo Tomás. Experienced and shrewd colonials, they urged the Crown to base its exploitation of native economies upon a respect for the traditional relationships and prerogatives of Andean society. To the greatest extent consistent with Crown interests, royal policy should siphon off surplus goods and labor from ongoing native economies rather than reorganize or control them directly.[68]

Extracting a surplus by allying with the chiefs of autonomous and rather wealthy economic systems was, for the conquistadores, a realistic path of least resistance, but it soon led to a dead end. The kurakas controlled the basic processes of production and reproduction that sustained the colonials' economic, social, and political positions. If the kurakas were not at all "inferior" to the Europeans but in fact directed the social relations and dynamic economies crucial to the survival of colonial enterprise, why should they accept a subordinate position in society? On the contrary, their indispensable position tended to reinforce their posture as collaborating allies rather than dependent inferiors. In a real sense, the colonials remained foreign, extraneous elements superimposed upon an autonomous economy in which they served little purpose. As we shall see, such a limitation did not augur well for an aspiring ruling class's hegemony, its long-run capacity to dominate a society and capture the wealth it produced. As soon as the specific advantages of the kurakas' alliance with the Spaniards began to run out — because the Europeans demanded too much, or because Andean kinfolk resisted the demands made on them by the alliance — the colonial system would enter a crisis. The dependence of Europeans upon native elites for access to exploitable labor in agriculture, transport, public works, manufactures, and mining exposed the artificial character of foreign hegemony. The economy erected by the post-Incaic alliances was deeply vulnerable to changes in the natives' cooperative policies. Disillusion with the Europeans could spell disaster. And sure enough, disillusion set in, disaster struck.

CONTRADICTION AND CRISIS

To understand why disillusion set in, we need to remember that the native-white alliances had always been uneasy and contradictory. The encomenderos cultivated working relations with local chiefs and societies in order to rule over the Andes and to extract as much wealth as possible. The natives accepted an alliance with the victorious foreigners as a way to advance local interests and to limit colonial demands and abuses. The contradictions of the post-Incaic alliances thus bore within them the seeds of severe disillusion. The violence and arrogance endemic in the Europeans' early relations with the Indians warned of the limitations of such alliances for both sides.

In many ways, Huamanga's native societies had fared relatively well by allying with the Europeans. Their adaptations freed them of onerous bonds with the Incas, found them allies in struggles with rival native groups, and offered them the opportunity to accumulate wealth in the form of precious metals. The combined effects of epidemic disease, war, and emigration of yanaconas took their toll upon the several hundred thousand natives of Huamanga, but the post-conquest decline was not as irrevocably devastating as that in other Andean areas. The first, and probably most devastating, Old World epidemic struck the Andean zone in the mid-1520s, well *before* European conquest in 1532. Despite the epidemics of typhus or plague, smallpox, and influenza which shook the Andes in 1546 and 1558–59, the Lucanas peoples of southern Huamanga claimed in the 1580s that their population had actually increased since the turbulent reign of the Inca Huayna Capac (1493–1525).[69] For Huamanga as a whole, a high birth rate, the relative immunity of remote high-altitude areas to disease, shrewd politics, and good luck helped cut net population losses to an average rate of perhaps 0.5

percent a year or less, or some 20 percent over the 1532–1570 period.[70] Such a loss posed hardships for a labor-intensive system of agriculture, but was not by itself disastrous. Indeed, the rich herding economies of the high punas of Lucanas, Chocorvos, and Vilcashuamán served as a kind of "insurance" against a decline of labor-power available for agriculture.[71] Successful adaptation to colonial conditions had enabled Huamanga's Indians to maintain traditional relationships and economic productivity. Inspections of southern Huamanga in the 1560s turned up many local huacas, presumably supported by retaining rights to lands, animals, and ayllu labor. Several years later, Viceroy Francisco de Toledo was so impressed with the wealth of the Lucanas Laramati peoples that he nearly tripled their tribute assessment. Huamanga's kurakas probably joined other Andean chiefs in offering King Philip II a dazzling bribe to end the encomienda system — 100,000 ducats more than any offer by the Spanish encomenderos.[72]

Nevertheless, the alliance with the Europeans had created ominous trends. First, even though Huamanga's rural societies weathered the effects of epidemic, war, emigration, and population decline relatively well, these were nevertheless disturbing events. Economically, unpredictable drops and fluctuations in the population available for local tasks augured poorly for the long-run dynamism of ayllu-based society. A certain expected level of available human energy was a prerequisite for the maintenance of the traditional economic prerogatives, relationships, and exchanges which tied together producers. Ideologically, Andean societies tended to interpret misfortune — especially disease or early death — as the result of poorly functioning, "unbalanced" social relationships within the community of kin groups and gods. Illness, in particular, was often considered the work of neglected or angry huacas. War and epidemic disease raised the specter of fundamentally amiss relationships which might bring about a major catastrophe far more devastating than earlier trends.

Second, colonial relationships created humiliations and dependencies that undercut the ethnic freedom gained by liberation from Inca hegemony. Aside from the individual abuses and extortions that natives confronted everywhere, local societies found themselves relying upon colonial authority to defend their interests. Using an alliance with Europeans to protect against encroachments by outside ethnic groups was one matter. But dependence upon Europeans to settle internal disputes or to correct colonial abuses was quite another. Unfortunately, such a dependence grew increasingly frequent. Given the internal strife which plagued decentralized ethnic "families," it was difficult to avoid turning to Europeans as a source of power in local disputes over land rights, tribute-labor obligations, and chieftainships. By the 1550s, Huamanga's Indians commonly travelled as far as Lima to redress local grievances.[73]

Finally, the new relationships generated demands for labor that might go beyond what local societies were willing to offer in exchange for the benefit of alliance with the colonials. The number of Spaniards, of course, increased over the years. Moreover, the demands of any particular set of colonials did not necessarily remain static. Consider, for example, relations with Catholic priests. The rural priests (*doctrineros*) theoretically lived among ayllu Indians to indoctrinate them on behalf of the encomenderos. In practice, the utopian phase of Spain's "spiritual conquest" had spent itself in Mexico, and many Peruvian doctrineros were "priest-entrepreneurs" who used their positions to enhance their commercial interests.[74] At first, many communities probably accepted the necessity of an alliance with the priests. To ally with the Europeans without cooperating with their gods was senseless from an Andean point of view. The powerful Christian deities had defeated the major Andean huacas at Cajamarca, and like the native gods, could improve or damage the material wellbeing of the living. Since the Catholic priests mediated relations with the pantheon of Christian divinities (including saints) who affected everyday welfare, Indians did not rebuff the priests or their demands lightly. By the 1550s, churches and crosses—however modest—dotted rural society, and their priests demanded considerable labor services for transport, construction, ranching, household service, and so forth. By 1564, the rural priests' ability to extract unpaid native labor inspired jealousy among the urban encomenderos.[75] But as the priests' demands escalated, when would native societies judge them far too excessive for the supposed advantages offered by favorable relations with Christian gods?

The kurakas, as guardians and representatives of the community, could not ignore such evaluations of the relative advantages and disadvantages of cooperation with colonials. The kurakas who mobilized labor for European enterprise did not, in the long run, enjoy complete freedom to will the activities of their peoples. The chiefs bolstered their privileges and "influence" by fulfilling obligations to guard the communitarian unity and welfare. The traditional interchanges of reciprocities which enabled chiefs to mobilize the labors of kinfolk created expectations that might be difficult to reconcile with a unilateral flow of goods, labor, and advantages to European society. Traditional reciprocities also placed limitations upon the kinds of requests a kuraka could make of his ayllus and households. Production of textiles for the Europeans through a "putting-out" system similar to accepted Andean practices was one matter. As we shall see, sending workers to distant mines was quite another. Natives would be more reluctant to comply, and once at the mines might never return to the domain of local society.

Evidence shows that labor demands became a matter provoking resentment among Indians even when the labor was sought for activities superficially similar to traditional Andean practices. If labor demands were originally the price for the relative advantages of working relationships with the encomendero elite, the advantages could dwindle over time, and the price could rise unacceptably high. In local society, for example, canal-cleaning had normally been an occasion for celebration on the agricultural and ceremonial calendars. In ritual led by the native elite, a community of "relatives" reaffirmed the importance of such tasks for the collective welfare of the group. But the same activity carried an onerous flavor if viewed as uncompensated labor to the exclusive benefit of others. The Huachos and Chocorvos Indians complained in 1557 that they were forced to sweep clean the great canal "with which the citizens [of Huamanga] water their [farms] and ditches." The Indians did not benefit from or need the water.[76] Under such conditions, kurakas could not transfer the celebratory aspect of Andean work to colonial canal-cleaning even if they had wanted to. A kuraka who felt compelled to satisfy colonial labor demands could not assume that his call for labor would be accepted as justified by his kin. He risked an erosion of confidence which would undermine the reciprocal exchanges that made ayllus responsive to his requests.

In the 1560s, the contradictions inherent in the post-Incaic alliances imposed themselves more sharply than ever. The growing dependency of Indians upon Europeans to settle disputes;[77] economic shortages or hardships imposed by colonial extraction, emigration, or population decline;[78] the tendency of encomenderos, local priests, and officials to demand increasing shares of ayllu goods and labor — all these eventually would have provoked a reassessment of native policies towards the colonials. What made the need for a reevaluation burn with urgency, however, was the discovery of rich mines in the 1560s. Gold and silver at Atunsulla (1560), and mercury at Huancavelica (1564) fired Spanish dreams of a thriving regional economy whose mines would stimulate a boom in trade, textile manufactures, crafts, construction, agriculture, and ranching. The only obstacle or bottleneck would be labor. If European demands escalated far beyond the supply of individual laborers, or of contingents sent by kurakas, how would the colonials stabilize an adequate labor force?

By 1562, the labor problem merited an official inquiry by the distinguished jurist Juan Polo de Ondegardo. Polo investigated Indian complaints, set out to reform and regulate labor practices, and ordered native societies to turn over a rotating force of 700 weekly laborers for the Atunsulla mines. The labor regime imposed by the European miners had been repulsive and harsh. Miners bent upon achieving riches sought to maximize their exploitation of native laborers. Natives personally carried heavy loads of fuel, salt, and other supplies from distant areas; in the mines themselves, laborers confronted brutal production quotas; after fulfilling their labor obligations, they faced a struggle to receive their wages.[79] Small wonder that the Indians asked a noted defender, Fray Domingo de Santo Tomás, to inspect the mines. Santo Tomás found that "until now the Indians have been paid so poorly, and treated worse . . . that even if they went voluntarily [these abuses] would wipe out [their willingness]." Hopeful that Polo's reforms— boosted by higher salaries—could attract enough voluntary labor, Santo Tomás warned that the Indians and kurakas would resist attempts to force natives to work under the abusive conditions of the past, "even if they knew they would have to spend all their lives in jail." Santo Tomás found the Indians restless about demands for mine labor. The Soras and Lucanas peoples, farther away than other groups from Atunsulla, were particularly vexed about working for greedy entrepreneurs in cold, distant mines.[80]

Polo's reforms changed little. The supply of native laborers forced or coaxed individually or through the kurakas remained irregular and insufficient. The corregidor of Huamanga complained in 1569 that work on the region's fabulous deposits sputtered because of the labor shortage.[81]

The mines made obvious the limitations of previous relationships to both sides. For the Europeans driven by the international expansion of commercial capital, alliances with native societies meant little if they could not supply a dependable labor force to a growing mining economy. For the Indians —kurakas as well as their kinfolk—collaboration with the colonials offered few benefits if the Europeans insisted upon draining ayllu resources in a drive to develop a massive mining economy beyond the control of local society. The Europeans wanted favors which the kurakas could not or would not give them. Yet the colonials still lacked effective state institutions that could force the chiefs to turn over large contingents to the mines.

At this very moment, contradictions between metropolis and colony encouraged the Indians to rethink the necessity of cooperation with encomenderos. In Spain, the Crown had long debated whether to abolish the encomienda system and convert the Indians into direct vassals of the Crown. Famous priests argued that phasing out the encomiendas upon the death of their holders would benefit the Indians. Their insistence carried weight in Spain, where royalists also saw the encomendero elite as an obstacle to metropolitan control. By 1560, the Crown had received impressive bribe offers from both sides—the encomenderos, and the native kurakas—but without reaching a decision. A commission sent to report on the merits of the encomienda issue dispatched Juan Polo de Ondegardo (pro-encomienda) and Fray Domingo de Santo Tomás (anti-encomienda) to conduct an inquiry. The pair toured the Andean highlands in 1562. In Huamanga as elsewhere, they organized meetings of natives to participate in a public debate of the encomienda issue. The Indians, of course, always sided with Santo Tomás.[82] Royal interests and moral sensibilities, spurred by deep frictions between encomenderos and the Church, had created a spectacular debate. In the very years when mine discoveries made the basic antagonisms between natives and whites ever more weighty and ominous, the Crown's distinguished representatives advertised political instability, elite divisions, and receptivity to the idea that the encomendero elite was dispensable to Crown and native alike!

If growing disillusion with labor demands inspired an impulse to sabotage or overthrow colonial relationships, the apparent vulnerability of such relationships to reform imposed by the metropolis could only give further impetus to such urges. Soon after 1560, the spread of native discontent expressed itself in a decade of growing withdrawals from cooperation or alliance. In 1563, kurakas in seven different Huamanga encomiendas refused to send Indians to the city plaza for corvée duty. The mines continued to suffer from an irregular labor supply. Many of Huamanga's peoples—especially the Soras and Lucanas peoples—confirmed Santo Tomás's warnings by stubbornly rejecting calls for laborers to work the mines. Indian shepherds cost their encomendero, Diego Maldonado, a claimed 7,000 sheep through robbery or neglect. Encomenderos blamed priests for the natives' growing tendency to ignore previously accepted obligations; another observer placed the blame on popular rumors that the Spaniards would kill natives for medicinal ointments in their bodies.[83] In an economy where the Europeans depended greatly upon alliances with native elites to gain access to exploitable labor, the spread of such disillusion and resistance could poison enterprise. In a society where the neo-Incas maintained a military presence in the montaña between Cuzco and Huamanga, and the colonials had not yet organized an impressive state apparatus, growing hostility posed strategic dangers as well. The corregidor of Huamanga warned the acting viceroy, Lope García de Castro, that a rebellion might break out. In neighboring Jauja and Andahuaylas, alarming discoveries of stored weapons confirmed that traditions of Indian-white alliance and cooperation were no longer reliable.[84]

Demands for mine labor on a new scale, the encomenderos' political vulnerability, and the neo-Incas' probable willingness to lead a revolt created a conjuncture that compelled second thoughts about the post-Incaic alliances. The spread of sabotage and subversion in the 1560s was a symptom of growing misgivings. From the beginning, the inherent contradictions of the early alliances had created the likelihood of disenchantment. Despite the relative success of their adaptation to colonial conditions, Huamanga's native peoples confronted trends which could eventually undermine local autonomy, relationships, and production. Demographic decline and instability, humiliation and dependence, growing demands for labor—all tended to expose the erosive consequences of an alliance among partners whose fundamental interests clashed. The discovery of major gold, silver, and mercury mines brought such contradictions to a head, and reinforced the typically Andean fear that disease and untimely death derived from ill-constructed social relationships which, if left uncorrected, could herald a major catastrophe. Suddenly, a desperate wave of fear and disillusion swept Indian society, and spelled the demise of the post-Incaic alliances.

3

A Historical Watershed

CRISIS IN INDIAN SOCIETY, RADICAL DREAMS

In 1564, the Spanish priest Luis de Olivera stumbled upon a subversive heresy which gripped the Indians of his parish in Parinacochas. As messengers of the native Andean deities, the *taquiongos* who disseminated the contagion preached that, very soon, a pan-Andean alliance of deities would defeat the chief Christian god and kill the Spanish colonizers with disease and other calamities. Indians who wished to avoid the same fate and to enter a new, purified era of health and abundance should worship the vengeful huacas and reject all forms of cooperation with Europeans. Alarmed by the nativist revival's appeal to all sectors of the Indian population, Olivera sent word of his discovery to ecclesiastical authorities in Lima, Cuzco, and Charcas. Later, a painstaking inspection by the curate Cristóbal de Albornoz revealed that the *Taki Onqoy* sect had gained thousands of active adherents in the Lucanas, Soras, Chocorvos, and Río Pampas regions of Huamanga. Outside of this "core" area, the revival seemed to spread rapidly north towards Jauja and Lima, and east towards Cuzco and Charcas. Only after Albornoz's thorough anti-idolatry campaign, which consumed two to three years and condemned more than 8,000 Indians, did this messianic revival lose its vigor.[1]

Scarcely twenty years after the founding of Huamanga, a deep moral crisis, which gave rise to radical dreams of a new post-Incaic era purged of Hispanic elements, swept through native society. The Taki Onqoy revival broke out around 1560, and expressed the generalized sense of misgiving and disillusion which infected that decade of crisis. Since the gods normally played a critical role in great cataclysms, native fears that continued cooperation with Europeans would lead to disaster necessarily entailed a religious dimension. Indians would have to reevaluate their relations with the Andean

51

huacas, as well as the Catholic deities. Fortunately for the historian, the anti-idolatry inspection which "reformed" Huamanga of its heresy by about 1570 left behind considerable data on the movement's ideology and activities, its social composition and leadership, and its capacity to withstand countervailing pressures.[2] With a certain sensitivity to the meaning of religious symbols and expression in native Andean society, and a historical understanding of early colonial relationships in Huamanga, such data affords us a long glimpse into the convulsion which wrenched native society at this time.

RELIGIOUS CONTAGION

Suddenly, without apparent warning, excitement jolted Indians out of malaise, or resignation to inexorable trends. The Andean huacas — no longer confined to rocks, waters, or hills — swept down on the natives, literally "seizing" them, entering their bodies, and causing the "possessed" to shake, tremble, fall, and dance insanely.[3] Taki Onqoy literally meant "dancing sickness," and much of its ritual focused on the apparently uncontrollable singing and dancing of those possessed by the "sickness." The seizure spiritually purified the possessed, who renounced Christianity and spoke for the reinvigorated native gods. The huacas might seize anyone — even children. One Spaniard saw "six or seven Indian boys and girls . . . who walked around like fools and people who [had] lost their senses." The imminence of a cleansing revolution created a contagious fever. In their possessed state, the gods' messengers — the taquiongos — exhorted kinfolk "with such excitement that those who heard them . . . took it for certain that they spoke the truth."[4]

The taquiongos promised their followers a millenarian upheaval which would wipe out the disturbing trends of the past. A pan-Andean alliance of native gods, organized into two great armies, would do battle with the Christians' God. Pizarro's victory at Cajamarca in 1532 had reflected the results of a wider cosmic struggle in which the Christians' God had led the Spaniards to victory over the Andean huacas and peoples. Now, the Andean huacas would reverse the results. "All the huacas . . . whom the Christians had burned and destroyed had come back to life. . . . They had joined together to battle God, . . . whom they had just about beaten." The resurgent huacas would destroy Spanish colonizers as well. "Soon the Spaniards of this land would be done away with because the huacas would send all of them sicknesses to kill them." The triumph would herald a new era purified of Hispanic traces. The gods would "now turn the world around, and leave God and the Spaniards beaten this time and all the Spaniards killed, and their cities flooded" by the destructive tide of a rising ocean. The flood had to occur "because there should be no memory of [the Spaniards]." Out of the destructive cataclysm would come regeneration. The revindicated huacas would create a "new world" inhabited by "other peoples." The reborn world would be an Andean paradise—free of colonizers, materially abundant, unplagued by disease. Significantly, major gods of the Incas, who still represented a potential threat to ethnic independence, were not to play a leading role in the armies of Andean gods.[5]

The end result, predicted the taquiongos, would be paradise for those loyal to the huacas and their messengers, cruel vengeance to traitors. The huacas "wandered through the air, thirsty and dying of hunger because the Indians no longer sacrificed to them, or offered chicha [beer]." Angry that the Indians had abandoned them, the huacas would kill disloyal natives along with the Spaniards: "They had planted many fields of worms, to put them into the hearts of the Spaniards, their livestock from Spain and the horses, and also in the hearts of the Indians who remained Christian."[6] To avoid the reprisals, natives would have to renounce the call of Catholic priests and reject Spanish religion, names, food, and clothing. The taquiongos implored their followers to withdraw from contact and cooperation with European society. Natives should neither enter churches nor serve priests. They should abandon tribute payments and reject labor drafts.[7] Only by allying themselves to the rebellious huacas and their human messengers could Indians enjoy the material benefits of good health, peace, and prosperity after the coming upheaval. "Worshipping the said huacas and doing the ceremonies that the [sect's] inventors and teachers . . . told them to do, all their affairs would go well. They and their children would enjoy health, and their fields would yield handsomely." The disloyal, on the other hand, "would die and walk with their heads on the ground and their feet above, and others would be turned into guanacos, deer, vicuñas and other animals."[8]

Indians took the wild taquiongos seriously. In Parinacochas, "they would place [the taquiongos] in some enclosures and there the Indians would go to worship them as the huaca or idol that they said had entered the body."[9] The taquiongos supervised the ritual feasts, confessions, and fasts with which their followers hoped to regain the huacas' favor. Such gatherings not only gave the taquiongos an opportunity to receive a stream of llamas, cloth, silver, corn, beer, and other offerings, but also provided an authoritative forum from which to preach the sect's ideology and to generate formidable anti-Hispanic pressures.[10] As their prestige boomed, the taquiongos became moral guardians of the community. "From time to time they made sermons to the people, . . . threatening the Indians if they did not leave Christianity totally; and they berated the cacique [kuraka] or native who would use a Christian name . . . and wore a shirt or hat, sandals or any other clothes from Spain."[11]

What appalled Spanish observers was precisely the taquiongos' capacity to command the respect or participation of everyone. Women and men,

Idolatry. The scene depicted here may have been based on events associated with Taki Onqoy. Note the prominent role of women, the loss of self-control by a drunk Indian, and the notion that the huacas—here represented as the devil—"seized" the victim.

young and old, kuraka and peasant, ayllu Indian and Hispanized yanacona
—all seemed vulnerable to their message or succumbed to outright seizures.
More than half the taquiongos were women.[12] In an area whose total population numbered no more than 150,000, Spanish authorities claimed to find
some 8,000 active participants.[13] Even worse, complained the secretary of
the anti-idolatry campaign, "everybody believed in it and kept what [the ta-
quiongos] said, chiefs as well as Indians, and old people as well as boys and
girls."[14] Observers feared that the contagion would spread irresistibly all
over the Andean highlands.[15] Most ominously, the anti-European heresy
wiped out earlier gains and patterns of cooperation. Supposedly Christian-
ized natives lapsed into idolatry.[16] Once cooperative ethnic groups and communities had transformed themselves into hotbeds of discontent, hostility,
and passive resistance. Strategic native groups now proved suspect. In the
rural encomiendas, a Hispanizing and collaborating native elite had played
an indispensable role as mediators between ayllu Indians and the European
elite. The participation or consent of kurakas made the Taki Onqoy revival
an extremely dangerous heresy, "the most damaging that there has been
since this land was conquered."[17] For colonial society as a whole, the growth
of a sector of Spanish-oriented Indians and yanaconas played a key role in
sustaining European rule. The yanaconas' loyalty to European patrons and
society swelled the effective numbers of colonizers. But now even city Indians and yanaconas renewed their Andean loyalties, and some gained
prominence as leaders of the movement. Albornoz complained bitterly that
acculturated Indians "raised amongst us" now travelled throughout the
highlands "begging and exhorting everyone who had been loyal to their
master" to believe in the coming upheaval.[18]

THE MEANING OF TAKI ONQOY'S MESSAGE

Native society thus leaped to swell the ranks of the taquiongos. Why, however, did the "possessed" and "insane" natives who preached cataclysm ac-
quire credibility as the huacas' chosen messengers? Why did they not suffer
the ridicule or neglect heaped upon mere lunatics?

The taquiongos spoke in an idiom consistent with popular logic and world
views. The belief that a coming convulsion would create—or restore—a
"new" world cleansed of the imbalances, disorders, and evils of the past corresponded to a cyclical view of history shared by all Andean peoples.[19] The
view that disease reflected the anger of huacas or the misguided quality of
social interchange belonged to an age-old vision of the causes of misfortune.[20]
Divination, too, was an accepted Andean practice, and the Lucanas and
Soras peoples so prominent in the Taki Onqoy agitation enjoyed a reputation as great soothsayers.[21] Even spirit possession was accessible to the experience of Andean logic. Though the huacas had normally been embodied in

the form of what we call today "inanimate objects" (waters, hills, or rocks), the separation between nature and humanity was not as stark in Andean thought as in the world view created by Western society's capitalist revolutions. Certainly the huacas had appeared before to speak in the dreams or minds of chosen spokesmen. They had also displayed a certain geographical mobility, an ability to enshrine different places at once.[22] The consistency of Taki Onqoy with accepted explanatory idioms gave the sect a certain intellectual plausibility which blunted immediate rejection as a mad frenzy whose internal logic was ridiculous or unintelligible. But a degree of intellectual credibility does not explain why a movement gains *social* credibility. Why did natives find themselves compelled to believe *in this particular instance* that the taquiongos, instead of being misguided fools, were indeed chosen mouthpieces of reinvigorated Andean huacas about to launch a cataclysm?

The impressive appeal of the taquiongos derived from their ability to pull together and articulate perceptions and impulses which were beginning to crystallize in their kinfolks' consciousness. As we have seen, events in the 1560s created a critical juncture of disillusion, resistance, and reassessment in once cooperative native societies. Local societies had joined the post-Incaic alliances to further traditional Andean goals and norms—communal or ethnic autonomy, economic self-sufficiency and wealth, favorable edges in local conflicts among ayllus or communities, "balanced" interchange with human and supernatural personages related to the community. Once and for all in the 1560s, and despite their rather successful adaptation to post-Conquest conditions, Huamanga's peoples saw that such alliances would prove untenable over time. The encomendero-led Europeans would inexorably seek to transform diverse ethnic allies and clients into a caste of mere "Indians" organized for colonial extraction. The huacas, through the taquiongos, confirmed the truth of the natives' worst fears, spelled out the implications of such truths, and galvanized lurking temptations to sabotage colonial relationships and purge native society of their influence. Yes, it was true that an implacable conflict of interest between Hispanic-Catholic society and Andean-pagan society far transcended the original premises of collaboration. Yes, it was true that unless the natives withdrew their willingness to appease the Europeans, they would collaborate in their own destruction. Yes, it was true that in order to rid itself of colonialism, native society would have to purify itself of Hispanic-oriented elements tied materially and mentally to the oppressors. Taki Onqoy expressed the painful truth dawning upon local societies—that conflict between the Andean and European elements of colonial society was at once inescapable, irreconcilable, and decisive.

The great truth of Taki Onqoy, native-white conflict, was embodied in two moral principles: resistance against the Hispanic world, solidarity within the Andean world. As we shall see, each of these principles was not easily realized in practice. For they asked that natives transcend adaptations, traditions, and genuine ambivalences which still governed their behavior towards Europeans and towards one another. Precisely because Taki Onqoy demanded new and different patterns of behavior, the revival exposed an emerging moral crisis.

The first principle, resistance, meant that Andean society would have to unlearn previous adaptations. The natives' "open" strategies towards Hispanic people and gods had facilitated colonialism. Now they would have to resist contact, interchange, and service to these colonial entities. Native societies would have to reject their "open" habits, even though interchange with powerful colonials might bring certain benefits or seem necessary to avoid reprisals. Only by reforming themselves of such habits could natives avoid participating in their own destruction and enjoy the fruits of the coming cataclysm.

Nowhere did such a change of strategy pose a more widely felt moral dilemma than in the case of relations with the European gods attacked by Andean huacas. The Christian pantheon of gods (God, Jesus, the saints and revered figures), like the Andean huacas, affected everyday material welfare. The Spanish victory at Cajamarca had proved the Christian gods' power and superiority over the major Andean deities assimilated to the Inca State. Only fools could ignore such consequential facts. As in other peasant societies, the authority of Andean gods and chiefs rested in part upon a pragmatic base. Their continual success, their demonstrated impact upon the course of material life, sustained their prestige and authority.[23] The Spanish conquest raised doubts about the continuing potency of the Andean gods, while "proving" the risk of offending the Christian deities. Huamanga's peoples thus chose to follow a time-honored Andean strategy. Instead of rejecting the powerful foreign deities imposed upon local life, they sought to absorb them into the pantheon of supernatural powers with whom native peoples sought "balanced" relationships.[24] For the Indians, such relationships would not have to exclude a continuing commitment to local Andean gods. Indeed, the sheer number of local huacas and "sorcerers," organized by ayllu, uncovered by Albornoz's entourage belies the huacas' collective complaint that their peoples had abandoned them.[25] Only the major regional or supraregional gods, whose prestige outstripped local ethnic affiliations, whose assimilation to the Inca State had left them discredited, and whose shrines and resources had been obvious targets of plunder, stood to lose. Yet as the fundamental conflict between European and Andean societies grew clear, who could doubt that service to the supernatural patrons of the colonizers, and disloyalty to the rights of some native gods, would only weaken Andean gods and societies as a whole?

Taki Onqoy condemned this accommodation to the Europeans' presence and defined the Andean peoples' choices in uncompromising terms. *Any* co-operation with the Europeans or their Church, however loyal in spirit to indigenous local huacas, placed one in the camp of the would-be destroyers of Andean gods. The basic conflict between European and Andean interests now limited religious strategies to all-or-nothing categories. The taquiongos, in the name of the once discredited major huacas and the lesser huacas allied to them, called upon the Indians to reform themselves, to purge the desire to placate prestigious Christian gods, to overcome any crisis of confidence in the power of the Andean gods.

Such resistance to Hispanic cultural ties would permit the community to affirm its less wavering, more complete commitment to Andean loyalties and relationships. By returning, under the supervision of the taquiongos, to the enthusiastic performance of age-old ceremonial obligations, native communities would regain the favor of the reinvigorated Andean huacas and live in health and prosperity. "They should fast five days in their manner according to their custom in the Inca's time, not eating salt nor ají nor maize nor having intercourse with their wives."[26] Well-known practices such as these carried out the traditional ritual purpose of balancing or readjusting reciprocity relations with the gods. Now, however, ritual celebrations acquired an added social function defined by the struggle against colonialism. They would celebrate the unlearning of ties to colonial society, and the revindication of *exclusively* Andean loyalties, relationships, and values.[27]

The corollary of resistance to Hispanic society was solidarity with the Andean world. Yet here too, Taki Onqoy called for changes which posed difficult moral dilemmas. On the one hand, the Andean mode of production had long tended to divide people into rival ayllus, communities, and ethnic groups. On the other hand, Spanish conquest created conditions that weakened traditional means of achieving cohesion. Worship of major regional or supraethnic gods had probably grown more difficult and irregular, and colonial dynamics threatened to divide native society into opposed classes — one a native elite tied to the colonial power structure and Hispanic relations of property and labor, the other an indigenous peasantry whose labors sustained the native elites and other colonial lords. Despite the germ of class contradiction which had always impinged upon relations between kurakas and ayllus, the chiefs had theoretically acquired privileges and authority in their capacity as recognized wards of the collective identity and interest of their "families." In small-scale societies, community imperatives held in check incipient class dynamics. The fertilizing impulse of Spanish colonial penetration now encouraged the embryo of class contradiction to grow and develop, producing, as a poisonous by-product, a crisis of confidence in the old ways that weakened the internal unity of native community life. The kurakas' enthusiasm for Hispanic symbols and their collaboration with the colonials linked them to the yanaconas and socially mobile ayllu Indians whose strategies and aspirations threatened to convert them into agents of colonialism. Hispanism and collaboration with the colonial regime tended to erode the chiefs' prestige or legitimacy once their people came to see them as acting to the advantage of the Spaniards and against their own interests and traditional expectations.

Taki Onqoy condemned the dynamics which tended to divide native individuals and communities into opposing camps. The huacas and taquiongos expressed the gnawing anxiety that natives who assumed Hispanic styles of religion, clothing, food, and custom were becoming enemies tied to colonialism and Christianity. In addition to symbolizing the community's renewed commitment to interchange with the Andean gods, the anti-Hispanic ritual gatherings directed by the teachers of Taki Onqoy provided a means of pressuring Indians whose Hispanic orientations differentiated them from the community and its struggles. Only by participating in Andean rituals of revindication and purification led by the taquiongos could Christian natives —even if they had observed their pagan obligations—placate the angry huacas. Only by shedding their Hispanic accouterments could relatively "acculturated" natives, particularly kurakas, overcome suspicion and regain the confidence of suspicious or moody kinfolk. Only by submitting to such pressures could an incipient class of Hispanic Indians avoid destruction alongside the Spaniards and join the natives' passage to health, abundance, and autonomy.[28]

Taki Onqoy aimed at a solidarity transcending not only newly emergent class divisions, but also traditional disunities along community and ethnic lines. Indeed, Taki Onqoy called for a consciousness of pan-Andean unity revolutionary to traditional thought and identification. In their battle against the Christian God, the huacas themselves set an example. The taquiongos spoke in the united name of "Titicaca, Tiahuanaco, Chimboraco, Pachacamac, Tambotoco, Caruavilca, Caruarazo and more than sixty or seventy other huacas."[29] Similarly, native affiliations to ayllu or ethnic groups, as rivals of other such kin networks, should lose priority before the importance of new realities which welded all natives into a single caste subordinated to Spanish rule. For the first time, the natives began to think of themselves seriously as "Indians." The Taki Onqoy preachers seemed to use "the Indians" and "the huacas" as new, less particularistic categories of interest and identity.[30] Significantly, the taquiongos used a notoriously multiethnic encomienda as a central gathering area which united participants from diverse encomiendas and ethnic groups.[31] Just as the huacas themselves had buried latent rivalries to make the Andes safe for indigenous gods and peoples as a whole, so should the Indians recognize their common position vis-à-vis the Europeans. To put it another way, Andean peoples projected onto their gods a desire to throw aside structural divisions and conflicts which made them all more susceptible to colonial domination.[32]

The leaders of Taki Onqoy sought to prove that in a battle against the Christian God, the united Andean huacas would inevitably win. For the taquiongos to dismiss the power of the Christian God as insignificant would have been foolhardy, in view of Spanish victories at Cajamarca and elsewhere, the colonials' continuing dominance, and the persistent lure of cooperation with Hispanic men and gods. The taquiongos conceded "that God was powerful for having created [the Spanish kingdom of] Castile and the Spaniards and the necessities which they grew in Castile."[33] From an Andean point of view, the material fortunes of a people in war reflected to a great degree the power of its gods. The success of the colonizers who represented the distant kingdom of Castile proved the very real power of the chief . deity, God, whom they worshipped.

Rather than deny such power outright, the taquiongos countered with a material argument that weighed the relative strengths of the gods in their native homelands. If it was true that the Spanish gods were impressive providers who reigned supreme in Spain, where they directed the process of material creation, then it was also true that the Andean huacas enjoyed superiority in Peru, where they alone sustained the material base of life. In the Andes, it was "the huacas [who] had created the Indians, this land, and the provisions which the Indians once enjoyed; *and thus they took away from [God] his omnipotence.*"[34] In an economy where the colonials still remained an extraneous element, dependent upon kuraka allies and Andean-style relationships to oversee production and deliver them a surplus, such an argument expressed a deep colonial truth. The Europeans had so far failed to integrate themselves as functionally necessary parts of local society and economy.[35] If we recall the intimate ties of religious relationships, cooperative labor, and economic production in traditional Andean society, we will understand why Andean peoples, even today, tend to draw parallels among relationships between humans in society and those between their gods in the cosmos.[36] The irrelevance of Europeans for the success of a native-run economy proved the underlying irrelevance and impotence of their gods. As several key leaders put it: "It was not God who gave [the Indians] their foods."[37]

Thus relations with Hispanic gods, as with their peoples, were fundamentally dispensable. Christianity was extraneous, unnecessary, and demonstrably inferior. The taquiongos "would put a cross . . . in a corner . . . and they talked in the said house with their huacas." To their listeners they would point out: "Look how that [Christian] stick did not speak through the cross. He [the Andean huaca] who speaks to us is . . . our god and creator and it is he that we must adore and believe." The gods taught by the Christians were "a laughing matter." [38] Having recognized that collaboration with the Spaniards, ethnic rivalry, and emergent class oppositions were weaknesses aiding colonial domination, Taki Onqoy also recognized the fundamental strength of native people and gods—the management and internal organization of economic production in the Andes remained largely in their hands. The close ties of material and religious dimensions of life allowed the taquiongos to "prove" the Andean gods' superiority in Peru by virtue of the Andean peoples' economic vitality, self-reliance, and ultimate superiority.

Taki Onqoy spoke truths which all sectors of native society could appreciate, and evoked moral dilemmas which touched upon everyone. The contradictions of colonialism affected ayllu Indian, kuraka, and yanacona. Discontent with the consequences of cooperation among partners with conflicting interests, rejection of further willingness to collaborate with European people or gods, revindication of the traditional norms and relationships of community or "family," desires to overcome divisions which eroded native society's solidarity against exploitation, dreams of a convulsion that would herald a new, purified cycle of history: all these understandably appealed to the restless, pent-up energy of disenchanted ayllu Indians in the 1560s. The ayllu Indians, after all, bore the primary burden of sustaining a demanding colonial society and economy.

The truths and moral dilemmas espoused by Taki Onqoy, however, appealed also to kurakas. The native elite, as guardians of the communitarian welfare and as mediators whose success depended upon their continuing "influence" with kin, could not simply ignore discontent or the harmful trends sapping ayllu society. On the contrary, European demands for labor in distant mines must have alarmed them. By further eroding the effective network of human energy available to local society, such demands would inevitably drain away the traditional prerogatives of the native lords. For the kurakas who sought to rid the Andean highlands of the encomienda system, Taki Onqoy promised a veritable utopia: autonomous local societies free of the Incas, free of the Europeans, and subject only to their natural chiefs.[39]

Nor were the yanaconas immune from Taki Onqoy's message. They had to endure a personal dependence upon European masters, which left them vulnerable to humiliations, abuses, and labor obligations that blurred their differentiation from ayllu Indians. We may hypothesize that with the mining boom of the 1560s, the temptation to use yanaconas as Indian slaves to supplement the labor of encomienda Indians surged dramatically.[40] Furthermore, individual isolation from the ayllus, communities, and human-god landscapes of traditional society alienated yanaconas from the collective subsoil which, in Andean culture, nurtured individual identity, psyche, and affect. As in other colonized areas, the social and psychological void of such "individualization" could create a profound crisis of the spirit. In Taki Onqoy's anti-Hispanic rituals, patterned after traditional Andean ceremonies and customs, yanaconas could, together with ayllu Indians and kurakas, recapture a lost sense of community immune to the corruptions of Spanish colonialism.[41] As "outsiders" of ayllu society, yanaconas who experienced misgivings about native-white cooperation were uniquely capable of attaining perspective on the consequences of colonialism for native groups as a whole, as a caste of Indians rather than a heterogeneous conglomeration of ayllus and ethnic groups. Having loosened their active ties to ayllu society, the yanaconas could propagate one of Taki Onqoy's prime tenets with a special fervor—that the shared experience of becoming "Indians" superseded by far the traditional ethnic and ayllu rivalries which pitted native groups against one another.

Taki Onqoy, then, spoke to needs increasingly felt throughout native society in a moment of crisis, criticism, and yearning for change. It expressed painful truths which, in a more diffuse and inchoate way, had begun to alarm native societies and individuals by the 1560s. It harnessed these truths to a moral evaluation of earlier native adaptations to Spanish conquest, found them faulty and destructive, and demanded change. Finally, Taki Onqoy offered the hope that its adherents could transcend discouraging divisions and weaknesses and usher in a new era free of colonial domination. Small wonder indeed that everyone in native society seemed eager to embrace the subversive heresy!

VULNERABILITY OF THE MOVEMENT

Alas, it was not that simple. Taki Onqoy did not command a homogeneously committed loyalty from all Indians, or even from all its followers. Taki Onqoy called for resistance to Spaniards and Hispanism, revindication of the native Andean world, and solidarity among all Indians precisely because so many social forces continued to pull the other way. Divisions and conflicts internal to native society did not disappear with a proclamation of the coming cataclysm, nor did the temptation to ally with, or at least placate, the colonials. Taki Onqoy exacerbated the moral crisis of Indian society precisely because at a moment of severe disillusion and misgiving, it condemned strategies, adaptations, and traditions which, in practice, too many natives would find difficult to renounce. When sensing a Spanish victory, even adherents of the sect slipped into searching for a benign European patron to protect them from severe punishment.[42] From the outset, some Indians defied the rules of Taki Onqoy by allying actively with the colonials. A kuraka betrayed two leaders of the sect, and Albornoz's anti-idolatry entourage enjoyed the services of Indian functionaries and informants.[43] As we shall see, the dynamics of class, ethnicity, and collaborationism which came under attack in the 1560s conditioned the movement's social composition, leadership, and cohesion in the face of pressure.

CAPITVLOPRIMERODEVECITA-DOR

CHRISTOBA·DEALBOR

nos uus m dor gene ral dela s madre yglecia buena justicia

jues   cristobal

Cristóbal de Albornoz on his anti-idolatry campaign. Note the use of an Indian intermediary, and the public humiliation imposed on the victim held by rope. An image of the devil is attached to his head, and he holds a lit candle as a symbol of penitence. Poma de Ayala served Albornoz as an interpreter, and praised the ecclesiastic for incorruptible integrity.

In administering punishment to Indians guilty of participation in the her-esy, the Spanish authorities recognized different levels of leadership, com-mitment, and potential threat. The Albornoz campaign sent truly active na-tive chiefs or notables to Cuzco along with the sect's leaders and "inventors" for public punishment and confessions; other ayllu Indians and followers of the movement remained in their local areas to hear sermons denouncing their mistakes and explaining the road to Catholic salvation.[44] Inspection lists distinguished between leading preachers and their accomplices (*predica-dores, maestros, dogmatizadores*) and the larger group of taquiongos who made up a core of active followers.[45] The most dangerous subversives suffered temporary or permanent exile from their homelands. Some would serve the Church or hospital in the city of Huamanga; others were assigned to serve priests in other encomiendas. Albornoz condemned lesser leaders to live in special houses next to their districts' churches, which they would serve indef-initely. The vast majority of taquiongos did not suffer alienation from their encomiendas and ayllus, but their heresy allowed the Church to increase its demands on their labor-time. Ninety-five taquiongos from Huacaña (Soras), for example, had to see their priest three days a week for religious instruction and to serve the church in nearby Morocolla "in whatever was needed."[46]

The potential for class contradictions within local society made the rela-tionship between traditional native elites and popular heresy at best prob-lematic or ambivalent, and at worst antagonistic. Though Taki Onqoy ac-quired impressive support among the kurakas and lesser elites, the data we have hints that, as a social group, the native chiefs did not throw their influ-ence and prestige into enthusiastic leadership or backing of the movement. In Cuzco, the sect's chief leaders publicly "confessed" that they had propa-gated a deception: "they did not know anything but to be poor and to ac-quire food through the offerings."[47] To the extent that such forced confes-sions had any credibility, they belie an equation of the wealthy major kura-kas with the movement's leadership. Few known kurakas appear on the lists of key Taki Onqoy leaders meriting exile.[48] In the important Lucanas re-gions, kurakas appear to have split on the Taki Onqoy issue despite the com-mitment of them all to more conventional "idolatrous" practices. In Lucanas Laramati, for example, the chiefs of both Guacguas and Caroancho were guilty of general idolatry, and the peoples of both groups participated in Taki Onqoy. The lists of guilty taquiongos, however, cite the chiefs of Guacguas but not of nearby Caroancho. In the *Hanan* (Upper) division of Lucanas La-ramati, eight of ten chiefs guilty of worship of customary local huacas were accused also of connections to Taki Onqoy. In the *Hurin* (Lower) group, however, only five of eleven such chiefs had participated.[49] A kuraka of Juan de Mañueco's encomienda, a central gathering area of the conspirators,

went so far as to take two important taquiongos to Huamanga for punishment.[50] Significantly, Spanish authorities phrased their accusations against
many kurakas and lesser elites in terms suggesting alliances *with* the sect
rather than outright leadership *of* the revival. The Albornoz inspection usually punished chiefs not as preachers, teachers, inventors, or propagandists
(*predicadores, maestros, inventores, dogmatizadores*) but as "consenters" or "con-
cealers" (*consentidores, encubridores*) who should, presumably, have restrained
or exposed the revival.[51]

The evidence as a whole not only differentiates traditional native elites
from the instigators of the sect,[52] but also suggests that ambivalent ties, latent oppositions, and outright conflicts existed between them. One recalls
that the kurakas themselves were the obvious targets of popular pressures to
abandon cultural Hispanization in favor of solidarity against colonialism.
As a social group, their relationship to the revival varied from betrayal to
Europeans, to reluctant support in order to maintain their standing among
kin, to more willing support and, in some cases, active leadership. However
affected they were by the growing intensity of native-white opposition in the
1560s, and however much Taki Onqoy envisioned a kind of utopia for chiefs
of free ayllus and communities, the kurakas stood to lose the most if the
revival, rather than extirpate the Europeans, only unleashed their wrath
and vengeance. However primitive or embryonic their distinction as a class
from the community's households and ayllus, and however vulnerable they
were to the message of Taki Onqoy, the prospective rewards or penalties
faced by the chiefs differentiated their choices from that of commoners.
However loyal and genuinely committed many were to the anti-Hispanic
revival, their *potential* as a class integrated into a colonial power structure
uniting various "lords" in the mutual exploitation of the peasantry imparted
a special ambivalence to such decisions.

Taki Onqoy was literally a popular outburst, not easily controlled by traditional elites or relationships, and originating partly in rivalry or opposition to governing native elites. The "very disorderly"[53] character of the
revival violated the conventional forms of control characteristic of Andean
religion. The evidence cautions against viewing even the traditional religious elite as the prime force behind the revival. Many had been able to
work out a local *modus vivendi* with Catholic priests who overlooked paganisms. Moreover, Albornoz learned of gatherings in which the taquiongos
killed local native priests (huacacamayos).[54] Such conflicts pitted the traditional huacacamayos of local gods against taquiongos, including yanaconas
marginal to the community, who threatened their authority by claiming to
speak for more famous Andean deities, and for the huacas as a whole.

If the ambivalence of native elites to Taki Onqoy limited the strength of
the movement, so did the disunities and antagonisms inherent in a society

organized through rival networks of kinship and ethnicity. Taki Onqoy cried out, of course, for a pan-Andean unity capable of superseding such divisions. But without an effective, organized commitment to unity on the part of chiefs of diverse ayllus and communities, the call to solidarity would be difficult to realize in practice. To the extent that the natives could not vent their hostility directly against the colonials, an impulse to conflict and violence may actually have unleashed itself internally, within native society.[55] In any case, the resurgence of bitter land conflicts among ethnically variegated groups south of the Río Pampas in the 1570s indicated the difficulties of suppressing old hostilities basic to native social and economic organization.[56]

Even within an ethnic group, its decentralized organization may have operated subtly to pluralize the levels of enthusiasm, loyalty, and commitment won by the taquiongos, particularly since the chiefs themselves varied in their reaction to the revival. Among the Lucanas Andamarcas peoples, for example, the accusations levelled against sixty-nine kurakas and lesser elites, many of them minor chieftains who were working members of their kindreds, offer suggestive clues to such variations. The elites of the ayllus of Andamarca and Omapacha were punished merely as "consenters," while those of Uchucayllo as "consenters of the said sect and for having given favor and help to the dogmatizers."[57] Ethnic fragmentation, like incipient class dynamics, constituted a formidable counterweight to Taki Onqoy's appeal for a resolute pan-Andean unification.

Finally, a curious inner vulnerability to defeat or submission plagued the anti-Hispanic resolve of even committed taquiongos. Spaniards boasted that many Indians appeared voluntarily before Albornoz's entourage to "confess" their sins and ask for mercy.[58] Many such "confessions" surely involved a tactical shift to submissiveness among natives anticipating the victory of Albornoz's anti-idolatry campaign. But we should not automatically exclude the possibility of genuinely remorseful motives. In view of native society's internal divisions, and the Christians' victory at Cajamarca, the decision to abandon collaborative dispositions altogether entailed great risks if the colonials and their gods once more proved victorious. The taquiongos had never denied completely the power of the Christians' God; they had simply labelled him an implacable enemy of the native huacas, who would have sufficient strength to defeat him. One of the most striking examples of voluntary "repentance" by taquiongos involved a group of self-styled "saints" named after Mary, Magdalena, and so forth.[59] From an Andean point of view, these Christian saints formed part of a pantheon of Hispanic huacas headed by God. These women taquiongos, who were feted as Christian saints rather than Andean huacas, expressed a desire at the very core of the Taki Onqoy movement to ally with some elements of Hispanic supernatural power while simultaneously battling God. The attempt to gain the favor of some of the lesser Christian gods, in the midst of an anti-Christian war, exposed a crisis of confidence in the capacity of the Andean gods, by themselves, to control the course of events.

As a result, a certain ambivalence common to colonial situations colored the nativist revival's rejection of Hispanic ties, and diluted its resolve in the face of Spanish pressure. Despite the disillusion with the Europeans in the 1560s, collaborative postures might offer relative advantages over conflictual stances inviting reprisals. Taki Onqoy arose in response to an emerging moral dilemma precisely because the natives' anti-Hispanic impulses were tempered by their continued inclinations to placate the colonials and their powerful gods.

Taki Onqoy's truths exerted an infectious pull upon all sectors of native society, but these very truths also betrayed weaknesses which haunted the movement. In condemning Hispanizing Indians who bound themselves to colonial power, together with those internal antagonisms which traditionally divided ayllus and ethnic groups, and generally collaborative adaptations toward the colonials and their gods, Taki Onqoy pinpointed precisely the forces which eroded its own capacity to challenge colonial society. Incipient class dynamics, ethnic division, and collaborationism all loomed over Huamanga's popular heresy, and confined its effective scope to spiritual issues. The first made links between the elite and the movement ambiguous and contradictory; the second weakened the natives' capacity to organize a truly united force or strategy; the third tormented natives sensitive to Taki Onqoy's moral command to purify themselves of ties to the Hispanic world.

MILLENARIANISM AS SOCIAL CRISIS

With the seizure of natives by the Andean gods, radical dreams of upheaval blasted their way through all of native society, and left no sector unscathed. The ideological core of "revolutionary millenarianism"—then and now, in the Andes and elsewhere—has been the desperate vision of an imminent, totally comprehensive transformation which, by the power of supernatural forces and the insurgents' own moral purification, will soon destroy an evil social order and regenerate a new, perfect world in its place. Historically, such movements have appealed to sharply disaffected social groups who experience a profound crisis of confidence. They not only find it difficult or impractical to launch a more direct political or military assault against the sources of their discontent, but have also lost confidence in the moral integrity of their own lives. The mixture of radical disaffection, political impotence, and inner doubts imparts to such crises an especially spiritual or moral character, even though the discontent stems from socioeconomic processes. Particularly in colonial situations, such a crisis is often experienced as a profound ambivalence between two competing sets of relationships and values. The continuing prestige and allure of the white man's world of power and wealth adds to the already difficult burden of oppression and political disability a terrible trial of inner conviction.[60]

Taki Onqoy responded to the emergence of just such a crisis in Huamanga. By the 1560s, an explosive mixture of fearful perceptions, subversive impulses, and severe misgivings reshaped many natives' attitudes toward themselves and toward native-white alliances. The taquiongos openly proclaimed that the post-Incaic alliances had constituted a source of evil rather than a strategy for survival and adaptation. They spread the burning message that only through a radical departure from past strategies and postures could the emerging caste of "Indians" purify themselves, and turn back the catastrophic fate which doomed them. As we have seen, however, existing social forces continued to pull Indians in directions condemned by Taki Onqoy. Despite the heresy's impressive appeal throughout native society, the taquiongos could not fully neutralize the stubborn dynamics of class, ethnicity, and collaborationism which weakened the political potential of any rebellious outburst. Nor could they sweep away the inner crisis of confidence and values which made it difficult even for taquiongos to reject Hispanic ties irrevocably. The limits of Taki Onqoy's success underscored the impasse of radical disillusion, political weakness, and moral uncertainty in which native society found itself imprisoned in the 1560s.

It was precisely the spiritual crisis created by this impasse — and not the supposed stresses of anarchic breakdown or disorganization, nor the alleged pre-political thrust inherent to peasant protest[61] — which explains why a millenarian revolt emphasizing moral reform inflamed Huamanga. By means of the post-Incaic alliances, Huamanga's native societies — especially in the south, where the heresy made its greatest headway — had managed to preserve a degree of economic vitality and internal coherence which belie images of anomie, disorganization, or "destructuring" often used to explain revolutionary millenarianism. The radical disaffection which engulfed Huamanga in the 1560s arose less from pressures of social disorganization or impoverishment than from a growing consciousness, among groups who had adapted more or less successfully to colonial conditions, that the contradictions of colonialism would lead to unbearable results. Nor can we say that the millenarian dreams which dominated the character of the subversion in Huamanga reflected a predisposition of pre-modern agricultural peoples to mount ineffective, "pre-political" forms of struggle against oppression or deprivation. As we shall see, Andean societies whose circumstances differentiated them from Huamanga seemed perfectly capable of organizing politico-military forms of struggle against colonialism. It was the special moral character of the crisis experienced in Huamanga, not the *inevitably* pre-political quality of protest among archaic societies, which bred millenarianism. Indeed, the inability of Huamanga's fragmented peoples to relieve their discontent by organizing war against the Spaniards contributed profoundly to their spiritual crisis.

Taki Onqoy offered its believers a way to overcome the demoralization inherent in the disenchantment, impotence, and inner doubt which tormented native society. A war fought by the native gods, and a return to moral purity by their loyal peoples, would suffice to effect the restoration of a pristine past purged of colonial and Incaic corruptions. In practical terms, the path to liberation would focus internally upon the misdeeds of native society rather than externally upon the European agents of evil. Moral reform and passive resistance, not organization for a direct human assault on the colonials, would usher in the native utopia.

What distinguished the millenarian crisis which inflamed southern Huamanga from other anticolonial movements was this predominance of an inward-looking moral drama. The neo-Incas ensconced in the jungles of Vilcabamba (see Chapter 2) had adopted more direct political and military strategies — a combination of war and diplomacy — against the Europeans from the 1530s on. While nativist religious inspirations played an important ideological role in their military raids and insurrectionary conspiracies, their independence and fairly consistent anticolonial stance relieved them from a crisis of moral purity. Like Huamanga's local societies *before* their crisis of confidence, the neo-Incas proved receptive to Hispanic cultural accouterments. Even in their most militant phases, the neo-Incas did not reject Hispanic symbols or religion. Indeed, they aggressively plundered and traded for Spanish commodities, particularly horses and weapons which would improve their military effectiveness.[62]

Similarly, the Huancas north of Huamanga plotted a bloody uprising in 1565. The Huancas, bitter foes of the Incas, had allied themselves to the Spanish conquistadores. But like Huamanga's societies, they apparently had reached a crisis of disenchantment with the Spaniards. Although Taki Onqoy may have played a significant ideological role among the Huancas, its reliance upon preaching internal reform and passive resistance, and upon elevating the battle against the Spanish to the realm of the supernatural, did not define the nature of the Huancas' subversion. The Huancas' solution to their discontent took the form of a military conspiracy, coordinated with their former Inca enemies and conceived as part of a more general revolt throughout the Andean highlands. The Huancas, like the neo-Incas, had escaped the impasse of extreme disenchantment, organizational weakness, and moral uncertainty that lay behind the stalemated politics and spiritual crisis infecting Huamanga. The Huancas had been a powerful, strategically important, and ethnically unified regional kingdom, sharply different in character from Huamanga's ethnically variegated societies, which permitted large-scale organization centralized in the leadership of several recognized ethnic chiefs. The Huancas could function, more effectively than Huamanga's fragmented societies, as an ethnic kingdom with an independent regional army. More than Huamanga's peoples had done, the Huancas also had thrown themselves unsparingly into the Spaniards' military battles and gained notoriety as an allied ethnic army. This experience, more than familiarizing the Huancas with Hispanic culture, enabled them to adopt Spanish military skills and technologies as their own. Rather than "purify" themselves culturally of Hispanic attachments, the Huancas set up primitive factories which produced thousands of Spanish pikes, battle-axes, and other weapons for the coming anticolonial war. Rather than reaffirm a rigid, absolute loyalty to all Andean customs, the Huanca chiefs gave priority to the tasks of organization. They refused to redistribute agricultural surpluses among needy households or ayllus, preferring instead to accumulate huge stores of foodstuffs to answer the needs created by war.[63]

The secular threat posed by Huamanga's spiritual convulsion was less immediate than that of the Huancas' and neo-Incas' military schemes. One could argue with some truth that Taki Onqoy's inward emphasis on moral purification was politically defeatist, that rejection of Spanish society was ambivalent, that millenarian dreams failed, in practical terms, to heal the weaknesses and resolve the dilemmas which had generated this profound spiritual crisis in the first place. In this sense, Taki Onqoy provided Huamanga's peoples renewed spirit and hope, but not a path to effective liberation.

Such an argument should not be overdrawn, however, for the millenarian fever which gripped Huamanga presented a grave challenge to the emerging colonial society. Whatever its inward-looking focus, the historical context and consequences of Taki Onqoy had important economic, political, and military repercussions for society at large. Economically, the colonials depended greatly upon their alliances with native elites to gain access to goods and exploitable labor, and had not yet erected a sophisticated state apparatus that could force chiefs to turn over a consistent, regular flow of goods and labor to colonial enterprise. Taki Onqoy undoubtedly encouraged the surge of hostility, withdrawal from cooperation, sabotage, and passive resistance which frustrated Huamanga's economic development in the 1560s. Politically, the heresy threatened to reverse cooperative strategies, and appealed to the indigenous loyalties of ethnic groups, native elites, and Hispanizing yanaconas who had once sustained colonial rule. Even if the rebellion focused on spiritual issues, it encouraged the growth of attitudes and relationships which could improve the prospects of successful Indian rebellion. It propagated a consciousness of shared identity and interest which sought to downplay divisions between rival kindreds or communities, or between Hispanizing elites and indigenous peasants.

Given the existence of Indian societies plotting war, any movement which taught pan-Andean unity and hatred of the Europeans posed military dangers. Conspirators and rebels, including the neo-Incas, allied themselves with Taki Onqoy, in which they hoped to find tools to encourage military cooperation to wreck Spanish rule.[64] Who could say that a contagious mobilization of anticolonial hatreds and millenarian expectations would not, in the end, be absorbed into an active military assault? The corregidor of Huamanga, like his counterparts in Huánuco and Cuzco, warned Acting Viceroy García de Castro that rebellion might break out.[65]

Thus Taki Onqoy was more than a regional crisis of Huamanga; it constituted one part of a more general crisis menacing the Peruvian viceroyalty as a whole. Outside of Huamanga, nativist religious revivals threatened Christianity's inroads on Andean life. Economically, Europeans in Cuzco and Lima contended with Indian rebelliousness and resistance to labor demands. Moreover, a sharp decline in silver production at Potosí threatened to bring the colonial economy to a standstill, while Spain's fiscal difficulties worsened in Europe. Politically, the kurakas and Spanish priests had stalled a favorable resolution of the debate on whether to perpetuate or abolish the encomienda (see Chapter 2). In addition, creole jealousies and intrigues, and mestizo conspiracies threatened to plunge colonial society into another series of civil wars. Militarily, the neo-Incas' raids on Jauja and Huamanga, their contacts with tribes attacking frontiers in Charcas, Tucumán, Chile, and northern Peru, and the discovery of arms and plots in Jauja, Andahuaylas, and elsewhere made large-scale insurrection a concrete danger, not merely a theoretical possibility.[66]

In Huamanga, an aspiring ruling class had pegged its political and economic strategies to a system of post-Incaic alliances. Now, however, the subversive dreams which infected the native allies in Huamanga and elsewhere threatened to shatter the imperial venture.

CRISIS IN IMPERIAL SOCIETY, REFORMIST SOLUTIONS

"The more I go on looking at the matters of this land, the more I come to feel how necessary it is to remedy the bad rule of the past, as much in spiritual [matters] as in temporal."[67] These were the words of Peru's acting viceroy, Governor-General Lope García de Castro, in 1565. The crisis of the 1560s inspired radical dreams of utopia in native society; in imperial society, the crisis gave rise to a critical, reformist spirit which searched for solutions.

A TIME FOR INNOVATION

As Guillermo Lohmann Villena has shown so well, the sudden collapse of the Spanish success story in the 1560s preoccupied statesmen and intellectuals concerned with the collective welfare of an emerging ruling class. Leading colonials, like García de Castro, consciously understood that Spanish rule in Peru had reached a critical watershed. Bedeviled by native resistance and the specter of wholesale insurrection, intra-European and mestizo strife, and economic bottlenecks, they would need to reconstruct society on terms more favorable to the colonial elite's long-run, uncontested dominance. This was a classic task faced by all ruling classes, which the subversive restlessness of the natives had finally forced the Europeans to confront. How to mold Spanish and Indian societies into a single, organic polity blessed with internal stability, while simultaneously structuring the new society to favor the economic and political interests of the colonial elite, was the burning issue that lay behind an outburst of criticism, ethnographic investigation, and proposals for reform. Suddenly, a near-utopian impulse to endow colonial Andean society with a sense of the "common good," to erect a more effective state apparatus, and to establish systematic rules which would command the respect of all, took hold of the colonials.[68]

Juan de Matienzo, a distinguished jurist and wealthy entrepreneur,[69] best exemplified this desire to lay a stronger foundation for a colonial society in the Andes. His outstanding treatise on "the governing of Peru," written in 1567, presented a moral and political blueprint to revitalize Spanish imperialism. Matienzo saw the encomendero elite as the keystone of society and therefore viewed the encomenderos' function and interests as the basic source of social stability, economic development, and moral progress. They defended Spain's American outposts against insurrection, supported an array of dependents who swelled the colonizing population, mobilized mining and commerce by levying and spending tributes, and hired priests to indoctrinate the natives. "It is certain," he argued, "that the encomenderos sustain the land, and without them there could not be a commonwealth."[70]

Instead of confining himself to a narrow defense of the encomenderos' interests, however, Matienzo spelled out what the times needed — a comprehensive, organic vision of the general welfare which harmonized the presumably complementary interests and social functions of natives and Europeans. With remarkable fervor, Matienzo repeatedly emphasized his desire to reorganize society in a way that would defend the natives against abuses, short-sighted policies, and eternal damnation. "I wish all the good to the Indians and Spaniards, and that everyone [should] benefit with the least harm possible to the Indians, and even with no harm to them. As this land gives us such riches, it is just that we not pay them with ingratitude."[71]

In a systematic effort to impart moral integrity to colonial rule, Matienzo articulated a view of native history which railed against the Incas and extolled the benefits of Spanish conquest. Imperialist world views have always held that the foreigners brought progress and liberation to downtrodden peoples. Writing a colonial's history of Andean society, Matienzo interpreted Spanish conquest as the liberation of a racially inferior people. The Indians had fallen under the enslavement of Inca tyrants and the devil, who manifested his evil in the natives' pagan gods. "Born and raised to serve" rather than command, the natives were too lazy and unintelligent to work or live in a civilized way on their own initiative. Having liberated the native peoples from tyranny, the Spaniards could now bring them progress and salvation. "Let us compare," Matienzo moralized, "what the Spaniards receive and what they give to the Indians, to see who is indebted to whom. We give them religious instruction [*doctrina*], we teach them to live like men, and they give us silver, gold or things worth [them]." Quoting Biblical authorities who praised the superior value of wisdom and intelligence to material riches, Matienzo concluded that the natives held the advantage! In exchange for the "inestimable" value of Catholic civilization, the Indians had given up mere "rocks and mud."[72]

A serious statesman, Matienzo advocated several policies to back the moral philosophy of conquest with a sophisticated reorganization of politics and society. First, the Crown would have to stabilize the internal government of Spanish society, "upon which depends execution of the laws regarding the Indians and all the rest."[73] Fully conscious that a continuation of intra-Spanish and mestizo wars and conspiracies against the encomendero elite would endanger colonial rule, Matienzo searched for ways to promote Spanish unity and stability. He inveighed against vagabonds and pretenders to noble status, proposed ways to reinvigorate the institutions and authority of the state, and argued for policies favoring small and medium agriculturalists. The owners of modest farms known as *chácaras* would swell the Hispanic population with a stabilizing force of conservative settlers, some of them petty lords of dependent yanaconas.[74]

Second, Matienzo hoped to extend the apparatus of the colonial state more directly into reorganized native communities. The natives' scattered settlement patterns and relative autonomy weakened colonial control. Matienzo proposed a massive inspection and resettlement program, which would "reduce" the dispersed households of ayllus and communities into towns and villages, yield reliable demographic and economic information, set reasonable tributes and labor obligations, distribute land rights, and subject the reorganized communities to the control of the colonial state's local representatives. A Spanish corregidor, or chief magistrate, would represent the colonial juridical system and oversee local life. Next to the corregidor's residence on the town's central plaza would stand the local jail. Spanish authorities would choose Indian functionaries for a municipal council, modeled after the Spanish cabildo, which would share with the kurakas responsibility for the internal government of native society. Just as the Indian lay assistants of Catholic priests expanded the number of local agents of the Church, so the Indian cabildo would swell the effective power of the colonial state.[75]

In addition to placing reorganized native communities under more direct control of the state, Matienzo sought to neutralize the neo-Incas' political and military presence. Negotiations between Titu Cusi, ruler of the Neo-Inca State, and the Spanish viceroys had faltered by 1565, when the neo-Incas terrorized traffic through Huamanga and Cuzco. With the discovery of the Huancas' conspiracy in Jauja, and the pressure of repeated attacks by hostile tribes along the viceroyalty's perimeters, plausible rumors spread "that the Inca had agreed with some chiefs of the kingdom that all would rise up and kill the Spaniards."[76] Matienzo sought to breathe new life into nego-tiation with Titu Cusi, and himself held a remarkable interview with the mercurial Inca. Negotiations culminated in a peace treaty in 1566, but Titu Cusi held off from leaving his jungle fortress for Cuzco. Matienzo, like his contemporaries, recognized that a peaceful arrangement which allowed an independent Inca kingdom to stand would not suffice. The neo-Incas' au-tonomy, military capacity, proximity to Cuzco and Huamanga, and heri-tage as displaced imperial rulers could inspire subversion and conspiracies enlisting discontented local peoples. The only way to end the neo-Incas' po-litical and military presence once and for all would be to integrate them into colonial society, and Matienzo suggested a systematic policy of enticement which would lure Titu Cusi into Cuzco.[77]

Finally, Matienzo sought to rationalize policies, rules, and institutions into a system of interdependent parts promoting social stability and economic development. Matienzo's originality lay not in his ideas, many of which an-tedated the 1560s, but in his ability to conceptualize them as parts of a sweeping, interlocking design for systematic reform. The modest owners of chácaras would not only stabilize Hispanic politics, but also contribute to economic diversification. To balance the dynamic mining centers, the state would encourage agriculturalists, ranchers, artisans, and owners of sugar mills and obraje cloth factories to supply a growing market for foodstuffs, processed goods, manufactures, and handicrafts.[78] How would miners, farmers, and other entrepreneurs find labor to exploit? First, the state would make permanent the yanacona status of native retainers held since 1561 or earlier, while disallowing further emigration of yanaconas to or from encomiendas. This demographic "freeze" would at once stabilize a core resi-dent labor force in European homes, lands, and enterprises, and seal off the native communities from demographic outflows or from the return of politi-cally disruptive, acculturated yanaconas. Second, the inspections, resettle-ments, and revamped community power structures would create an appa-ratus of state power capable of supplementing the core group of yanaconas. The inspecting judge or the corregidor of a rural district would assign Span-ish enterprises with rotating contingents of native laborers for temporary service periods. In these conditions, however, how would the state minimize

the use of force to fulfill the labor needs of the colonial economy? The inspection and resettlement program would set reasonable tributes based on a
tributary population count of adult males, aged eighteen to fifty. To pay the
monetary portion of their tributes, the natives would have reason to hire
themselves out for wages some seventy days a year.[79]

How would the colonial system maximize a flow of precious metals into
the Spanish economy? The state would allow for a flourishing trade in commodities, particularly coca, needed by native workers in the mines. The Indians' purchases of coca, corn, cloth, and other goods would pry loose the
impressive sums of silver and gold accumulated by natives in the mining
centers. These sales would stimulate the commercial economy and rechan-
nel money into the diversifying Hispanic economy.[80] How would the system
reproduce itself in the long run? The state would peg colonial extraction of
tributes and labor contingents to a realistic estimate of the surplus capacity
of self-sufficient communities, and thereby avoid damaging the reproduc-
tive capacity of ayllu economies. The state would also install an effective
power structure to enforce society's rules, and maintain an accessible system
of justice to expose and correct abuses. Detailed regulations of social and
economic institutions would prevent unfettered exploitation of Indians
which, in the long run, could undermine the colonial system's ability to reproduce itself.[81]

The times favored reform. In Huamanga, Cristóbal de Albornoz launched
his sweeping campaign to correct the religious life of the natives. Determined
to root out messianism and idolatry, Albornoz plunged colonial power directly into the intimacies of local life. For more than two years, he sought
out ethnographic information and experience; he rewarded collaborators
and informants with economic resources or promotion to kuraka positions;
he differentiated punishment according to degree of threat or leadership;
he subjected key figures to public rites of repentance and humiliation, including whipping and haircutting; he exploited native fears of reprisals by the
Christian gods; and he offered salvation to the repentant. To give local
Catholic institutions a new lease on life, Albornoz replaced incompetent
priests, ordered new church construction, and funnelled the labor of punished natives into the revitalized churches.[82]

García de Castro, the acting viceroy from 1564 to 1569, understood that
the viceroyalty's crisis demanded bold innovations. The governor backed
the successful peace negotiations with Titu Cusi. With less success, he tried
to resettle the natives into villages and towns and to install new Indian functionaries. Most important, García de Castro began to experiment with placing corregidores—judge-administrators of municipalities and their districts
—in the rural encomiendas. These new *corregidores de indios* would complement the *corregidores de españoles* who already supervised Spanish municipali-

ties such as Huamanga. Writing the king in 1565, the governor explained that "all these natives had agreed to rebel." A corregidor-system in the rural provinces would enhance security, regularize administration, obviate the need for costly tours of inspection, and prevent kurakas from robbing poor Indians at the expense of the Crown's and encomenderos' legal tributes. But García de Castro lacked the force of personality, political skill, base of support, and vision to put through even his own reforms, much less the more ambitious reorganization favored by Matienzo.[83] If, by the close of the decade, García de Castro, Matienzo, Albornoz, and others had forestalled the threat of immediate insurrection, they had nevertheless failed to lift Peru out of economic stagnation and political crisis.

VICEROY TOLEDO'S REFORMS

The ruler who finally put Matienzo's vision into effect was Don Francisco de Toledo.[84] Energetic, forceful, and ambitious, the great viceroy was a person whose skills in organization, planning, and politics flourished in the atmosphere of crisis gripping Peru. During his twelve years of rule (1569–1581), Toledo's government conducted oral inquiries on Inca tyranny which supported the morality of Spanish conquest; invaded the neo-Inca kingdom and publicly executed its militant ruler, Tupac Amaru; undertook a massive inspection of the entire viceroyalty; "reduced" the natives into Hispanic-style settlements under the control of Spanish corregidores and Indian functionaries; set up a system of tribute and rotating forced labor, the colonial *mita*; organized a prosperous mining economy fueled by the mita labor system; tied the colonial elite's economic wellbeing to the institutions of a revitalized state; and left behind a huge corpus of legislation to govern the politics and economics of the reorganized regime.

To accomplish this much, Toledo spent five years (1570–1575) travelling throughout the Andean highlands on an audacious *visita,* or tour of inspection, designed to implement an effective, direct reorganization once and for all. Mobilizing a distinguished array of jurists, ecclesiastics, and veteran encomenderos and functionaries,[85] Toledo collected at first hand knowledge and experience for rulings on regional and local problems, and dispatched subdelegations to all corners of the kingdom to carry out the *reducciones* (resettlement program) which would reorganize native life. The bulk of his creative work Toledo did in the highlands, personally in touch with the milieu in which problems arose, and bringing the glitter and symbols of his office directly to bear upon various regions. In Huamanga, Toledo attended to organizing and providing labor to the Huancavelica mines under the state's control; in Cuzco he ordered the dramatic execution of Tupac Amaru; in Potosí he directed construction of a huge hydraulic power and refining complex which, together with a new amalgamation technique, would rescue the moribund silver mines. In Vilcashuamán Toledo symbolically sat himself in the throne atop the magnificent sun temple built after the Inca conquest of Huamanga.[86] The end result of Toledo's efforts was a systematic reorganization which, by raising the productive forces in the mining economy, creating a centralized system of forced labor, and destroying the neo-Inca presence, surpassed even Matienzo's plan in its sweep.

My purpose here is not to offer the specific details of Toledo's work and legislation — a story readily available elsewhere.[87] In the next chapter, we shall see more precisely what Toledo's reorganization meant for the native societies of Huamanga. Of more importance for the moment is an understanding of the historical significance of his work as the logical culmination of a colonial crisis which demanded reform. Even weaker personalities like García de Castro understood that the alternative to reform was at best decadence, at worst destruction.

What remains puzzling is *how* Toledo managed to accomplish such a massive reform program despite considerable opposition. The reducciones campaign conflicted sharply with traditionally dispersed settlement patterns designed to exploit a series of scattered Andean microenvironments. Peru's natives offered Toledo 800,000 pesos to abandon the resettlement idea, and in Huamanga in fact Indian residence in the new towns grew somewhat precarious and irregular by the 1580s.[88] How, then, could Toledo carry through his reorganization of local life? We still await the documentation needed to write an "inside history" of Toledo's visita, but we can suggest a plausible line of explanation.

A profound demoralization must have gripped native Andean societies by 1570. On the one hand, hoped-for insurrections by the neo-Incas, Huancas, and other groups never materialized. On the other, messianic promises of a Spanish-free paradise vanished before Albornoz's campaign against heresy. Taki Onqoy had forestalled an already lurking despair, and sought to galvanize native society out of its deep moral crisis. Now, the defeat of the rebellious huacas dashed the inspired hopes of radical millenarians and once more demonstrated the superiority of the colonials' gods. Coming on the heels of such crushing blows, the public execution of Tupac Amaru in 1572 had a profound symbolic impact which moved Spaniard and Indian alike; finally, after forty years, Toledo had eliminated the Neo-Inca State, the last autonomous stronghold of a proud highland people.[89] In other colonized zones, the unrealized dreams of revolutionary millenarianism have often given way to "post-millennial" adaptations in which the defeated settle for less ambitious sects or reformist political groups.[90] In Peru, too, the natives had to accommodate themselves to the reality of defeat. The demoralization attending such adaptations augured poorly for the short-term collective will of native society to resist a determined European force.

Indeed, the end result may have been to turn frustrations inward in a divisive way which worked to the advantage of the *visitadores* (judge-inspectors) sent to reorganize rural encomiendas. We know that other colonized peoples, frustrated by their inability to attack their oppressors successfully, have sometimes undertaken traditional fratricidal struggles with renewed vengeance.[91] As we shall see, evidence from Huamanga suggests that a resurgence of intracommunity and interethnic struggles took place, which enhanced the authority of Toledo's inspection teams. Internal disunity offered Toledo a golden opportunity to replace kurakas judged disloyal or ill-suited for colonial tasks, and he made the best of it.[92] At moments of political instability, the kuraka families always spawned various pretenders to chieftainships — sons, cousins, nephews of the ruling kurakas — who each searched for a social base of support with which to depose incumbents or other aspirants.[93]

The crisis of the 1560s and its disheartening aftermath probably encouraged such struggles for power.[94] The taquiongos had first discredited reluctant kurakas, and Albornoz's campaign then discredited or replaced kurakas sympathetic to Taki Onqoy. Consider the testimony of Don Juan Llanto, a kuraka from Angaraes, in 1589. When Gerónimo de Silva visited his encomienda to implement Toledo's reorganization, he "made a public investigation of the cacicazgos [chieftainships] of my community *to restore the deposed and name caciques* [kurakas] *competent for good government* of the pueblos."[95] South of the Río Pampas, the inspection team led by Juan de Palomares found a resurgence of bitter land conflicts among a cluster of interspersed ethnic groups. The situation favored the authority of Palomares, who "ordered that the caciques make models of the said land, with the fruit trees, rivers, springs, lakes, pueblos and other [landmarks]." At least twenty chiefs from several ethnic groups collaborated in the making of "the said description, model, and painting." After ruling on land rights and other issues, Palomares extracted joint approval from the chiefs and ordered that his work be obeyed, "under penalty of loss of cacicazgos."[96] The evidence indicates that, with native society demoralized and caught in a web of internal strife, and with kurakas aware that their incumbency rested upon approval by the colonial state, the Indians could not mount effective opposition to the Europeans' tough-minded campaign to implant a state apparatus once and for all in local society.

Less difficult to explain is Toledo's ability to override coolness and antagonisms from European factions. He enjoyed certain resources. A special junta called in Spain a year before his departure vested in him full authority to implement thorough reform in the name of the Crown. In addition, Toledo possessed political skill sufficient to align the support of key intellectuals and other members of the colonial elite. Perhaps most important, the crisis of the

1560s must have affected the collective consciousness of the colonial elite. We may hypothesize that the air of near-misses with native insurrections chastened an emerging ruling class. A heightened sense of self-preservation probably cautioned against the carefree murders of unpopular authorities which prevailed in the disorderly 1540s.[97] Moreover, Toledo did not truly threaten the interests of the colonial elite. On the contrary, however much some of them grumbled about specific actions — such as expropriation of the mercury mines at Huancavelica, and assignment of concessions to work them in contracts with the state—Toledo demonstrated a capacity to organize a prosperous economy which would funnel to the colonial elite a flow of tributes, labor, and profits. The crisis of the 1560s had generated a willingness to recognize the need for law, as long as the lawgiver would promote the interests of a colonial ruling class.

The specter of revolution had created the reality of reform. In a deep sense, the founding of colonial Andean society began in earnest when Toledo departed for the highlands in 1570. After a generation of first attempts which ended in crisis, Toledo was to lay a more enduring foundation for the evolution of a colonial society in the Andes.

4

The Political Economy of Colonialism

IN THE 1570s, the local peoples of Huamanga finally became Indians. Toledo's reorganization did not erase their ethnic diversity, but subordinated it to a wider, more decisive set of relationships. For the Caviñas, Acos, Angaraes, Huayacondos, Huaros, Pariscas, Chilques, Papres, Totos, Tanquihuas, Quichuas, Aymaraes, Lucanas, Soras, Chalcos, Huachos, Yauyos, Chocorvos, and other peoples of the region, the contours of local ayllu and ethnic life would be forever defined by their shared incorporation into a new colonial category, the so-called "republic of Indians." Within the Indian caste, a large class of native peasants controlled by a revamped indigenous elite or directly by the colonials themselves would provide goods, labor, and profits to the Crown and to the other great caste, the "republic of Spaniards." Within the latter group, a ruling class of colonials with diversified interests in commercial production, mining, trade, agriculture, and administration would dominate the mixed-bloods and other Europeans, and reap the greatest rewards of exploitation of the indigenous peasantry.[1]

Because Toledo's economic design imposed harsh obligations on self-sufficient native communities, it required coercion to enforce compliance with the state's rules of extraction. The secret of Toledo's achievement was his construction of the "political arm" of colonization: the organization of coercive, violent institutions and relationships into power structures capable of implementing a grand design for economic development. By tying extraction to the institutions, patrimony, and repressive apparatus of a revitalized state, Toledo domesticated the colonial elite—a class of aristocrat-entrepreneurs who combined noble pretense with a sharp eye for trade and profit. When the state, its officials, merchants, and local elites accommodated one another, the game of political alliances and connections served up highly profitable economic opportunities to be shared by them all. Favored by access to political power, European enterprise, led by a dynamic mining sector, embarked upon a tremendous boom. Economic expansion and prosperity, we shall see later (Chapter 6), developed a dynamic of its own. Eventually, the colonials' economic dynamism and the peasants' deepening poverty would allow Huamanga's elites and lesser citizens to accumulate resources and exploit labor without having to depend as much as they had at first upon political favor or the formal patrimony of the state. But in the last analysis, the economic dominance which eventually permitted the elites to exploit large amounts of labor more directly, sidestepping the state, originated from the advantages bequeathed to entrepreneurs by Toledo's legacy, the political arm of colonization.

THE GRAND DESIGN AND ITS BURDENS

In Huamanga as elsewhere, Toledo dispatched inspection teams to collect the demographic and economic information needed to set up a planned system of extraction. The inspectors counted a total of 21,981 tributaries (healthy males eighteen to fifty years old), and a total population of 122,629 Indians, in Huamanga's twenty-three "core" encomienda districts, called *repartimientos*. The great visita pegged tribute liabilities to the various tributary counts of the repartimientos (Table 4.1), and converted the encomenderos into pensioners of the Crown. Of every ten "core" repartimientos, three held over 1,000 tributaries each—a high figure in greater Peru. Another five surpassed respectability by far, with over 500 tributaries each.

Table 4.1. Size distribution of tributary counts in Huamanga repartimientos, 1570–1575

	1,500 +	1,000–1,499	500–999	300–499	1–299
No. of repartimientos	5	2	11	2	3
% of repartimientos	21.7	8.7	47.8	8.7	13.0

Note: The boundaries of the Huamanga district changed somewhat during the entire colonial period. The figures cited for Huamanga's twenty-three core repartimientos exclude the Jauja repartimientos to the north, five small groups of mitmaq whose colonies lay in the Chocorvos district, but whose ethnic homelands were outside Huamanga, and several repartimientos on the peripheries of the Huamanga region.

Source: *Tasa de la visita general*, ed. Cook, 260–80.

In general, a repartimiento's Indians owed about four *pesos ensayados* (12.5 *reales* each) per tributary—nearly three in silver or gold, and the rest in kind. From each repartimiento's assessment, the state deducted administrative "costs": priests' salaries, a church fund, sums for the salaries of state officials and for "good works," salaries for major kurakas, and, in the beginning, a surplus assigned to community cash boxes. The remainder was "free" for the encomendero, other pensioners of the Crown, or the Crown itself. A rich repartimiento holding 1,000 tributaries or better turned over thousands of pesos in precious metals and marketable goods to its encomendero. A poorer repartimiento held only several hundred tributaries, but could still produce substantial annual pensions (see Table 4.2). Taken as a whole, the twenty-three core repartimientos produced a total annual tribute of 86,127 pesos ensayados. Of these, 37,553 pesos were distributed to administrative "costs" (the majority being priests' salaries), leaving a net regional tribute of 48,574 pesos for distribution to favored pensioners.[2]

To solve the colonials' labor problem, Toledo set up a draft system based on tributary counts. Traditionally, native society supplemented joint labor by the community as a whole with a rotation system. Peasants served a mit'a, or turn, out of the community's total labors. The rotations allowed communities and ayllus to distribute collective labor needs or obligations in accordance with local reciprocities, which called for equal contributions of labor-time by the community's kindreds. The Incas extended local mit'a traditions into a means of extracting labor which, as usual, sought to clothe peasant burdens in the well-known customs of communal life.[3] Toledo transformed the mit'a tradition into a colonial institution of forced labor, in which the state demanded contingents of up to one-seventh of a repartimiento's tributary population. (In this book the colonial labor draft is spelled "mita" and thereby distinguished from its pre-Columbian indigenous antecedent, spelled "mit'a.") The *mitayos,* as the temporary laborers were called, would work for specified periods outside their communities, until replaced by workers starting a new rotation. The state would regulate wages and working conditions, and assign mita quotas to colonial entrepreneurs. Mita labor on a grand scale, enforced by the authority of an effective state, would end the shortage of labor for dangerous work in mining. The mercury mines of Huancavelica would receive 3,000 mitayos drawn largely from Huamanga's rural districts; south and east of Huamanga, mita assignments drew some 14,000 workers for the fabulous silver mines of Potosí. The colonial mita would mobilize a plentiful, cheap, and reliable labor supply not only for mines, but also for obraje workshops, agriculture, ranching, general household service, and any other task or person deemed worthy of the state's patrimony.[4]

For the Indians, Toledo's grand design implied harsh burdens. Tribute in kind, for example, violated time-honored ways of protecting local self-sufficiency. Traditionally, Andean ayllus had given their authorities a tribute in labor only, rather than in finished products, on fields or herds set aside for ethnic chiefs, local cults, state shrines, and Inca rulers. In an environment where, year in and year out, no one could expect reliable harvests, prohibition on tributes in kind distributed the risks of sierra agriculture and pro-

Table 4.2. Variations in repartimiento incomes based on Toledo's visita

	Soras	Quinua	Huaros
Tributaries:[a]	2,441	876	321
Total population:	15,169	5,141	1,979
Tributes:[b]			
Silver	6,713	2,628	963
Cloth	1,500[c]	—	—
Corn	788[d]	510[e]	200[f]
Wheat	263[g]	285[h]	63[i]
Potatoes	126[j]	—	21[k]
Swine	188[l]	—	—
Footwear	188[m]	—	—
Chickens	—	81[n]	38[o]
Total	9,766 pesos	3,504 pesos	1,285 pesos
"Costs":			
Priests	2,400	827	298
Church	100	50	12
Judges	498	300	69
Kurakas	460	150	30
Surplus	1,002	300	81
Total	4,460 pesos	1,627 pesos	490 pesos
Net Tribute:			
In money	2,253	1,001	473
In kind	3,053	876	322
Total	5,306 pesos	1,877 pesos	795 pesos

[a]net tributary population (excludes kurakas removed from sum of taxable tributaries).

[b]All figures are monetary values for one year, as calculated in Toledo's visita, and rounded off to the nearest peso ensayado (of 12.5 reales).

[c]600 large textiles, at 2.5 pesos each.

[d]1,050 fanegas, at .75 pesos each (1 fanega =c. 1.5 bushels).

[e]680 fanegas, at .75 pesos each.

[f]160 fanegas, at 1.25 pesos each.

[g]350 fanegas, at .75 pesos each.

[h]380 fanegas, at .75 pesos each.

[i]50 fanegas, at 1.25 pesos each.

[j]505 fanegas, at .25 pesos each.

[k]42 fanegas, at .5 pesos each.

[l]125 adult head, at 1.5 pesos each.

[m]1,000 pair sandalwear, at .1875 pesos each (16 pair = 3 pesos).

[n]864 fowl, at .09375 pesos each (32 chickens = 3 pesos).

[o]300 fowl, at .125 pesos each (8 chickens = 1 peso).

Source: *Tasa de la visita general,* ed. Cook, 260, 270, 273.

tected local subsistence stocks. If a crop failed on Inca lands, the state had to accept the loss and rely on its reserves from previous seasons.[5] Colonial tributes in kind, in addition to claiming the community's "surplus" labor time, eliminated the protection of community and ayllu stocks. Though communities continued the tradition of producing taxes on lands set aside especially for that purpose,[6] they would have to make good on tributes even in years of poor harvests. In effect, the community would have to dip into harvests or warehouses assigned to local subsistence. To protect themselves, and to retain the option of selling surpluses on their own behalf when market prices rose, various ethnic groups won viceregal decrees which allowed them to commute payments in kind into equivalent money tributes (calculated at fixed prices).[7]

The most oppressive and fearful institution, however, was the forced labor of the mita. Consider what awaited the tributary who marched off with his ayllu's contingent to the mercury mines at Huancavelica, to the silver mines at Castrovirreyna or elsewhere, to the obraje factories scattered throughout Vilcashuamán, or to the central plaza of Huamanga, where the elite and lesser colonials received mitayo allotments for agriculture, ranching, construction, food processing (sugar, alcohol, grains), household duties, and any other "worthy" tasks.

For the next two to four months, the mita meant far more than a short work stint away from community life. The mitayo found himself consigned to a brutal relationship, in which colonial entrepreneurs tried to squeeze out the greatest amount of labor possible before the mitayo's time expired. Long work-days and high production quotas shaped a grinding, taxing existence. Mitayos followed the old practice of taking along wives, children, or other relatives to assist them, give company, and prepare meals in work away from their "core" residences. By bringing along relatives and foodstuffs from the community, the mitayos could hope to avoid purchasing food to supplement the rations given by their masters, and thereby take home most of their meager wages. Such practices, however, exposed a larger group of people to the harsh realities of mita labor. Colonials raped women, commandeered the labors of relatives for secondary tasks, and set impossible production quotas to force mitayos to utilize the labors of their families. In short, colonials increased profits by appropriating for themselves all the productive resources, including human labor-power, brought by the mitayos. In the obrajes, for example, the mitayos tended to be older men or children. Despite the long hours put in by the children, they could not meet daily production quotas without the help of parents, or brothers and sisters. In construction, the Europeans forced mitayos to transport building materials in their own *mantas* (carrying cloaks) until the tough textiles wore out.[8]

Long, hard work in dangerous conditions pressed in on health. Back-breaking, sweaty mine labor in the high cold climates of Castrovirreyna (silver) and Huancavelica (mercury) invited pneumonia and respiratory ailments. The worst work was underground. Laboring by candlelight, Indians hammered away at flint-hard rock, carried heavy bags of ore up hundreds of tortuous feet, and emerged — hot, exhausted, and thirsty — into the cold air. Some died in accidents, when underground support columns collapsed. Ore-rich columns, especially, were subject to theft during off-hours which weakened their stability. Occasionally, the raiders included overseers responsible for mines and Indian laborers during regular hours. In Huancavelica, poor ventilation, mercury vapor, and mercury-rich dust conspired to make poisoning a terrifying reality. Many miners who contracted the mercury sickness did not die quickly, but suffered long, debilitating illnesses. The malady ulcerated the respiratory tract, infected blood and bones with mercury, induced bouts of trembling, fever, and paralysis, and slowly led some victims to a merciful death. Those who survived or held off death for a year or two lived on in their home communities, disabled in varying degrees, visible reminders of the horrors of mitayo labor in Huancavelica.[9] Given the harsh regime endured by mita laborers, one needs little insight to understand why some twelve percent, or nearly one out of every eight mitayos sent from Lucanas to the silver mines of Castrovirreyna, found ways to escape rather than serve out their mitas.[10]

Even mitayos who escaped the dangers of mine labor could not assume that they would preserve their health. Work from sunrise to sunset in textile workshops must have stifled the physiological development of the children sent to obrajes. Mitayos diverted from farming or ranching for intense labor in hot sugar lands struggled against fatigue, which invited disease and accidents. Several died horrible deaths in the mills, ground up by the heavy wheels meant to press sugar cane.[11]

In exchange for two to four months of hard work under dangerous conditions, a mitayo earned not a remuneration sufficient to maintain his household's subsistence economy and pay off tribute assessments, but rather the right to struggle for such an outcome. The state's regulation of mita labor provided for a modest wage, along with food rations (including meat in the mines). But from the moment his service began a mitayo contended with pressures to enter commercial transactions which reduced his net pay. If daily rations and the foodstuffs brought from home communities proved insufficient to support the mitayo and the relatives who accompanied him, the peasant would need to purchase the remainder from his temporary master or in the market at large.[12] In a dynamic mining center, a *fanega* (c. 1.5 bushels) of corn, a standard ration for one adult for two months, cost well over twenty reales, or seven work-days in wages.[13] Even without a food deficit, mitayos had good reason to turn to the market. Rations did not generally include coca, an indispensable source of sustenance during Andean labor. Unless a mitayo enjoyed ample access to coca through ayllu kinship relations, he had no choice but to buy the prized leaf from one of the numerous merchants who flocked to cities and mining centers, and travelled through rural hinterlands.[14] Nor could a mitayo simply ignore traditional religious obligations or other festivities. Indeed, the release from misery and subjugation found in drunken celebrations and outbursts created dependencies upon liquor as well as coca which drew mitayos further into the market.[15] Moreover, a mitayo who kept a lid on commercial consumption during the official mita period often had little choice but to buy foodstuffs in the market while he waited for days or weeks after the mita to collect wages.[16]

In the race between debts and wages, spurred on by masters eager to save on wages by selling goods at inflated prices,[17] those gifted with luck, tremendous discipline, or substantial original resources stood the greatest chance to accumulate significant amounts of money. The native assigned to a relatively "easygoing" miner considered himself lucky to avoid working for a large, powerful, and demanding miner like Juan de Sotomayor. Everyone knew that Sotomayor drove his work gangs hard, leading them to physical exhaustion, high debts, attempted escapes, and even death.[18] A native whose homeland lay relatively near the worksite could send for needed food or clothes more easily than the mitayo from far away, and thus limit his dependence upon market transactions. Similarly, a wealthy peasant could mobilize kinfolk and community resources to support him during mita labor more readily than his poorer counterpart. A man who enjoyed good health could pile up wage credits for more work-days (or production quotas) than a frailer laborer whose poor health lowered earnings and raised expenses. If we are to believe the wage records available for 107 Lucanas mitayos who died or fled Castrovirreyna in the years 1597–1603 (Table 4.3), a small minority of mining mitayos (18.7 percent) did indeed manage to avoid debt, or at least hold indebtedness to less than a fifth of wages. But the majority of workers (51.4 percent) incurred debts amounting to over 60 percent of their mita wages, and one in seven (14.0 percent) earned no net wages at all!

These figures exclude market transactions independent of direct claims on wages by miners, and thus may understate true debt burdens. But even if we ignore the unrecorded obligations, the debts claimed by the miners alone prevented most workers from accumulating significant sums of money from

Table 4.3. Debts of Lucanas mitayos, Castrovirreyna, 1597–1603

% of wages	0	0.1–20.0	20.1–60.0	60.1–99.9	100 +
% of mitayos	16.8	1.9	29.9	37.4	14.0

Source: Wage records of 107 Lucanas mitayos who died or fled Castrovirreyna, discussed and listed in Appendix A.

mita labor. The records for sixty-five mitayos at Castrovirreyna who accumulated credits for twenty-five or more work-days (Table 4.4) indicate that nearly one in three (30.8 percent) netted no wages or less than one peso after debts. Another fifth (21.5 percent) netted one to four pesos, enough to meet tribute claims in part or in full, but with little or nothing left over. Fewer than one in ten (9.2 percent) enjoyed the economic resources, skills, or luck to end their mita labor with net wages amounting to eight pesos or more — enough to take home significant earnings after tribute deductions.[19] A mitayo in agriculture or obrajes earned only about half the daily wage of his counterpart in the mines,[20] and therefore relied upon a much smaller wage credit to cover debts and commercial transactions.

Table 4.4. Net wages of Lucanas mitayos, Castrovirreyna, 1597–1603[a]

	none	.01–.99	1–3.99	4–5.99	6–7.99	8 or more
% of mitayos	15.4	15.4	21.5	26.2	12.3	9.2

[a]in pesos ensayados (of 12.5 reales each).

Note: Excluded from this sample are records of Indians whose work-day credits totalled less than twenty-five days when they died or fled Castrovirreyna because such cases might underestimate the net pay of workers who survived or remained in Castrovirreyna during the full mita period. The work-day credits accumulated by Indians who stayed during the entire mita varied enormously, and the 25–102 range in this sample is, I believe, a fair one.

Source: Wage records in Appendix A.

Under these circumstances, a mita laborer was fortunate if his remuneration, after deduction for tribute, was sufficient to support him and the relatives who accompanied him during his labors, let alone compensate for the labor-time lost to his household's economy. In effect, the resources and human labor-power the mitayos brought along from home communities subsidized the colonial entrepreneurs, who were thereby freed from having to pay a salary which could, by itself, sustain and reproduce the labor-power of their work forces.[21] Yet the more a mitayo brought with him to avoid mounting debts which would consume more than he earned, the more he risked undermining his household's subsistence economy. As long as a mitayo and his close relatives were tied to mita life and labor, they could neither apply their labors to the ayllu fields assigned them, nor to the interchange of reciprocal labors which normally earned them the assistance of other households. Since the mitayo was likely to belong to the poorer segments of native society in the first place,[22] he enjoyed a smaller, less effective network of kin ties to mobilize for the care of fields and animals during his absence. A returning mitayo frequently encountered deteriorating or unworked fields, and an eroding network of relatives to call upon for reciprocal labor assistance. For such an individual — and there were many[23] — the mita, more than representing a discrete amount of labor-time lost to the household economy during the year, brought with it the corrosion of relationships without which families could not survive and reproduce themselves.

From the point of view of the wider community of ayllus, too, the mita disrupted access to vital resources and relationships. As often as not, a community contended with double the legal number of mita absences because, in practice, the mitas overlapped. Several days or a week before the official period of one mita expired, the next contingent would have to begin its trek under the watchful eyes of native and sometimes European functionaries. When the previous mita finally expired, the ex-mitayos would have to wait several days to over a month for wage payments before beginning their march home.[24] In rainy season, downpours slowed progress to a long, sometimes dangerous crawl across soggy paths and torrential rivers.[25] Since most mitas in Huamanga lasted only two months,[26] communities might face mita overlaps a total of five or six months every year. Consider, for example, the condition around 1600 of a populous repartimiento, in Andahuaylas, with some 3,000 tributaries. Among their mita liabilities, they owed 250 mitayos to mercury miners at Huancavelica every two months. In practice, however, they had to count on 500 absent heads of households.[27] In effect, at any given time of the year, they lost one of six, not one of twelve, of their vigorous men to Huancavelica alone. In real life, the overlaps could double the total mita assessment to nearly one of three tributaries, particularly if legal mita drafts had not yet been revised to take into account population decline.

In addition, communities could not even count on the return of all mitayos. As we have seen, records at the Castrovirreyna mines showed that, around 1600, some twelve percent of the mitayos sent from Lucanas escaped from the forced labor, disease, debts, and abuse closing in on them. Even if most of the escapees returned to their home communities, a net attrition rate of only three percent could prove extremely burdensome. For a repartimiento like the one in Andahuaylas, which sent 1,500 mitayos (six mitas of 250 each) a year to Huancavelica, such a rate would cost it some 45 tributaries annually, or one of every six or seven tributaries over a decade.[28]

The prolonged absences of considerable numbers of mitayos, who themselves tended to take along relatives to their temporary workplaces, and the attrition represented by mitayo flights, siphoned off high proportions of available labor-power. Particularly in labor-intensive agriculture, the mita's drainage inevitably forced communities to retrench the scope of their subsistence economies and restrict the production of surplus crops which would tide them over poor harvests. Perhaps more difficult than the loss of labor-power as such was the fact that traditional relations of production acquired a less dependable character. The absence of laborers on a temporary basis did not, by itself, constitute a new or disruptive element. As we have seen, ayllus and communities traditionally worked scattered pockets of resources which required considerable geographical mobility and significant absences from "core" settlement areas. A local mit'a system, integrated into a network of reciprocal interchanges of labor among a community of producer-relatives, had long played an important role in the subsistence economy. Expectations that labor assistance would be reciprocated later allowed absent producers to call upon relatives to tend to their interests until their return. The mit'a established by the Incas permitted such expectations to continue.

But the colonial mita made such expectations problematic, even foolhardy, not only because it reduced the total labor-time available for community work, but also because it disrupted the dependability of traditional forms of interchange. The mitayo and his relatives might never come back! Or if they returned, they might not arrive in time for crucial moments in the agricultural cycle, when their labors were most needed. Or the mitayo might return in time, but too sick to put in the work expected of a young man. By injecting new risks and uncertainties into local work relationships, the colonial mita induced a *collective* deterioration which undermined the efficacy of traditional institutions as a reliable source of labor. Only in this way can we understand the widespread complaint, in societies which had long managed to integrate labor rotations, geographical mobility, and temporary absences into their economic organization, that mitayos could not find people to tend to their fields while they were away.[29]

THE SURVIVAL OF AYLLU SELF-SUFFICIENCY

Ideally, the system of tributes and mita allotments, set by the supposed carrying capacity indicated in demographic counts, were to have supplied the colonial economy with a flow of money, commodities, and labor while preserving the basic self-sufficiency of autonomous native economies. As we have seen, reality proved far more complex. Tributes in kind and repeated demands for the community's surplus labor-time set in motion a process of hardship and attrition which, over the years, menaced subsistence stocks, shrank the core mass of available labor-power, and disrupted relationships and activities that had once constituted renewable annual cycles of ayllu production and reproduction.

Yet the state's extractive institutions did not immediately, in one blow, destroy the internal vitality or subsistence capacity of peasant economies. The process which ultimately undermined the economic independence of native societies took time, and was itself contradictory. For the very same forces—an expansive commercial economy driven by large-scale mining—which drove colonials to expropriate large amounts of labor and tributes also gave Indians a chance to exploit commercial opportunities. And the revenues Indians accumulated in trade could help them reverse setbacks or inroads on local subsistence. For at least a decade or two after Toledo's reorganization, access to sufficient lands, animals, labor-power, and other resources, together with creative local adaptations to the commercial economy, allowed most communities to meet their subsistence needs, and even to accumulate surprising cash surpluses.

Population decline, colonial interests, and the natives' own tactics helped preserve local self-sufficiency. Demographic decline reduced the total amount of lands, pastures, and labor time needed to sustain the remaining local populations. Unlike their eighteenth-century counterparts, whose expanding population hungered for land, Huamanga's sixteenth-century peoples usually held surplus lands which they could not work because of population decline and labor drafts for Spanish enterprise.[30] In addition, colonial extraction was premised upon exploiting the Indians' self-sufficiency, rather than eliminating it. The state, therefore, instituted policies designed to place limits on colonial expropriations. Toledo's inspection teams set aside lands for the exclusive use of the resettled communities and, as we shall see (Chapter 5), colonial juridical institutions allowed communities to revise their tribute and mita obligations downward in accordance with declines in the tributary populations. Just as important, the private interests of colonials as individual entrepreneurs also favored local self-sufficiency. Even wealthy miners—the entrepreneurs most capable of paying wages sufficient to support workers' families, and whose labor regime most threatened the subsistence economy of the mitayos' rural communities—relied on cheap labor, whose maintenance was subsidized by community economies, to increase profits and minimize risks.

The natives themselves developed strategies to protect their self-sufficiency. They sued in colonial courts to lower tribute and mita quotas, convert tributes in kind to tributes in money, fight off European intrusions on fertile lands, and the like (see Chapter 5). With the tacit consent of local officials, they abandoned residence in the new reducciones for more traditional, dispersed settlement patterns. The new resettlements, had they been enforced, would have eaten into labor-time available for production by stretching out travel to scattered holdings.[31] Most important, by connecting resilient and dynamic local economies to commercial networks, communities managed to generate a monetary income which could, for a time, pay off tributes, minimize labors in distant sites under conditions not easily controlled, and make up for shortfalls in subsistence storage or production. Natives sold excess lands,[32] worked local mines on their own account,[33] and marketed surplus animals, commercial crops, and processed goods such as wool and cheese.[34] Particularly in southern regions such as Lucanas, Soras, and Castrovirreyna (before the discovery of silver c. 1590), access to extensive pasturelands unexpropriated by colonial ranchers allowed communities to earn money by selling thousands of animals whose care required relatively little labor. (Colonial estancias first spread near the cities of Huamanga and Huancavelica and along the commercial route through Vilcashuamán.)[35]

In effect, many communities displayed an internal vitality that enabled them to survive — for a time — as relatively autonomous and modestly prosperous productive units. By producing and marketing a surplus on their own account, they could compensate for the inroads made by colonial institutions upon local self-sufficiency. In Parinacochas, for example, local kurakas sometimes entered the market for their repartimientos' tributes in kind, and bought back foodstuffs their ayllus had just turned over for tributes.[36] By the 1580s and 1590s, many ethnic groups were accumulating thousands of pesos in cash reserves deposited in community coffers. The reserves, coveted by local elites, colonial bureaucrats, and royal treasurers alike, grew into a headache for royal policy well before 1590.[37] The system of extraction set up by Toledo had not anticipated the kind of dynamic adaptations which allowed communities, after turning over goods, money, and labor to the colonial economy, to generate substantial surpluses and cash reserves for their own use.

Thus, though colonial tributes and mitas imposed hardship, disruption, and drainage which wore away at and ultimately impoverished local subsistence economies, the *process* of attrition took time. Communities reduced to a bare subsistence by 1620 or 1630, unable to pay scaled-down tributes or even to meet administrative "costs" (salaries for priests and functionaries, church funds), managed to put aside thousands of pesos after paying hefty tributes in 1580 or 1590.[38] Economically, Toledo's extractive regime functioned as a crude "siphoning" process drawing upon the labor and resources of independent, sometimes wealthy, local economies. At least until around 1590, the natives' access to resources and shrewd adaptations to colonial conditions enabled many communities to maintain an impressive subsistence economy, buttressed by cash accumulations.

As a result, ayllus had no economic reason to submit to the mita labor or tribute assessments imposed by Toledo. In societies where producers retain independent access and control of resources sufficient to provide for their subsistence, no compelling economic necessity drives them to deliver surplus goods or labors to prospective employers or masters. Even if producers maintain inadequate access to resources, barely able to eke out a living, some form of extraeconomic coercion or pressure often proves necessary to exploit their labors.[39] In the case of Huamanga's local societies, Toledo's reorganization imposed a harsh regime of extraction upon groups of producer-relatives who could, more than scratch out a living, generate considerable wealth on their own. Even had communities accepted money tributes as the price of "social peace," they would have had little economic reason to comply with mita labor drafts, especially in the mines, to earn wages. Their own resourceful adaptations to the commercial economy, and the comparatively high wages commanded by non-mitayo labor, provided less abusive alternative modes of accumulating money.

The irony of Toledo's extractive regime was that it imposed terrible burdens which ultimately menaced local economies and life rhythms, but did not immediately eliminate the natives' subsistence capacity or economic independence. Under these circumstances, only one force could translate the horrors of the mita, along with a tribute system, into workable institutions. That force was force itself.

THE POLITICS OF ENFORCEMENT

What was new after Toledo was not the tributes or mitas in themselves, but the state's ability to rationalize and implement them on a large scale. Under the system of post-Incaic alliances, Indians and colonials alike had dubbed the transport of tributes by natives to the city, and the natives' subsequent stay for a period of service to their encomenderos, as the fulfillment of a "mita."[40] To translate such practices into veritable institutions providing a regular flow of goods, money, and forced labor to an expanding European economy, including a prosperous mining sector, required the reorganization and integration of local power structures into an effective network of state power.

The corregidor de indios system begun by García de Castro, along with Toledo's massive campaign of local inspection and reorganization, provided the means to enforce the state's extractive institutions. The new settlements established by the visitadores (inspectors) did not last long as permanent residential centers, but as we saw earlier, the reorganization entourages which fanned out over Huamanga represented the true arrival of state authority to demoralized rural districts. The itinerant judges settled local disputes, supervised construction of new towns and churches, and made clear that the state would replace troublesome kurakas with more pliant functionaries. To centralize the lines of rural power, Toledo grouped Huamanga's twenty-three core repartimientos into four rural districts, or *corregimientos* (Huanta, Angaraes-Chocorvos, Vilcashuamán, Lucanas).[41] As the state's chief administrative agent, judicial officer, and jailer, the corregidor de indios ruled over the economic, social, and political life of his corregimiento. Like his counterpart in Spanish cities such as Huamanga and, later, Huancavelica and Castrovirreyna, he did so in alliance with the prominent powers of his district.[42]

A revamped indigenous power structure, dependent upon the state's benevolence for its tenure and privileges, would serve as local agents of the corregidor and colonial regime. The major kurakas, who retained their chieftainships subject to the consent of the state, would have to share authority with new native officials. Within the corregimientos, the principal towns of the repartimiento districts would seat Indian cabildos modeled after the Spanish municipal councils. The Indian *alcalde* (mayor), assisted by his administrative aides (*regidores*), policeman (*alguacil mayor*), and other cabildo officials, would together with the kurakas oversee local life and represent the natives before state authorities. The cabildo officials, like the kurakas and the Indian assistants of local priests, enjoyed exemption from tribute and mita levies. In addition, major kurakas and several other native functionaries received rights to modest salaries (10–100 pesos ensayados a year). In effect, the state sanctioned the creation of privileged civil and religious power groups, recruited partly from traditional elites but also from more humble "social climbers." In both cases, the natives' elevated position would depend greatly upon their commitment to the institutional arrangements of the colonial regime.[43]

When the reformed colonial power structure functioned well, it nurtured a series of local, regional, and supraregional networks of elites. By connecting themselves to one another and to state officials and institutions, these elites could work out alliances of coexistence, mutual favors, and distribution of the profits extracted from an Indian peasantry. At the local level, whether in rural Indian society or in the Spanish cities and mining centers, the corregidor or *gobernador* (governor) appointed by the viceroy held a strategic position. He was the primary judge who heard disputes, administered state institutions such as mita and tribute, and exercised the authority and police powers of the colonial state. Like any person who secured a major appointment from Lima, the corregidor was already a man of some means or influence. Eager to make a small fortune during his term of several years, a newly arriving corregidor often cultivated working relationships with regional elites whose interest, like his, lay in tying together opportunities in administration, commerce, manufacturing, mining, and agriculture. In rural society, the corregidor de indios and his lieutenants mediated key relationships between Indian communities and the colonials seeking to exploit them. The kurakas, Indian functionaries and municipal officials, corregidor and lieutenants, rural priests, locally powerful encomenderos, landowners, and other entrepreneurs, well-connected merchants, prominent outside individuals and groups with significant local interests (such as miners with rights to mita labor), and the Spanish, mixed-blood, black, and Indian managers, assistants, and officials linked to them—together these figures composed a power group that dominated rural society in any given locale and enjoyed influential ties with state officials and elites in cities like Huamanga, Huancavelica, or Lima.

In some respects a loose assemblage of competing powers at odds with one

The multi-racial character of rural power groups. A Spanish corregidor invites a mestizo, a mulatto, and an Indian commoner to dine with him.

another and with other such networks, at other moments a more tightly woven mesh of mutually cooperating exploiters who enveloped rural Indian society, the power group developed its own internal hierarchies, ties of kinship and friendship, patron-client relations, and contradictions. When competition for influence, clientele, and profit went too far, internal divisions and contradictory individual interests created favorable conjunctures for Indian resistance, sabotage, or assertion of legal rights. But taken as a whole, the local and regional elites depended upon their connections and loyalties to one another, and to state officials and institutions, for their authority and profits. They shared a common interest and interdependence, and they knew it.[44]

Hence, when Don Juan Manuel de Anaya arrived in Lucanas in 1578, he sought out the kinds of working relationships with established local elites which could turn his two-year term as corregidor into a highly lucrative venture. On the European side, he sent Indians to work the fields of powerful Hernando Palomino. Palomino was head of a high elite family which lorded over a rich local encomienda (Soras), housed skilled native silversmiths at Hernando's villa and base of operations on Huamanga's central plaza, organized large and small rural estates and farms throughout the region, owned huge herds of cattle which "by custom" supplied the Huamanga meat market, held several mines in gold- and silver-rich Parinacochas to the south, lent monies to colonial officials, other elites, and lesser residents, and spent thousands of pesos to carve out and decorate the main chapel of the awesome Dominican church in Huamanga.[45] On a more petty level, Anaya cultivated a friendship by arranging for the sale of 100 Indian llamas to Juan de Quesada at less than two-thirds the going price. Quesada, a rural priest, accumulated money and commodities sufficient to finance commercial networks stretching out to Ica and Lima on the coast.[46] On the Indian side, Anaya befriended and obligated native elites as well. Passing through on inspection of the vast Lucanas districts, the corregidor appointed Don Francisco Usco, an important kuraka, as his lieutenant and spokesman in Lucanas Andamarcas. In Lucanas Laramati, he vested his authority in yet another native "Don Francisco."[47]

Such alliances with local lords or notables, whether Indian or European, were normal procedure for a corregidor or his lieutenants. In Castrovirreyna, for example, Indians complained that the corregidor's brother and chief lieutenant gave 180 pesos in community money to one Don Juan Quilla "for being his compadre," or godfather of the Indian's child.[48] A rural corregidor frequently turned to local elites to post the *fianza,* a surety which guaranteed the Crown payment in case of fraudulent accounts, or to serve as the corregidor's local representative.[49]

In rural society, then, Toledo's reorganization created imposing networks of authority, formal and informal, in which the corregidor stood at the center, armed with the police powers of the colonial state. The "police powers" were real enough, for corregidores and other officials jailed and whipped people, and impounded their belongings, under the guise of enforcing laws and punishing criminals.[50] In a sense, each of the notables in a local power group operated in a similar way to cultivate working relationships with other prominent figures inside and outside of Indian society. Like the priest who learned to milk the local countryside, a corregidor had to avoid overreaching his effective power, or violating locally established boundaries of entitlement. If too greedy, he could create a strong group of enemies ready to embroil him in dangerous, costly litigation when an incoming corregidor conducted the standard *residencia,* or judicial review, at the end of his term.[51] But an intelligent corregidor found that all interested parties, from humble peasants to pretentious high elite families, sought to accommodate an authority whose favors they would need. Indians oiled the wheels of justice with petty gifts—fish, eggs, and the like. Among the expenses of an elite family was an entry for nine *arrobas* (about 225 pounds) of sugar, worth six months of abundant food and drink to a skilled Indian muledriver, spent to finance a huge feast during the corregidor's visit to their sugar estate.[52]

THE POLITICS OF PROFIT

The expense invested in the feast made good sense, because in the colonial society reconstructed by Toledo, possession of political power and influential connections, and the state's benevolence, paved one's way to enormous economic achievements. Given the breakdown of the post-Incaic alliances, the economic ambitions of the colonials, and the resilient self-sufficiency of ayllu economies, the mechanics of extraction had come to depend more than ever upon access to effective political force organized by a central state. Despite internal rivalries, the game of political partnership and mutual favors was one which all members of a power group had to play. The figure most likely to come out ahead in the short run was the corregidor—the combined judge, administrator, and jailer of any given district. By dominating the circuits of commerce and, in the countryside, plundering local economies, he could rapidly accumulate a small fortune and finance ambitious economic ventures.

Our figure from Lucanas, for example, Don Juan Manuel de Anaya, threw his energies into one driving purpose: to convert political eminence into quick profits. A career bureaucrat who later served as royal treasurer, and a man of considerable means before leaving the city for his corregimiento in 1578,[53] Anaya had no other reason to look forward to two years in a remote Indian hinterland. In an economy where investments in commercial capital could provide swift wealth, Anaya used his position at the hub of

local power to commandeer labor, seize money and goods, control and expand trade circuits, and back up ambitious commercial ventures. The corregidor passed out free or cheap labor to his friends, and demanded that ex-
pert native weavers supply him valuable luxury textiles at substandard
prices. Anaya's merchant-partners came to animal-rich Lucanas to "buy"
thousands of alpacas and llamas from unwilling Indians at pitifully low
prices. Then they made off for high-priced markets elsewhere. To a commercial partner, Antonio Troncoso, Anaya gave 5,200 pesos (of 12.5 reales)
from the local repartimientos' *cajas de comunidad* (community boxes for cash
reserves and legal documents). Acting on his own rather than in collaboration with local priests and kurakas, the corregidor created a minor scandal.
The 5,200 pesos, ostensibly withdrawn to buy "needed" ornaments and materials for local churches, were in fact used for a large commercial investment in Lima. Among the luxury goods bought with the Indians' money in
the cheaper Lima market were elaborate religious ornaments and silver-
work. Anaya promptly resold them at inflated "Huamanga prices" to the Indian parishes in Lucanas.[54]

Again and again, Anaya dipped into the cajas de comunidad for money
or capital. His responsibility for the repartimientos' financial affairs and records gave him enviable access to the silver and gold pieces, worth thousands
of pesos, accumulated by dynamic community economies. Moreover, he
violated legal ordinances by retaining all three keys to each caja. (Normally,
a kuraka and one other native should have held two keys, and the corregidor
a third.) More than fifteen years later, the Crown was still struggling to clear
up the muddled accounts left by this rapacious functionary.[55]

Anaya left behind a trail of notoriety and complicated litigation typical of
authorities whose greed overreached their effective power, but his actions
belonged to the mainstream of the colonials' prerogatives and abuses.
Throughout Huamanga, corregidores used political posts as a resource with
which to extract labor and tributes, plunder local economies, and set up
profitable commercial arrangements. Much to the Crown's chagrin, corregidores everywhere converted the cajas de communidad into private pools
of capital.[56] If a corregidor could work out an effective alliance with local
"lords"—native, Spanish, or mestizo—he could subvert the outflow of legal
tributes and mitayos which drained the local economy. In doing so, he could
channel more resources into exploitation by the rural power group.[57] Even
when they did not sabotage state-sponsored tributes and mitas, Huamanga's
corregidores funnelled labor to their friends, and, often with the consent of
the kurakas, set up putting-out systems to produce domestic manufactures
such as cloth or twine.[58] Through the putting-out method, and by confiscat-
ing or buying at low prices commodities such as animals, wool, leather, or
coca, the magistrates controlled the commercialization of local products in

outside markets.[59] In addition, they monopolized and expanded the inflow of commodities. Handling local repartimientos like captive markets, corregidores (or their friends) set up stores and managed a lucrative commerce in religious items such as wax or ornaments. In Castrovirreyna, the corregidor's brother and rural lieutenant plied a profitable wine trade. Not content merely to monopolize a modest local market for good wine at reasonable prices, the enterprising bureaucrat took advantage of his authority to unload numerous jugs of bad wine—"part of it vinegar"—upon the Indians.[60]

By converting his political base or advantage into a money-making operation, a corregidor simply followed a widespread colonial strategy. Any significant official—whether a corregidor, his lieutenant, a priest, or "protector" who represented the natives in legal proceedings—could command a certain stream of "gifts," bribes, and labor services from the natives in his jurisdiction.[61] Anyone who established himself or herself as an effective power, linked to an array of other potentates, passed through doors closed to others. A Catholic priest, for example, held the authority of the victorious Christian gods, and represented a powerful Church hierarchy charged with controlling religious life. The priest could bestow exemptions from the mita upon his favored lay assistants,[62] and heap abuses upon the troublesome by accusing them of idolatry.[63] By becoming a local "lord" to be reckoned with by the other lords, Andean or European, a priest could command tributes and labor drafts, set up a putting-out system to weave luxury cumbi textiles, and finance far-reaching commercial ventures. In the mines of Huayllay (in Huanta), even Spanish colonials fumed at the economic exploits achieved by "the powerful hand" of an ambitious priest.[64]

All the characters of an elite network—petty pretenders to noble status and powerful lords, permanent mainstays and officials passing through— knew that the accumulation of political favor and authority constituted the gateway to economic success. On an informal level, the entrepreneur or oligarch who cultivated the friendship of state officials expanded opportunities for profitable commercial arrangements, extralegal labor drafts to supplement mita contingents, a sympathetic hearing of petitions, or simple enforcement of legal rights to tribute and mita.

On a more official level, too, the state held the key to labor and wealth. Its mita drafts provided the bulk of exploitable energy for hard work in mines and obrajes, and a substantial share for agriculture and ranching. Its reorganization of Indian communities regulated a flow of tributes and salaries to encomenderos, other pensioners, and officials, and set up a convenient source of further capital in the form of the repartimiento cash boxes (cajas de comunidad). During the sixteenth century, when communities accumulated impressive precious metal reserves, regional elites and the royal treasury itself raided the cajas for censos, long-term loans whose principal was

Priests as members of power groups. Above, a priest and corregidor provide one another companionship and entertainment. Below, a Dominican priest uses his authority to sequester a native woman he accuses of idolatrous concubinage, and to set her to work weaving cloth on a traditional Andean loom. Poma de Ayala complained that such women were commonly transformed into concubines of rural priests.

paid back at the option of the borrower. The Crown lamented the anarchic accounts left by functionaries eager to rob the cajas or to pocket interest payments on outstanding censos, but never opposed the institution itself.[65] The state's official patrimony further included basic resources such as mines and lands. Toledo expropriated the Huancavelica mercury mines, and set up a contract system which leased the site to miners for a production quota sold back to the Crown. Even where the state did not itself own mines, rental contracts show that its control of mita labor determined their market value.[66] From the 1590s, land itself fell under the Crown's patrimony. Periodically, judges went out on *composiciones de tierras,* or inspections of land titles. In exchange for an agreed upon contribution to the royal treasury, inspectors awarded or confirmed rights to lands theoretically unneeded or unworked by the natives, but frequently coveted by Indians, whites, and mixed-bloods alike for their fertility or commercial value.[67] Finally, the state distributed lucrative bureaucratic posts and managed a juridical system which could back up labor drafts, tributes, and property rights with coercion.

Under these conditions, political weight and skill determined one's share of the economic spoils. In 1599, for example, 200 respectable Huamanga residents held rights to mita contingents of 681 natives sent to the city plaza for work in agriculture, ranching, or household service.[68] But 100 (50 percent) of the colonials could claim just 15.0 percent of the mitayos, or one (1.02) laborer each. By contrast, a mere twenty citizens (10 percent) commanded 41.1 percent of the mita contingent, an average of fourteen (14.0) natives each.[69] At least eighteen of the twenty were encomenderos from old local families, and ten belonged to a small circle of "high elite" families who had parlayed a background of encomienda and conquest politics into a set of tributes, farms, ranches, workshops, mines, administrative perquisites, and commercial interests.[70]

The figures actually understate the share of the politically powerful. Close relatives of the influential, for example, received allotments which upped the share of just nine high elite families to nearly a third (30.8 percent) of the contingent, or over twenty-six mitayos (26.3) per family.[71] Moreover, the 681 natives sent to Huamanga's plaza did not include direct allotments to rural estates which bypassed distribution in the city of Huamanga. For example, the powerful local figure Crisóstomo de Hontiveros, who was apportioned only six mitayos at the Huamanga plaza, enjoyed a direct allotment of twenty-nine others besides. Pedro Díaz de Rojas and Diego Gavilán, who each received eighteen mitayos at Huamanga, got another sixteen and twelve workers respectively, in direct allotments from their encomiendas.[72]

It was, in fact, the long-established leaders of Huamanga, joined by influential institutions, bureaucrats, and newcomers, who cornered the state's regional patrimony. In Vilcashuamán, distinguished figures such as Jerónimo de Oré and Hernando Guillén de Mendoza secured drafts of more than two hundred natives for obrajes set up among the families' encomienda Indians. The viceroy deemed Nuflo de Romaní and his haciendas worthy enough to accommodate his petition for supplementary labor with four extra mitayos. The Jesuits' political muscle earned the religious order a special two-year allotment of fifteen mitayos for construction.[73] In the mining centers of Huancavelica and Castrovirreyna, the powerful and rich included men such as Pedro de Contreras and Juan de Sotomayor, big miners with cruel reputations and allotments of several hundred workers. Though neither could claim membership in Huamanga's older high elite circle, their rise had been predicated upon political talent, an early local presence, and important ties to Huamanga and Lima.[74] Despite the openings which mineral-rich Huamanga gave to fortune-seekers and transplanted elites, some of them "citizens of Lima,"[75] old Huamanga leaders such as Amador de Cabrera and Crisóstomo de Hontiveros enjoyed sufficient means to hold on to impressive mining interests, or to develop new ones.[76]

In a society where access to influence constituted the lifeline of wealth and enterprise, high lords and petty tyrants alike spun complicated webs of kinship and placement which enhanced their political reach and stature. In the countryside, corregidores and other Spanish lords were not too proud to become godparents of Indian children. Local colonials even married the daughters of kurakas, who had their own reasons for such alliances.[77] In the city, distinguished citizens worked together on the municipal council, placed lesser sons in the priesthood which spread out over the Indian countryside, and sought out lucrative or powerful bureaucratic posts.[78] Marriage linked high elite families of Huamanga such as the Díaz de Rojas, Hontiveros, and Oré, or extended their ties to cities such as Arequipa or Lima.[79] Fat dowries confirmed the serious stakes committed to friendships consolidated through marriage. When Hernando Guillén de Mendoza betrothed his daughter Doña Micaela to the son of another encomendero of Vilcashuamán, he cemented the alliance with a promise to provide his son-in-law with herds of sheep, cows, goats, and horses, lands for farming and grazing, urban property in Huamanga and Lima, textile production from his obraje, and luxuries such as fine clothes and jewelry. The valuation of the dowry came to 15,000 pesos (of eight reales), equivalent to the market value of twenty-five or thirty healthy adult Africans on the Lima slave market.[80]

In the final analysis, the energy and wealth devoted to solidifying or extending points of loyalty and cooperation in various elite networks could make the difference between success and failure. In any given locale, the correlation of forces that shaped the final outcome of exploitative ventures could change, creating winners and losers. (For a more detailed discussion of cleavages within the colonial elite, see Chapter 5.) In more than one area, encomenderos closed out of local tributes and putting-out systems complained bitterly about the illegal extractions, which by draining communities of their surplus undermined the legal encomienda tributes. The partnership of corregidores and kurakas proved so effective, however, that the litigants failed to prove their case.[81] In a society where one's fortune reflected one's place in changing and contradictory alliances of power, no one enjoyed the luxury of neglecting political credibility or authority. A parish priest who seemed vulnerable to judicial charges found that his old Indian collaborators — even his cook — suddenly turned against him. Later, he managed to mobilize the political and economic resources necessary to swing the Indian chiefs back.[82] Even for a corregidor, political isolation or weakness invited setback and disaster. In Huamanga, one unlucky magistrate incurred the violent wrath of too many notables, and suddenly found himself mired in charges of treason which cost him his life! His beheaded visage, impaled on a stake for all to see, stood as a morbid reminder that in Huamanga, at least, any person who alienated social allies would face alone the inherent brutalities of a colonial society.[83]

VIOLENCE

And Huamanga was, indeed, a brutal society. Divided as they were by economic, ethnic, and racial geography, all the characters of colonial Andean society nevertheless shared at least one pervasive fact of life. From one angle or another, all knew first-hand the drama of confrontation backed by raw violence — physical, sometimes capricious, always a real-life possibility. The very nature of production and exploitation imparted a crude, direct quality to economic relationships. A series of tributes, labor drafts, and plunderings imposed upon a self-sufficient peasantry by right of superior power, in order to make prosper the mines, manufactures, rural estates, and high life styles of foreigners, could not easily mask its character as sheer usurpation. This was especially true since the impositions threatened to undermine local welfare and self-sufficiency. It was this crude character of economic extraction which made necessary such imposing networks of authority built around a revamped Indian power structure, an effective local bureaucracy, and an entrenched regional elite.

In such a society, extractive institutions and relationships required the repeated application of coercive energies simply to reproduce themselves. A mere preponderance of power through elite alliances was not, by itself, enough. Noise, threats, bribes, violence, sabotage, shows of prestige, even rituals of domination[84] — all constituted regular, necessary parts of exploitative relationships. Only a naive encomendero, for example, expected to receive Indian tributes automatically, or smoothly. Twice a year a repartimiento owed tribute payments, and twice a year the Indians had to evaluate the balance of political forces, and their economic capacity to satisfy the tributes. Each time they had to decide whether to pay the full amount, pursue delaying tactics, or plead economic incapacity to pay the entire quota. Tributes regularly fell into arrears, and an encomendero who failed to send a legal agent to enforce payment might lose a good share of the revenues. In Vilcashuamán, many communities refused to deliver tributes until legally forced to. "The kurakas and notables and account-keepers and other leaders declared that they retained [the tributes] in their power on the account of the encomendero, in order to deliver them when and if he would order them delivered." Ultimately, the corregidor's capacity to jail the kurakas and confiscate their property guaranteed the tribute payments. A census judge touring Andahuaylas in 1604 needed the assistance of various kurakas to count the Indians; in one town, he appealed to the corregidor "to free the kurakas that he held prisoner because of tributes." If the corregidor had reason to collaborate with the kurakas to subvert legal tributes, encomenderos might never manage to mobilize the political force needed to collect their pensions.[85]

The mitas, the most dreaded of the Toledan institutions, provoked repeated confrontations which tested the balance of political forces. Most labor drafts called for fresh contingents every two months, and from the very beginning the Indians indicated that they would comply only when forced to. A corregidor knew that to fill the mita calls reasonably well, he would have to muster considerable persuasive efforts. Sometimes a skillful mixture of favors and threats was not enough. Beatings, jailings, and sequestration of property might all prove essential to mobilize a mita contingent. Always, close physical supervision of the drafted laborers would be needed to insure their arrival relatively intact at the work center. Try as a corregidor might to pass on all such tasks to intermediaries, he could nonetheless find himself pressed to intervene personally in the process.

The Indians' unwillingness to comply with the mita except under pressure presented a corregidor with touchy political dilemmas. The magistrate, interested in exploiting his district's peasantry, frequently shared the Indians' concern about the outflow of local people to distant mita centers. Moreover, his authority and profits depended partly upon his ability to obligate a clientele of Indian elites and pretenders. By cooperating with local elites to sabotage the mita, a corregidor enhanced his position as a powerful patron. But if he dispensed with the labor drafts altogether, he could bring on disastrous lawsuits and charges of fraud by miners, treasury officials, and other mita interests. As a result, corregidores usually had to force some degree of compliance, but often tolerated or encouraged efforts to limit the drafts to incomplete, sometimes irregular rotations. To receive their allotted quotas, the mita interests normally had to commission special judges to visit the rural corregimientos, and force corregidores and Indians to comply more fully with legal rules.[86]

In the end, only force and superior political power made the mitas a viable institution. When the system of enforcement weakened, the exploitative relationship simply could not reproduce itself. In 1599, a Huamanga official complained that "it has not been possible to gather all the [mita de plaza] Indians in one day . . . even though many efforts have been made."[87] Even when mita contingents arrived with some regularity, the colonials had to reconcile themselves to a chronic deficit of mitayos "that the kurakas did not deliver."[88] At least once, sheer noncompliance forced authorities to consider native claims that mita quotas should be reduced in accordance with population decline.[89] The practicality of a demand depended greatly upon the authorities' ability to back it up with force. When the kurakas of Andahuaylas adamantly refused to send off a group of mitayos to Huamanga despite repeated orders, the corregidor jailed them and began to confiscate their property. Reluctantly, they dispatched the laborers. When a judge for a mining mita arrived in Ocopampa (Castrovirreyna), he resorted to a public show of force to stifle resistance to the labor drafts. The judge hanged ten Yauyos Indians.[90]

Violent discipline, then, served essential functions without which colonial relationships could not survive. Even had they wished to, the colonials could not have limited force to a mere option lurking in the distant background. Instead, they had to use physical punishment and humiliation as a living tool, a genuine threat, whose public display would prod natives into submitting to their political superiors. The social drama of punishment taught who commanded true authority, and how easily they could abuse those who dared to challenge them openly. When an Indian fisherman refused to give fresh fish demanded by the corregidor of Castrovirreyna, the "indignant" magistrate "held [the Indian] prisoner in the public jail . . . three or four days. Later he took him out and hung him in the stock by the feet and gave him fifty lashes. Then he cut his hair and took him prisoner to the jail another time. . . ."[91] The severity of the corregidor had a certain logic. A pretentious, arrogant, and abusive social style symbolized his authority, political superiority, and expectation of deference. Without it, a colonial did not command the respect needed to impose his economic will. In Tambo Quemado (Lucanas Laramati), where travelling Spaniards normally demanded meals, lodging, and labor from the Indians, "a poor sick Spaniard on foot" could not even get a meal. Timid colonials would not enjoy success, for as two citizens of Huamanga put it: "all that [the natives] do has to be very slow and by force."[92]

Neither colonizer nor colonized could escape the violent tenor of life in-

The role of violent discipline. Above, an encomendero and a corregidor hang an Indian chief who became a troublemaker. The corregidor's gesture dramatizes that the incident will be hushed up. Below, a corregidor has an Indian official whipped because a mitayo did not give the magistrate his customary two eggs.

herent in their socioeconomic relationships. In more than one case, priests resorted to beatings or led gang-style rampages just like any other colonial man determined to get his way. One priest carried a pistol on his person.[93] The precaution may have been a wise one; a prominent citizen who visited his Lucanas encomienda around 1574, apparently without much protection, paid dearly for his negligence with an ugly death, "by a stone throw that an Indian . . . gave him in the temples."[94] Two decades later, a well known colonial travelling up from the Pacific coast to Castrovirreyna never arrived. A search party failed to find him. Six years had passed when, almost by accident, the authorities learned that an Indian guide had murdered the Spaniard while they travelled alone across the high puna. The nagging fear of the colonials, at least in the sixteenth century, was that the Indians might organize their own violent potential into an open assault against Hispanic society. In 1589, a group of Angaraes mitayos plotted to destroy Huancavelica. Upon their arrival to replace the old mitayos, they planned to set fire to the city and to kill off the Spaniards. When the colonials discovered the conspiracy, they quickly gathered together their weapons and horses, and organized night patrols to prevent a rebellion.[95]

Most of the time, the colonials' control of rural life and the natives' internal divisions discouraged organization of an open assault. But even so, Indian violence, sabotage, or obstinacy exposed the crude character of economic relationships. Occasional fires destroyed harvests, or burned cajas de comunidad whose stores of money and documents the corregidores controlled. An authority who imposed putting-out systems had to guard against ayllu attempts to pass off goods specifically designed to ruin their market value. Miners at Huancavelica contended with workers who "do not take out the amount of mercury that they could, and besides . . . sell mercury to merchants for half or less its [true] value."[96] If a colonial misjudged the balance of political forces, or tried to impose new obligations upon the Indians, they might challenge him or her to a show of force which compelled the colonial to back off. In Vilcashuamán, Catholic priests convinced some of the kurakas and Indians to plant without pay nearly 300 hectares of wheat whose sale would benefit the church. But the pact ran up against so much resistance that the priests had to abandon the project.[97]

PROSPERITY

Indians resisted Toledan institutions, and the viceroy's reorganization did not satisfy entirely the needs of colonial elites. Eventually, the Indians' resistance and population decline would undermine the effectiveness of Toledan mitas and tributes (see Chapter 5). Even in its heyday, and even from the point of view of the colonials, the economic system consolidated by Toledo and his successors had certain defects. It restricted the independence of colonial elites by linking their economic fortunes to the institutions and patrimony of a powerful state. The state provided the elites mechanisms of political control and coercion to force "lazy" Indians to turn over goods, money, and human labor-power. But it could not offer the colonials an efficient, self-reproducing system of labor exploitation free of sabotage, resistance, and continual struggle. Despite these deficiencies, however, the resurgent Peruvian economy of the late sixteenth century had one "virtue" which every colonial appreciated: the revenues and profits it produced were enormous.

In mining, the strategic nerve center of the regional economy, the state's ability to mobilize a large labor supply generated dazzling wealth. Before Toledo, Huancavelica's annual production of refined mercury measured in the hundreds of *quintales* (c. 100 pounds each). By the 1580s, the average count of officially registered mercury shot up to 7,500 quintales a year.[98] Reorganization had transformed mercury mining into a massive primitive industry, whose heavy labors fell primarily upon a rotating force of over 3,000 mitayos. During a boom year like 1587, registered production totalled 9,700 quintales. The huge contraband trade probably raised total production to at least 13,000 quintales (some 650 tons). To produce this much mercury, workers had to dig up, haul, and refine thousands of tons of ore in a single year. At the official Huancavelica sale price of 94 *pesos corrientes* (nine reales each) per quintal, the year's production totalled 1,222,000 pesos — enough to pay the salaries of all the corregidores in greater Peru's seventy-one districts for an entire decade![99] With the discovery of rich silver deposits south of Huancavelica in 1590, the state's labor drafts ushered in yet another regional mining boom. The new mining city of Castrovirreyna enjoyed an allotment of over 2,000 mitayos, drawn primarily from provinces bordering on the Huamanga districts. Around 1610, well after the heyday of its early years, the Castrovirreyna mines still produced silver valued at 250,000–275,000 pesos corrientes a year.[100]

Miners, of course, could not simply pocket all this wealth. The Crown, merchants, and even labor held large claims on production. The royal treasury's share at Huancavelica in 1587 amounted to 578,000 pesos, nearly half (47.3 percent) the year's total output. At Castrovirreyna, the Crown took about a sixth of annual production.[101] Commercial capitalists siphoned off yet another large fraction. The merchants captured extra revenues by "underpaying" miners eager to dump contraband metals. In 1587, the take from underpayments at Huancavelica soaked up at least 128,700 pesos, or a fifth (20.0 percent) of the wealth left unexpropriated by the Crown.[102] In addition, merchants charged inflated prices for the food and drink, textiles, animals and slaves, raw materials and tools, and equipment consumed in production. Stiff terms of credit tended to subject medium and small miners to utter dependence on merchants for subsistence goods, for certain factors of production, and in Huancavelica, for silver itself.[103] Even wages could add up to large claims on production. The official caravans of silver sent to Huancavelica to pay Indian wages in 1587 totalled 223,600 pesos.[104] Crown entitlements, underpayments by merchant capital, and official wage costs thus appeared to leave the miners "only" 291,700 pesos — less than a fourth (23.9 percent) of the year's production — for subsistence, costs of production beyond mita wages, and profits. If, as seems reasonable, the non-mita costs of production absorbed over 100,000 pesos,[105] the revenues left for subsistence and profits in a boom year shrank to less than 200,000 pesos.

But to compute the profits of miners in this way, either in absolute terms or as a percentage of "capital invested," profoundly distorts the dynamics of colonial enterprise. In particular, assignment of a monetary value to the various factors of production (labor, lands, raw materials, capital construction and improvement, etc.) fundamentally misconstrues the historical basis of profit-making before the rise of industrial capitalism. The data available from colonial mines, workshops, and haciendas suggests that colonial producers, like their grain-exporting contemporaries in Eastern Europe, amassed huge liquid profits precisely because they could avoid, or at least minimize, paying monetary equivalents for the true costs of production.[106] In a productive process where cheap mita wages might account for two-thirds the calculated value of the factors of production, mining profits depended greatly upon holding wages far below the subsistence needs of Indian family economies. For this very reason, miners eagerly sought to pocket a good share of the Indians' wages for themselves, by indebting workers or by outright fraud.[107] In 1587, avoiding payment of half the nominal wages would have increased the Huancavelica miners' revenues well over 100,000 pesos, boosting profits by 50 percent or more; for a miner with rights to 100 mitayos, the increase represented several thousand pesos of income a year.[108]

In an economy where merchant capitalists raided wealth by acquiring commodities cheaply, often by underpaying producers, in order to sell them dearly, the successful miners were those who themselves adopted the techniques of commercial capital. Large miners defrauded workers even of cheap mita wages, set up cattle ranches to avoid purchasing their workers' meat rations in expensive local markets, and produced commercial crops to exploit the needs of other producers and their dependents in high-priced markets.[109] The encroachments of commercial capital siphoned off profits from production and reduced many small miners to dependence; but the powerful enjoyed access to good mines, plentiful labor, and the means to hold market costs of production to a relatively modest proportion of gross revenues. And the gross revenues could be quite large: even after discounting the Crown's take, a Huancavelica mining operation sufficient to utilize the labors of 100 mitayos brought in at least 15,000 pesos corrientes a year.[110] In Castrovirreyna, a fine mine-hacienda complex could command annual rents as high as 7,000 pesos.[111]

Huamanga's mining prosperity, and its importance as a zone of passage between the Lima, Cuzco, and Potosí markets, presented outstanding commercial opportunities to those equipped to exploit them. Entrepreneurs who produced, bought, or otherwise acquired cheap commodities resold them at higher prices to urban and laboring populations, to small and large producers, and to the itinerant merchants who swelled Huamanga's cities and mining centers, and cluttered its commercial routes. The cities of Huancavelica, Castrovirreyna, and Huamanga all constituted important markets for food and drink (corn, wheat, bread, fish, meat, cheese, fruits, vegetables, sweets, wine, chicha, brandy), coca leaf, woolen and cotton textiles, raw materials and accessories of production (wood, salt, candles, carrying sacks), handicraft products (leathers, shoes and good clothing, furniture), and labor itself (slaves and animals for sale, mitayo and "free" Indian labor for rental).[112]

Given these opportunities, the mining boom represented simply the most spectacular and dynamic part of a broader phenomenon. In a region where an annual income of five or six hundred pesos corrientes could support a Spanish majordomo or hacienda administrator in modest prosperity,[113] the patrimony and institutions of the colonial state enabled powerful citizens to accumulate fortunes worth tens of thousands of pesos in a few years or less. A large encomienda alone could finance substantial commercial investments by providing its holder money and commodities worth several thousand pesos a year. An encomendero who set up a rural obraje and acquired cheap mita labor easily earned several thousand pesos in a good year; a corregidor who controlled an extensive putting-out system might accumulate as much as 20,000 or 30,000 pesos from the textile trade in three or four years.[114] Opportunities in commercial agriculture sparked an aggressive response. Each year, Huamanga produced about 75,000 bushels of wheat, whose market value normally exceeded 100,000 pesos in the city of Huamanga in the late sixteenth century. Yet the revenues available in the inflated mining markets were even higher, and Huamanga was plagued by wheat shortages imposed by merchants and producers eager to market foodstuffs in Huancavelica or Castrovirreyna.[115] As usual, those with political power and connections dominated access to the labor, tributes, land rights, and markets needed to realize large profits. The fertile Chaquibamba plains, for example, produced over 20,000 bushels of wheat and were located along the main commercial road within easy reach of Huamanga. Not surprisingly, the landowners who dominated production in this lucrative zone belonged to Huamanga's old elite, which also captured a huge share of the mitayos available for farm work.[116]

Mines and markets. Castrovirreyna springs up as a bustling commercial center high in the mountains (about 3950 meters above sea level). Today, the old silver city is desolate.

The expansive regional economy encouraged a process of considerable investment and reinvestment in production and commerce. True, the leading figures of Huamanga, Huancavelica, and Castrovirreyna lived high and well, and eagerly engaged in "wasteful" ostentation and aristocratic pretense. But such displays contributed to the political and social prestige which was, as we have seen, a necessary condition of the aristocrat-entrepreneurs' economic exploits. To be a good entrepreneur, one had also to be a good aristocrat.

Moreover, the region's elite citizens did not simply squander their fortunes, live off rents, or retreat to economic stagnation on unproductive estates. In mining, producers engaged in limited experimentation to improve productivity.[117] In agriculture, Huamanga's powerful figures tended not to bury their wealth into single, expanding, autarchic estates, but to accumulate a lucrative portfolio of scattered properties, some huge and others modest in size. The diversified land tenure patterns reflected energetic responses to various branches or zones of profit-making which attracted all sorts of people — from petty producer, to substantial citizen, to members of the high elite (see Map 3).[118] A single person might hold a mine in Huancavelica, a coca plantation in the montaña of Huanta, a rural obraje near encomienda Indians in Vilcashuamán, wheat fields and vineyards near the city of Huamanga.[119] As we have seen, the logic of profit demanded that owners avoid paying monetary equivalents for the true costs of production. But in their quest to expand production and wealth in a booming regional economy, the aristocratic entrepreneurs channelled considerable revenues into buying up lands; improving them through irrigation and other works; acquiring trees, vines, animals, seed, and other start-up materials; constructing buildings and equipment to mill grain, process cheese, press and refine sugar cane, crunch and smelt mining ore, weave and dye textiles, and the like; purchasing heavy work animals and African slaves to perform specific labors in the productive process; buying commodities and hiring pack animals and drivers for commercial investments; and lending money to other producers bent on setting up or expanding enterprises.[120] A minor elite figure of Huamanga, who began his career as a notary, built up a lucrative agricultural complex in the Huatata Valley near Huamanga. He spent only several hundred pesos for the lands themselves, but then poured 6,000 pesos into improving them. The valuation of a sugar refinery's animals, buildings, and machinery easily surpassed 15,000 pesos. A leading Castrovirreyna miner spent probably over 20,000 pesos to accumulate and improve an enormous ranch, situated near traffic to and from the mines, complete with specialized pastures and corrals, feeding sites, cheese manufactures, and a tannery.[121]

The elites of the late sixteenth century built their economic careers around the aggressive pursuit of growing profits, but their activities did not

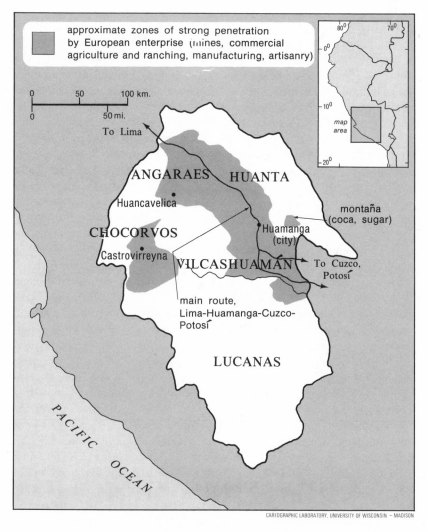

approximate zones of strong penetration by European enterprise (mines, commercial agriculture and ranching, manufacturing, artisanry)

0   50   100 km.
0   50 mi.

To Lima

ANGARAES   HUANTA

Huancavelica

CHOCORVOS

Castrovirreyna

VILCASHUAMAN

Huamanga (city)

montaña (coca, sugar)

To Cuzco, Potosí

main route, Lima-Huamanga-Cuzco-Potosí

LUCANAS

PACIFIC OCEAN

map area

CARTOGRAPHIC LABORATORY, UNIVERSITY OF WISCONSIN – MADISON

Map 3. Zones of European enterprise, Huamanga, c. 1600

herald the development of a capitalist economy. (By a capitalist economy, I mean a productive system and set of social relations based upon the employment of free wage laborers, whose labor-power is a commodity purchased along with other "factors of production" by investors, for the purpose of making a profit — i.e., converting the liquid revenues invested into more liquid revenues.) Freely contracted wage labor played a secondary role in production, and in earning peasants their subsistence; the latter fact imposed definite limits upon the expansion of both the labor market and the market for subsistence goods. Where they could do so profitably, the elites reinvested considerable sums in a diverse and expanding economy. But even had they wished, they could not have found lucrative outlets sufficient to reinvest most of their fortunes. Even after spending large sums on ornamental metal work, imported luxury goods laden with jewels, and the like, a wealthy miner might accumulate large amounts of silver for which he or she had little use.[122]

As in many areas of Europe, the obstacles to further economic development grew most apparent during the course of the seventeenth century; the age of basic economic construction and expansion was over, the importance of wage labor had increased, but too great a proportion of the rural population maintained access to the means of production. By the late seventeenth century, stagnant mines and markets, internal and external, could not support a high level of investment and reinvestment. Significantly, it was from the mid-seventeenth century on that Huamanga's churches began to absorb a huge share of the region's wealth and landed property, donated or sold by a colonial elite whose investment opportunities were extremely constricted.[123]

The decades immediately following Toledo's government, however, were times of heady prosperity and economic expansion. The state's capacity to organize violent coercive institutions brought to fruition patterns of development under way in the early decades after conquest, then frustrated by the crisis of the 1560s. As Huamanga's mining, manufacturing, agricultural, and commercial sectors gained mature shape, an aging encomendero might have marvelled at the success of Toledo's reforms. But the encomendero's heir would not have had the luxury of such musings. For as we are about to see, he would be too absorbed in a struggle to protect Toledan privilege against the Indians' legal assaults.

5

The Indians and Spanish Justice

As HE STRODE PAST the soft white stone of Our Lady of Mercy, Huamanga's oldest monastery, Don Miguel de Bendezú seethed with anger. A refined young aristocrat, Don Miguel had recently come into possession of a modest family encomienda. Ever since, the deceitful Indians, led by the kuraka Don Pedro Astocuri, had taken unfair advantage of the Spanish laws. In 1622, when Don Miguel was still a legal minor, the natives managed to win a *revisita,* or reinspection, which bypassed the customary legal citation giving notice of the proceeding to interested parties. By pushing through their claim that nearly two hundred tributaries had died or fled, they lowered the annual tribute assessment by some 700 pesos ensayados. Now, just two years later, Don Pedro and his people were at it again. This time, Don Miguel had been cited to respond to their petition for a new count of the tributary population. As he made his way toward the plaza to declare his answer before a notary, the exasperated young patrician determined not to fall prey again to the "ignorance and malice" of Don Pedro and his followers. He would appeal to the royal court in Lima to cancel the revisita. Another inspection, he explained desperately, would bring "the complete ruin of the said repartimiento, because the said cacique, to avoid paying tributes and complying with the Huancavelica mitas, will send off the Indians. They [the kurakas] will order them to hide and claim them for dead or escaped, as is their custom."[1] As the more experienced citizens of Huamanga might have told him, Don Miguel would have to master the formal and informal rules of the legal game quickly, if he wanted to protect his income. By learning how to assert some legal rights of their own, the natives, source of so much wealth, had also become a source of great trouble.

For Don Miguel and others like him, the political revitalization of Peru brought mixed blessings. On the one hand, Toledo's regime established reins of power effective enough to fashion an unparalleled economic boom. On the other hand, it tied elites to a colonial state which defined legitimate and illegitimate rules of exploitation, and whose judges and bureaucrats would decide upon their implementation. Spanish legal philosophy associated sovereignty with the idea of jurisdiction, conceived as responsibility for reconciling life on earth with the principles of a higher, divinely ordained law. The state was fundamentally a dispenser of justice, and its officials were invariably known as "judges" or the like.[2] The resurgent role of the colonial state in the 1570s gave new life to this tradition. The great burst of legislation and political reform sponsored by Toledo included detailed statements of the natives' legal rights and procedures for claiming them. In addition, the state's administrative network included bureaucrats like the "protectors of Indians," whose stature, money-making possibilities, and power depended upon their potential as formidable legal defenders of the natives. In short, the juridical institutions which sponsored the extractions of a colonial ruling class also gave the natives an opening by which to constrict exploitation. As long as some bureaucrats or colonial powers found it in their interest, in some cases, to back an assertion of the natives' legal rights, the Indians could find ways to impede, obstruct, or subvert extraction.

The natives made the most of the opportunity, and entangled the colonials' exploitative practices in labyrinthine adjudications whose final outcomes were often uncertain. As we shall see, the Indians' struggle for Spanish justice, in the end, weakened their capacity to mount a radical challenge to the colonial structure, and thereby contributed to the dominance of a colonial elite. Along the way, however, resistance within Spanish juridical frameworks locked the colonials into a social war which hammered away at specific privileges, and left the ultimate victors with a good many bruises and headaches.

THE LEGAL BATTLES OF A CONTENTIOUS PEOPLE

From early on, the natives earned a reputation as litigious peoples. By the 1550s, they were flooding the viceregal court, or *audiencia,* in Lima with petitions and suits, the majority of them between native communities, ayllus, or ethnic groups. Two decades later Toledo hoped that local administrative reorganization might streamline the litigation process and avoid overtaxing the Lima jurists.[3] In practice, however, consolidation of a harsh exploitative system administered through a set of justices charged with enforcing legal guidelines did little to discourage litigation. Instead, the natives learned how to press aggressively for the "rights" allowed them. By the 1600s, they had developed legal forms of struggle into a major strategy for protecting individual, ayllu, and community interests.

Even at this time of decline in the native population, some of the conflicts with colonials concerned land. The Spaniards and other proprietors coveted areas whose ecology, fertility, or location promised high rewards for commercial agriculture. Despite the absence of generalized land pressure,[4] competition in the prized zones sparked fierce conflicts. Spaniards enjoyed the advantages of a legal system which enhanced their claim on lands. The composición de tierras institution permitted Crown inspectors to award a community's "unused" or surplus lands to petitioners.[5] Since Andean agricultural technology depended on a rotation system which let many lands lie fallow, the composiciones of the 1590s, 1620s, and 1630s offered landgrabbers an opportunity to claim essential community lands which lay unworked in any given year.[6] Communities which spent money and energy to contest the legality of Spanish or even mestizo claims faced great risks. Spanish law officially devalued the credibility of native witnesses,[7] and colonials enjoyed more resources to spend on litigation and bribes. The judges shared social affinities and sympathies with Hispanic claimants. Even if a judge ruled on behalf of the natives, a corregidor or his lieutenant might neglect enforcement. With the balance of forces tipped against them, and their funds eaten up, the natives sometimes withdrew their suits.[8]

Yet despite the disadvantages of law, economics, social prejudice, and their modest political clout, Indians won important local victories. In Socos, near Huamanga, a literate Indian woman fought skillfully to fend off the incursions of a local landowner on several prized hectares. When, in the 1590s, Don Cristóbal de Serpa tried to claim vast tracts of valuable lands just south of the Río Pampas, the community of Tiquihua won a decree by the viceroy in Lima which kept Serpa out. Even when natives could not carry through a struggle to a final victory, their litigation might prove costly and disruptive to a colonial entrepreneur. One family, eager to invest funds to improve lands in the prosperous Huatata Valley near Huamanga, paid its encomienda Indians 500 pesos (of eight reales) to withdraw their lawsuit.[9]

The legal battles from which the natives simply refused to withdraw concerned labor rather than land. Though the colonials accumulated a good share of valuable land, the most threatening feature of the Toledan system for ayllu society was the mita. The labor drafts drained away native energy, threatened the health of individuals and the ability of communities to reproduce themselves, and undermined the reciprocity relations on which native society was built. By the 1590s, communities were waging an aggressive campaign to protect themselves from "excessive" demands which violated official guidelines. Kurakas from Huanta and Vilcashuamán empowered the solicitor of suits at the Lima audiencia "to present certain provisions that we have won . . . about the mita of Indians that we have to [send to] Huancavelica."[10] The Tanquihuas Indians cut in half the contingent of 120 natives they had sent to their encomendero's obraje.[11] Since the mita legally drafted up to one-seventh of the tributary population (able-bodied males, eighteen to fifty years old), a repartimiento with declining population could seek a revisita to revise its mita quota downward. With the ascent of the sympathetic viceroy Luis de Velasco, a major reinspection effort got under way around 1600. At least ten, and probably more, of Huamanga's original twenty-three core repartimientos had their tribute and mita assessments lowered.[12]

The Indians threw their most dogged efforts into resistance against the mita. The kuraka of one ayllu sued for at least three years to avoid turning over just one native for a *mita de plaza* in Huancavelica. (A mita de plaza did not send laborers to mines, but rather to serve in the households, farms, and ranches of a city's citizens and residents.) His ayllu, "warm-weather" (*yunga*) natives who lived in low-lying ecological zones near Luricocha (Huanta), enjoyed legal exemption from work in cold climates like that of Huancavelica. To clinch his case, the chief mobilized testimony by Indians and Spanish miners to prove that his ayllu never had to contribute to a special contingent of 100 laborers designated to work local mines, and later shifted to the Huancavelica mita de plaza.[13]

Much of the energy that the colonials expended to drive the natives to comply with the hated labor drafts involved drawn-out legal battles. In Andahuaylas, for example, kurakas backed their unwillingness to fulfill a mita order with a legal ruse which disrupted the draft. Ordered in October 1606 to turn over an allotment of fifteen mitayos for two years to the Jesuits in Huamanga, the Chanca kurakas replied with a statement opposing the draft. Their repartimiento legally owed one-seventh of its tributary population to mita service. With no more than 3,000 tributaries, they should have to provide no more than 429.5 natives. Since, by the kurakas' count, they had already turned over 462 natives, the chiefs appealed the legitimacy of the order. But their count included 112 functionaries of Indian municipal and church government. Legally, the municipal officials and lay assistants enjoyed special exemption from mita service, but communities held no right to count this "reserved" group among its quota of natives fulfilling mita duties authorized by the state. Like other groups, the Chancas tried to stretch the individual exemptions into a means of reducing the communities' total mita liabilities (in this case, from 429.5 to 317.5 natives).[14] The Jesuits' priest-lawyer contested the legality of their count, and in December won an order to force compliance.

Still, the kurakas proved obstinate. In April 1607 they claimed that the enforcement order issued by the highest court in the land, the royal audiencia in Lima, was illegal! After all, they argued, it demanded that Indians send more than the one-seventh quota to mita service. For months, the Chancas simply reappealed unfavorable decisions with legal arguments of their own until in October the corregidor threw them in jail. Even then, the chiefs held out. Only after the corregidor approved the Jesuits' request to seize the kurakas' property and keep them in jail indefinitely did the chiefs submit. Finally, from the jail of Andahuaylas, they dispatched fifteen mitayos off to Huamanga, "without prejudicing our right and what we seek to plead before Your Excellency." The kurakas' recalcitrance had held up the mita order for a full year.[15]

In their search for legal techniques to erode or disrupt forced labor requisitions, the Indians sometimes uses shrewd tactics. From the 1580s, the Tanquihuas Indians had gained considerable experience in a protracted struggle with Hernán and, later, Diego Guillén de Mendoza over mitayos and other natives working on the family's obraje-hacienda complex. In 1615, the group failed to send some twenty peasants to Huancavelica for the September-October mita. At a time of year when ayllus had to prepare and plant fields for Guillén as well as themselves, they probably could not spare any hands. When a judge commissioned at Huancavelica arrived later to investigate, the Tanquihuas blamed the incident on "the many Indians that their encomendero Don Diego Guillén de Mendoza has working." The tactic worked brilliantly, for it shifted the focus of the investigation to the hacienda complex and its impact on the Huancavelica mita. In the end, the legal actions inspired by the miners' complaint cost Diego Guillén over 600 pesos.[16]

The Indians' inferior social, legal, political, and economic status of course threw up great obstacles to their success at law and reduced some "victories" to insignificance. The residencias, judicial reviews taken by incoming officials of the conduct and accounts of outgoing functionaries, theoretically offered a forum for redress against abuses by corrupt officials. But even when the natives could break through the notorious tendency of incoming and outgoing corregidores to collude in the residencia, their "victory" often amounted to very little. Many penalties and fines were owed to the Crown courts rather than to the natives. Even worse, the long process of appeal gave the functionary time to mobilize well-placed friends to back up arguments on his behalf. In more than one case, officials initially sentenced to stiff penalties managed to reverse or lighten the results.[17] Politics clouded the "justice" of other proceedings as well. When, around 1600, the Indians sued for an investigation of labor practices at the obraje of Chincheros, the findings condemned the powerful Oré family to the tune of thousands of pesos. The natives' triumph gave them a legal excuse to abandon the workshop, but on appeal the victory proved elusive. The family managed to have the penalty reduced to a mere 100 pesos, and mobilized the bureaucracy to force the Indians to return to work.[18]

Still, the well-known corruptions, abuses, and collusions which made a mockery of Indian "rights" did not constitute the whole story. Indeed, the first obraje built by the Oré family had been shut down when an investigation supported complaints that the workers could not collect wages. When Jerónimo de Oré built a new obraje in 1584 he made sure, said the Indians later, to pay the workers well at the start.[19] As we have seen, the natives fended off some incursions on their lands, won revised mita quotas in accordance with population declines, and constructed legal arguments against specific cases of forced labor. Even when legal actions failed to prevent abuses or exactions, they delayed the colonials, carved out a bit of breathing space to plant crops, or earned the Indians payoffs to withdraw their suits. Thus the Indians succeeded enough to make legal action a viable form of struggle. But we may ask why, in a system created to exploit the native peasantry, such redresses were possible.

THE OPPORTUNITY:
CLEAVAGES WITHIN THE COLONIAL ELITE

The exploitative system consolidated under Toledo functioned not as a monolithic bloc of power, but as an alliance of various local, regional, and supraregional elite networks. Though in its overall structure this system transformed the native Andean peoples into "Indians" available for colonial appropriation, the elite networks were beset by sufficient internal contradictions to give the natives room to maneuver. In addition, Spanish colonial institutions gave law and, more generally, the juridical system central importance in the administration of rationalized extractive institutions such as tribute or mita. By mastering the art of defending themselves in alliance with appropriate bureaucrats or colonial powers, the Indians—despite general disadvantages which hampered their success in litigation—improved their chances of winning specific victories.

Any figure who sought to carve out a local fiefdom of privilege and profit had reason to defend Indian clients against excessive greediness by a rival elite. Consider, for example, the encomendero who had long held lands near "his" (or occasionally, "her") Indian communities. Interested in tributes, fertile or well-placed lands, and native workers for his hacienda, an encomendero-hacendado frequently opposed competing landholders whose claims might undermine the self-sufficiency or productivity of his encomienda Indians. By assisting the natives against the usurpation of others, the encomendero also enhanced his capacity to demand favors from his clientele. Again and again, encomenderos supported the struggles of their Indians against land claims by other colonials or by rival natives.[20] Indeed, colonials caught in land fights tended to blame European patrons rather than the natives themselves for their troubles! As one besieged landowner, himself an encomendero, put it: "Doña Teresa de Castañeda, for her own ends, goes about settling two Indians of Luis Palomino her son [also a local encomendero-hacendado] in order to disturb and upset my peaceful, long-standing possession."[21] The elites of any given locale, of course, often worked out mutually beneficial relationships which allied them in the exploitation of the natives. Nevertheless, attempts by outsiders to establish themselves, or efforts by the established to expand their share of the spoils, sparked conflicts. As with the encomenderos, such conflicts provided the Indians with willing, if unreliable, defenders. In the mines of Huayllay, Spanish miners spoke with vehement outrage when accusing a priest-miner whose usurpations cut into their own privileges.[22]

More important, perhaps, than factional divisions within a local terrain were the endemic contradictions between local and supralocal interests. In a certain sense, all local lords shared with the natives an interest in subverting tribute and mita allotments to distant centers which undermined the local economy or drained away its surplus. All supralocal claimants, on the other hand, sought to squeeze out a maximum of goods, money tributes, and labor from distant hinterlands. The conflict pitted local exploiters against outsiders. An encomendero-hacendado, joined by local kurakas and corregidor alike, denounced the destructive effect of the Huamanga mita de plaza on his repartimiento's Indians and requested that mitayos sent to the city of Huamanga be assigned instead to his local haciendas.[23] Royal officials, city residents, and miners always suspected that local corregidores, kurakas, and priests conspired against formal mita and tribute institutions. By manipulating population counts, contending that it was unrealistic to expect complete mita contingents, and documenting that it was "impossible" to collect tributes from the impoverished natives, local officials extended their ability to command unofficial tributes, to set up putting-out systems, or to organize a lucrative local commerce.[24] These extractive relationships, and the continuing vulnerability of poor Indians to mita drafts, differentiated the interests of local lords, Hispanic or Andean, from that of the poorer peasantry. Nevertheless, the elites' interest in maintaining viable local economies supported ayllus and communities in their most serious struggle — the attempt to minimize the requisition of forced labor away from local homelands.

What compounded these cleavages within the elite was the resurgence of the Spanish colonial state, under Toledo, as a vital patron of exploitation. Law and juridical administration grew into a serious fact of life, an undeniable component of the field of forces confronted by colonials and Indians alike. The support natives enlisted from jurist-bureaucrats did not necessarily imply that administrators acted as disinterested executors of legal guidelines. Though some displayed a certain integrity or commitment to legal rules, the vast majority deserved their reputations for corrupt patronage and money-making. More to the point than a disinterested sense of integrity was the way in which jurist-bureaucrats found it in their interest to support some of the natives' struggles. As we have seen, corregidores had good reason to support native sabotage of institutions which sapped the local economy. In cities such as Huamanga, Huancavelica, or Castrovirreyna, the "protector of natives" enjoyed social influence and attracted offers of bribes by virtue of his capacity to represent the natives aggressively.[25] The eye on money-making which rendered bureaucrats corruptible by Spanish clients also opened the door to bribery by the natives. The citizens of Huamanga appointed one of their own, Juan Nuñez de Sotomayor, to take legal action to correct the chronically incomplete mita contingents sent by the natives. To their chagrin, however, Sotomayor's loyalties faded before his private business interests. Travelling through the rural provinces, Sotomayor "converted the mitas into his benefit, and allowed that the [tributary counts] be lowered."[26]

By legal or illegal means, the natives gained access to a more or less working juridical system and, as much as they could, pressed it into their service. In the long run, all colonial elites shared a common general interest in exploiting the Indians through political coercion. This shared interest found conscious expression in mutually beneficial alliances, marriage and kinship bonds, diversification of economic interests, and a disposition to accommodate one another rather than invite conflict. Still, they were in the colonial world to make money, and their narrower interests as competing exploiters often clashed. For native Andean peoples, these contradictions, in conjunction with a juridical system susceptible to their claims, represented an opening to defend themselves on issues concerning labor, lands, and tributes. The Indians saw their opportunity, and they took it.

FROM DEFENSE TO MANIPULATION

As a result, legal tactics mushroomed into a major strategy of Indian life. By the 1580s, kurakas commonly gave Spaniards general powers of attorney to represent their legal interests.[27] At least one ethnic group, the Acos of Huanta, institutionalized its legal activity. "Each new year," declared seven kurakas in 1597, "we are accustomed to naming solicitors to use our power in all our [legal] causes." With license from a Spanish alcalde and protector of natives in Huamanga, eight chiefs appointed three persons—two kurakas and a Spanish solicitor in Huamanga—to look after the group's legal interests.[28]

As the natives grew more adept at defending their rights, the distinction between defensive action against colonial disregard of legal guidelines and more aggressive manipulation of the juridical system to sabotage the colonials grew increasingly blurred. In particular, the legal correlation of tribute and mita burdens with repartimiento tributary counts (healthy males, eighteen to fifty years old) lent ayllus and communities a potent tool with which

The rising importance of legal documentation. An Indian notary writes a petition and serves as caretaker of the growing assortment of documents relevant to native life.

to fight colonial extraction. By petitioning for revisitas (reinspections) of their populations, native peoples lowered their legal tribute and mita quotas in accordance with real and pretended demographic declines. By the early seventeenth century, the revisita institution had become the battleground of a social war fought to control official population figures and tax liabilities. Rather than offering a reliable guide to the human resources available to Huamanga's native societies, the revisita counts expressed the outcome of this ongoing struggle.

On the one side, encomenderos, miners, royal treasury officials, and others interested in maintaining current tribute and mita levels tried either to postpone the revisitas or to minimize their impact. In almost any legal proceeding, the affected parties held the right to participate and defend their interests. In the revisitas, encomenderos received an official citation giving them notice of the coming recount, and led the attempt to maintain the status quo. By appealing the legality or necessity of a revisita to the Lima audiencia, or objecting to the proposed judge, an encomendero or pensioner could postpone or slow down the process.[29] In the meantime, the beneficiary held rights to the old tribute levels. Once a reinspection was under way, the opposed parties did whatever they could to have the claims of the natives thrown out. Asserting that kurakas hid tributaries and then pretended they had died or fled to unknown parts, encomenderos and like-minded judges demanded rigorous proof of the native contentions. If an alleged death did not appear in the local priest's "book of deaths," a judge often recorded the Indian as a living tributary unless proved otherwise.[30] In one inspection, even a Spanish priest's testimony that he had indeed buried the Indians did not suffice to reverse this practice![31] Similarly, kurakas had to offer proof that escaped natives had truly fled their homelands and eluded their kinfolk's attempts to locate them.[32] In a revisita, Indians and ayllus always had to contend with colonial efforts to inflate or maintain the list of tributaries liable to taxes and mita. One encomendero persuaded an inspector to reverse the exemption of local Inca descendants from normal tributary status.[33] By the conclusion of a revisita, colonial recipients might still enjoy tribute and mita rights based on census lists which included dead or long-gone males among the tributaries.

On the other side, the natives did all they could to use the revisita to lessen ayllu burdens. Kurakas mobilized the testimony of priests and Indians to certify deaths and flights, and to explain the faultiness of parish mortality books; they had Spanish doctors confirm mercury sickness and endorse the removal of the ill from tributary rolls; they led inspectors on tours of crumbling, abandoned homes to prove that natives had fled the community.[34] Within several years of a completed revisita, they came back with evidence that tributes and mita assessments should be lowered further.[35] To the extent that native groups, in alliance with judges or priests or on their own, managed to include hidden tributaries among the dead or absent, they might even push through a reduction which exceeded true population declines. The powerful Hernando Palomino, whose Soras Indians pressed aggressively for reductions by the early 1600s, complained that local priests confirmed the "deaths" of hidden tributaries "in order to employ them in their trade and business and to satisfy the caciques." The priests who certified forty-four deaths between 1607 and 1609, Palomino observed pointedly, "did not say that they *buried* the natives." Instead, they went along with the natives' story on the strength of "having seen their wives dressed as widows."[36]

The day-to-day process of a revisita mirrored this tug of war. At the beginning of his tour, and at each village to which he came, the judge usually delivered a standard warning in his public announcement to the throng gathered at the plaza. "Those who may know that the caciques or other persons have Indians hidden should declare them. If they do so, they will be rewarded and likewise those uncooperative . . . will be punished."[37] The identity and political sympathies of a judge concerned the natives as much as it did the colonials. One ethnic group petitioned for appointment of their corregidor as judge of a revisita. Since the corregidor already received a salary, they argued, he could perform the revisita without subjecting the natives to the salary and costs of another official. Probably the Indians also thought that their corregidor held enough interest in local exploitative relationships to cooperate with their efforts to cut back tribute and mita. When the viceroy tried to sidestep possible collusion by appointing an independent judge, the natives' strenuous objections held up the revisita for seventy-four days.[38]

Once they began, the revisitas dragged out into painstaking expeditions — village by village, ayllu by ayllu, household by household — which recorded each individual, checked age and death classifications against parish records, demanded written proof for all contentions, and earned the judge a mounting daily salary.[39] The inspections took on a quality of hide-and-seek played with documents, witnesses, payoffs or political alliances, and elusive settlement patterns. The nucleated population clusters sponsored by Toledo had broken down sufficiently to allow ayllus and kurakas to settle natives "in hidden and remote parts" which escaped inspection. The possibility of native subterfuge, on the other hand, gave harsh judges a rationale to dismiss Indian claims as suspect. When two kurakas, supported by a "protector of the natives," organized written testimony to prove the death of a Lucanas tributary in Castrovirreyna, the judge declared "that it is not enough [to have] Indians testify in it and not a Spaniard." Most Indians, he went on to observe, "do not hesitate to perjure themselves in order to remove [natives]" from their ayllus' tribute and mita rolls.[40]

The results of the recounts thus reflected the relative skills, advantages, and luck of the interested parties as much as they did demography. The Soras Indians, with 2,441 tributaries in 1570–1575, managed to lower their count by a mere 46 tributaries around 1600 despite the important epidemic of smallpox (and perhaps also epidemics of typhus and/or influenza) which struck the Huamanga region in the mid to late 1580s. The toll exacted by epidemic disease in these years is unknown, but the net decline of male tributaries among the Soras peoples from Toledan census levels surely amounted to more than 200 tributaries (8.2 percent) in the year 1600. Less than a decade later, the Soras Indians lowered the tributary count by an impressive 439 tributaries despite the *absence* of major epidemics. Between 1600 and 1610, they had clearly learned how to use the revisita institution more effectively.[41] In a less fortunate case, the Chancas of Andahuaylas lowered their count by a large proportion, only to find that subsequent investigation of the revisita's accuracy wiped out most of their relief. The original revisita of 1604 revised the 1594 count by compiling figures of 1,429 male deaths, 456 men who had passed fifty years of age, and 1,117 new tributaries who had reached eighteen years of age. The net decline was 768 tributaries, from a total of 3,277 in 1594 to 2,509 in 1604. The Andahuaylas encomienda had reverted to the Crown, which received substantial tributes from the Chancas by the 1600s. Crown officials objected to the credibility of the recount, claiming that the judge was too interested in personal profit to double-check alleged deaths or to include some 500 able-bodied young males in the count of new tributaries. By 1606, the accusations of fraud against the royal treasury led to the appointment of a special judge to investigate, with power to replace kurakas if necessary. Aided by "discord among the caciques," the new inspector claimed to discover an undercount of 641 tributaries, and raised the count to 3,150 (a net decline of only 127 from 1594).[42]

By the early seventeenth century, the Andean peoples of Huamanga had developed sufficient skills in local politics, juridical procedures, and subterfuge to lower the official tributary population by dramatic proportions. By 1630, revisitas had cut the regional count from over twenty-two thousand in 1570–75 to some four thousand (see Figure 5.1). The drop cut gross tributes from over 85,000 pesos ensayados to only 15,000 pesos, and choked the once plentiful flow of over three thousand mitayos to six hundred or less. In the initial period of 1570–1600, repartimientos in Huamanga only managed to lower official counts to some eighty percent of the Toledan tributary population. But between 1600 and 1630, the evidence suggests growing native skill and experience. Revisitas proliferated until they reduced the count to a mere fifteen to twenty percent of the Toledan figures.

What is more, by the 1620s many revisita figures may have underestimated the human energy available in local ayllu economies. Anyone famil-

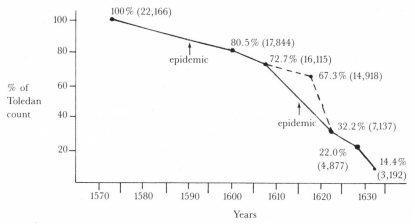

Figure 5.1. Official counts, Huamanga tributary populations, 1570–1640

Note: Dashed line is curve based on counts for only two repartimientos, whose 1606–1610 percentage seemed abnormally high (17.3% higher) when compared with the regional count based on twelve repartimientos.

Sources: Census counts of Huamanga's twenty-three core repartimientos and Sancos during five-year intervals, as given in Appendix C. The regional percentages and estimates assume that the revisitas found in the extant documentation are fairly representative of the recounts in the region as a whole. The percentage given for the year 1600 (80.5%) consolidates figures for 1596–1600 and 1601–1605, particularly since I have not been able to specify exactly which of these five-year intervals is appropriate for some of the recounts.

iar with Andean terrain and indigenous settlement patterns knows how easily a determined social group could hide a portion of its human, animal, or even agricultural resources from outsiders. An investigation of idolatry in the Huancavelica-Castrovirreyna district showed that ethnic groups concealed some of the newborn even from local parish records. Several major huacas each enjoyed the services of twenty or thirty men and women reserved for the cults. To protect the servants from discovery, and from mita labor in the mines, the Indians "would hide them when [they were] children and would not baptize them so that they would not appear in the priest's books."[43] The Bishop of Huamanga, who toured the region extensively during 1624 and 1625, noted that so many adult males had either died or fled to live in hidden places away from villages that "it is impossible that one could fulfill the mita of Huancavelica." Finding hidden natives was not easy, since "those who look for them do not want to find [the natives] but rather their money."[44]

In addition to this concealed population, a community built access to a significant group of able-bodied males legally exempt from its tributary count. Flight from home communities had created a sector of immigrant Indians known as *forasteros*. Some opted to live in new rural community settings rather than attach themselves to European estates or enterprises, or live in cities or isolated montaña regions. These community forasteros often married native ayllu women and participated actively in local economic life.[45] Until the eighteenth century, however, they were legally exempted from the tribute-mita counts of their adopted communities. The bishop who toured Huamanga in 1624–25 certainly exaggerated when he said that the total native population of rural parishes had remained fairly stable, if one included children, hidden people, and forasteros (of all kinds).[46] But a 1683 census of Chocorvos ayllus settled in Vilcashuamán confirmed that the community forasteros constituted an important, if hitherto unquantified, sector of seventeenth-century ayllu economies. Twenty-seven forasteros expanded the communities' population of able-bodied males aged eighteen to fifty by 33.8 percent. All but one lived in one of the two towns inspected, where they raised the count by 54.2 percent.[47]

The sharp cutback in tribute and mita thus represented a considerable native achievement against formidable odds rather than an inescapable consequence of objective demographic trends. Even had the revisita figures reflected these accurately, population losses in themselves had not led automatically to commensurate reductions of tribute-mita levies. As we have seen, the rate and scale of tributary count reductions were the result of hard-fought juridical wars. Nor did population loss, by itself, necessarily undercut the objective capacity of communities to support tribute-mita levies based on high male tributary counts. The viability of alternative means of extracting large profits from native communities (Chapter 6) casts doubt on the assumption that ayllus simply could not have satisfied quotas whose ratio per male-headed household exceeded that established by Toledo. Indeed, Indian communities or individuals unwilling or unable to satisfy mita quotas in persons frequently paid money equivalents as an alternative, or hired other natives to replace mitayos. Kurakas who managed to accumulate monies paid tributes for men who had fled the community.[48] Finally, the effect of hidden Indians and forasteros, combined with the developing skills of native petitioners, meant that the official tributary counts, in at least some cases, seriously underestimated the total human network available to local societies. Andean communities, to be sure, suffered appalling losses to disease (especially in the epidemics of 1585–88 and 1610–15), abuse, and flight which high birth rates or in-migration could reverse only partially.[49] The net effect may have cut the region's ethnic populations by half or more between 1570 and 1630, from over one hundred twenty thousand to a measure in the tens of thousands. But the dramatic drop in tributary counts to a fifth or less of the Toledan census was not a direct index of the decline in human resources or economic surplus available from ayllu society. It measured instead the effects of the Indians' never-ending sabotage campaign against tribute and mita.

THE IMPACT OF JUDICIAL POLITICS: THE COLONIAL ELITE
For the colonials, the natives' juridical activity constituted far more than an occasional nuisance. By the early seventeenth century, the revisitas had undermined the reliability of the state's official extractive institutions as suppliers of adequate labor and revenues to a developing economy. The total effect of the natives' campaign against exploitation, however, did not subject Huamanga to a generalized crisis. Mercury production — a key measure of economic dynamism and markets — suffered occasional setbacks due to technical and labor problems, and never recaptured the heady boom years of the 1580s and 1590s. Nevertheless, Huancavelica continued to compile a reasonably consistent record of prosperity (Figure 5.2),[50] and colonial Huamanga escaped sharp economic decline until much later in the seventeenth and early eighteenth centuries. But the Indians' struggles sparked a series of local or temporary crises which disrupted enterprise and incomes, shut down workshops, and pinched production with labor bottlenecks. Cheap mita labor grew scarce and unreliable. The natives' growing ability to evade or lower mita-tribute quotas, and to entangle exploitative relations in legal battles, gave the colonials strong incentive to find alternative sources of profit more independent of state authority or patrimony. As we shall see (in

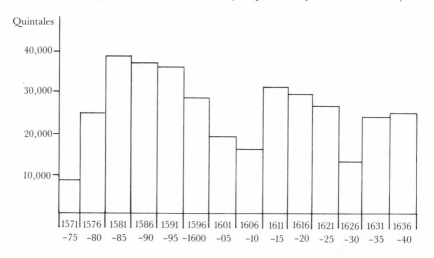

Five-year intervals

Figure 5.2. Mercury production registered at Huancavelica, 1570–1640

Source: Lohmann, *Las minas,* 452–54.

Chapter 6), the colonial elites turned increasingly to more direct modes of exploiting Indian labor, based on economic dependencies and forms of political control which escaped official state supervision, to shield their enterprises from vulnerability to legal action.

Even the early revisitas of the 1590s had saddled an expanding commercial economy with labor shortages. The boom of the 1580s and 1590s encouraged investment in farms, ranches, and hacienda estates, but mita cutbacks imposed significant hardships. By 1600, ninety-eight petty beneficiaries of the mita de plaza received only one native each. Prominent citizens coped with fewer mitayos to work vast holdings. An allotment of forty-one laborers for Crisóstomo de Hontiveros was cut to twenty-nine; Pedro Díaz de Rojas lost ten of twenty-six mitayos; Alonso Hernández Alvitez complained of losses "because of lack of help" when a revisita dropped his share from sixteen to thirteen mitayos. On the expanding complex of farm and pasture lands held by Francisco de Castañeda, a labor shortage posed severe problems by 1595. "The eighteen [mita] Indians we used to have were very few to take care of the herds and fields which we have in this district and [elsewhere]." Now, with his quota down to just twelve mitayos, Castañeda lagged desperately behind in the agricultural cycle. "It is now the middle of the month of November and beyond; I do not have the wheat harvested . . . on account of not having Indians with which to do it." Castañeda held some 300 hectares of farmland suitable for corn, wheat, potatoes, and other crops, but dared plant only about 120. Perhaps exaggerating, Castañeda claimed that thirty Indians alone were needed to care properly for his rapidly multiplying herds of over 8,000 sheep, 400 mares, 150 mules and donkeys, 700 goats, 100 swine, and 25 oxen. In 1595, the labor squeeze had cost him over 300 sheep and goats.[51]

By the seventeenth century, the mita de plaza lost its credibility as a major supplier of labor to complement yanaconas in agriculture and ranching. The mita reductions caused by the revisitas, and the rural corregidores' cooperation with natives to sabotage enforcement of the remaining quotas, grew into an inescapable fact of life. In 1606, and again in 1625 and 1645, Huamanga's cabildo appealed to the viceroy for a more effective mita de plaza. These repeated pleas indicated that the viceregal decrees issued in response could not reverse the political, economic, and demographic realities conspiring against the mita.[52]

The mining sector, of course, enjoyed the highest priority in economic policy, but even so had to contend with shrinking mita supplies. The opening of a major silver mining city at Castrovirreyna in the 1590s shifted mitayos away from significant, but secondary, gold and silver deposits at Atunsulla. Within a decade, eighty mitayos normally distributed to Atunsulla fell to twenty, and shortages of cheap labor threw the once thriving mines into decline.[53] By extending the geographical reach of Huamanga's mining mitas to new provinces, redistributing mitayo assignments to favor heavy mining work, and maintaining mita quotas in excess of ratios warranted by the revisitas, colonial authorities shored up the labor drafts. Still, these measures could not forestall indefinitely the advent of mitayo scarcity, and greater dependence upon more expensive voluntary laborers. In the late sixteenth century, Huancavelica's surplus production and plentiful labor supply facilitated cutbacks in mitayos to accommodate competing enterprises and declining community populations. But by the 1610s and 1620s, miners fought a losing battle to maintain and enforce hefty mita quotas. The Huancavelica mita dropped to 1,400 laborers in 1630 (see Table 5.1), but authorities expected only half that number to show up.[54]

Table 5.1. Huancavelica mita assignments, 1575–1645

	1577	1590	1604	1618	1630	1645
Mitayos	3,280	2,274	2,400ᵃ	2,200	1,400	620

ᵃIncludes supplement of 800 mitayos which revised initial quota.
Source: Lohmann, *Las minas,* 103, 145, 178, 186, 253, 284, 331.

Earlier, in 1618, the viceroy Francisco de Borja y Aragón had recognized that only drastic measures could save the Huancavelica mita. By his own analysis of revisitas, seven rural districts (six of them in Huamanga) deserved a reduction of 800 mitayos, which would cut the total allotment to fewer than 1,500 workers. Even more serious, the incompleteness of contingents arriving at the mercury mines had grown into a serious headache which made the quotas more apparent than real. Yet, Borja thought, the chronic deficit "is not so much because of Indian mortality . . . [as] from them having abandoned their reducciones, fleeing from the mitas and services assigned them." Local kurakas, corregidores, and priests all had reason to send only partial contingents, to hide natives, and to protect forasteros from their original communities' tax and labor obligations. Other interests, too — urban dwellers and artisans, ranchers and farmers, owners and administrators of haciendas, textile workshops, and sugar and coca plantations — welcomed migrants who wished to escape ayllu burdens.[55]

To revitalize the mita, Borja commissioned an ambitious project which was unrealizable from the beginning. Don Alonso de Mendoza, corregidor of Huanta, would take a census of all the Indians — visible and hidden, local and forastero — in the cities, farms and estates, obrajes, communities, and countryside of twelve districts which owed mitayos to Huancavelica. Mendoza should force forasteros to return to their original communities, or if they had come from over twenty leagues (fifty to sixty miles) away, he could provisionally enroll them in the tax-paying population of the closest Toledan village. Though Borja later claimed success, and Mendoza managed to extend mita and tribute obligations to some new Indians, the corregidor quickly recognized that wholesale repeal of unofficial migration and labor patterns was politically and economically unfeasible. Threatened with loss of Indian retainers, various "citizens and residents" of Huamanga voiced their opposition with "great feeling, setting forth the irreparable harm which would befall them." Mendoza backed away from Borja's ambitious proposals, and the viceroy had little choice but to accede to a more modest reform. Mendoza would inspect farms and estates in the area of the city of Huamanga. Where he managed to record yanacona retainers, the corregidor would obligate the Indians' masters to either deliver a native whose mita turn had arrived, or to pay a sum to hire a substitute laborer.[56] In the end, the project made little practical difference. Huancavelica would have to adjust to the growing shortage of cheap labor caused by declining mita allotments, and spotty enforcement of the quotas themselves.

Similarly, the formal tributes grew less and less significant as sources of revenue or capital. By the 1600s, the Crown had assumed control of assigning encomienda tributes upon the death of pensioners. In 1625, Crown control already channelled tribute revenues to the royal treasury and to an absentee Inca noble in four of every ten rural parishes.[57] In addition, the decline in regional tributes from some 85,000 pesos ensayados to about 15,000 pesos by the 1630s reduced all encomienda incomes to modest proportions. Six decades earlier, five of Huamanga's twenty-three core repartimientos held more than 1,500 tributaries. Another eight had counts over 700. Thus, over half the repartimientos had generated revenues ranging from nearly 3,000 to over 10,000 pesos. Even after the deductions for salaries and administrative costs, a dozen or so encomienda families could each count on net annual tributes worth thousands of pesos. By the 1630s, the revisitas had relegated such pensions to the past. Tributes regularly fell into arrears, and an encomendero was lucky to hold rights to a net revenue of several hundred pesos.[58]

The natives not only squeezed the flow of mitayos and tributes to painful levels. Perhaps worse, their judicial tactics imposed crisis and disruption upon colonials who enjoyed nominally plentiful quotas of tribute or labor. As we saw earlier, litigation shut down the Oré family's obraje in 1584, and disrupted work at a second obraje in 1601. Enforcement of mita or tribute rights always ran up against peasant resistance and juridical tactics. In 1607, when the Soras still owed a large annual tribute, their encomendero complained that the Indians used a dispute over tributary counts as an excuse to cease payment on thousands of pesos.[59] Even after population decline and Indian petitions cut back the initial Toledan allotment of workers to the Cacamarca obraje in Vilcashuamán, the owner still held rights to sixty mita-yos. But around 1610, his encomienda natives, embroiled in continual fights over labor practices and obligations, temporarily crippled production by getting the Lima audiencia to cancel the mita altogether! Later, the drafts were reinstalled, though revisitas reduced them to insignificance. In 1642, local natives won an order (subsequently reversed) to close the obraje. By this time, the new owner, like his predecessor, understood that only by culti-vating direct relationships with a controlled clientele of dependent workers could he shield production from community litigation.[60]

THE IMPACT OF JUDICIAL POLITICS: NATIVE SOCIETY

The Indians' juridical strategy inflicted considerable hardships upon many colonials, but nevertheless brought unfortunate consequences to native An-dean society. Given the bitter conflicts over lands, kurakazgos (chieftainships), and mita-tribute burdens which shaped ayllu and ethnic life, one could not expect that the natives would limit judicial politics to peasant actions against colonial exploitation. Andean litigants used their juridical rights and skills against one another, a practice which left native society divided and depen-dent upon colonial authorities to settle internal disputes. In addition, access to Spanish power and legal institutions encouraged a certain individualiza-tion, or privatization, of interest and perspective on the part of natives who acquired private land titles, secured legal exemptions from mita or tribute, mediated ayllu relationships with corregidores or other colonial powers, and the like. By reinforcing ayllu and ethnic strife, and fostering class dynamics which tied privileged Indians to the colonial power structure, a working sys-tem of colonial justice weakened the capacity of native societies to unite for a more ambitious, radical assault upon the exploitative structure as a whole. A more fragmented strategy pursued more limited victories — the particular causes of particular native groups or individuals. And the Indians grew in-creasingly dependent upon the legal institutions and favor of their exploiters to advance such causes, even when the disputes involved only Indians.

For many native groups, the most persistent land fights stemmed not from colonial incursions, but from rivalries with other ayllus and ethnic groups. Particularly in regions such as the Río Pampas or Huamanga-Huanta-Angaraes, a proliferation of interspersed ethnic groups generated centuries of conflict over lands and pastures. To settle such disputes until the next outbreak, local groups could resort to war, negotiation, or appeal to outside authority. Access to a legal system which presumed to resolve local disputes may actually have intensified them. A group too weak to win a vio-lent battle, or to accept a modus operandi based on local power balances, could try to compensate by securing legal backing from a Spanish judge. But rival groups, particularly if they were stronger, could not very well renounce their own claims simply because their enemies held legal title to the prized resources. Ethnic disputes repeatedly flared up, and the group able to back up its claims with legal precedents always turned to colonial judges to help protect its local interests.[61]

Even within an ethnic group, access to colonial juridical institutions fostered conflicts which undermined its internal authority and cohesion. Succession to major chieftainships had always constituted a difficult, thorny process in Andean societies. The potential heirs of a kurakazgo almost always included several rivals among the sons, and even nephews or brothers of the incumbent chief.[62] Since a major kuraka was identified more closely with one of the several ayllus constituting a community or ethnic group, his practical authority and acceptance by all the ayllus in his domain depended upon his political skills and fulfillment of popular expectations.[63] The identities of the major kurakas held crucial economic implications, since the kurakas supervised distribution of tribute and mita burdens among the various ayllus. The endemic rivalries between individual aspirants could spill into such social divisions, tearing apart a community or ethnic group. In more than one case, the ensuing civil war led to "many deaths and misfortunes" among warring "brothers."[64]

By offering defeated aspirants a tool with which to overturn the status quo, access to colonial judges kept disputes and local polarization alive, and left ethnic chiefs dependent upon Spanish power to back up their standing even with local kin. Two Soras cousins revived a dispute between their fathers until the aggressive challenger displaced his cousin as kuraka in 1594. The Angaraes chief Don Juan Llanto complained that his nephew, a source of trouble to local notables since the 1570s, had curried "the favor . . . of the corregidor and notary." With their help, the upstart had gotten two chiefs replaced and threatened to do the same to his uncle. The resulting "rebellion over cacicazgos" sent Llanto to Huamanga in 1589 to commission a lawyer to present his case before the audiencia in Lima. In Huanta, a conflict over succession turned into such a bloody and costly affair that the three rivals, each apparently backed by a significant following, agreed to settle upon an uneasy truce in 1596. Litigation, they discovered, "has no end" and burdened the Hurin Acos ayllus with costly legal fees and trips to Lima.[65]

Spanish judicial authority developed into a major internal force used by Indians against their own authorities. By obtaining the favor of Spanish judges, complained an embittered Lucanas native, a "tributary Indian pretending to be kuraka reserved all of his people from the mines and [mita labor] without consulting the cacique principal [chief kuraka]."[66] A sick peasant ordered by his kurakas to pay tribute and serve mita turned to the protector of Indians for an appeal to the corregidor which undercut the chiefs' orders. When Don Bernabé Sussopaucar passed fifty years of age, he got the corregidor of Huanta to issue an order reserving him from tribute and mita. Still, his chiefs pressured the wealthy native, a minor lord himself and holder of private title to irrigated lands, to contribute to the mita burdens of the community. Don Bernabé responded by securing a viceregal provision threatening to depose the kurakas if they persisted. The Anta ayllu of Huamanguilla included wealthy natives who, as ethnic descendants of the Incas, legally enjoyed exemption from mita and tribute. Higher kurakas, particularly those of more powerful ayllus, looked askance at the Incas' privileges and wealth. Even as an old man, an Inca descendant complained, "they force him to [serve] the said mita or to hire someone in his place." By winning a viceregal order, presenting it to the corregidor, and securing his public promise to enforce the order, the Inca descendants could defend their economic advantages.[67]

Indeed, Spanish legal authority encouraged Indians to develop individualized interests and privileges shielding them from the lot assigned to the poorer peasantry. Legal immunity from mita or tribute enabled municipal and church functionaries, Inca descendants, and artisans to sidestep burdens which impoverished kinfolk.[68] Dependence upon colonial authorities to uphold a kuraka's tenure, or to protect him from personal liability for the mita and tribute obligations of his ayllus, encouraged a native lord to work out private arrangements which accommodated the exploitative practices of local functionaries. Such arrangements enabled the chief to avoid the physical abuse, jailings, and confiscations of wealth which befell kurakas of "delinquent" taxpayers; to secure needed help in his efforts to sabotage state-sponsored labor drafts and tributes; and to mediate native-white relationships which yielded profits to all the collaborating elites.[69] The periodic composiciones de tierras gave further incentive to a process of privatization by which Indian elites might differentiate themselves from poorer kin. Legally, the judge of a composición could sell any community lands deemed "surplus" to petitioners for private title. But the composiciones also allowed wealthy Indians to purchase the auctioned lands, and kurakas to "privatize" their traditional land use rights. Huamanga's chiefs responded aggressively to the opportunity; one lord converted himself into a spectacular landowner by listing over seventy sites, totalling thousands of hectares, which "I have always possessed since my ancestors."[70]

It is doubtful that a lord could truly emancipate *all* such resources, if he wished to maintain his local standing and mobilize labor to work the lands, from the traditional claims of ayllu society. But individual title allowed him to begin to superimpose private property rights on a traditionally ayllu domain. An Indian with individual title to lands could sell them as one's own, and protect landed wealth from the usurpations which threatened collective ayllu property. As one successful petition put it: "the said lands [are] not common but rather their own individual [property] from which [the petitioners] cannot be despoiled."[71]

The natives' very success at using Spanish juridical institutions created forces in everyday life and struggle which undermined the possibility of organizing a wider, more unified and independent movement on behalf of the peasantry. First, judicial politics reinforced socially costly internal divisions along ayllu, ethnic, and even class lines. Notarial accords among ethnically distinct chiefs testify that common subjection to mita and tribute spawned efforts to unite diverse groups with similar interests and complaints.[72] But as we have seen, in practice juridical tactics could also pit Indians against one another. Ethnic groups fought over lands, rival elites battled for recognition of kurakazgos, and individual natives searched for ways to accumulate and protect wealth and privileges. During a revisita of the Chancas, all ayllus shared an interest in corroborating claims of death which lowered their collective mita-tribute quota. But a Spanish judge adept at polarizing the endemic bickering which plagued a ranked hierarchy of ayllus and kurakas discovered hundreds of "false" deaths. (The techniques of Spanish judge-investigators probably involved finding and interrogating potential informers who, threatened with punishment or offered a reward, might reveal a local secret — at least one concerning "other" ayllus or kin groups. Armed with one or several such "wedges," a shrewd investigator could proceed to try to exploit internal rivalries and divisions of loyalty to crack the community or ethnic group's wall of secrecy.)[73]

Second, a strategy of defense which depended upon colonial institutions to resist exploitation tied the natives more effectively than ever to Hispanic power. Indians who evaded or cut back mita burdens, or protected landholdings, or enforced murky claims to kuraka status through the "grace" of powerful colonials used the rules, formal and informal, of Hispanic dominance to defend themselves. Those rules demanded acceptance of colonial relationships which ultimately impoverished the Andean peasantry. Indians who won limited but important victories by securing the favor of colonials and their institutions held a certain interest in avoiding wholesale challenges of authority which invited punishment or revocation of their achievements. Moreover, judicial politics fostered loyalties among Indian elites and Hispanic patron-allies which held dangerous implications for the peasantry. Over time, the means by which ayllus battled state-sponsored extractions encouraged alliances which assimilated native elites to the colonial power structure, substituted extralegal exploitation in place of the old "legal" burdens, and differentiated the interests and perspectives of native elites — as an emerging class — from those of peasants.[74]

The juridical strategy developed by 1600 made good sense for its time, given the defeat of Taki Onqoy's radical vision, the decline of ayllu popula-

The King as dispenser of justice. Poma de Ayala imagines himself presenting his long illustrated "letter" to the King of Spain. Presumably, the King would read the treatise and adopt
the reforms proposed by Poma to end colonial abuses. The letter, some 1,200 pages in length,
was discovered by Richard Pietschmann at the Royal Library in Copenhagen in 1908.

tion and wealth, the extension of outposts of colonial power throughout the countryside, and the possibility of genuine inroads against the Indians' most hated and feared burden, the colonial mita. Aggressive use of the colonial system of justice, complemented by "laziness,"[75] flight, and anonymous forms of sabotage (hidden populations, mysterious fires)[76] offered "realistic" means of resistance. By mastering the art of judicial politics, ethnic groups, ayllus, and even individuals won battles on pressing real-life issues such as mita, tribute, and land rights.

But on another level, the natives' achievement cost them a great deal. From the point of view of a society's ruling class, a system of justice functions successfully if it represents a pact on the part of social groups and individuals not to go to war over their differences, but rather to settle conflict within the framework of rules established by society's dominant forces. Turning established rules or institutions to one's favor does not, of course, by itself signify an unwillingness to use force or to organize more radical strategies. But to the extent that reliance on a juridical system becomes a dominant strategy of protection for an oppressed class or social group, it may undermine the possibility of organizing a more ambitious assault aimed at toppling the exploitative structure itself. When this happens, a functioning system of justice contributes to the hegemony of a ruling class. This was the case, in Huamanga at least, by the early seventeenth century. By then, subversive religious movements spoke not of eliminating Hispanic society or power, but simply of resisting cooperation with Spaniards "unless forced to."[77] The Indians' struggle for Spanish justice subjected a good many colonials to constraints and hardships, and even forced some of them to search for alternative ways to extract labor and profits. What it could not do, however, was challenge colonialism itself. Spanish justice, in some instances and on some issues, favored the natives against their oppressors. But for that very reason, it set into motion relationships which sustained colonial power, weakened the peasantry's capacity for independent resistance, and rooted exploitation into the enduring fabric of Andean society.[78]

6

The Political Economy of Dependence

THE SECRET of an enduring exploitative system is, on the one hand, its capacity to organize coercion on behalf of the rulers, and, on the other hand, its ability to make the exploited "need" their exploiters. On the one side, coercive violence equips society's leaders to punish defiance of major rules and institutions. On the other side, dependency promotes "voluntary" consent to oppressive relationships. To the extent that the exploited rely on their superiors for basic needs, they must accept or even initiate obligatory relationships which subject them to continued exploitation. The subtle coercion of dependence supplements the naked coercion of force, and extractive relationships acquire greater sophistication. In an industrial capitalist society, for example, the economic dependence of proletarians is so extreme that entrepreneurs need not resort to extraeconomic compulsions to find workers. The pressure of economic necessity suffices to drive men and women to "volunteer" themselves for exploitation. Free labor, cut off from access to the means of production, has no alternative but to sell its labor-power to capitalist producers, in exchange for wages to pay for subsistence. (The rise of extensive social welfare programs in some countries has not provided alternative subsistence strategies to large enough numbers of people to change the general pattern of dependence on wage work.)

In Huamanga, by contrast, the colonial regime consolidated by Toledo was premised upon exploiting economically self-sufficient ayllus and communities. This meant that extraeconomic compulsions, including physical force, played a prominent role as the indispensable activators of extractive relationships. As we have seen, the tributes and mitas sponsored by the state, and the extralegal exactions mediated by corregidores and local power figures, met with repeated resistance which only strong coercive measures could overcome. Over time, of course, control of power and violence enhanced the ability of colonial elites to create dependencies which pressured Indians into more "voluntary" compliance. Indian village officials retained political posts subject to approval by the colonial state; ayllus and communities turned to Spanish juridical institutions as a source of protection; pagan Indians placated Catholic priests who mediated relations with the powerful Spanish gods. These "extraeconomic" dependencies added to the colonials' repertoire of weapons more subtle instruments of discipline. But unless they eroded the material self-sufficiency of peasants, they did little to make the *economic* process of exploitation more sophisticated. The essential dynamic behind the Toledan institutions remained political—the repeated mobilization of superior power, in naked or subtle form, to coerce tributes and labor drafts out of an economically independent peasantry.

Yet we have also seen that by the early seventeenth century, Indians increasingly sharpened skills enabling them to circumvent certain coercive pressures. In a context of declining population, Indian resistance—flight, subterfuge, and adroit judicial politics—crippled the state-sponsored mitas and tributes which had fueled the prosperity of the late sixteenth century. Indeed, one might expect the rapid decline of legal tributes and labor drafts to have plunged Huamanga's commercial economy into depression.

But the colonial economy of Huamanga did not stumble into a prolonged decline until much later in the seventeenth century. Somehow, early seventeenth-century entrepreneurs found alternative means to exploit labor, without depending as greatly upon the largesse or coercive power of the colonial state. In many cases, they did not need to apply any coercion at all to attract laborers. To understand why, we will need to consider the economic forces unleashed by Toledo's reorganization. The revitalized regime of the late sixteenth century saddled the Indian countryside with severe economic demands accompanied by a growing commercialization of relationships. The combination tended to weaken the self-sufficiency of local economies, to increase the monetary needs and obligations of the Indians, and to stimulate a certain degree of internal differentiation into rich and poor. By 1600, a growing sector of poor ayllus and households had no choice but to rely on occasional wage labor to cover their monetary obligations, and to make up for shortfalls in subsistence. In addition, increasing numbers of Indians decided to escape the heavy burdens of ayllu life entirely by emigrating to new settings of life and work. In both cases, the poor and the émigré often had little choice but to "volunteer" for exploitation by wealthier colonials who, presumably, provided their clienteles with lands, subsistence, wages, and protection. This chapter explores how such dependencies arose, and made it possible to avert a crisis of the commercial economy during the years 1600–1640.

ORIGINS OF THE LABOR PROBLEM

The crisis of the official state institutions derived from two elements. First, the Indians learned ways to weaken the original Toledan institutions. In a context of declining demography and substantial emigration from communities, aggressive judicial politics enabled Indian groups to shrink the legal pool of tributes and labor drafts to a much smaller scale by the early seventeenth century. Moreover, the Indians tended to disrupt the remaining quotas at every turn. Individuals escaped from mine work; ayllus backed noncompliance with dilatory legal tactics; chiefs conspired with corregidores to sabotage enforcement of legal tributes and mitas; and communities brought suits to shut down mita-powered obrajes (see Chapter 5).

Second, economic and demographic trends increased the demand for exploitable labor. Huamanga's mining and commercial prosperity encouraged producers to expand agricultural, ranching, manufacturing, artisanal, mining, and commercial enterprises. In addition, dynamic economic zones such as the cities of Huancavelica, Huamanga, and Castrovirreyna, and certain districts of Angaraes-Huanta-Vilcashuamán attracted an inflow of fortune-seekers and independent producers. The inflow of migrants compounded the natural increase of a Spanish-mestizo population less susceptible than Indians to death caused by microbes of European origin, or by overwork and abuse. By the early seventeenth century, a growing mass of thousands of Spaniards and mestizos aspired to exploit Indian labor and to profit from an expanding economy.[1]

The squeeze on state-sponsored supplies of labor and tributes thus occurred at a time when economic and demographic forces boosted the Spanish-mestizo sector's thirst for labor. A tiny elite of thirty or forty people grabbed most of the shrinking regional patrimony (see Chapter 4). Even for the high elite, this patrimony grew less and less adequate to sustain expanding enterprises or provide revenues for investment, and a growing sector of lesser elites, pretenders, and petty producers were closed out of major shares of the state's labor drafts and tributes in the first place. An early revisita of the region, around 1599, cut the mita de plaza allotment of ninety-eight lesser citizens of Huamanga, many of them farmers, to only one Indian each.[2] A modest farmer who depended on the year-round labors of two or three mitayos could not easily absorb a reduction of one or two workers. Like the high elites, he would search for alternative means of securing labor that would save him from scaling down his operations.

ALTERNATIVES AND SOLUTIONS

The adaptations available to alleviate the shortage were diverse and well-known. During boom times, legal mitas and tributes, complemented by the extralegal exactions of corregidores and other functionaries,[3] had supplied massive amounts of labor, goods, and money revenues to an expanding commercial economy. But the colonials had never relied exclusively on mita, tributes, or extralegal coercions by officials. They had supplemented their access to surplus labor and products with a range of alternative relationships: slavery of Africans and in some cases foreign Indians; personal servitude imposed on yanaconas and other dependents; and wage labor contracts or agreements for varying time periods.

These relationships had emerged in "civil society," as expressions of "private" relations and coercions relatively free of direct sponsorship by the formal political structure of the state. Mita and tribute functioned as official extractive institutions; their very dynamic continually bound exploiter and exploited to the legal coercive authority of a strong central state. Slavery, personal lordship, and contracted labor, on the other hand, bound exploiter and exploited directly to one another. The colonial state, at various moments and in different degrees, legally sanctioned, encouraged, and even purported to regulate such relationships. But the initiation, internal dynamics, and socioeconomic significance of these relationships reflected private or extraofficial initiative more than state edict.[4]

As long as the mita supplied plentiful cheap labor, its success limited the attraction of alternative labor arrangements to an auxiliary level. Africans were comparatively expensive, justifiable mainly for social prestige and to fill positions demanding special training, productivity, or trustworthiness on the part of ethnically isolated slaves.[5] Yanaconas carried more economic and demographic weight, especially in agriculture and ranching. They required no purchase price, and they could learn to perform tasks requiring Andean or Hispanic skills. Still, the possibility of obtaining cheap infusions of fresh labor for limited time periods dampened the usefulness of long-term relationships with dependents who demanded lands, goods, and reasonable treatment for their labors, which the Spaniards often thought they performed negligently. On large estates owned by powerful men and women, resident yanaconas probably represented a numerically modest, though essential, source of labor in the sixteenth century.[6] The availability of mita labor similarly restricted the demand for wage laborers. Dynamic mining centers like Huancavelica and Castrovirreyna attracted a stream of experienced mine workers who had loosened or abandoned ties to their home communities. But these laborers earned twice the wages of mitayos, and were attractive primarily to supplement the extractive work of mitayos in especially rich veins, or to perform skilled work in other phases of the productive process.[7]

What distinguished patterns of labor in Huamanga in the early seventeenth century was not the existence of slavery, *yanaconaje* (long-term personal bondage), or wage labor, but their increasing importance in production. Even in enterprises where the mita continued to supply the bulk of the work force, judicial politics and changing community demography made the state-run labor drafts an outmoded institution of the past, destined to decline as a reliable source of labor. Alternative relationships arranged in "civil society," which circumvented dependence upon the labor patrimony of the state, represented the dynamic, growing forces of the future. By creating a large, varied clientele of personal dependents and contracted laborers, a colonial could protect production from labor scarcities and disruptions which, increasingly, accompanied state-controlled labor.

Thus even African slavery, relatively costly in a highland economy where profits depended on large inputs of cheap labor, grew into a significant economic force by the 1600s. The prestige attached to owning slaves had always guaranteed a certain demand for blacks, especially for household and urban services. The suitability of ethnically isolated Africans for extremely intense or skilled labors widened the market, and a brisk slave trade flourished in Huamanga. In the seventeenth-century countryside, slave labor dotted the vineyards, sugar haciendas, and farms of prosperous zones. A census of Huancavelica in 1592 counted over 240 slaves in the city. In certain mines with major refining mills, slavery could reach surprising (though still modest) proportions. In 1616, the half-owner of a Castrovirreyna mine-hacienda complex held eighteen slaves to complement the labors of fifty-two mitayos.[8]

More impressive than the spread of slave labor was the growing importance of yanaconaje in agriculture, ranching, obraje manufactures, and even mining. Conditions of long-term bondage varied considerably, even within single enterprises, but normally implied an obligation by the master to provide for the subsistence and needs of dependent Indians by granting rights which usually included lands and an annual wage credit. In exchange, the yanaconas owed certain labor services to their masters, who expected personal bonds to take precedence over ayllu bonds.[9] But the work and loyalties of Indian serfs often displayed the "neglect" and sabotage normally associated with dependent labor. "It is now about five years . . . ," complained the lord of a notoriously troublesome native, "that he plants [for himself] on my lands without helping me in anything."[10] Moreover, the wage credits accumulated by many yanaconas over the years, if uncancelled by debits and sales of overpriced goods, could prove burdensome.[11] The evidence suggests that elites and other substantial citizens did not resort to yanaconaje on a large scale if they could obtain labor drafts for limited time periods, with fewer long-term obligations, from the mita, extraofficial corvées arranged by Spanish or Indian functionaries, or other means. In 1577, a rural estate of a powerful citizen utilized the labors of twenty-seven community peasants, but only five yanaconas and four Indian "cowboys" (vaqueros). Similarly, a farming partnership between two local grandees in 1601 relied on mitayos for at least three-fourths of the full-time labor force. Another part-

nership, in 1609, on lands sufficiently productive to warrant hiring a Spanish administrator, placed only six yanaconas on the consolidated holdings.[12]

But whatever the initial preferences of the elite, the declining credibility
of the mita and the strong demand for labor guaranteed that yanaconaje
would grow more attractive. Lesser figures with modest political influence,
of course, had always needed to search for alternatives to the state's labor
patrimony. By the 1600s, powerful families and institutions were engaging
in the same search. In 1618, an inspection of a Jesuit hacienda near Huamanga counted sixteen yanaconas, eleven of them heads of families. With
relatives, the "attached" residents on the hacienda totalled forty-four Indians, thirty-two of them old enough to work.[13] That same year, accounts
from a leading gentlewoman's hacienda in Vilcashuamán identified ten of
twenty-nine workers as yanaconas. Just as important, the estate tended to
convert the other nineteen laborers, technically "community" Indians, into
long-term residents whose life and work relations, in practice, resembled
those of yanaconas. Of the nineteen "community" Indians, ten had lived on
the hacienda at least two years; of these, probably six had been residents six
years or more.[14] Earlier, rural labor strategies focused on labor drafts to
complement a modest "core" of resident Indians. Now, the emphasis had
shifted somewhat, to expanding the "core" of resident laborers and to securing outside labor unrelated to the mita.

Obraje manufactures witnessed a similar shift of emphasis. To counter
conflicts with communities which lowered or disrupted mita labor drafts,
the owners tended to pull ayllu Indians more fully into the orbit of the obraje
complex. By settling natives on obraje lands, and taking care of their tribute
or mita obligations, an entrepreneur, in effect, assimilated ayllu Indians to
yanacona-like status as indefinitely resident dependents.[15]

By 1620, the yanaconas had become so integral to Huamanga's social and
economic structures that no authority could rewrite the new demographic
map. Toledo had hoped to stabilize the yanacona population by legalizing
bonds formed well before his reign, but prohibiting new retainers except
with special license.[16] By the 1600s, a growing sector of lesser colonials and
powerful elites had acquired considerable numbers of new Indian retainers
who now played an expanded role in the production of food, textiles, and
craft goods for Huamanga's mines, cities, and commercial networks. This
was the context in which Viceroy Borja tried unsuccessfully to revive the
Huancavelica mita in 1618 (see Chapter 5). The reform plan was to revitalize the mita pool in part by sending "new" yanaconas back to their ayllus. In
Huamanga, "the citizens and residents, seeing . . . the great harm that
would befall them for removing the Indian yanaconas from their haciendas,"
protested loudly. Borja reluctantly accepted the advice of his appointed representative, Don Alonso de Mendoza, that he legalize the yanaconas (pro-

vided that masters would pay to hire replacements for retainers who skipped their ayllus' mita obligations). Borja prohibited further expansion of yanaconaje, but Huamanga's Spaniards continued to "hide all the [mita] Indians who leave Huancavelica in estancias and haciendas . . . throughout this bishopric."[17]

To supplement their expanded forces of personal retainers, Huamanga's colonials turned increasingly to various forms of labor contracting. Given the limited number of potential yanaconas, stiff competition for them, and the obligations imposed by long-term seigneurial relationships, few colonials of significant economic stature could rely on such relationships to supply most all their labor needs.[18] The growth of yanaconaje, and to a lesser extent slavery, expanded the "core" labor forces attached to various colonials, but could not eliminate the need for additional labor from the outside.

To fill out one's labor force, and to secure an infusion of extra laborers during busy times, an entrepreneur "rented" Indians for limited time periods in exchange for a remuneration which often included money wages. The records of a sugar estate in the 1630s, for example, made plain that only by hiring wage laborers, from nearby communities and from far away, could the hacienda satisfy its fluctuating demand for labor. Indian wages, especially to cut, transport, and mill sugar cane during harvest season, accounted for the great majority of the administrator's expenses. The managers of an obraje responded to the strong market for textiles in the 1590s by hiring Indian laborers, for periods ranging from several days to several weeks or more, to supplement their force of mitayos and yanaconas. In obrajes, as in agriculture, the decline of the mita heightened the importance of personal retainers and hired laborers. In mining, a key source of income for the entire regional economy, the expansion of wage labor relationships played a crucial role. Despite the presence of hired Indians, the mining boom of Huamanga in the last quarter of the sixteenth century had been built chiefly upon the labors of large mita contingents. By 1630, the mining mitas had dropped off sharply, and the market was expanding for skilled mine workers who commanded twice the wages of mitayos. By mid-century, production at Huancavelica continued at a healthy rate, but the demand for labor had driven the wages of voluntary workers up even further, to three and a half times the daily wage of mitayos.[19]

In the city of Huamanga, notaries recorded a series of *asientos,* labor contracts between individual Indians and prospective masters, which proliferated from the 1590s on. A survey of seventy-eight such contracts in the period 1570–1640 shows that they normally represented more than a simple exchange of labor-power for money or commodities.[20] The Indian turned himself (or, on rare occasions herself) over to a master for a substantial period, usually a year, both as a repository of labor-power and, more broadly, as a client human being. The native promised to stay with the employer

throughout the time of the contract, and often to do "all that might be ordered him." The master agreed not only to pay wage money, but also to
commit himself to the broader welfare of his dependent. He would provide a
specified amount of subsistence goods, especially food and clothing, restore
the Indian to good health in times of sickness, and might even look after the
native's religious instruction. The contract might specify a promise to teach
the native a trade, or to protect him from the mita.[21] For general work in agriculture, ranching, or domestic service, the monetary component of the exchange was usually modest (12–24 pesos of 8–9 reales a year), and might
represent simply one of several mutual obligations. In two out of three apprenticeships, the Indian apprentice held no rights at all to monetary compensation for his labor.[22] Only in the case of skilled or specialized labor by
Indian artisans, *arrieros* (muleteers, drivers of animal trains), and the like
did the monetary aspects weigh more heavily. Artisans earned 40–60 pesos a
year, and arrieros 80–130 pesos. In addition, their contracts sometimes
spelled out special rights which increased the hired Indian's income or earning capacity. One arriero held the right to use his master's animals to make
"all the trips that he wishes . . . from this city to other places."[23]

In truth, the range of relationships generated through labor contracts and
agreements varied considerably, and to equate them with modern wage labor would distort their character. Various degrees of compulsion lay behind
some of the "agreements," which turned out to mask more coercive relationships. Receipt of wages was by no means automatic, and a contracted
worker whose subsistence was provided for might have to work six months
before he could claim a wage.[24] Some contracts, particularly in the case of
putting-out systems or seasonal harvests, represented collective sales of labor-
power by ayllus and ethnic groups rather than direct, individual contracts.[25]

Even in the case of freely hired individuals, which grew increasingly important from about 1600 on, we find a broad spectrum of relationships. At
one end were relations which constituted early forms of wage labor. The pre-
dominant feature of the bond was the worker's sale of labor-services in exchange for a money wage, or in some cases a share of the commodities he
produced. Continuation of the relationship depended on short-term agreements and personal decisions. In mining, textile production, and agriculture, this kind of relationship enabled entrepreneurs to hire Indians on a
temporary basis without assuming too many responsibilities to dependents
in the long run.[26] At the other end of the spectrum were agreements which
imbedded the "sale" of labor-power in a much broader set of human bonds
applicable for a year or even longer. This kind of relationship, more seigneurial in flavor, enabled colonials to hire Indian workers who temporarily
expanded the colonials' clienteles of "attached" dependent laborers. To the
extent that a master could impose debts upon a hired Indian, he or she
might wipe out the laborer's wage credits, lengthen the term of service re-

quired to "pay back" debts, and eventually enmesh the contracted Indian in a long-term, yanacona-like relationship.[27] In a sense, many asientos represented a kind of rental of yanaconas. An Indian rented to the master broad authority over the native's life and work for a year or longer, in exchange for subsistence, wage credits, protection, and other services. The colonials themselves sometimes referred to such hired Indians as "yanaconas in accordance with the contracts and agreements which have been made with them."[28]

But in all these cases, labor contracting bore witness to the growing importance of a certain kind of market for the services of individual Indians who hired out their labor-power. In some cases, the item sold was labor-power pure and simple, unencumbered by other bonds, and freely traded for money or precious metals. Often, the sale of labor-power was enmeshed in a broader set of mutual obligations which linked masters and dependent laborers, and tended to reduce the practical significance of the monetary element in the transaction. To talk of the kind of generalized labor market associated with nineteenth-century industrial capitalism would, therefore, misconstrue the comparatively narrow, embryonic character of voluntary wage labor in Huamanga. The "market" for free labor was primitive at best: shallow in scale, irregular in supply, vulnerable to political control, and colored by compulsions which rounded up "vagrants," robbed workers of wage payments, and tied some laborers to long-term, coercive relationships.[29]

Nonetheless, despite all these limitations, the contracts offer some evidence of a labor market mechanism. Peasants who descended from Huamanga to work in the vineyards and farms of coastal Ica, where Indian labor was comparatively scarce, earned five to ten pesos more a year than their counterparts in Huamanga.[30] As the seventeenth century wore on, the demand for hired labor tended to press wages upward. In the city of Huamanga, the average annual salary promised to asiento contract Indians for unspecialized labors was, besides subsistence, about fifteen pesos in the period 1596–1602 (sixteen contracts). By 1609, the average had climbed to about twenty pesos a year (eight contracts); ten to fifteen years later, wages averaged about twenty-four pesos (ten contracts).[31] In Huancavelica, the daily wage owed to non-mitayo workers climbed from some seven reales around 1600 to as much as twelve reales in mid-century.[32] Increasingly, colonials who lacked sufficient access to mita and other forms of forced labor had little choice but to offer wages and other remunerations to Indians who "volunteered" to work.

THE ROLE OF INDIAN CONSENT

Indeed, the remarkable aspect of the rise of yanaconaje and labor contracting was the degree of voluntary consent by Indians to such relationships. To be sure, colonials continued to use force to recruit laborers. And as we have seen, once a bond was initiated, whether by choice or compulsion, coercive pressures frequently shaped the texture and further evolution of the relationship.

But the evidence suggests that, by the seventeenth century, many producers came to depend upon the willingness of Indians to work for colonials. Huamanga's Spaniards "promise the moon," complained a knowledgeable observer, to lure ayllu Indians to become resident yanaconas on rural estates.[33] Colonials offered rising wages to contracted workers precisely because they could not counteract labor shortages by force alone.[34] In many cases, Indians migrated long distances to work for employers with whom they were unlikely to have had significant bonds previously, coercive or not. Two out of every three "unspecialized" Indians who entered asiento contracts with Europeans in the city of Huamanga came from rural provinces beyond the immediate countryside surrounding the city; the city itself contributed less than a tenth of the Indians (see Table 6.1). Most of the migrants appear to have joined relatively unknown masters, people who had not enjoyed much influence or stature in the Indians' original homelands.[35]

Colonial masters, of course, battled against having to count on voluntary compliance by migratory Indians. Entrepreneurs frequently sought to "tie down" contracted workers and yanaconas alike in long-term relations of debt, mutual dependency, and personal lordship. Or they held back on full wage payments to increase the likelihood that a temporary laborer would return later. To collect payment on past labors, an Indian might have to submit to yet another round of labors.[36] Such measures were significant and widespread, but we ought not exaggerate their success. Many Indians held enough power or alternatives—including escape[37]—to collect some wages and leave after limited stints of duty.[38] A colonial who sought to lure and maintain access to contracted laborers and, to a lesser extent, yanaconas had to live with that fact of life. More than he or she might have wished, the

Table 6.1. Places of origin, Asiento Indians,[a] 1570–1640

	City of Huamanga	Immediate rural environs	Rural provinces of Huamanga	Outside Huamanga (the region)	Unknown
No. of cases	4	6	30[b]	3	7
% of all cases	8.0	12.0	60.0	6.0	14.0
% of identified cases	9.3	14.0	69.7	6.9	—

[a]Natives contracted in the city of Huamanga to serve European masters, excluding cases of skilled Indian specialists such as artisans and arrieros.

[b]Includes one case from Andahuaylas, one from southern part of "valley of Jauja," and two from Parinacochas—all regions that bordered on the formal hinterland of Huamanga.

Source: Appendix D, Table D.1.

colonial relied upon a certain measure of consent on the part of the Indian. From time to time, enterprises which paid considerable wages to hire temporary or contracted laborers halted production "because nobody showed up" to work.[39]

Fortunately for the colonials, however, dependents and workers seemed to gravitate towards them. Dynamic zones and enterprises functioned as economic poles or magnets which drew Indians to work in mining, agriculture, ranching, crafts and other skilled specialties, manufactures, transport, and domestic service. To some extent, prosperous centers had always exerted such a pull on the ayllu countryside. But colonial producers had earlier depended heavily on the state's coercive power to raid ayllus for labor in mines, textile workshops, sugar or coca plantations, and commercial farms or ranches. By the 1600s, as the stream of peasants and vagabonds looking for work or for masters rose to new heights, many colonials found that they need not rely as heavily on coercion to recruit and hold laborers. A person of means could tap the flow of Indians into Huamanga, Huancavelica, Castrovirreyna, Vilcashuamán (the trading center), and other commercially prospering zones. The emphasis of Indian grievances began to shift subtly. Now, many Indians complained not that they had been forced to work, but that entrepreneurs reneged on fair payment of wages.[40]

The options available to colonial entrepreneurs had changed dramatically. In 1570, the economic self-sufficiency of ayllu society constituted a roadblock to the extraction of surplus labor. Only repeated applications of force, under the aegis of a powerful state, could spur the development of the colonial economy, especially in mining. Fifty years later, the colonials still could not dispense with force to exploit Indian labor. But coercion was more private or extraofficial in character, less bound to the formal legal institutions of the state. Moreover, coercion often could not meet the needs of major and minor entrepreneurs. Voluntary agreements between Indians and their employers or masters came to play a crucial role in continued production, above all in mining.[41] Ayllu access to land and labor still posed constraints upon the exploitation of Indians, but no longer in the same way. What had changed?

THE DECAY OF AYLLU SELF-SUFFICIENCY

What had changed was the capacity of Indians to meet economic needs and obligations independently. For colonials, mining and commercial capital constituted the cutting edge of economic enterprise and development. For ayllu Indians, the development of a prosperous mining and commercial economy controlled by colonials generated forces which, over time, disrupted their self-sufficiency. The prosperity created by Toledo's regime imposed severe burdens on Indians and at the same time, induced a certain

monetization of obligations. As a result, ayllu Indians contended with growing needs for money or its equivalent just as colonial relationships tended to
undermine their capacity to earn money independently by marketing a surplus of commodities. Moreover, local commerce tended to exacerbate internal differentiation into rich and poor which distributed economic burdens,
and the resources to satisfy or avoid them, in highly unequal ways. By the
seventeenth century, an emerging population of poor Indians needed to
work for colonials to meet economic needs or obligations, or to escape the
burdens of ayllu life entirely. Originally, Toledan institutions relied on superior political power to exploit independent ayllu economies; eventually,
these very institutions generated economic conditions which limited ayllu
independence, and thereby reduced the necessity of political coercion.

A certain portion of the Indians' "need" for money was, of course, simply
a direct expression of coercive relations. The state regularly demanded tributes in silver or gold; corregidores, priests, and their allies used their positions to "sell" commodities to captive Indian markets at inflated prices; legal
regulations forced native communities to pay salaries to schoolteachers, or
fees to itinerant judges.[42] Colonials used monetary equivalencies to collect
on unfulfilled tributes or mitas, or to impose new burdens. An Indian
blamed for the death or loss of a pack animal owed the owner a debt worth at
least a year's wages.[43] These politically imposed obligations—tributes,
forced sales, salaries and fees, debits—forced Indians to earn substantial
amounts of money or its equivalent.

But the colonial regime also promoted more subtle and willful needs for
money, or for goods and services which cost money. From the start, Indian
communities had adapted aggressively to commercial opportunities available in an expansive colonial economy. They used revenues not only to meet
colonial demands, but also to fund new needs or choices. In a prospering,
commercialized economy almost any obligation became a commodity with
a market price, and Indians often *preferred* to commute tribute and mita into
monetary equivalents. By substituting money payments for that portion of
tributes originally designated in kind, ayllus protected harvests and herds
assigned to subsistence.[44] By paying mita claimants the money needed to
hire substitute workers, ayllus reserved more of their people for local life and
work. By paying off chiefs and notables who oversaw distribution of mita
burdens, individual Indians escaped designation as mitayos. And once designated, a peasant might avoid the cruel work regime by "renting" an Indian
to replace him in the mita. The price commanded by a mitayo replacement
soared as high as thirty-six pesos (of eight reales)—nearly six times the annual tribute owed to the state.[45] To protect their interests Indians, as we
have seen, mastered the art of judicial politics; litigation, however, cost considerable sums of money for fees, bribes, travel, urban living, and the like.[46]

The conversion of colonial obligations into commodities. A "mita captain" rents an Indian laborer to substitute for a peasant whose previous mita duty had struck him with the "mercury disease."

The colonial situation thus generated new needs; indeed the Indian market for Hispanic-style goods and services was not entirely artificial. Items such as shears, knives, and candles served useful purposes; knick-knacks, games, and puzzles exerted a more exotic appeal.[47] Hispanic symbols and attire held the prestige associated with power. Their lure extended more broadly than the wealthy Indians who most easily afforded them. Consider, for example, the careful specifications of an Indian boy's contract to work for a citizen of Ica. The boy, who had migrated from Huanta, would receive twelve pesos a year, and "a very gallant set of whatever [American-made] clothes he chooses—shawl, shirt, pants, hat, shoes, and blanket."[48] More than ever after the defeat of Taki Onqoy, Indians had to respect the power of Christian gods, including saints. Such respect implied a market for religious objects, wax and candles, painters of churches, and other goods and services offered to the deities.[49] Away from their homelands, mitayos contended with strong pressures to enter market transactions, especially in the mines. Such experiences led to tastes and dependencies which created a certain market for brandy and wine.[50]

Now as long as ayllus produced sufficient goods for subsistence and market sale, a certain need for revenues by no means drove large numbers of Indians to work voluntarily on colonial enterprises. By selling a surplus of coca, animals, wool, textiles, foodstuffs, Spanish or Indian handicrafts, and other commodities, Indians could earn needed funds. This is precisely what happened in the 1570s and 1580s, when many groups accumulated impressive cash reserves.[51] The problem was that, over time, colonial relationships despoiled ayllus of the capacity to produce and control a surplus, or even enough for their subsistence. Royal officials siphoned off community cash by outright fraud, or by arranging long-term loans never paid back. Spanish and Indian entrepreneurs laid claim precisely to the lands and resources most suited for profitable commerce or production. Expropriation of strategic resources—irrigable lands, coca plantations, valuable herds, beautiful cumbi textiles as well as everyday cloth—constituted a double blow.[52] The expropriations not only damaged the ayllus' capacity to earn revenues, but also to produce goods needed for subsistence and ritual. Having to purchase such essentials expanded further the need for revenues. When ayllu revenues fell short, chiefs might sell surplus lands unworked by declining community populations. But such expedients restricted further the long-run potential of subsistence economies.[53]

Indeed, the cumulative effect of colonial extraction and Indian population decline threw the subsistence economy itself into precarious straits. Tribute and mita drained away needed goods and labor-time, and disrupted expectations and reciprocities essential for local production. The combined impact of population losses, tribute, and mita shrank the amount of human energy regularly available for ayllu and household economies. Declining productivity could prove disastrous to societies whose kin groups had always relied on large reserves to tide them over poor harvests.[54] As local peoples lost their ability to fill warehouses in "good" years, the crop failures which normally plague sierra agriculture every few years took on new significance. To survive, peasants would have to purchase foodstuffs.[55] As the resources, labor-time, and storage capacity of subsistence economies deteriorated, the scope of local commodity exchange expanded. Markets probably fluctuated widely from year to year and place to place. But significantly, rural Indians began to need money or credits for essentials once produced and distributed independently — coca, salt, maize, ají, even coarse cloth for everyday use.[56]

Not all Indians shouldered such burdens equally; nor did they all have to. On the contrary, given an unequal distribution of power, resources, and burdens in native society, the colonial regime tended to stimulate further differentiation into rich and poor. Major kurakas, municipal functionaries, lay assistants of priests, village artisans, women heads of household, and forastero migrants enjoyed legal exemption from mita and, in most cases, tribute. Not surprisingly, Indians who accumulated surpluses tended to emerge from these privileged groups.[57] The families of common tributaries, on the other hand, had to use whatever "extra" resources they could muster to bribe officials or to "rent" substitute laborers, if they wished to avoid the mita. The poorest tributaries might have little choice but to indebt themselves to pay for a substitute, or else serve the mita. But if they served, their meager economic base decreased the likelihood that they could save significant wages, or mobilize kin to look after fields during their absence. Deteriorating fields, of course, left them more vulnerable than ever to commercial relations.[58] As commodity circulation and a certain monetization of obligations penetrated local life, those with political or economic advantages gained while other floundered in a sea of tributes, corvées, debts, and subsistence problems. The process of differentiation was, by modern standards, incomplete since the poorest ayllu peasant almost invariably retained access to some land, labor, and redistributive rights.[59] But equally as significant, land itself began to circulate as a commodity even among Indians. In commercially active zones, forasteros, local Indians, and entire ayllus bought lands from individuals and ayllus short on funds.[60]

By choice and by compulsion, Huamanga's people had become integrated into an expansive commercial economy which redefined the needs of households and individuals. Itinerant merchants of all races established personal contacts in the Indian countryside. In certain zones, the small storekeeper — the vendor of coca, maize, salt, candles, cloth, wine, brandy, and other wares — became a notable rural figure.[61] The upper levels of Indian society, of course, formed the readiest market for Hispanic wine, clothes, foods, weapons, horses, and the like. But as we have seen, rising needs for revenue burdened the lower levels of society least able to afford them. Ayllu peasants financed purchases by elites, shared collective responsibility for coerced tributes and sales, supported costly legal battles, developed tastes of their own for "Hispanic" commodities, strained to earn funds needed to avoid the mita, and suffered subsistence deficits which drove them further into the market.[62]

By the seventeenth century, money and debt weighed heavily on ayllu life. For an emerging population of poor Indians, access to ayllu lands and resources, labor, and redistributive rights simply no longer sufficed to provide for unavoidable necessities. Even if precious metals did not change hands much, necessities now included the means to pay off debts or earn monetary credits. The wills of wealthy Indians began to record lists of debts collectible from other natives. The debts, often petty by Hispanic standards, included not only direct loans of money, or sales of "luxuries" like wine. The lists also mentioned basic subsistence goods: several bushels of corn here and there, and in at least one case chuño, the freeze-dried potatoes usually eaten as a food of last resort.[63] Occasionally debts landed Indians in jail.[64] More often, probably, rising needs for revenue gave monetary advances new force in Indian life. One out of six asientos in Huamanga linked the labor contract to a prior debt or money advance. Juan Moroco, for example, received an advance of nineteen pesos "that he paid an Indian [to replace him] in the mines of Huancavelica." Others hired themselves out to employers who agreed to pay off creditors and thereby keep the debtor out of jail.[65] In the 1570s the corregidor of Lucanas had relied on sheer coercion to extract a surplus. A half-century later, his counterpart used money advances, credit, and commercial relationships to build a more sophisticated repertoire of devices to persuade Indians to comply with unwelcome demands.[66] Growing monetary needs, a severely strained subsistence economy, and substantial internal differentiation had undermined the vital, independent ayllu economies encountered by the first conquistadores of Huamanga.

POVERTY AND DEPENDENCE

Over time, then, colonial relationships gave rise to economic dependencies driving natives into the arms of colonials. On the one side, pauperized ayllus and households depended on occasional wage labor to earn needed funds or credits. Only the most fortunate or wealthy could generate enough revenues independently—by producing a marketable surplus, controlling local trade, or pursuing relatively autonomous work as artisans or muleteers. From time to time, the rest had to volunteer their labors to entrepreneurs who controlled dynamic sectors of the commercial economy. On the other side, the burdens of ayllu life weighed so heavily that a certain proportion of Indians fled outright. To escape the onslaught of tributes, mitas, sub-sistence shortfalls, and debts, they left for new lives as forasteros, outsiders. As we shall see, at least some of the runaways depended on colonials for eco-nomic sustenance or social protection. Like poor ayllu Indians, émigrés often found that they "needed" their exploiters.

In the case of émigrés, we ought not underestimate the trauma inherent in their decisions to flee their old lives. Escape brought relief from ayllu bur-dens, but it also cut people off from the society where their ancestors had lived; where ethnic and ayllu gods looked over the wellbeing of their chil-dren; where people acquired individual identities and sustenance *because* they lived as members of larger social groups; where a person dreaded social isolation and depended on bonds with local relatives, ayllus, hills — with na-ture itself.[67] We ought not assume that emigration, in a social rather than physical sense, was always permanent or absolute from the start. In some cases forasteros retained significant links with relatives in their original homelands; in others, those bonds took time to erode.[68]

But whatever the difficulties of a decision to flee, however strong their re-luctance, people abandoned ayllu life. Sometimes, Indians made fateful choices at moments of extreme duress. We know, for example, that a certain proportion of mitayos ran away while laboring in mines away from their homelands.[69] More generally, some evidence suggests that young, single males experienced a special kind of life crisis. As they approached the grim threshold of marriage, household responsibilities, and tributary status, what could they look forward to? As *hatun runa*, "big men," they would enter a stage of life in which they enjoyed greater status and claims to ayllu land and resources. Yet once they committed themselves to life as "big men," they would assume family responsibilities restricting their mobility further, and faced a potentially miserable lot as poor tributaries. At this junction in the life cycle, apparently, a number of people broke away. An inspection of one district, ayllu by ayllu, listed over three-fourths of the men who fled as single rather than married; most of the older absentees, men forty or fifty years old, were said to have left as youths — "over twenty years ago," or "since a boy."[70] (A somewhat different life crisis is suggested for young women in Chapter 7.)

Some migrants undoubtedly shielded themselves from colonial society fairly successfully. They descended to remote, often treacherous jungles east of Huamanga; they gained access to land through semi-clandestine relation-ships with ethnically alien Indian communities; or they swelled vagabond populations as far away as Lima.[71] But all these options had definite limits. The tropical *selva* was ecologically and socially forbidding to many sierra In-dians. Life amidst foreign ayllus was not always possible or welcome from either side's point of view. Nor did it immunize a forastero from the mone-tary economy, especially if the outsider had to buy or rent lands, or married

into a community. Finally, even vagabonds might seek occasional employment, or protection from Indians and officials who hunted runaways to collect on tributes or mitas.[72]

Out-migration thus generated people who turned to colonials for wages,
subsistence, or protection. The émigrés expanded the force of skilled wage
laborers who kept the mining economy going; merged into the population of
yanaconas living on Hispanic farms, ranches, and haciendas; sought out
apprenticeships with urban artisans; drifted in and out of work as day laborers; or agreed to long-term asiento contracts in cities like Huamanga. Given
the Indians' limited alternatives, a colonial patron competing to lure servants might offer relatively attractive conditions of life. Consider, for example, the case of Anton Yucra, who agreed to serve on the haciendas of Pedro
Serrano Navarrete for two years. In exchange for his service, Yucra earned
rights to twelve pesos and a set of clothes each year, a ration of corn, and use
of some fields "in whatever location he wishes, at the cost of the said Pedro
Serrano, using his oxen and plowshares." Perhaps most important from Yucra's point of view, the contract specified that Serrano "has to free and save
him from the mitas of Huancavelica and Chocolococha [Castrovirreyna]
and other personal services."[73] In Vilcashuamán, Yucra's original province,
ethnic groups complained bitterly that the owner of an obraje-hacienda
complex lured ayllu Indians away, further sapping the economic base of
ayllu society.[74]

The Indian countryside thus expelled a stream of pauperized ayllu Indians who left temporarily to accumulate funds or pay off debts, forasteros
who fled permanently to establish new lives, and others caught in a more
ambiguous, transitional situation.[75] In varying degrees, the lives of all reflected the rise of dependencies which expanded the options available to colonial entrepreneurs. Whether or not Indians left ayllu society behind, from
time to time they turned to wealthier people for wages, lands, subsistence,
credit, protection. Economic dependence was not, of course, complete or ir-
reversible. Yanaconas often held plots of land or pastured their own animals,
and as we have seen, Indian laborers were more mobile than colonials might
have liked. Even in mines, where voluntary wage labor was most important,
employers probably contended with a semi-independent work force. An Indian miner who commanded high wages might withdraw for a while, live off
accumulated funds, or buy lands which allowed him to earn a livelihood as a
petty cultivator.[76] But whatever its limited or partial character, the Indians'
economic dependence was real, and represented a sharp departure from the
more self-sufficient Andean past.

THE POLITICAL ECONOMY OF COERCION AND CONSENT

Huamanga's elite built its prosperity on contradictory trends. The very
forces which drove colonials to bind laborers to serfdom also compelled

them to rely more heavily on voluntary agreements, including wage labor. Ayllu resistance, in the context of an expansive colonial economy and a changing demographic map (declining total Indian population, and within the total, a rising proportion of semi-clandestine forasteros), undermined the success of state-sponsored labor drafts. Forced to adjust to disruption and labor scarcity, entrepreneurs placed greater emphasis on developing exploitative relations in "civil society."

One such adaptation was to extend extraofficial and private forms of coercion. Gerónimo de Oré, for example, rented his obraje to the rural constable, who also happened to represent the local corregidor; this powerful functionary overstepped the formal boundaries of authority to rob hired workers of wages, impose illegal corvées, and the like.[77] Colonials went beyond such extralegal arrangements with bureaucrats, however, to cultivate direct lordship over personal dependents. One such practice, the purchase of African slaves to assume a more prominent role in production, sidestepped Indian society altogether. Other such practices expanded yanacona populations and, as we have also seen, enmeshed temporary workers in relations tending to convert them into long-term dependents.

But it was precisely because Indians did not succumb easily to coercive pressure, and even escaped if pushed beyond certain limits, that colonials came to rely also on a second adaptation: the use of voluntary agreements, contracts, and early forms of wage labor to secure native services. Forced labor alone, even if extraofficial and private in character, could not supply the needs of a dynamic regional economy. Indeed, the very existence of colonials eager to attract labor probably lessened the willingness of retainers to accommodate themselves to severely coercive masters.

Yanaconaje and wage labor, both on the rise in the early seventeenth century, did not simply represent alternative or complementary labor strategies; they also represented extreme cases of opposite, contradictory tendencies. Because coercion was inadequate, colonials hired natives who agreed to work for wages. But because the labor market was shallow and irregular, and techniques of production tied profits closely to low labor costs, colonials could not rely on "volunteer" labor alone to provide a steady work force or high profits. Thus even as they turned to an emerging marketplace to find labor, entrepreneurs could not dispense with coercion. They continued to use force to recruit and hold on to laborers, and to minimize wage payments. They continued to defend mita quotas, shored up alliances needed to operate effectively as members of local and regional power groups, and imbedded purchases of labor-power in more seigneurial relations which constricted monetary exchange and bound laborers to overlords. Out of such contradictory tendencies arose apparent paradoxes: yanaconas who "rented" themselves by contract; servile forms of labor in which accounts of wages and debits played an important role; hired laborers whose employers owed back wages for years.[78] A single unit of production could exploit mitayos, wage laborers, slaves, life-long yanaconas, and dependents whose rights and obligations distinguished them both from yanaconas and wage laborers.[79]

One could express the matter in another way. On the one side, severe exploitation and a commercializing economy despoiled the native countryside enough to disrupt its capacity to support itself. Sheer survival or economic necessity therefore drove Indians to work more willingly for colonial patrons or employers. On the other side, colonial accumulation did not proceed so far that it cut people off from a subsistence economy altogether. The ability of natives to maintain or to reestablish access to a subsistence economy limited the rise of markets or freer forms of labor to an uneven, partly reversible process. Thus colonials could recruit a willing clientele of wage laborers and prospective dependents, yet they required considerable coercive power to insure that Indians would not slip out of their grasp, that they would perform unwelcome labors despite access to their own subsistence economy, that an enterprise need not depend solely on cultivating a voluntary laboring clientele for its wellbeing. Given the limits on entrepreneurs' ability to exploit Indians or mestizos, imported Africans assumed an important role even in the highlands.

Salaried and servile labor, despite their contradictions, both reflected the rise of new dependencies in "civil society." There was a certain irony to the natives' bitter struggle against mitas and tributes. Even as they made inroads against formal extractive institutions mediated by a coercive state, Huamanga's Indians fell under the more direct sway of employers and masters. Integration of the natives into a commercial economy had taken on a life of its own, and generated a clientele of natives who turned to wealthier people for money or credit, or for a new subsistence shielded from outside demands. The new dependencies not only made it easier for colonials to find "voluntary" sources of exploitable labor, including wage laborers; they also broadened opportunities to bind serfs and clients in a tangle of mutual obligations, antagonisms, and loyalties.[80] The rise of these new social and economic dependencies had not led to a sharp, absolute rupture with an earlier history of extraction based on violence and coercion. Nor had it led to a society whose ruling class could ignore the power of state officials. But coercive extraction had grown more private and extraofficial in character, and could be supplemented or reinforced by arrangements of mutual consent, including wage labor, which reflected the decline of Andean self-sufficiency. In short, an exploitative society had grown more sophisticated; it had made the exploited "need" their exploiters.

7

The Tragedy of Success

In Huamanga, if one saw a gallant figure dressed in rose velvet breeches with fine gold trim, bright doublet beneath a dark velveteen cape from Segovia, broad felt hat, and a pair of good shoes, one probably expected to see the face of a wealthy colonial, or perhaps even a mestizo. Sometimes, however, the face belonged to an Indian.[1] The growing poverty of Andean peoples by the early seventeenth century could lead us to overlook the rise of natives who escaped severe burdens imposed upon most Indians, in some cases climbed the social ladder, and accumulated considerable wealth.

Yet our story has already suggested the historical importance of privileged strata within the "republic of Indians." We have seen the embryonic potential for class divisions among Huamanga's societies before Spanish conquest, and the institutions which stifled their further development. After conquest, the strategic position of Hispanizing kurakas as mediators between natives and colonials intensified incipient contradictions in native society; the post-Incaic alliances caught native elites between traditional roles as protectors of ayllu interests, and new opportunities and demands as "friends" of the conquistadores. During the crisis of the 1560s, the taquiongos pressured collaborators of the colonial regime to purify themselves and renew exclusively Andean loyalties, but the tenuous and guarded relationship of Indian elites to Taki Onqoy mirrored their ambivalent, contradictory position. A decade later, Toledo's reforms organized a network of state power to coerce a surplus out of a self-sufficient ayllu peasantry; the system worked in part because its power groups incorporated Indian as well as Hispanic lords.

The Indians eventually undermined Toledan mitas and tributes, but not the emergence of multiracial power groups. Indeed, judicial politics encour-

158

aged mutually beneficial arrangements among native elites and Hispanic patrons who sometimes profited by subverting state-sponsored extractions. The economic boom of the late sixteenth century integrated local societies into a highly commercialized economy; local commodity-circulation patterns induced internal differentiation even further, concentrating Indian resources in fewer hands, and privatizing a proportion of ayllu lands. From the first years of conquest, but with increasing force in the seventeenth century, ayllu society lost migrants to cities, mines, commercial centers, Spanish patrons, and foreign Indian communities. Some of the migrants learned skills or developed connections which saved them from the fate of poor Indians, and enabled them to join the ranks of those who profited from the commercial economy.

The personal strategies and achievements of successful Indians, who assimilated in important ways to Hispanic-mestizo society, bear a close relationship to the broader history of European exploitation and Indian resistance. Their achievements stimulated a process of class differentiation within native society, inserted European-style relationships, motivations, and culture more directly into peasant life, and furthered the shrinkage of traditional Andean rights and resources. The tragedy of Indian success lay in the way it recruited dynamic, powerful, or fortunate individuals to adopt Hispanic styles and relationships, thereby buttressing colonial domination. The achievements of native individuals, in the midst of a society organized to exploit indigenous peoples, educated Indians to view the Hispanic as superior, the Andean as inferior.

PATHS TO SUCCESS

Despite conditions which severely impoverished most natives by the early seventeenth century, a minority managed to accumulate sufficient funds to buy or rent valuable rural and urban property. A sample of fifty-two transactions shows that many Indians who bought or rented lands and homesteads spent sums far beyond the economic horizons of most natives. Fully half (50.0 percent) the purchases cost 40–90 pesos (of 8 reales); another fourth (28.3 percent) required 100 pesos or more.[2] These represented large sums for an Indian. The state's annual tribute, a heavy burden for many, amounted to less than ten pesos; an unskilled asiento Indian earned perhaps twenty pesos for an entire year's service; an expenditure of thirty pesos to rent a mitayo replacement was unrealistic for a poor peasant.[3]

Even by Hispanic standards, some Indian purchases represented significant accumulations. One woman bought part of a fine city lot owned by a distinguished encomendero family. The 300 pesos she spent equalled eight or nine months of the profit expected by a master who rented out a skilled slave artisan. Juana Payco and Don Pedro Pomaconxa each bought valuable lands from foreign ayllus for 600 pesos. That amount of money sufficed, in most years, to buy a prime African slave. Some transactions, especially purchase or rental of city residences by Indians whose economic base remained in the countryside, fulfilled prestige desires. To establish a respectable residence in Huamanga, one kuraka shunned a site in the city's Indian parishes; instead, he rented homes in the finer, more expensive Spanish section.[4]

Even as monetary obligations and debt became increasingly oppressive forces in the lives of poor Indians, an emerging sector of natives accumulated enough liquid wealth to become creditors. We have seen that the wills of prosperous Indians recorded lists of uncollected petty debts.[5] Native artisans and other "credible" figures served as bondsmen of Indians in debt or in trouble.[6] Some loans were more than petty in size. Lorenzo Pilco, born to a wealthy Indian family in the city of Huamanga, and owner of valuable lands in rural Angaraes, loaned 300 pesos to an impoverished kuraka. Pilco eventually had the chief jailed for lack of payment. Doña Juana Yanque Molluma financed the purchase of 300 cows and bulls by her daughter for 1,650 pesos. Significantly, even Spaniards turned to wealthy Indians for credit on occasion. One Spaniard secured a one-year loan of 140 pesos from Doña Juana Mendez; another paid 50 pesos of interest a year on a long-term loan of 700 pesos from Catalina Reinoso, an Indian gentlewoman who owned a vineyard in the Nazca Valley descending from Lucanas to the Pacific coast.[7]

The historical question which we must ask is how an emerging sector of wealthy Indians earned such funds, and protected themselves from expropriations which confined most natives to a meager existence. The economic and political means by which a minority of Indians achieved success, in a society which had despoiled most ayllus and peasants of the capacity to produce and market a surplus, warrant close examination.

In a thriving commercial economy heavily dependent on artisanal or craft technologies, those who sold skilled services might earn substantial incomes. Experienced mine workers commanded handsome wages in the seventeenth century. Inflated prices controlled by outside merchants, respites from a harsh existence in drinking and gambling, and fraudulent abuses by mine owners often consumed wages quickly. But some Indians probably managed to accumulate savings, by setting aside significant amounts of wages or stealing valuable ores.[8] More attractive than mining were artisanry and transport, relatively independent forms of work for which there was high demand. Huamanga's economy relied heavily on skilled trades and crafts for construction and manufactures, and Indian artisans assumed a prominent role in all kinds of "Hispanic" occupations, as silversmiths, painters and gilders, masons, stonecutters, carpenters, joiners, tanners, tailors, shoemakers, and the like.[9] Martín de Oviedo, a Spaniard with a strong reputation as a "master sculptor" and architect, was hired in 1609 to refurbish the interior of the Dominican church for 4,600 pesos; Oviedo, in turn, subcontracted for Indian carpenters, painters, and gilders to work on the project. An independent Indian craftsman could earn a very respectable income. In two months, a stonecutter could fashion a water wheel worth sixty pesos. Juan Uscamato, a carpenter, earned 150 pesos by agreeing to build a flour mill in six months. His expenses were low, and he probably did not have to work full time on the mill, since the contractor agreed to supply needed materials, including carved stone and iron tools, and six Indian laborers to work under Uscamato.[10]

The asiento labor contracts of Huamanga (described in Chapter 6) show a dramatic income gap between skilled Indians and unspecialized laboring peons. Artisans hired in asientos earned double or triple the wages promised for general service, some 40–60 pesos a year besides subsistence. Arrieros (muleteers, drivers of animal trains) earned at least twice as much again, some 80–130 pesos a year. The nonmonetary components of the compensation often included special rights which widened the gap further. One tanner received ten semifinished hides which, in effect, subsidized his independent work. Arrieros received a few extra yards of cloth to stock their wares. More important, the drivers' work helped them consolidate independent trading connections, and lower their own business costs by transporting commodities on employers' animals, as in the previously mentioned case of the employer who formally agreed that his hired arriero could make "all the trips he wants with [the employer's] animal train."[11]

Concessions such as these mattered because those who engaged in substantial trade or commercial production could accumulate great wealth. Indian merchants, like Spaniards, speculated in commodities. Artisans, unlike arrieros, could not pursue commerce on a full-time basis, but ambitious craftsmen engaged in varied mercantile transactions on the side.[12] Indians, like Spaniards, carved out private landholdings for commercial production of coca, wine, maize, wheat, vegetables, wool, meat, hides, cheese, and the like. Indeed, Indian entrepreneurs tended to focus their accumulations of private property in the very same zones which attracted their Spanish counterparts: the well-located and fertile valleys of the Angaraes-Huanta district, the city of Huamanga and its surrounding valleys, the coca montaña of eastern Huanta, and, to a lesser extent, fertile pastures and farmlands along the road which cut across Vilcashuamán to Cuzco and Potosí (see Map 3 above, Chapter 4).[13]

Marketable skills and services, commercial production, and trade itself earned Indians considerable revenues, but they do not explain how a successful minority protected its wealth from expropriation. Ayllus too had earned very impressive incomes in the sixteenth century, but colonial control made such accumulation increasingly difficult, if not impossible, for most ayllus in the seventeenth century. The economic function of the colonial power structure was, after all, to usurp Indian resources and to siphon the surplus of a native society reduced to bare subsistence. Kurakas enjoyed greater access to revenues than common households, but redistributive obligations presumably limited the capacity of chiefs to accumulate personal resources while kinfolk slid deeper into poverty. Indeed, the chiefs' personal liability for community obligations, especially tribute and mita, sometimes forced them to sell valuable lands or animals, and subjected their wealth to confiscation by corregidores.[14] As we have seen, the periodic composiciones de tierras permitted colonial judges to award title to "surplus" Indian lands requested by Spanish petitioners. In practice, the land inspections made ayllu land tenure a precarious proposition. To avoid dependence on a European overlord, a forastero might seek a livelihood in a new Indian community setting. But earning the acceptance of foreign ayllus might entail new kinship bonds, or payments of rent for land-use rights, which limited accumulation.[15]

Under these circumstances, earning a respectable income did not, by itself, insure one against impoverishment. Indians could achieve lasting economic success only if their socioeconomic "strategy" shielded them, in part at least, from colonial expropriations and from redistributive obligations to poorer Indians. A key shielding device involved "privatizing" property rights. Individual title to land, recognized by Spanish law, protected the owner from legal confiscations which befell ayllu property. Private ownership of property also provided a weapon against overlapping or collective claims by ayllus and ethnic groups, especially if the owner accumulated lands in "foreign" zones, i.e., outside the domain traditionally claimed by the Indian's ayllu or ethnic relatives. But even within a given ayllu or ethnic domain, a process of privatization transferred a proportion of property rights to powerful or wealthy local Indians, and to wealthy outsiders of all races. During the first composición de tierras, held in 1594, some of Huamanga's kurakas secured private title to extensive land-use rights traditionally allotted them by ayllus. A kuraka who wished to protect his prestige, or to work the lands by calling upon traditional ayllu relationships, probably could not alienate such lands from collective claims in an absolute sense. But we know that kurakas sold or rented some of these lands to outsiders, and that in later generations, children who "inherited" lands from deceased chiefs defended their property rights against Indian relatives.[16] Even if a chief (or his heirs) did not privatize ayllu property for his own use, he held authority to sell community lands in order to pay tributes or to hire mitayo replacements. Such sales alienated property from ethnic and ayllu domains in a more permanent sense. Fertile lands once held by ayllus circulated as commodities on a surprising scale in the seventeenth century, especially in dynamic commercial zones of northern Huamanga (from the Río Pampas north, with special intensity along the Angaraes-Huanta-city of Huamanga axis). And as we have seen, the buyers of valuable property included Indians as well as Spaniards and mixed-bloods.[17]

Another form of protection lay in escaping tribute and mita obligations. A household continually drained by contributions to pay ayllu tributes or hire mitayo replacements could hardly expect to accumulate money sufficient to buy lucrative property, even if it earned a significant monetary income. The colonial regime, however, exempted certain natives from mita and tribute, and Spanish law failed to incorporate the large forastero population systematically until the eighteenth century.

The evidence suggests that the privilege of exemption brought considerable benefits. Tributary status did not apply to independent women heads of household, and women accounted for over a third (35.8 percent) of Indian purchases or rentals of property. Forasteros and artisans also played a conspicuous role in private accumulations of property.[18] The forasteros' ill-defined legal status freed them from mita and tribute as long as they escaped tax collectors sent from their original communities; artisans, both village and urban, held legal exemption from the mita. Finally, major kurakas, municipal functionaries (mostly officers of the Indian cabildo), and lay assistants of Catholic priests all enjoyed exemptions from mita and, some of them, from tribute. A few earned modest salaries as well.[19] Within ayllu society, therefore, appointments to municipal and church posts distributed privileges which allowed some people to accumulate resources while others eked out a bare existence or fell into debt.

A third form of shielding, and one which increased opportunities for economic gain dramatically, exploited privileged ties to the colonial power structure. Within ayllu society especially, access to power often proved a decisive determinant of revenues and obligations. Powerful ayllus and favored relatives of kurakas paid lighter tributes than others, and the kurakas themselves levied extra tributes.[20] The Toledan regime had reorganized the countryside by establishing a series of multiracial power groups, with a Spanish corregidor at the center, but including a contingent of Indian functionaries and assistants. The revamped Indian power structure drew its members from important kuraka families, socially mobile commoners eager to benefit by association with Hispanic power, and (in the seventeenth century, at least) a few forasteros integrated into local ayllu societies.[21] Judicial politics further cemented alliances between Indian elites and Hispanic patrons. The assistance of Hispanic patrons brought with it a *quid pro quo*: loyalty to the interests of "friends," cooperation in local schemes of extraction. In effect, local alliances assimilated an elite fraction of ayllu society to the Hispanic power structure, and thus to the conversion of political advantage into private wealth. The liability of kurakas for community tribute and mita, for example, theoretically subjected chiefs to confiscations of wealth which might have impoverished them in the seventeenth century. Some confiscations did indeed occur, but often kurakas enlisted the aid of corregidores and priests to "prove" that mita and tribute quotas had been set too high. Instead of losing resources to pay for tributes in arrears, a kuraka could earn thousands of pesos by joining Hispanic friends in mutually profitable schemes, such as putting-out systems to sell cloth or rope woven by ayllus.[22] The burden of such schemes, and the reduced quotas of legal mitas and tributes, fell most heavily on the least powerful and poorest segments of native society.

The differentiation of native society into rich and poor reflected the ability of a minority to free itelf from constraints which bound most Indians. We ought not underestimate the difficulty of such achievements, especially for natives who did not inherit advantages by birth into powerful or wealthy Indian families. For the great majority the road to success was closed. Daring decisions did not guarantee prosperity. Emigration from the society of one's relatives, perhaps the boldest step an Indian might take, led some individuals to success, but prosperous emigrants were a minority. Most forasteros lived a more modest existence as yanaconas, day laborers, petty producers, community peasants integrated by marriage into foreign ayllus, vagrants, and the like. Artisanry exerted a special appeal precisely because it offered the surest path to economic improvement and independence. Prospective apprentices flocked to cities to find artisans willing to teach them a trade in exchange for their labors. As a result, in a regional economy where labor was usually in short supply, and wages tended to rise, apprentice labor constituted a glaring exception. In two of three apprenticeship asientos, the hired Indian's compensation did not include a monetary wage at all; a chance to change the course of one's life was compensation enough.[23]

Those who earned relatively high incomes, of course, did not automatically accumulate "private" resources shielded from overlapping or redistributive claims by poorer relatives. Women heads of household, for example, enjoyed legal exemptions from mitas and tributes, and participated heavily in commercial production and trade. But ties of kinship and obligation meant — in some cases, at least — that apparently "private" resources in fact helped to shore up the faltering economic base of poorer kinfolk, including male tributaries.[24] In these cases, "success" was less individualized, more subject to a web of overlapping rights which redistributed accumulations.

By the seventeenth century, however, an emerging strata of ambitious Indians superseded such obstacles, and accumulated impressive personal wealth. As we shall see, the success of these natives changed the very texture of Indian life.

THE SOCIAL SIGNIFICANCE OF INDIAN HISPANISM

Above all else, Indian success rested upon one's capacity to imitate Hispanic strategies of accumulation, or to develop close ties with Hispanic-mestizo society. The successful Indians of the seventeenth century were independent producers and merchants, many of them women or forasteros or both, who owned private property and invested in commerce; artisans and others whose special skills, whether Andean or Hispanic, earned them incomes sufficient to purchase property or engage in commerce; political and religious functionaries of the colonial villages who enjoyed mita-tribute exemptions, and who profited from their position in the colonial power structure. The material wellbeing of these Indians no longer depended, as it had for their ancestors, on their ability to mobilize traditional forms of property, reciprocal obligation, and loyalty within an ancient family of ayllu and ethnic relatives. Their economic welfare came to depend primarily upon their capacity to privatize interests in a commercial setting: to accumulate private property, exploit commercial opportunities, and convert political influence, service, or privilege into liquid wealth. For these Indians, rural commodity circulation and a certain monetization of obligations represented an opportunity, not a burden or a symptom of declining self-sufficiency. The penetration of commercial capital into the countryside created opportunities to buy lands, to extend commercial networks, to consolidate influence as creditors to those trapped in a quagmire of tributes, corvées, subsistence problems, and debts.

A certain Hispanization of property and relationships, linked to the emergence of successful natives, thus began to remold the internal structure of Indian society. The process of Hispanization, like the internal differentiation it mirrored, was only partial or incomplete. Ayllu reciprocities and property rights still constituted an important resource for many Indians.[25] But those who continued to depend exclusively upon "traditional" rights were condemned to poverty, and by the early seventeenth century, relations between rich and poor Indians began to take on a more "Hispanic" tonality and texture. Wealthy Indians no longer depended upon the collective claims of ayllus and ethnic groups for access to property; they acquired private title to the best Indian lands, both in ayllu homelands and among foreign Indians. Commercial transactions and debt forged new bonds and dependencies superseding those of kinship and reciprocal obligation. Wealthy and powerful natives looked beyond traditional Andean reciprocities for access to labor, and resorted to Hispanic methods of labor exploitation. Indian miners, coca planters, and hacendados attached dependent laborers to their properties, and hired temporary workers for wages.[26] On occasion, a prominent Indian even secured an official mita allotment! In 1598, Viceroy Luis de Velasco granted the Indian Doña Isabel Asto, a rich miner and widow of a Spaniard, sixty mitayos to work her mines in Huancavelica.[27] In one of ten (10.3 percent) asiento labor contracts in Huamanga, the hired Indian worked for an Indian master. The employers, some of them artisans hiring apprentices, were clearly men and women of considerable means. One Indian merchant could afford to pay a hired arriero 100 pesos a year in wages. Another employer, Catalina Cocachimbo, recruited a yanacona by lending an Indian 150 pesos. Adopting both the form and content used by Hispanic colonials, she contracted the peon to work for her at 20 pesos a year to repay the debt; after one year, he would receive a plot of land to grow his own food.[28]

An especially significant result of these changes is the way they affected bonds between related ayllu Indians. In the case of "unrelated" Indians, such as a forastero establishing a presence among ethnically distinct ayllu Indians, or a city Indian hiring a poor ayllu peasant, we might expect private property holdings, commercial and debt relations, and nontraditional claims to labor to play an important role. But the new forces also conditioned relations among *originarios*, local ayllu Indians descended from common ancestor-gods (as distinguished from immigrant forasteros descended from foreign ayllus and ancestors). Even among originarios, a wealthy minority and pauperized majority might head in opposite directions. In June 1630, for example, the Indians and chiefs of Guaychao had to sell valuable community lands to an outsider to raise funds. Yet in the very same month, Pedro Alopila, a local ayllu Indian, bought for himself some twelve hectares of irrigable maize lands from a Spanish landowner. Internal differentiation opened the door to new relationships far removed from traditional bonds among originarios. Consider, for example, the career of Juana Marcaruray, a woman who retained her ayllu presence and identity until her death. Within the region of her ayllu homeland, she accumulated seven private properties (including two coca fields), indebted various members of the community, and collected rent from Indian tenants on her property.[29]

The case of Don Juan Uybua and Sebastian Cabana, ayllu Indians of the same village, is also revealing. Uybua, a local kuraka, paid a debt of 90 pesos owed by Cabana, who was accused of losing four cows and three horses. But Uybua's act hardly represented the traditional generosity expected of a chief bound by long-term reciprocities with kinfolk. The two Indians apparently belonged to different (though related) ayllus, and Uybua used the debt to make a typically "Hispanic" arrangement. To "repay" the loan, Cabana had to agree to a labor asiento binding him to Uybua for almost seven years! Uybua would placate the indebted peon's kurakas by paying them the annual tribute owed by Cabana.[30]

The emerging Indian elite of the seventeenth century thus embraced strategies and relationships drawn from the dominant, exploiting sector of

society. Increasingly, Hispanic models of advancement offered the only way
out of confines which shackled most Indians. Those whose personal success
required a Hispanization, however partial, of their economic lives included
originarios as well as forasteros, socially mobile commoners as well as kurakas, permanent city dwellers as well as Indians who maintained homes and
bases in both city and countryside. Not surprisingly, the material culture
and technology of Indian production bore witness to the process of Hispanization. Artisans used Spanish tools and materials in their shops; ranchers
raised herds of cows and sheep; farmers harnessed plows to oxen to till
wheat fields. To a certain extent, the spread of Hispanic material culture was
more generalized than that suggested here, particularly as growing numbers
of Indians produced "Spanish" commodities such as eggs or beef, or served
as peons to Spanish overlords. But the material "Hispanization" of Indian
production was more closely associated with wealthy Indians, including
chiefs.[31]

The spread of Hispanic "culture," moreover, was not confined to resources used in material production. Wealthy Indians bought and used the
accouterments of cultured Spanish folk. They wore fine clothes (made in
Europe), travelled on horse and saddle, bought furniture, jewelry, and trin-
kets for their homes, enjoyed wine with meals, and owned Spanish firearms
and swords.[32] The successful (or pretentious) appropriated the Spanish titu-
lature of Don or Doña, and acquired urban predilections. Even if their livelihood kept them in the countryside much of the time, wealthy Indians established second homes in which to live and do business in Huamanga or
other cities.[33] A few cultured natives even read and wrote Spanish.[34] In 1621,
the Jesuits opened the Royal School of San Francisco de Borja, a boarding
school in Cuzco which taught Spanish language, religion, and culture to
sons of major kurakas from Huamanga, Cuzco, and Arequipa. The new
school represented a small part of a much broader educational process, formal and informal, long under way, which created a growing sector of *ladino*
Indians. The ladinos were people of Indian parentage whose culture, demeanor, and lifeways took on a more mestizo or even Spanish character.
They knew the ways of Spanish-mestizo society, dressed in nontraditional
garb, understood and spoke Spanish, and in some cases even cut their hair.
In cities and mining centers especially, ladino traits spread through the Indian population far beyond the successful, prospering elites. But the most
"Hispanic," least "mestizo" or "Indian," of the ladinos were those whose socioeconomic stature allowed them to buy fine clothes, mix in Spanish circles, get an education, and the like.[35]

Apparently, the successful valued their Hispanism highly. Juana Hernández, owner of at least eighty-five hectares of wheat and corn fields near Jul-
camarca (Angaraes), proudly called herself "a ladina Indian, and very intel-

Changing styles of Andean dress. Above, "creole Indians" of the city participate in one of the fiestas of Hispanic-mestizo society. The dress of the male is more fully Hispanized than that of his partner. Note especially her use of the traditional *lliclla* (mantle) fastened by a decorative *tupu* (pin). Below, Poma de Ayala depicts the contrasting appearances of Indian elite and commoner.

ligent in Spanish language." Indians spent considerable sums—200 pesos for a suit of clothes, 50 pesos for a gun—to collect Spanish items. Don Fernando Ataurimachi of Huamanguilla (Huanta), descendant of the Inca Huayna Capac, related by kinship to Spaniards, and owner of urban property and irrigated corn lands, collected Spanish guns, lances, halberds, and swords. The proud Ataurimachi made a point of showing off his collection at great public festivals.[36]

Some of the Hispanizing Indians took Christian religion quite seriously. The defeat of Taki Onqoy, of course, made plain that all Indians needed to avoid the wrath of powerful Christian gods. To placate the gods and their priests, peasants submitted to a thin overlay of Christian ritual.[37] Catholicism might have enjoyed somewhat greater acceptance among city Indians cut off from rural kin networks and ancestor-gods.[38] But the evidence suggests a striking enthusiasm on the part of wealthy Indians in both city and countryside. Ataurimachi of Huamanguilla married his Indian wife in a Christian ceremony supervised by a Catholic priest. Successful Indians led the native *cofradías* (Catholic lay associations), sought Christian burial in places of honor—"inside the church next to the pulpit"—and had masses said for their souls. Some donated lands, animals, and money to the church, or set up ecclesiastical benefices to look after their souls. Some Indians, of course, had good reason to profess Christianity; they had climbed in social and economic station by serving Catholic priests as sextons (*sacristanes*), choir leaders (*cantores*), and the like.[39]

But others, too, developed close bonds with Christian gods and their representatives on earth. Catalina Pata, a city Indian of Huamanga, bought a huge crucifix which stood a yard and a half tall in her home. Her son, a wealthy artisan, donated lands to the Augustinians "on the condition that the day I die they accompany me . . . and give me a burial inside their church and sing a mass [for my soul]." The will of Don Diego Quino Guaracu, a minor chief of Andahuaylas, named Friar Lucas de Sigura executor of the Indian's estate. Quino gave the priest, apparently a close friend, control of a handsome ecclesiastical benefice of lands sufficient to support nine or ten peasant families. In addition, Quino ordered that his daughter be raised in Huamanga's convent of Santa Clara, "where she might grow up civilized and Christian."[40] For these Indians, Christianization—which by no means excluded continuance of traditional paganisms—constituted far more than a superficial overlay. Like the secular symbols of Hispanism, Christian religion expressed relationships and aspirations which deeply touched their lives.

In a society where "cultural" and "economic" dimensions of life interpenetrated one another deeply, Indian Hispanism had profound symbolic importance. Andean culture esteemed cloth highly as a ritual article, and as an emblem of ethnic affiliation and social position. Natives who wore fine Hispanic clothes vividly expressed an aspiration to move beyond a condemned Indian past and merge into the upper strata of colonial society. Andean thought interpreted "religious" relationships as a mutual exchange which provided material reward to those who served the gods. Christian devotion by wealthy Indians symbolized their attempt to nurture a mutually beneficial interchange with the Hispanic world, its gods (including saints) as well as its people.[41]

Symbolically, then, cultural Hispanism expressed the socioeconomic orientation of an emerging Indian elite whose acquisition of private property, pursuit of commercial gain, and social relationships tended to differentiate them from the Andean peasantry, and to assimilate them to an exploitative class of aristocrat-entrepreneurs. Even in the case of modestly successful Indians (small farmers, urban artisans, and the like) who did not develop direct relationships with ayllu peasants, dependent retainers, or contracted laborers, their differentiation as a class of small independent producers represented a drain on the resources and labor-power available to ayllu society. And the most impressive success stories tended to create a strata of "Europeans" with Indian skin and faces, a provincial elite whose Andean heritage and connections enabled it to inject Hispanic-style relationships, motivations, and culture all the more deeply into the fabric of Indian life.

But the ties between Hispanism and Indian success were sometimes more direct than those implied by mere imitation of European models, or a reproduction of Hispanic styles and relationships within native society. One recalls that Doña Isabel Asto, Don Fernando Ataurimachi, and Don Diego Quino Guaracu all had Spanish relatives or friends. As we have seen, ambitious Indians sought Spanish allies or benefactors for protection or advancement; Spanish individuals and power groups, in turn, enhanced their authority and economic potential by cultivating a clientele of Indian allies and functionaries. Success drew an Indian into Hispanic-mestizo circles, and oppression created desires to find a better life by associating with non-Indian sectors of society. A minority of Indians developed close social bonds outside native society. They bought Indian lands on behalf of colonials, donated or willed property to non-Indian friends, and appointed Spaniards executors of their estates.[42] In a number of cases, the bonds between Indians and Spaniards even included marriage and kinship.

To the Spanish elites, marriage to native women from influential or wealthy families brought social connections and dowries. Even a high elite family consented to such arrangements if the Indian woman enjoyed a sufficiently noble background. The descendants of Antonio de Oré, an esteemed pre-Toledan encomendero, proudly documented their aristocratic Spanish genealogy. The Oré pride, however, did not prevent Antonio's son Gerónimo from marrying an Inca noblewoman.[43]

More often, lesser or aspiring elites sought to gain or extend footholds in the countryside of Huanta, Angaraes, and Vilcashuamán by marrying Indian women. Juan Ramírez Romero had a notoriously exploitative reputation when he served as lieutenant of a rural corregidor from 1601 to 1606. This ambitious hacendado and "citizen" of Vilcashuamán, owner of extensive ranches, farms, and sugar fields, probably made his first inroads by marrying Doña María Cusiocllo. Ramírez observed that "my father-in-law," a local kuraka, had given him much of the property as a dowry. Not far away, an Indian-white couple, Doña Beatriz Guarcay Ynquillay and Don Cristóbal de Gamboa owned sixty hectares of land donated by her brother, chief kuraka of Vischongo, "to cancel his sister's rights . . . in the property of their father Don Juan Pomaquiso." The families created by such marriages could amass enviable wealth. Isabel Payco of Quinua (Huanta), a dynamic zone with a substantial stratum of wealthy Indians, married Juan Enríquez, a commercial farmer-hacendado. Payco brought perhaps 100 hectares of wheat and maize lands to the marriage, and a home in the village. Payco and Enríquez made out well; their mestiza daughter inherited hundreds of hectares of land, and several urban properties in Lima.[44]

For some Indian women, marriage or informal conjugal relations with outsiders had its attractions. The daughters of Indian chiefs may have had little choice in the matter, but wealthy or ambitious women shared the Hispanic orientation of their male counterparts. María López, an Indian, acquired several urban properties in Huamanga during her marriage to a respectable Spanish resident. When her husband died, she established an informal relationship, and had a child, with Gaspar de Arriola, a wealthy "citizen" of Huamanga "to whom I am much obligated for good works." Arriola contributed valuable lands to the support of López and their illegitimate son.[45] More humble Indian women, too, had reason to pursue relations with outsiders. Earlier (Chapter 6), we saw that young males seemed to experience a kind of life crisis on the threshold of marriage and tributary responsibilities; some fled and swelled the forastero population. Young women facing the grim burdens of ayllu life must have experienced crises and tensions of their own, especially if they had a chance to "escape" by marrying outsiders—forastero Indians, free blacks, mixed-bloods, or Spaniards. Among the originario population, women usually outnumbered men anyway. Some women made the jump and did well. Juana Curiguamán, for example, married a free mulatto, Alonso de Paz; not far from her homeland in Soras, they bought a modest hacienda worth 600–700 pesos.[46] Describing the situation, Felipe Guaman Poma de Ayala of Lucanas complained that Indian women "no longer love Indians but rather Spaniards, and they become big whores."[47] His remark expressed male resentment; it underestimated the importance of force and sexual assault in many Indian-white relationships, and ignored the women whose lives and resources remained

Women as spoils of conquest. Colonial relationships are depicted here as a struggle to control the destinies of native women. Indian mother and father are both present, but in Poma de Ayala's view, men are the active contestants.

bonded to Indian kinfolk (of both sexes). Nevertheless, Poma's exaggeration corresponded to a very real social pattern, to a Hispanic allure which attracted both female and male.

At its highest levels, Indian success signified a fuller emergence of class relationships within seventeenth-century native society. Hispanism was a path to success for a small minority, but it also tended to transform the prosperous into foreigners — people whose economic relations, social bonds, and cultural symbols differentiated them from poorer, more "Indian" counterparts, and imparted a Hispanic-mestizo dimension to their identities.[48] In any given rural terrain, the emerging provincial elite included a strong component of "outsiders" anyway — forastero Indians, Spanish colonials and officials, mestizos (some of them heirs of Indian-white marriages among local elites), occasionally a black or mulatto. But even a local ayllu Indian acquired a more alien character if success violated community norms or assimilated the native to outside exploiters. Poma de Ayala observed an erosion of major kurakas' legitimacy among kinfolk; social climbers who had usurped chieftainships from rightful heirs, and chiefs whose social and economic activities allied them with hated colonials "are no longer obeyed nor respected."[49] Consider also the will of Juana Marcaruray, a wealthy ayllu Indian with no children. Marcaruray left her considerable estate to her friend Doña Mariana de Balaguera, wife of the municipal standard bearer of Huamanga, "in view of [my] having received very many good works, worthy of greater reward, from her household." Traditionally, property rights would have reverted to ayllu relatives if the deceased left no spouse or children.[50]

Success tended to draw the most dynamic and powerful members of native society — originarios as well as forasteros, villagers as well as city folk — into the world of aristocrat-entrepreneurs, and thereby widened the social basis of colonial exploitation. The question we may ask is whether this tendency met with any kind of resistance. As we shall see, considerable tension and conflict marred the achievements of successful Indians.

STRIFE, TENSION, AND PURIFICATION

In a society where ethnic loyalties continued to set communities against one another, forasteros who intruded on ayllu domains contended with hostilities which sometimes flared into open conflict. Catalina Puscotilla, an "Indian hacendada," held 130 hectares of prime land near the village of Espíritu Santo, midway between the urban markets of Huancavelica and Huamanga. The zone's waters, ecology, and location made it especially important for commercial agriculture, and Puscotilla's Indian husband had agreed in 1625 to pay the Crown 298 pesos (of 8 reales) for legal title to the land. The local Quiguares Indians bitterly disputed the award of valuable property to outsiders, however, and a classic hacienda-community conflict festered for decades. In the 1640s Puscotilla, now a widow, was still fending off the Quiguares, as well as a mestizo rival who had entered the fray.[51] Lorenzo Pilco, a wealthy city Indian and "master shoemaker," encountered similar problems in the countryside. To end litigation with the Angaraes Indians of Pata, Pilco resorted to an expedient well known to Spanish entrepreneurs. He simply paid the Indians, who could ill afford protracted legal struggles anyway, seventy pesos to withdraw their suit.[52]

Outsiders could gain more acceptance by integrating themselves into community life and responsibilities, but such integration gave local Indians a means to exert pressure for redistribution of wealth. In 1642 Clemente de Chaves, a ladino from Huamanga, spent thirty pesos to buy a modest amount of land from a wealthy ayllu Indian of Huanta. The fact that Chaves married and settled in the area, and "helps [the community] serve the mitas of Huancavelica" undoubtedly stabilized his presence.[53] A wealthier forastero, Don Diego de Rojas, married Teresa Cargua of Lucanas Andamarcas. Rojas apparently won the esteem of his new kinfolk, for he served as chief of their small ayllu.[54] Acceptance of Rojas's leadership probably derived from his willingness to submit to local reciprocities which demanded "generosity" on the part of chiefs. An Indian as wealthy and powerful as a Lorenzo Pilco, who had a kuraka jailed for failure to pay a debt,[55] might shun obligations which limited one's capacity to accumulate or privatize wealth. But if he did, the intruder risked the same conflicts and litigations which afflicted Spanish entrepreneurs.

Conflict between ayllu Indians and wealthy forasteros is readily understandable, but the changing texture of relationships among originarios generated analogous tensions. Poma de Ayala's observation that kurakas lost "respect" as they were integrated into the colonial political and economic structure suggests the development of more precarious, forced relations between chiefs and "their" people. At times, loss of confidence in the reciprocal exchanges which bound chiefs and ayllu peasants erupted in outright refusals to obey an "illegitimate" request. In Vilcashuamán, for example, some Papres and Chilques kurakas and Spanish priests decided that ayllus ought to plant nearly 300 hectares of wheat to earn funds for local churches and cofradías. When the peasants discovered that they would not be paid for their work, resistance grew so fierce that the project had to be abandoned.[56] A chief who lost legitimacy among kinfolk faced serious problems beyond those of simple disobedience. Emigration of ayllu Indians might increase; complaints to Spanish officials might undermine ethnic or ayllu authority; rivals to a chieftainship might secure a following and embroil local society in a civil war.[57]

A new tension thus entered the relationship of major chiefs and ayllu peasants. To shore up the legitimacy which made ayllu households responsive to their requests, chiefs had to demonstrate loyalties and perform services for ayllus and ethnic groups. Probably such services included skillful leadership in judicial politics and other defenses against extractive relations; "generosity" in redistributing wealth to poorer kinfolk; enforcement of a "fair" distribution of burdens and rights within the community of producer-relatives; and as we shall see later, symbolic expressions of solidarity with ayllu and ethnic relatives. These services enhanced prestige among kin, but they also limited the degree to which a chief could privatize resources and interests, or function as a reliable partner of colonial power groups. The structural position of ambitious chiefs thus embodied a deep contradiction. To operate effectively, with minimal force, required that chiefs earn the confidence of kin, but too zealous a defense of ayllu interests handicapped their ability to accumulate wealth or pursue private gain. Kurakas were conspicuous among the Indians whose "Hispanic" success differentiated them from the seventeenth-century peasantry, but their success eroded some of the "influence" associated with traditional reciprocity relationships. The result was a more strained, suspicious relationship in which conflict, coercion, and economic power acquired added importance.

Similar tensions probably accompanied the success of originarios who never held an important chieftainship. In the final analysis, ayllu Indians did not readily accept the legitimacy of a complete alienation of resources from the fabric of community life and authority.[58] Wealthy ayllu Indians, kurakas or not, faced a network of relatives, ayllus, and ethnic groups who claimed overlapping rights to "private" lands and revenues. Indeed, kurakas sometimes used their position as spokesmen of the community to expropriate or redistribute the "private" property of wealthy ayllu rivals, including women. Ayllu enemies countered with legal suits to protect their resources.[59] Such conflicts exacerbated the erosion of the chiefs' moral authority, and hardly lessened resentments created by networks of private interest and wealth, much of it beyond the control of ayllu society. Beyond a certain point, privatization of resources alienated not just the resources attached to the owner, but the owner too, from ayllu Indians.

By the early seventeenth century, then, the success of a minority amidst growing pauperization created new strains in native Andean life. Indian Hispanism — as a socioeconomic strategy, and as a set of cultural symbols — constituted for some a path to economic success and at least the pretense of social respectability.[60] But to those left behind, especially the ayllu peasantry, it represented a powerful, oppressive force in the very heart of rural society. Hispanism symbolized the conversion of Indian society's foremost figures into partners of colonial rule and exploitation, a widening split of interests, loyalties, and orientations which accompanied differentiation into rich and poor. It symbolized, too, a loss of "confidence" which touched all sectors of

Andean society. Poor Indians understood very well the temptation to escape or soften burdens by allying with the world of the colonials, in a search for personal gain which weakened community solidarity and confirmed the superiority of the Hispanic over the Andean.[61]

At moments of crisis, these tensions exploded in nativist outbursts which sought to purge Andean society of Hispanic-Christian influence. The data available on these internal convulsions is extremely scarce, but the Jesuits recorded one such instance in 1613 when an epidemic swept western Huamanga (the Castrovirreyna-Huancavelica zone settled by the Huachos and Yauyos peoples).[62] In this case, at least, Indian nativism generated fierce loyalties and violence. Indians not only killed two Catholic priests, but also (as we shall see later) one of their own chiefs! Quickly, Catholic extirpadores of the idolatry dragged 150 pagan priests to the city of Castrovirreyna for the standard public spectacle and proceedings: whippings and haircuts for the worst offenders, a bonfire to destroy Andean articles of worship (including the huacas themselves), "confession" and eventual rehabilitation of the idolaters. But some of the offenders refused to submit, and staged a spectacular show of defiance. Within five days, thirty of "the most obstinate" leaders, "exasperated and desperate," had killed themselves "with poison that they took by their own hand."

As in the 1560s, when millenarian upheaval inflamed Huamanga, the huacas served as a medium of popular protest and calls for change. In the Taki Onqoy movement, the Andean gods had literally "seized" the bodies of Indians, transforming previously uninfluential natives into authoritative voices of angry gods. This time, the huacas voiced popular impulses by appearing to a variety of people in visions and dreams. "Three times they appeared in public to many people, and preached and taught them what to do. . . ." The huacas rebuked the Indians for supposed disloyalty and neglect of the native deities, who had taken vengeance by sending disease and hard times to the land. And they issued a series of anti-Christian "commandments." The Indians "should not recognize any other god except their huacas," and should know "that everything that the Christians teach is false." The natives should perform the traditional rites and services owed to ancestor-gods, and should avoid any collaboration with Spaniards, who were "enemies of the huacas." The Indians "ought not go to serve the Spaniards, nor deal with them, nor communicate, nor ask [their] advice . . . unless forced to."

The qualification "unless forced to" conceded a harsh fact of life. In the context of the early seventeenth century, the colonial power structure was too secure to be smashed or challenged overtly. But the Indians should not collaborate willingly. Instead, they should close ranks around a purifying hatred of colonials and Christian influence. "The day that a cleric or priest leaves town . . . ," ordered the huacas, "[the Indians] should catch an all-black dog and drag him along all the streets and spots where the priest had walked." Afterwards, the natives should kill the animal at the river, "and where [the river parts into] two branches they should throw in [the body], in order that . . . they purify the places walked by the priest." In Andean culture, the juncture of two streams had special ritual significance as a symbol of perfection, or the achievement of "balanced" social relationships (Chapter 1).

What distinguished the religious turmoil of 1613 was not its "idolatrous" nature, but rather its intense nativism — an attempt to wipe village society clean of Hispanic-Christian influence. Idolatry itself was neither exceptional, nor especially anti-Hispanic. Huamanga's Indians had long adhered to traditional religious practices, sometimes concealed beneath an overlay of Christian symbols and holidays. From an Andean point of view, "pagan" traditions balanced relationships with ancestor-gods who vitally affected the material welfare of the gods' children. Most Indians, therefore, could scarcely abandon their service to Andean gods. At crucial moments in the ritual calendar or life cycle, alcohol and coca lowered inhibitions, and "the most Christian [Indian], even if he [could] read and write, [chant] a rosary, and dressed like a Spaniard," reverted to Andean paganisms.[63] Indeed, successful or Hispanized native elites, including lay assistants of Catholic priests, often led traditional religious practices. This form of idolatry, though it sometimes expressed a muted hostility to Christian gods, tended to encourage coexistence and eventual interpenetration of Andean and Hispanic gods, symbols, and practices. In this sense, it promoted a syncretic religious culture through which Hispanizing Indian elites could maintain traditional sources of prestige and influence among kinfolk, while pursuing strategies and relationships drawing them ever more tightly into the world of Hispanic exploiters.[64]

The nativist idolatry which erupted in 1613, on the other hand, promoted fiercely aggressive anti-Hispanic sentiments, and spoke directly to the internal crisis symbolized by Indian Hispanism. For syncretism or coexistence, it substituted internal purification.[65] For tradition led by a native elite, it substituted visions and dreams beyond the control of local authority. Before affirming the prestige of Hispanized Indians, it first put their loyalties on trial. At bottom, nativist currents and outbursts represented a protest against internal trends which sapped the strength and unity of Andean society. The message of anti-Hispanism, we ought to remember, was directed at Indians, not Spaniards. The huacas' commandments called upon all natives to reject the temptation to forsake the Andean for the Hispanic, in a quest for personal success which weakened community solidarity and confidence in the adequacy of Andean tradition. The most pointed targets of such

Religion and wellbeing in Andean culture. In the two scenes on top, the huacas—represented by Poma de Ayala as the devil—speak through dreams and fire. The bottom scene depicts a native priest, controlled by the devil, healing a sick Indian by sucking out the impurity.

"commands," however, were those who had already made such a choice. To regain the favor of the huacas—and of poor peasants—successful natives would have to drop Hispanic aspirations which converted them into willing partners of colonial enemies. By reaffirming a purer loyalty to native Andean relationships, successful natives could demonstrate solidarity with the more "Indian" peasantry. Those who rejected the call of the huacas risked extreme alienation from local Indian society, and even violence. Nativists turned against ethnic elites who shied away from religious purification, and in one case poisoned "a kuraka of theirs, a good Christian, for not coming to their rites nor wanting to worship their idols."[66]

But murder remained the exception rather than the rule. We do not know to what extent wealthy forasteros participated in nativist idolatries. But among the originarios, at least, a good many elites responded to the pressure of local sentiment, and participated in the condemnation of their Hispanic-Christian ways.[67] The threat of social alienation could become a tool of resistance which conditioned social and economic behavior. Indeed, to the extent that ayllu peasants could mobilize such a tool to redistribute the resources of successful Indians, they placed limits on the process of privatization and internal differentiation reshaping rural life. But why, we may ask, should a notable fraction of the successful Indians adopting "Hispanic" strategies and relationships prove so vulnerable to the threat of alienation from Andean gods and peoples?

BETWEEN TWO WORLDS

One answer, at first sight adequate, lies in the realm of physical safety and material interest. We have already seen that Indians feared antagonizing Andean gods who ruled over one's health, economic wellbeing, and the like. Equally as important, many successful Indians retained important economic ties in the ayllu countryside. Presumably, they could pursue those interests and protect their persons more effectively if they built loyalties and cooperative relationships, or at least avoided gratuitous antagonisms. Social isolation, beyond a certain point, invited violence, disruptive conflicts, and perhaps expulsion from valuable property. Even forasteros assumed relationships and obligations which stabilized their presence. Successful originarios depended upon "traditional" rights and obligations for some part of their access to resources and labor. A kuraka who enjoyed prestige among "his" people could set up a lucrative putting-out system with little trouble. A chief who had lost the "respect" or confidence of ayllu households, on the other hand, contended with uncooperative, resistant people. By this logic, those Indians who depended upon a certain esteem among ayllu peasants to maintain or enhance their material wellbeing could not afford to ignore pressures to participate in the nativist idolatries of an aroused peasantry.

Yet this answer is true only up to a certain point. After all, the direction of change limited the material vulnerability of wealthy Indians to declining esteem. An Indian elite which controlled considerable wealth and had integrated itself into provincial power groups enjoyed the same weapons of coercion and economic domination held by colonial aristocrat-entrepreneurs. They had powerful friends and relatives, and sufficient wealth to contract laborers, recruit dependent clients and retainers, accumulate property independent of ayllu control, invest in commerce, indebt (and jail) poor Indians, and the like. Indeed, deteriorating self-sufficiency and commercial penetration of their communities left peasants dependent on wealthy superiors of all races for money, subsistence, credit and protection. As wealthy Indians developed "Hispanic" patterns of accumulation, they emancipated their *economic* lives from the esteem of kinfolk. The wealthiest Indians could indeed afford to withdraw themselves from the traditional burden of prestige and reciprocal obligation, and some in fact did.[68]

But others did not. The structural position of successful Indians, as a group, was laden with a deep contradiction which inhibited their social acceptance among Spaniards and Indians alike, and generated ambivalent loyalties and identities. As an emerging class, the successful Indians held interests and aspirations joining them to the colonial Hispanic world whose social, economic, and cultural patterns they emulated. But the stain of their racial origins linked them to the Indian peasantry, and generated social barriers which normally prevented their complete merger into Hispanic society and culture. Ruling classes tend to consider those whose labor they exploit as "lazy" or inherently inferior. In a colonial situation, where class relationships have their genesis in the conquest of one people by another, this characterization applies to entire castes defined by their racial and cultural origins, in this case the "republic of Indians."[69] The achievements of an Indian minority, judged by the Spaniards' own standards, flew in the face of the natives' supposedly inherent degradation. Dynamic Indians competed with Spaniards for land, labor, and profits; they recast themselves in the trappings of Hispanic culture, and found Spanish suitors, allies, and friends. In some cases, they even mastered reading and writing skills known by only a minority of Spaniards. These wealthy and acculturated Indians flagrantly violated the world view and psychology of colonialism.

The Spanish response to ladinos, elites, and social climbers was, therefore, highly contradictory. On the one hand, colonial entrepreneurs and officials pursued the contacts they needed to exploit or control the Indian countryside. Their natural allies and friends were powerful, wealthy, and ambitious Indians. But dynamic Indian figures also disturbed the racial hierarchy which legitimated colonial exploitation, and entitled all whites — even those who could not break into high elite circles — to a respectable social and economic position. Hence acculturated or wealthy natives also aroused the hostility and contempt heaped upon pretenders who deny their "true" origins. (It is true that money or wealth could help one surmount racial barriers, but the economic success of many Indians, even if impressive and disturbing to racial hierarchies, was nonetheless modest when measured by the standards of high elite circles of Spanish colonial society.)

In general, then, successful Indians could not simply abandon their racial origins and find social acceptance and identification in a Hispanic world. But strong ambivalences also colored relationships with the bulk of Indian society. On the one hand, poor Indians "needed" wealthier, more acculturated counterparts. Their wealth could shore up deteriorating household and ayllu economies, or save an Indian debtor from jail. Their cultural knowledge of Hispanic society could strengthen juridical and other defenses against European enemies, or establish contacts which might serve the community. In addition, poor Indians probably looked upon successful natives with a certain amount of pride; like Spaniards, they understood that Indian dynamism provided a symbolic counterpoint to stereotypes condemning natives to inferiority and subordination. In certain respects, then, a wealthy ladino whose loyalties and commitments joined him or her to Indian society could prove to be an exceptionally valuable and popular leader.[70]

But there, alas, was the rub—in the question of loyalties and commitments. A widening gulf of suspicion, tension, and conflict accompanied the differentiation of Indian society into rich and poor, and for very good reason. Success assimilated the most powerful and dynamic fraction of Indian society to an exploitative class of aristocrat-entrepreneurs; the more modest success stories often represented a drain from ayllu society of needed people, skills, and resources, and weakened its internal solidarity. The cultural Hispanism of ambitious Indians expressed their weakening commitment to an onerous Andean heritage, and their conspicuous aspiration to blend into the dominant sectors of colonial society. Thus even as poor Indians "needed" their more Hispanized counterparts, and might take some pride in their achievements, they lost confidence in the loyalties of a new, more alien Indian elite. One response, especially against forasteros, was open conflict. But another, probably more widespread, was more subtle. Social pressure forced wealthy Indians to demonstrate their loyalties to the people to whom they "belonged," or else suffer an awkward, alienated relationship governed by colonial rules of coercion and economic domination.

The Indian elite, especially its poorer and more rural segments, was vulnerable to the pressure of social ostracism precisely because contradictions of class and race blocked their fuller acceptance into Spanish society. The structural position of ladinos suspended them between two social worlds, Hispanic and Andean, without fully welcoming them into either. Somewhat ill at ease in Spanish circles, yet estranged or suspect in peasant society, at least some acculturated Indians endured considerable psychic strain and inner conflict. We know, for example, that Andean huacas haunted "Christian" Indians in dreams and visions, sometimes for years. Often the native gods first presented themselves to both men and women as attractive sexual partners luring the unfaithful to return to Andean loyalties.[71] Indians whose "Hispanic" wealth, socioeconomic strategies, and aspirations tended to differentiate them from the peasantry nevertheless found that they could not make a final break from Indian society. At least some continued to search for esteem or social acceptance among Indians, and responded to pressures to demonstrate loyalty to Andean society.

And on occasion, a popular hero emerged from the ranks of the fortunate and powerful. Don Cristóbal de León, son of a middle-level kuraka in Lucanas Andamarcas, was a cultured ladino: Spanish in dress and hair style, Christian in religion, and known for his learning and ability. Given his political and economic privileges, and his acquired culture, León was in a position to integrate himself into the provincial power group exploiting the local peasantry, or to leave for a respectable life in a Spanish city. But León departed from conventional patterns and incurred the wrath of local colonials. León continued to live in his ayllu homeland, opposed drafts of peasant laborers to transport wine from Pacific coastal valleys across Lucanas to Cuzco, and condemned putting-out arrangements run by kurakas and corregidores to sell cloth in lucrative markets. At one point, he even set out to Lima to denounce local abuses before the viceroy. The local corregidor imprisoned León, "punished" him, and threatened to end the matter by hanging him. The incident marked the first of several confrontations between León and local corregidores. In 1612, a corregidor and visiting priest finally killed the persistent troublemaker. Significantly, other chiefs and notables had avoided helping León out of his scrapes.[72]

The tragedy of Indian success stemmed ultimately from the way it secured the participation of a defeated people in its own oppression. The colonial regime rewarded Indians whose advantages, skills, or luck enabled them to adopt Hispanic forms of accumulation, and punished those whose identification with the peasantry was too strong or aggressive. The political implications were profound. The lure of success and the threat of loss recruited Indian allies to the colonial power structure, discouraged overt challenges which invited repression, and fragmented the internal unity of Andean society. The economic implications, too, were far-reaching. Success stimulated class differentiation within the "republic of Indians," dividing it into the rich and more acculturated on the one side, the poor and less acculturated on the other. The achievements of an Indian minority accelerated the erosion of traditional resources and relationships, while implanting Hispanic property, relationships, and culture deeply within the "internal" fabric of Indian life. The emergence of a colonial Indian elite generated new sources of social conflict, tension, and protest in native society. Yet here, too, was an element of tragedy. For in pressuring Indian elites to demonstrate their loyalties and service to the community, peasants acknowledged that they needed "Hispanic" wealth and skills to survive and defend themselves against colonial exploiters. And in the end, though peasant pressure placed certain limits, at given times and places, on the differentiation of Indian society into rich and poor, it could not reverse the overall trend.[73]

For many of those left behind by Indian success, the only escape was escape itself, flight in search of a better life. Among the fugitives, a small fraction would themselves join the ranks of the successful Indians. As they rebuilt lives in a more Hispanic-mestizo mold, they would gain distance from a condemned Andean heritage left to the peasantry. But they could not escape entirely. A welter of memories, habits, relationships—and snubs— would bind them and their children to their Indian origins.[74]

8

Huamanga's Colonial Heritage

THE PRESENCE OF THE PAST

A VISITOR TO AYACUCHO (the modern name of Huamanga) finds that, four centuries later, the heritage of Spanish colonization still looms large. The very architecture and physical layout of the city conform to a sixteenth- and seventeenth-century mold unbroken by urban growth or industrial expansion. Indeed, the city's economy faded in the nineteenth and twentieth centuries; its population—less than 30,000 in 1970—has only recently surpassed its colonial apogee, and continues to include large numbers of peasants and ex-peasants among its day laborers, servants, artisans, peddlers, and university students. In what the colonial city called its "Indian parishes," native Quechua is still the language of many households. And in the countryside, the legacy of the past is even more conspicuous. Ayacucho remains one of the most "Indian" regions of Peru—that is, an area populated predominantly by poor peasants whose language and culture, socioeconomic institutions, and historical memory link them to the indigenous past, setting them apart from "creole" society. For people such as these, the clash of the indigenous and the foreign outsider still has great meaning. In dances, ceremonies, and mythology Indian peasantries continue to commemorate scenes and events of the Spanish conquest. For them, colonialism created forces and relationships that continue to govern, in important respects, the shape and texture of everyday life.[1]

It would be foolish, of course, to claim that nothing has changed in modern times, or even in the late colonial period. The twentieth century, in particular, has witnessed the growing predominance of capitalist industry and relationships in Andean South America. Accompanied by a demographic explosion, the effect has been to constrict the scope of the "subsistence econ-

184

omy" available to the population to an ever narrower, more vulnerable compass. Wage labor has become increasingly important for economic survival, the internal market has expanded on a new scale, and a few cities are flooded with rural migrants. Yet the present seems to superimpose itself upon the past, not destroy it. The Indian peasantry shrinks as a proportion of the population, but refuses to disappear. The subsistence sector of the economy grows ever more backward relative to industrial advance, yet continues to serve vital functions, by providing a source of cheap goods and labor for entrepreneurs, and an economic backdrop from the point of view of the "underemployed" and unemployed.[2] To deny momentous changes would betray historical realities. Yet certain patterns — however modified or reconstituted by a changing context — have endured and had their beginnings in the period when a colonial society was founded.

The most dramatic creation — and legacy — of the first century of colonization was Indian poverty. In Huamanga, at least, the decisive phase began not with the defeat of the Incas, but with Viceroy Toledo's reorganization and its aftermath. The European invaders encountered dynamic local societies whose skillful adaptations to a harsh highland environment yielded great wealth. The initial plunderings and early epidemics that followed European arrival did not destroy, in one generation, the resources and skills developed over centuries of human settlement in the Andean highlands. On the contrary, ethnic freedom from Inca hegemony and aggressive adaptations to commercial opportunities allowed local Andean societies to accumulate wealth that inspired Spanish envy, and that to some extent counteracted colonial expropriations.[3] Indeed, during the period of the post-Incaic alliances, the dependence of colonizers on negotiation with chiefs of wealthy, relatively independent native societies limited the Spaniards' capacity to accumulate further riches. In Huamanga, the discovery of major mines in the 1560s led not to the creation of a prosperous mining economy by the colonials, but rather to labor bottlenecks, a souring of the early alliances, and finally, a major colonial crisis.

It was only after a thorough reorganization, led by Toledo, that colonials held sufficient power to change the scope of economic extraction. The revamped power structure funnelled massive supplies of cheap Indian labor to hated mines and other enterprises (the mita), absorbed revenues earned by native communities (tributes and control of the cajas de comunidad), and transferred prized lands to favored entrepreneurs (the composiciones de tierras). Colonial expropriation proceeded on a new scale, and unleashed new economic forces. Huamanga's mines and manufactures, commercial agriculture and ranching, artisanry and crafts, and trade and transport enjoyed a wave of prosperity. But the consequence for the bulk of the Andean peasantry was, by the early seventeenth century, poverty.

The interaction—and interpenetration—of commercial and subsistence sectors constituted a second legacy. Colonial rule integrated rural native society into a commercial economy, regional and international, and left ayllu peasants dependent upon occasional wages, credits, or money advances from patrons or entrepreneurs. Poverty meant not simply that Indians eked out a meager existence independently, falling behind while a dynamic commercial sector prospered, and raided the peasantry for goods, labor, and land. In Huamanga, at least, the penetration of the commercial economy reached the point of redefining the "necessities" of households, inducing a relative "monetization" of needs and obligations, and undermining the capacity of poor Indians to survive economically on the basis of household or ayllu production alone. A century of colonial expropriation and commercial expansion had reduced the native peasantry to something less than self-sufficiency, despite continuing access to land. Partially separated from the means of production, ayllu peasants had little choice but to earn, from time to time, wages or credits by serving outsiders. For those who did not flee from homelands entirely, temporary migration to shore up local subsistence would become a common feature of life.

Indeed, emigration to cities, mines, and other economic "poles" constituted another enduring legacy. Long ago, Indian society began to lose its grip on people. Centers of dynamism shifted elsewhere, and even those who remained committed to ayllu homelands found that at times they might have to leave temporarily to earn subsistence or wages, or pay off debts, by working for economic superiors. Others left permanently and swelled the populations of laborers, servants, petty producers, peddlers, fortune-seekers, and vagabonds who clustered around colonial cities and mining centers. The scale of such emigration has reached massive proportions in this century, but had its beginnings with the decline of the Indian countryside, and the rise of new centers of work, prosperity, and refuge.

The Indian countryside thus became poor and "backward" not simply in economic terms, but in a social and ideological sense as well, and this constituted a fourth legacy. Colonialism created "Indians," and defined them as an inferior, degraded race. Local Andean peoples might easily reject such ideologies at first, and indeed, the early colonials themselves often admired the skills, wealth, and achievements of Andean peoples. But over time, and especially after the 1570s, objective conditions changed. Rural native society declined into impoverishment and dependence, dynamism on the "outside" pulled away people, and the colonial power structure could crush a challenge or revolt quite easily. As colonial "superiority" manifested itself on many levels—economic, social, political—and as the achievements of indigenous peoples receded into the past, the "inferiority" or "backwardness" of Indian society and tradition found internal expression and confirmation among the natives themselves. There were countertendencies which limited such a process, of course, but even these betrayed the superiority of the colonial world. A successful Indian minority proved that native peoples were as capable as whites, but significantly, native achievement rested on superimposing a layer of "Hispanic" skills, strategies, and relationships upon an Andean essence or background, gradually changing the latter and transforming the Indian into a ladino. Nativist currents and outbursts revindicated the worth of the Andean, and condemned the Hispanic; but significantly, even angry huacas cautioned against challenging the colonials openly. By the early seventeenth century, European dominance was unquestionable. The specific extractions and abuses of aristocrat-entrepreneurs could be — and were — resisted and fought in numerous ways. But to conceive of a massive destruction of colonial power, as the Taki Onqoy movement and the neo-Incas had done in the 1560s, was out of touch with the times.

FOUNDATIONS OF COLONIAL HEGEMONY

How are we to explain the emergence of colonial hegemony in Huamanga, the contrast, say, between 1565 and 1635? As we have seen, the reorganization of political power in the 1570s brought the ayllu countryside under the more direct control of a complex web of local, regional, and supraregional power groups. A more effective political apparatus made peasant assault more difficult. But still, the mobilization of superior force to coerce a surplus from an independent peasantry would, by itself, have constituted a crude system of dominance. It required considerable violence and a continual show of authority, generating confrontations that under certain circumstances provoked defiance or rebellion (see Chapter 4).

Three colonial trends fostered more subtle dependencies, and a willingness — up to a point — to accommodate to the "reality" of colonial dominance. The first, judicial politics, was a consequence of resurgent state power, and of contradictions among colonial elites (including bureaucrats charged with enforcing the legal system). Indians appropriated a workable system of "justice" on their own behalf; despite great disadvantages in legal struggles, they used judicial institutions shrewdly, and with surprising success. As a result, the peasantry made great inroads against its most hated burden, the colonial mita. But the emergence of judicial politics as a viable strategy of resistance also promoted dependencies on colonial patrons and power, encouraged strong bonds and mutual loyalties among Indian and colonial elites, and exacerbated internal rivalries and conflicts that undermined native authority and cohesion. The ability of Indians to employ the tactics and institutions of Hispanic politics to reshape, within limits, the boundaries of their existence lent greater sophistication to the *political* dominance of colonials.

A second trend promoted economic dependencies. When the Europeans first arrived, from an economic point of view they were extraneous. As foreign allies and conquerors, they superimposed demands on autonomous native economies, but had little role in the internal organization or production of life's necessities. Toledo's reforms, at first, simply rationalized this relationship on a new scale, and backed it with the force of a revitalized state. Mitas and tributes siphoned energy and wealth from economically independent, self-sufficient ayllus. But over time, the disruptions and expropriations wrought by colonial institutions, in the context of an expansive commercial economy and declining ayllu demography, led to increasing economic dependencies upon Europeans. Among émigrés from the burdens of ayllu life, a certain fraction turned to colonials for protection and subsistence in the form of wages, subsistence goods, land rights, or a combination thereof. Among ayllu Indians, the colonial regime changed the definition of "necessities," and shrank the resources available to peasant households for their own use. Thus ayllu peasants, too, would "need" patrons or employers for money advances, wages, credits, and even subsistence goods.

Finally, the emergence of successful natives contributed to a more subtle Hispanic dominance. Success or, more modestly, improvement of one's condition divided natives into different, to some extent antagonistic social strata (despite the common features of their oppression as a race or caste of "Indians"). Indian success compounded preexisting rivalries and disunities, and on its highest levels reproduced within native society class contradictions first imposed by Spanish colonials. Redefinition of personal success according to European standards furthered, moreover, a kind of cultural hegemony, a recognition from within native society that European ways and power, however repugnant or disliked, were "superior." The foremost strata of Indian society belied the truth of racial stereotypes, but under colonial conditions they could do so only by taking on Hispanic-mestizo skills, strategies, and social styles. Indians succeeded not *because* they were Indian, but because they could, to a certain extent, recast themselves as Europeans *despite* their racial inheritance.

By the early seventeenth century, then, a sophisticated political, economic, and social system had emerged, and a ruling class of aristocrat-entrepreneurs had achieved a pervasive hegemony over the indigenous peasantry it exploited. Under these conditions, a radical millenarian mobilization like that of Taki Onqoy, which envisioned the imminent and total destruction of the European presence, was less likely to sweep native society. In its place emerged the myth of a messianic savior, a long defeated "Inkarrí" who would return, someday, from the distant past to avenge Indian society and restore the cosmos to its proper order. Inkarrí entered the oral tradition of a defeated peasantry, and as recently as the 1970s, anthropologists still recorded the myth in Huamanga.[4]

SOCIAL CONFLICT AND INDIAN LABOR

The emerging hegemony of a colonial ruling class, however, did not free society of conflict, contradiction, or the seeds of future political crisis. This grew clear in the eighteenth century, when the colonial elite experienced a profound crisis of hegemony, some of whose elements issued from the very trends discussed above.[5] Even in the early seventeenth century, the colonials' hegemony meant only that the Indian peasantry could not launch a direct challenge to the prevailing structure of power, relationships, and ideologies. Within more restricted boundaries, conflict and resistance conditioned the everyday realities of both ruler and ruled; shaped the specific character and limits of the accommodations which did take place; and over time, might modify the social and economic structure itself. Indeed, when we look closely at the evolution of the colonial labor system in Huamanga, we find that the patterns of exploitation which prevailed by 1630 or 1640 — and the basis, therefore, upon which an emerging ruling class established its hegemony over society at large — reflected the outcome of a long, sometimes bitter struggle.

Over the course of a century, colonials in Huamanga resorted to three principal paths to gain access to Indian labor or its products. One method, which I shall call the "indigenous form," mobilized native labor on the basis of traditional Andean norms and relationships. Europeans and Indian chiefs negotiated agreements or understandings that called upon the kurakas to provide native labor or products. The kurakas, indispensable mediators of the relationship, assumed responsibility for mobilizing and managing labor relationships, within the context of the traditional norms, reciprocities, and expectations binding chiefs and their kin. The Spaniards would enjoy the fruits of native labor, but direct European control of the production process or of the native labor force would be severely limited. A second mode of extraction, the "state form," used the formal legal institutions of the state to mobilize a labor force (the mitas), or to gain access to revenues (tributes). This form of exploitation facilitated more direct control of productive processes and labor relationships by colonials, despite dependence upon the state for access to labor. A third path, the "private form," involved extraofficial relations arranged directly between colonials and the Indians they exploited. These more direct relations included long-term servitude such as yanaconaje; wage labor agreements; more ambiguous arrangements, such as asiento contracts, that mixed elements of long-term bondage and free sale of labor-power; and extralegal coercions to serve the personal (extraofficial) interests of state functionaries and their allies. Though not necessarily illegal, nor completely divorced from formal or informal uses of state power, these kinds of extractions reflected the emergence of forces in "civil society." They circumvented the official labor-tribute patrimony of the state, as well as the limits imposed by kuraka mediators who operated within the traditional norms of Andean labor. These arrangements enabled entrepreneurs to assert their most direct control over production and labor.[6]

Indigenous, state, and private forms of exploitation coexisted and complemented one another as labor strategies during Huamanga's first century of colonization, but their relative importance changed greatly. Until the 1570s the indigenous form proved vital to the development of the colonial economy. This was the period of the post-Incaic alliances, a time of early testing when the colonial state was relatively weak, and a handful of encomenderos and priests pioneered relationships with local Andean societies. Colonials depended greatly upon uneasy alliances with ethnic societies and their chiefs to secure the labor and goods they needed: labor for construction, transport, mines, textile manufactures, artisanry, agriculture, and ranching, and goods ranging from precious metals to basic foodstuffs to an enormous variety of handicrafts. Although a considerable yanacona population lent some importance to the private form of extraction,[7] the strategic pattern adopted by colonials relied on indigenous authority to mobilize a flow of ayllu labor and goods on behalf of colonial allies. Indeed, the limits imposed by European dependence upon such a labor strategy became most apparent after the discovery of major mines in the 1560s. European demands for large, stable supplies of native labor catalyzed a profound crisis, inherent in the contradictory nature of the early alliances, which blocked the development of Huamanga's mining economy, and threatened to shatter the entire colonial venture.

The failure of the post-Incaic alliances, and the indigenous form of extraction associated with it, created a new historical conjuncture. Toledo's thorough reorganization of colonial politics, economy, and society responded to a "historic necessity" imposed by the Indian threat, and ushered in a new era in the history of labor relations in Huamanga. From the 1570s, a transitional decade, until around 1600–1610, the state form of extraction powered a tremendous economic boom. Indigenous and private forms of exploitation played a secondary role in the production, expansion, and expropriations of the commercial economy. The state's tributes and mitas— the bulk of them distributed to small, partially overlapping elite groups centered in Huamanga, Huancavelica, and Castrovirreyna—mobilized a vital flow of revenues and cheap labor. The mitas, especially, made it possible to mine and refine large quantities of mercury and silver, to manufacture textiles in obrajes employing the labors of a hundred or more Indians each, and to advance commercial agriculture and ranching.

This second stage of Huamanga's labor relations represented far more than the achievement of a great personality such as Toledo; it represented the answer of a colonial elite, led and "domesticated" by officials sent from the metropolis, to the crisis that culminated an earlier period. Political and economic problems similar to those plaguing Huamanga had also emerged in other important Andean regions, including Jauja, Cuzco, and Potosí. In Huamanga as elsewhere, European weakness in the face of Indian resistance and subversion, and the handicaps of an economic system too dependent on indigenous tradition, meant that an aspiring ruling class had little choice but to accept thorough reforms implemented by a revitalized state.[8]

Yet the state form of extraction would not predominate forever, and over the 1600–1640 period grew less and less capable of supplying European needs for Indian labor in Huamanga. By 1630 or 1640 private forms of exploitation had grown increasingly important. Yanaconaje and other forms of peonage, wage labor and work contracts, extralegal tributes and corvées arranged through corregidores or other functionaries — these, along with African slavery, represented the dynamic, growing forces of the early seventeenth century. The state form tended to decline into a source of supplementary revenue or labor which cheapened the costs of enterprise,[9] and the indigenous form had become a relic of the sixteenth century. In part, the proliferation of exploitative relations in "civil society," already under way in the late sixteenth century, reflected the expansion of society's "middle" strata. Lesser colonials, mestizos, and petty proprietors demanded Indian labor, but had never enjoyed substantial rights to the state's labor-tribute patrimony. To run farms, ranches, workshops, small mines, transport services, or other enterprises, the lesser citizens and residents of Huamanga had to innovate alternative modes of extraction. In part, too, the ability of colonials to develop such alternatives reflected changes in ayllu life which, by the 1600s, created a growing pool of poor peasants willing to serve new masters, work as wage laborers, and the like. And finally, native population decline affected the quantity of tribute and mita quotas that colonials could legally extract. Over time, one could expect a declining number of Indian tributaries to undermine the economic significance of the state's mita-tribute institutions.

Yet in truth, the causes listed above do not suffice to explain why Huamanga's colonials, especially the region's high elite, made such a rapid transition to new labor strategies in the early seventeenth century. Expansion of the "lesser colonial" sector, declining Indian demography, and the rise of a "voluntary" clientele of pauperized ayllu emigrants constitute partial explanations, but are especially inadequate in the case of rich, powerful families forced to resort to new strategies of exploitation. Unlike lesser colonials, high elites dominated access to the state's patrimony; political clout spared them, at first, the search for alternatives. Later, even the drop of the Indian population from its Toledan levels did not constitute the irresistible economic force it might appear to be at first sight. Presumably, Huamanga's powerful citizens could have used their "influence" to impede the downward adjustment of tributary counts, and to claim larger proportions, if necessary, of the tribute-mita quotas which remained. Huamanga's leading figures fought hard to maintain inflated quotas, and they had good reason to do so despite the growing availability of "voluntary" Indian laborers and dependents. Mita labor was cheaper, more intensely exploitable, and imposed no long-run responsibilities on the employer.[10] As long as the mita supplied reasonably plentiful and reliable labor, the desirability of alternatives was strictly limited.

In the end, the state form of extraction declined as dramatically as it did because the Indians' resistance made mita labor scarce and unreliable even for the elite. By the 1600s, Indians were forging judicial politics into a formidable weapon of ayllu defense. Huamanga's native peoples adapted to the rise of state-sponsored extraction by engaging in aggressive, persistent, often shrewd use of Spanish juridical institutions to lower legal quotas, delay delivery of specific corvées and tributes, disrupt production, and the like. Threatened with instability, legal entanglements, and a growing squeeze on their labor supply, elites had to resort to alternatives that might shield them from judicial politics, and assure more direct control over a clientele of laborers and dependents. Otherwise, colonial mines, obrajes, and agriculture — all of them labor-intensive operations — might decline into decadence. Whatever their preferences, from a narrow economic point of view, for mita labor, Huamanga's colonials found that ayllu attacks had rendered state-sponsored extraction less and less reliable. Increasingly, the labor problem impelled them to abandon old strategies in favor of private forms of exploitation.

The labor system which matured in early seventeenth-century Huamanga thus differed sharply from the one with which the colonials began. Exploitation had evolved in three distinct stages, and in each case the transition from one phase to the next bore witness to the impact of native resistance on colonial policies and strategies. In the 1560s, Indian activity led to a crisis of the colonial system as a whole. Politically, radical subversion (Taki Onqoy and other heresies or conspiracies) enjoyed widespread appeal, and certain Indian groups (the neo-Incas, the Huancas, and tribes on the peripheries of colonial settlement) held significant military potential. Economically, ayllu resistance blocked the huge infusion of cheap Indian labor needed to jolt the mining economy out of its moribund state. In the 1570s a powerful reformist state rescued the colonials and launched a new era of political control and economic prosperity. A half-century later, Indian resistance no longer threatened European hegemony or the social and economic structure as a whole. But conflict had continued, and native activity created a labor problem which, again, forced elites to modify social and economic strategies. Shortages, bottlenecks, and disruptions affecting specific enterprises, rather than a generalized crisis of colonial rule and extraction, rendered official Toledan institutions obsolete, and spurred a further evolution in Huamanga's history of labor.

A process of social conflict, then, shaped the contours of Huamanga's colonial economy, and of its labor system in particular. At bottom, a fundamental contradiction pitted against one another not simply opposed peoples or castes, but opposed classes in formation — on the one side the aristocrat-entrepreneurs who dominated both European and Indian society, on the other the indigenous peasantry who supplied the bulk of exploitable energy, on the sidelines or caught in between a colonial Indian elite and a sector of lesser colonials and petty producers. Within native society, struggles against expropriations of labor, tributes, and land affected the economic survival of the peasant majority most directly, and Indian resistance itself had a contradictory dimension related to the internal development of class forces. One tendency united kinfolk and their chiefs against the oppressions imposed upon peasant society; another differentiated the interests of Indian elites and commoners, transforming peasant victories against one form of extraction into a basis for alternative, competing extractions. An important aspect of peasant resistance, therefore, was the attempt to assert internal solidarities which strengthened defenses, and imposed pressures on Indians to remain loyal to their own people. The reluctance of kurakas to send large contingents of laborers to the mines in the 1560s, and the aggressive sabotage of extractive institutions in the early seventeenth century, were necessary elements of the attempt by chiefs to preserve or enhance their standing among peasant kinfolk.[11] In this sense, they represented a response to social pressures from below.

The story of Huamanga's first century of colonization reveals a history not simply of native defeat, victimization, and exploitation. It is also a tale of resistance, partial victories, and the changing terms of oppression. The peasants in the end succumbed to the hegemony of a colonial ruling class, but they also made great inroads against their most hated burden, the colonial mita. Though Indians were incapable of doing away with the exploitative structure as a whole, their actions forced crises, innovations, and reforms which determined the specific forms and limits that their exploitation took. Today, an indigenous peasantry faces not the aristocrat-entrepreneurs of early modern Europe, but capitalist entrepreneurs and corporations of the modern world. In this new context, the challenge of conquest continues, and is Huamanga's most enduring heritage.

Reference Material

Appendix A

Debts, Wages, and Work in Castrovirreyna, 1597–1603

Table A.1 lists the work-days, wages, and debts recorded for 107 mitayos from Lucanas (Lucanas Laramati, Lucanas Andamarcas, and Soras) in six mining mitas at Castrovirreyna during the years 1597–1603. The six mitas whose wage records are available in the extant documentation are dated as follows: December 1597 to March 1598, August to November 1598, August to November 1602, December 1602 to March 1603, April to August 1603, and September to December 1603. Wage credits were listed for all 1,724 Lucanas mitayos in the six mitas, but debt figures were available only for 107 individuals who died or fled during mita service. The work-days may reflect production quotas rather than actual days of labor; wages were 2.75 reales per work-day (3 reales minus .25 reales automatically deducted to fund the state's administrative expenses). The figures in Table A.1 provided the data on debts and wages summarized in Tables 4.3 and 4.4, and discussed in Chapter 4.

Table A.1. Debts, wages, and work in Castrovirreyna, 1597–1603

Case	Workdays	Wages (reales)	Debts (reales)	Debts as % of wages
1.	10	28	0	0.0
2.	30	83	0	0.0
3.	8	22	0	0.0
4.	3	8	0	0.0
5.	18	50	24	48.0
6.	16	44	24	54.5
7.	7	19	0	0.0
8.	25	69	8	11.6
9.	25	69	0	0.0
10.	17	47	0	0.0
11.	14	39	32	82.1
12.	12	33	32	97.0

197

Case (cont.)	Workdays (cont.)	Wages (reales) (cont.)	Debts (reales) (cont.)	Debts as % of wages (cont.)
13.	8.5	23	24	104.3
14.	17	47	36	76.6
15.	25	69	68	98.6
16.	19	52	12	23.1
17.	31	85	24	28.2
18.	52	143	148	103.5
19.	45	124	124	100.0
20.	67	184	182	98.9
21.	59	162	160	98.8
22.	55	151	152	100.7
23.	59	162	160	98.8
24.	53	146	146	100.0
25.	45	124	148	119.4
26.	16	44	44	100.0
27.	41	113	60	53.1
28.	8	22	24	109.1
29.	11	30	44	146.7
30.	30	83	84	101.2
31.	57	157	156	99.4
32.	53	146	156	106.8
33.	60	165	164	99.4
34.	48	132	72	54.5
35.	74.5	205	204	99.5
36.	74.5	205	204	99.5
37.	35	96	28	29.2
38.	28.5	78	24	30.8
39.	6	17	0	0.0
40.	7	19	0	0.0
41.	27.5	76	54	71.1
42.	10	28	22	78.6
43.	9	25	22	88.0
44.	15	41	0	0.0
45.	29	80	24	30.0
46.	28	77	56	72.7
47.	80	220	108	49.1
48.	76	209	120	57.4
49.	48	132	32	24.2
50.	30	83	48	57.8
51.	42	116	100	86.2
52.	27.5	76	48	63.2
53.	27.5	76	48	63.2
54.	64	176	112	63.6
55.	71.5	197	0	0.0
56.	14	39	0	0.0
57.	30	83	60	72.3
58.	47	129	96	74.4

Case (cont.)	Workdays (cont.)	Wages (reales) (cont.)	Debts (reales) (cont.)	Debts as % of wages (cont.)
59.	28	77	52	67.5
60.	31	85	0	0.0
61.	9	25	31	124.0
62.	32	88	52	59.1
63.	37	102	48	47.1
64.	37	102	60	58.8
65.	23	63	44	69.8
66.	28	77	24	31.2
67.	18	50	48	96.0
68.	18	50	48	96.0
69.	12	33	24	72.7
70.	63	173	76	43.9
71.	23	63	56	88.9
72.	54	149	48	32.2
73.	44	121	120	99.2
74.	16	44	24	54.5
75.	23	63	48	76.2
76.	12	33	24	72.7
77.	23	63	48	76.2
78.	24	66	40	60.6
79.	14	39	32	82.1
80.	21	58	0	0.0
81.	5	14	12	85.7
82.	44	121	56	46.3
83.	66	182	60	33.0
84.	6	17	0	0.0
85.	10	28	0	0.0
86.	6	17	0	0.0
87.	33	91	48	52.7
88.	42	116	72	62.1
89.	32	88	80	90.9
90.	33.5	92	36	39.1
91.	34	94	36	38.3
92.	18	50	36	72.0
93.	4	11	0	0.0
94.	54	149	98	65.8
95.	102	281	48	17.1
96.	43.5	120	124	103.3
97.	74	204	104	51.0
98.	32	88	88	100.0
99.	34.5	95	64	67.4
100.	10	28	16	57.1
101.	74.5	205	92	44.9
102.	33	91	24	26.4
103.	31	85	88	103.5
104.	30	83	80	96.4

Case (cont.)	Workdays (cont.)	Wages (reales) (cont.)	Debts (reales) (cont.)	Debts as % of wages (cont.)
105.	58	160	84	52.5
106.	55	151	84	55.6
107.	68	187	96	51.3

Sources: Cases 1–38, mita of December 1597 to March 1598, BNP, A233, 1598; cases 39–44, mita of August to November 1598, BNP, A230, [1598]; cases 45–68, mita of August to November 1602, BNP, B968, 1602; cases 69–86, mita of December 1602 to March 1603, BNP, B971, 1603; cases 87–94, mita of April to August 1603, BNP, B895, 1603; cases 95–107, mita of September to December 1603, BNP, B806, 1604.

Appendix B

Guide to Colonial Land Tenure Documents for Huamanga

Patterns of European enterprise and land tenure emerged from an enormous number of documents, and I can offer only a partial guide to them here. I traced varying intensity of European penetration by grouping properties according to geographical zones, and within the zones, by earliest recorded dates of European tenure. The zones were: Huamanga (city and surrounding environs), Huanta-Angaraes (including the rich "isla de Tayacaja" district bounded by the southern Mantaro river system in northern Angaraes), Huancavelica-Castrovirreyna, Vilcashuamán, Lucanas, and (less systematically) Andahuaylas and Parinacochas. Land titles from the Huamanga region are abundant in the AGN, especially in the Títulos de propieded (TP) section. Relevant documents from the latter section are:

> C.8, 1568; C. 10, 1576; C. 21, 1594; C. 26, 1589; C. 28, 1596; C. 39, 1595;
> C. 54, 1598; C. 62, 1615; C. 63, 1629; C. 69, 1639; C. 132, 1604; C. 138, 1627;
> C. 168, 1627; C. 169, 1631; C. 174, 1647; C. 207, 1622; C. 239, 1615; C. 245,
> 1648; C. 246, 1651; C. 260, 1614; C. 261, 1616; C. 266, 1623; C. 305, 1604;
> C. 306, 1606; C. 311, 1636; C. 332, 1596; C. 335, 1627; C. 349, 1602; C. 370,
> 1607; C. 371, 1606; C. 380, 1659; C. 388, 1636; C. 642, 1627–1698; C. 645,
> 1637; C. 663, 1618; C. 665, 1650; C. 682, 1602; C. 685, 1641; C. 747, 1625.

The AGN documents may be supplemented by transactions recorded in the notarial books of the ADA, PN collection. Also valuable are documents from the BNP, whose "Astete Concha" manuscripts include very extensive data from Huamanga. I found the following BNP manuscripts especially useful:

> A393, 1594; A473, 1597; B75, 1626; B405, 1669; B733, 1625; B846, 1618;
> B890, 1616; B1042, 1627; B1111, 1637; B1227, 1648; B1231, 1644; B1516, 1633;
> B1525, 1647; Z303, 1586; Z304, 1591; Z309, 1600; Z312, 1594; Z313, 1616;
> Z315, 1686; Z323, 1616; Z335, 1631; Z339, 1626; Z428, 1574; Z436, 1595;
> Z439, 1619; Z888, 1646; Z891, 1594; Z1067, 1685; Z1088, 1656; Z1124, 1631;
> Z1268, 1590.

The composite picture yielded by the AGN, ADA, and BNP can be confirmed independently. The value of church tithes varied roughly in accordance with a zone's commercial value and degree of European penetration; seventeenth-century tithes recorded for the Huamanga region in the AAA (Siglo XVII, Estante 1, Exp. 18; Estante 3, Exp. 2; Exp. 21; Estante 4, Exp. 10) corroborate the subregional variations suggested by Map 3 (see Chapter 4). Also useful are descriptions of Huamanga's various districts, in *RGI,* 181–248; AGI, V, Lima 308, Description of the Bishopric of Huamanga, 1624–1625 (based on the inspection of Bishop Verdugo); Antonio Vázquez de Espinosa (1629), *Compendio y descripción de las Indias Occidentales,* ed. Charles Upson Clark (Washington, D.C., 1948), 486–507. I suspect that the colonial titles included in the RPIA (and the equivalent land registry in Huancavelica) would confirm the general pattern, though I was not able to use them to trace European land tenure.

Appendix C

Official Counts of Huamanga Tributary Populations, 1570–1635

Table C.1 compiles demographic counts discussed in Chapter 5, and illustrated in Figure 5.1. The repartimientos listed correspond to the twenty-three "core" districts of Huamanga mentioned in Chapter 4 and in Table 4.1, *plus* Sancos, for which separate data was available. The inclusion of Sancos explains why the regional tributary count given for 1570–1575 is slightly higher in Chapter 5 (Figure 5.1) than in Chapter 4. The tributary figures exclude kurakas officially exempted from tribute and mita duty.

Table C.1. Official counts of Huamanga tributary populations, 1570–1635

	1570–75	1596–00	1601–05	1606–10	1611–15	1616–20	1621–25	1626–30	1631–35
Soras	2,441	2,395		1,956					
Lucanas Laramati	2,793			1,736			793	369	286[a]
Lucanas Andamarcas	2,065			1,530				501	444
Angaraes (2)[b]	1,842			1,288[c]					
Guayllay	662			707[c]					
Calamarca	117			89[c]					
Quiguares orejones	185			168	149				
Huaros	321			160[c]			118	98	
Guaytará	1,073			771[c]					
Huachos Chocorvos	683			572	435				
Quinua	876	689							
Parija	1,500	1,431[c]							183
Caviñas	102	91	71[c]						
Angaraes de Hontiveros	902	473[c]	473[c]						
Tayacaja	793	396[c]	396[c]						

	1570–75 (cont.)	1596–00 (cont.)	1601–05 (cont.)	1606–10 (cont.)	1611–15 (cont.)	1616–20 (cont.)	1621–25 (cont.)	1626–30 (cont.)	1631–35 (cont.)
Quichuas y Aymaraes	1,964	1,734		1,303				552[d]	
Tanquihuas	739	510					242	181	
Totos	378	207					132[d]	64[d]	
Papres	578	546	477						
Pacomarca	595	380							
Hanan Chilques	772		619						
Hurín Chilques	600		413						
Sancos	185						139	94	

[a]Modified by correction in 1636 of the 1635 count of 300 tributaries.

[b]*Two* Angaraes repartimientos; figures listed are their combined counts.

[c]Best estimate of revisita date; when unable to specify the five-year interval with certainty, I have listed data in the two most likely intervals.

[d]Figure based on average of two counts during the five-year interval.

Sources: Figures are based on tributary counts, total mita quotas, and revisita dates drawn from the following: *Tasa de la visita general de Francisco de Toledo (1570–1575)* (Lima, 1975), ed. Noble David Cook, 260–75, 276–80; Antonio Vázquez de Espinosa (1629), *Compendio y descripción de las Indias Occidentales,* ed. Charles Upson Clark (Washington, D.C., 1948), 653–55; BNP, B1505, 1644, ff. 3v–5r, 10v–16r, 24r, 26r–30r; BNP, B1441, 1634, ff. 34r–35r, 46r–47v; AGN, DI, Leg. 4, C. 62, 1616; BNP, B1079, 1629, esp. ff. 61r–62r; AGN, JR, Leg. 24, C. 65, 1618, f. 295r and the "Testimonio de la retasa" directly following; BNP, A18, 1599, loose folio recording changes in total mita of various districts; B620, 1636; AGN, JR, Leg. 23, C. 62, 1617, ff. 30r–31r, 43v–44r, 56v–57v, 69v–70v, 82v–83v, 95v–96r, 105v–106r, 113v–114v, 126v–128r; BNP, B1159, 1629, ff. 3r–5r.

Appendix D

Asientos of Indians in the City of Huamanga, 1570–1640

The three tables in this appendix list data from seventy-eight asientos, labor contracts joining Indians to prospective employers and masters, often for a year at a time. The contracts were found in a survey of the ADA, PN series of notary books, and are discussed at some length in Chapter 6. As the reader will note in these tables and in Chapter 6, asientos hired Indians for a variety of services and under diverse circumstances. The remuneration frequently involved both monetary and nonmonetary aspects, and in a number of cases, the latter were more important. For the purposes of this book, I divided the asientos into three categories. Table D.1 lists asientos with European employers for "unskilled" or general work which earned Indians relatively low pay: agriculture, ranching, domestic service, apprenticeship, and the like. Table D.2 lists Indians hired by Europeans for "skilled" or special services drawing, usually, a higher monetary remuneration. Table D.3 lists asientos contracting Indians to serve *Indian* employers. The tables list the year of the contract; the place of origin (original spelling preserved) of the hired native; the age/gender of the laborer; the monetary component of the promised compensation, at an annual rate of pesos of 8–9 reales (not all contracts were clear on this point); the service period, in years or months, specified in the contract; and comments. In Table D.2, the "comment" column tells the occupation or kind of work performed by the hired Indian. In Table D.3, the "comment" specifies, among other things, the socioeconomic identification of the Indian *employer*.

Table D.1. Asientos with European masters for "unskilled" work, 1570–1640

No.	Year	Origin	Age/ Gender	Yearly pesos	Service period	Comment
1.	1577	Carauantes[a]	boy	0	1 yr.	
2.	1585	San Juan (Lucanas)	man	12[b]	1 yr.	tanner's apprentice
3.	1585	Socos	man	20	1 yr.	tanner's apprentice

No. (cont.)	Year (cont.)	Origin (cont.)	Age/ Gender (cont.)	Yearly pesos (cont.)	Service period (cont.)	Comment (cont.)
4.	1585	Valenzuela[c]	woman	25	1 yr.	
5.	1585	Sanco	man	12	1 yr.	
6.	1585	Cangallo	boy	0[b]	2 yrs.	tailor's apprentice
7.	1596	Guanta	man	25	1 yr.	
8.	1596	Guanta	man	25	1 yr.	
9.	1596	Mañueco[c]	man	12	3 yrs.	prior debt
10.	1596	Omasayos Indians	man	24	1 yr.	
11.	1596	Guamanga	man	12	1 yr.	
12.	1596	Mollebamba (Cuzco)	man	20	1 yr.	
13.	1596	Cuicara	man	12	1 yr.	
14.	1596	Guanca Guanca	man	12	1 yr.	
15.	1596	?	woman	6	1 yr.	
16.	1596	Andaguaylas	man	12[b]	1 yr.	receives land
17.	1596	Guánuco	man	0[b]	1 yr.	carpenter's apprentice
18.	1596	Lucanas	woman	8	1 yr.	hired with No. 17
19.	1596	Arequipa	man	6[b]	2 yrs.	carpenter's apprentice
20.	1597	Santiago (Chocorvos)	man	12	1 yr.	hired by Dominicans
21.	1598	Chumbe (Parinacochas)	man	0[b]	2 yrs.	
22.	1598	Vilcasguamán	man	12	2 yrs.	
23.	1598	Vincho	man	20	1 yr.	
24.	1601	Ocros	man	12(?)[b]	?	cowboy; prior debt
25.	1601	Cuenca	man	12	1 yr.	
26.	1601	Quilla	woman	6	1 yr.	hired by woman
27.	1602	Cayara	man	0[b]	2 yrs.	tailor's apprentice
28.	1602	Sarhua	man	12	6 mos.	
29.	1602	Laramati	woman	6	2 yrs.	
30.	1602	Acoria	woman	6	4 yrs.	
31.	1609	Pausa	man	18	2 yrs.	prior debt
32.	1609	Xauxa (valle)	man	8	1 yr.	ranching
33.	1609	Larcaya (Soras)	man	12	2 yrs.	
34.	1609	Vischongo	man	40[b]	1 yr.	
35.	1609	Guamanga	boy	12	1 yr.	
36.	1609	San Juan de Cayara	man	27[d]	1 yr.	
37.	1609	?	man	15	1 yr.	
38.	1609	Canaria	man	12[b]	2 yrs.	receives land
39.	1609	Xulcamarca	man	30	1 yr.	
40.	1619	Guanta	man	15	1 yr.	tend to goats

No. (cont.)	Year (cont.)	Origin (cont.)	Age/ Gender (cont.)	Yearly pesos (cont.)	Service period (cont.)	Comment (cont.)
41.	1619	Ticllas	man	30[e]	6 mos.	hired by Augustinians
42.	1619	Ticllas	man	30[e]	6 mos.	hired by Augustinians
43.	1619	Santo Miguel Pichigura	man	48	6 mos.	
44.	1625	Guillén de Mendoza[c]	man	12	2 yrs.	cowboy
45.	1625	Cangallo	man	30	1 yr.	
46.	1625	Guamanga	man	37[f]	1 yr.	prior debt
47.	1625	Guambalpa	man	12	2 yrs.	ranching
48.	1625	Sanco	man	12	1 yr.	cowboy
49.	1625	Ocros	man	12	4 yrs.	cowboy
50.	1636	Guamanga	man	0[b]	2 yrs.	shoemaker's apprentice

[a]repartimiento district.
[b]Besides routinely promised nonmonetary and subsistence items, there was another significant compensation in kind.
[c]encomienda of.
[d]includes promise to rent an Indian replacement for the mita (15 pesos).
[e]salary of 2 reales per day of work, conservative estimate of 120 work-days a year.
[f]includes promise to pay off a prior debt (to a third party) of 25 pesos.
Sources: These contracts, in the order of their chronological listing, are in ADA, PN, Romo 1577, f. 113v; Cárdenas 1585, ff. 6r, 7r, 44v, 92r, 68v; Peña 1596, ff. 324r, 324r, 252v, 248r, 296r, 281v, 284v, 55v, 292v, 294v, 303r, 303r, 289v, 318r; Soria 1598, ff. 88r, 155r, 716r; Soria 1593/*1601*, ff. 46v, 210v, 195v; Padilla *1602*/1613, ff. 317v, 319r, 402r, 436v; Palma 1609, ff. 82v, 104r, 389r, 395r, 175v, 207r, 310r, 316r, 323r; Palma 1619, ff. 549r, 655v, 655v, 621r; Palma 1625, ff. 174r, 269r, 558r, 824r, 851v, 891v; Silvera/*Mesagil* 1636–1637, f. 329v.

Table D.2. Asientos with European masters for "skilled" work, 1570–1640

No.	Year	Origin	Age/ Gender	Yearly pesos	Service period	Comment
1.	1577	Xauxa (valle)	man	35[a]	2 yrs.	tutor of children
2.	1596	Puerto Viejo	man	50[a]	1 yr.	arriero
3.	1596	Córdova[b]	man	40	1 yr.	majordomo on ranch
4.	1597	Cuzco	man	50[a]	1 yr.	butcher (?)
5.	1598	Guamanga	man	60	1 yr.	shopkeeper
6.	1609	Chuche	man	50[a]	1 yr.	tanner
7.	1609	San Gerónimo de Raure	man	60[c]	1 yr.	tanner
8.	1609	Guamanga	man	130	1 yr.	arriero
9.	1609	?	woman	100[a]	1 yr.	church aide

No. (cont.)	Year (cont.)	Origin (cont.)	Age/ Gender (cont.)	Yearly pesos (cont.)	Service period (cont.)	Comment (cont.)
10.	1613	?	man	80	1 yr.	arriero
11.	1613	Chile	man	130[a]	1 yr.	arriero
12.	1613	Tambillo	man	80	6 mos.	arriero
13.	1619	Tiqua	woman	35[c]	7–8 mos.	nurse a baby
14.	1619	Guamanga	woman	24[a]	2 yrs.	nurse and tend a baby
15.	1619	Espíritu Santo	man	120	6 mos.	arriero
16.	1625	Cabana	man	40[a]	1 yr.	tanner
17.	1625	Condesuyos (Arequipa)	man	144	6 mos.	arriero
18.	1627	Condesuyos (Cuzco)	man	100	1 yr.	arriero
19.	1630	Guamanga	man	120[a]	6 mos.	arriero
20.	1630	Xauxa (valle)	man	120	3 mos.	arriero

[a]Besides routinely promised nonmonetary and subsistence items, there was another significant compensation in kind.

[b]encomienda of.

[c]14 pesos for 7–8 months of work plus cost of renting a substitute Indian to serve a mita de plaza.

Sources: These contracts, in the order of their chronological listing, are in ADA, PN, Romo 1577, f. 62r; Peña 1596, ff. 310r, 111r, 320r; Soria 1598, f. 154v; Palma 1609, ff. 103r, 132r, 164v, 327r; Padilla 1602/*1613,* ff. 64v, 150r, 183r; Palma 1619, ff. 9v, 266r, 290r; Palma 1625, ff. 115v, 379r; Navarrete 1615–1618/*1627*/1630, f. 622r; Morales 1630, ff. 290r, 332r.

Table D.3. Asientos with Indian masters, 1570–1640

No.	Year	Origin	Age/ Gender	Yearly pesos	Service period	Comment
1.	1596	Cancha	man	12	?	hired by kuraka; prior debt
2.	1619	?	boy	12[a]	1 yr.	apprentice of master shoemaker
3.	1619	Guamanga	boy	0[a]	1 yr.	apprentice of master shoemaker
4.	1619	Canaria	man	30	1 yr.	aide to master curer of hides
5.	1619	Sancos	man	100	6 mos.	arriero hired by arriero/ merchant
6.	1625	Canaria	man	20	?	hired by woman; prior debt; receives land

No. (*cont.*)	Year (*cont.*)	Origin (*cont.*)	Age/ Gender (*cont.*)	Yearly pesos (*cont.*)	Service period (*cont.*)	Comment (*cont.*)
7.	1636	Guamanga	boy	13[a]	1 yr.	aide to master shoemaker
8.	1639	?	man	0[a]	1 yr.	aide to master chair-maker/ saddler

[a]Besides routinely promised nonmonetary and subsistence items, there was another significant compensation in kind.

Sources: These contracts, in the order of their chronological listing, are in ADA, PN, Peña 1596, f. 266r; Palma 1619, ff. 225v, 314v, 315r, 513r; Palma 1625, f. 707r; Silvera/*Mesagil* 1636–1637, f. 390r; Mesagil 1637–1639, f. 382r.

Notes

ABBREVIATIONS USED IN NOTES AND BIBLIOGRAPHY

AAA	Archivo Arzobispal de Ayacucho
ADA	Archivo Departamental de Ayacucho
ADA, PN	ADA, Protocolos Notariales
AGI	Archivo General de Indias (Seville)
AGN	Archivo General de la Nación (Lima)
AGN, DI	AGN, Derecho Indígena
AGN, JR	AGN, Juicios de Residencias
AGN, TP	AGN, Títulos de Propiedad
BMA	Biblioteca Municipal de Ayacucho
BNP	Biblioteca Nacional del Perú, Sala de Investigaciones (Lima)
CDIAO	*Colección de documentos inéditos relativos al descubrimiento, conquista, y organización de las antiguas posesiones españolas de América y Oceania,* 42 vols. (Madrid, 1864–1884).
CDIE	*Colección de documentos inéditos para la historia de España,* 113 vols. (Madrid, 1842–1945).
HAHR	*Hispanic American Historical Review*
HC	Harkness Collection, Library of Congress (Washington, D.C.)
RGI	Marcos Jiménez de la Espada, ed., *Relaciones Geográficas de Indias — Peru,* vols. 1–2, reprinted in *Biblioteca de Autores Españoles,* vol. 183 (Madrid, 1965).
RPIA	Registro de Propiedad Inmueble de Ayacucho
YC	Latin American Collection, Yale University, Sterling Library, Department of Manuscripts and Archives (New Haven, Ct.)

CHAPTER 1: PRE-COLUMBIAN LANDSCAPES

1 Wendell C. Bennet, "The Andean Highlands: An Introduction," in *Handbook of South American Indians,* ed. Julian H. Steward (7 vols., Washington, D.C., 1946–

59), 2:2. For a guide to titles of manuscripts cited in notes throughout this book, see the Bibliography.

2 For a fuller discussion of Andean ecology, see Javier Pulgar Vidal, *Las ocho regiones naturales del Perú* (Lima, 1946); Jaime Rivera Palomino, *Geografía general de Ayacucho* (Ayacucho, 1971), especially the maps on 58/59 and 66/67.

For sixteenth century descriptions of ecology and economic potentials in the Huamanga region, see Damián de la Bandera (1557), "Relación general de la disposición y calidad de la provincia de Guamanga," *RGI,* 176, 177, 179; Pedro de Carabajal (1586), "Descripción fecha de la provincia de Vilcas Guaman," *RGI,* 206-18; Pedro de Ribera y Antonio de Chaves y de Guevara (1586), "Relación de la ciudad de Guamanga y sus terminos," *RGI,* 182-83, 192; Luis de Monzón et al. (1586), "Descripción de la tierra del repartimiento de los Rucanas Antamarcas," *RGI,* 238, 244-47; id. (1586), "Descripción de la tierra del repartimiento de Atunrucana y Laramati," *RGI,* 227-30, 232-34; id. (1586), "Descripción de la tierra del repartimiento de Atunsora," *RGI,* 220-21, 223-24.

3 See AGN, DI, Leg. 6, C. 107, 1642, f. 14r; Juan Polo de Ondegardo (1571), "Relación de los fundamentos acerca del notable daño que resulta de no guardar a los indios sus fueros," in *Colección de libros y documentos referentes a la historia del Perú* (4 vols., Lima, 1916), 3:71.

4 On the consequences of this phenomenon for Andean soil cover, see Carl Troll, *Structure Soils, Solifluction, and Frost Climates of the Earth* (Wilmette, Ill., 1958).

5 See the case studies in John V. Murra, *Formaciones económicas y políticas del mundo andino* (Lima, 1975), 59-115. Cf. Domingo de Santo Tomás to the King, Lima, 1 July 1550, in *La iglesia de España en el Perú,* ed. Emilio Lissón Chaves (4 vols., Seville, 1943-1946), 1: no. 4, 195-96; Bandera (1557), "Relación general," 176. My discussion of Andean political economy and settlement patterns relies heavily on the pioneering work of Murra, whose essays were collected in *Formaciones.* Murra suggested many of the terms ("archipelago," "verticality," "outlier," etc.) now common in Andean scholarship. I am also indebted to Karen Spalding for numerous conversations, and for sharing a manuscript entitled "The Web of Production."

6 AGN, JR, Leg. 24, C. 65, 1618, ff. 252r-v, 268r; RPIA, tomo 13, partida LV, 331; Monzón et al. (1586), "Descripción . . . de Atunsora," 224.

7 AGN, DI, Leg. 4, C. 61, 1616, ff. 86r-v, 93v-97r; RPIA, tomo 21, partida XLVII, 459; Bandera (1557), "Relación general," 176-77. Cf. Murra, *Formaciones,* 64, 70-71, 78-80; Karl Marx, *Pre-Capitalist Economic Formations,* trans. Jack Cohen, ed. E. J. Hobsbawm (New York, 1965), 70.

8 Contrast the pattern found in coastal societies by María Rostworowski de Diez Canseco, *Etnía y sociedad: costa peruana prehispánica* (Lima, 1977), 221-24, 231, 235, 260-62.

9 Marriage outside the ayllu was depicted in this way in AGN, DI, Leg. 6, C. 119, 1648, ff. 110v, 111r, 111v, 115v, 120v, 121r, 125r.

10 On the simultaneously endogamous and exogenous orientation of ayllu lineages, and the potential for tracing descent matrilineally or patrilineally, see R. T. Zuidema, *The Ceque System of Cuzco* (Leiden, 1964), 26-27, n. 10; Billie Jean Is-

bell, "Parentesco andino y reciprocidad," in *Reciprocidad e intercambio en los andes peruanos,* ed. Giorgio Alberti and Enrique Mayer (Lima, 1974), 132.

11 See, for example, Francisco de Avila (c. 1598), *Dioses y hombres de Huarochirí,* trans. José María Arguedas (Lima, 1966), 63, 65, 139, 141; and the lists of ancestor-gods in Cristóbal de Albornoz (c. 1582), "Instrucción para descubrir todas las guacas del Pirú y sus camayos y haciendas," ed. Pierre Duviols, in *Journal de la Société des Américanistes* 56. 1 (1967), 20-21.

12 I am heavily indebted in this discussion to Karl Marx's comments on property relations in "Asiatic" societies. *Pre-Capitalist Economic Formations,* 69-70, 75, 80-82, 89-90.

13 Karen Spalding, *De indio a campesino: cambios en la estructura social del Perú colonial* (Lima, 1974), 69; John V. Murra, "The Economic Organization of the Inca State" (Ph.D. diss., University of Chicago, 1956), 72, 251, 308. Murra's thesis is also available in Spanish: *La organización económica del estado Inca* (Mexico, 1978).

14 ADA, Corregimiento, Causas Ordinarias, [Leg. 2], 1678, ff. 937v-938r.

15 See Polo, quoted in Murra, *Formaciones,* 28. For a helpful typology of reciprocity exchanges in contemporary Andean society, see Enrique Mayer, "Las reglas de juego en la reciprocidad andina," in *Reciprocidad,* ed. Alberti and Mayer, 45-62.

16 Diego González Holguín (1608), *Vocabulario de la lengua general de todo el Perú llamada qquichua o del Inca,* ed. Juan G. N. Lobato (Lima, 1901), 41.

17 The modifying particle *camayok* denotes a caretaker. González Holguín (1608), *Vocabulario . . . del Inca,* 49.

18 Entry added by the editor, Juan G. N. Lobato, ibid., 362.

19 Ibid., 362, 280, for all definitions.

20 See Tristan Platt, "Symétries en miroir. Le concept de *yanantin* chez les Macha de Bolivie," *Annales. Économies, Sociétés, Civilisations* 33 (1978), esp. 1106, n. 13; Paul Bohannan, *Justice and Judgment among the Tiv* (Oxford, 1957), 195 (cited by Platt); Meyer Fortes, *Oedipus and Job in West African Religion* (Cambridge, 1959), reprinted in *The Anthropology of Folk Religion,* ed. Charles Leslie (New York, 1960), 33. Cf. the remarkable short story of Enrique López Albújar, "Ushanan-Jampi," in his *Cuentos andinos* (Lima, 1920), 43-56.

21 Polo (1571), "Relación de los fundamentos," 115-16.

22 Murra, *Formaciones,* 34.

23 Avila (c. 1598), *Dioses y hombres,* 181.

24 I am grateful to Karen Spalding for making available her notes to colonial land litigation records. These document internal rivalries within a network of larger groupings and loyalties. Spalding found many costly court fights between ayllus of the same *waranqa* (a group of about 1000 units). In a fight with a lineage from another waranqa, however, an ayllu could expect to press its claims with the backing of its entire waranqa despite the intra-waranqa struggles.

25 See Monzón et al. (1586), "Descripción . . . de los Rucanas Antamarcas," 239, 241, 243; id. (1586), "Descripción . . . de Atunrucanas y Laramati," 228, 230, 232; id. (1586), "Descripción . . . de Atunsora," 221.

26 The Aymara verb is *aynisitha.* Ludovico Bertonio (1612), *Vocabulario de la lengua Aymara,* ed. Julio Platzmann (2 vols., Leipzig, 1879), 2:29.

27 See Monzón et al. (1586), "Descripción . . . de Atunrucana y Laramati," 231; Bandera (1557), "Relación general," 178–79; BNP, A371, 1594, *passim.* Although I know of no cases of female chiefs in Huamanga *before* the Spanish conquest, new research suggests the possibility that future scholarship will uncover extensive patterns of female authority and chieftainship. See Irene Silverblatt, "Andean Women in the Inca Empire," *Feminist Studies,* 4.3 (1978), 37–59; Silverblatt, "Andean Women Under Spanish Rule," in *Women and Colonization: Anthropological Perspectives,* ed. Mona Etienne and Eleanor Leacock (New York, 1980), 149–85.

28 See Bandera (1557), "Relación general," 178; Carabajal (1586), "Descripción . . . de Vilcas Guaman," 206; Monzón et al. (1586), "Descripción . . . de Atunrucana y Laramati," 231.

29 *Formaciones,* 215–16.

30 Ibid., 211–21, 225–42; Bandera (1557), "Relación general," 178.

31 Cf. Nathan Wachtel, *Sociedad e ideología: ensayos de historia y antropología andinas* (Lima, 1973), 59–78, esp. 64–69; Maurice Godelier, *Economía, fetichismo y religión en las sociedades primitivas* (Madrid, 1974), 176–97, esp. 188–89, 183; Godelier, "Modo de producción asiático y los esquemas marxistas de evolución de las sociedades," in Godelier et al., *Sobre el modo de producción asiático* (Barcelona, 1969), 20–24, 30–31, 46–54.

32 Monzón et al. (1586), "Descripción . . . de los Rucanas Antamarcas," 243. On the symbolic importance of cloth in Andean society, see Murra, *Formaciones,* 145–70.

33 Cf. Marx, *Pre-Capitalist Economic Formations,* 70, on more democratic or despotic forms of "oriental" organization; Godelier, "Modo de producción asiático," 55; Godelier, *Economía, fetichismo y religión,* 182, 191–92.

34 María Rostworowski de Diez Canseco has shown that coastal peoples frequently rejected the sierra ideal of "vertical" self-sufficiency — developing trade networks as an alternative — in order to rid themselves of onerous relationships with highland peoples. *Etnía y sociedad,* 21–95.

35 For histories of Huamanga before the Incas, Luis Guillermo Lumbreras, *Las fundaciones de Huamanga. Hacia una prehistoria de Ayacucho* (Lima, 1974); Medardo Purizaga Vega, *El estado regional en Ayacucho (período intermedio tardío, 1200–1470)* (Huancayo, 1972). See also Fernando de Santillán (1563), "Relación del origen, descendencia, política y gobierno de los Incas," in *Tres relaciones de antigüedades peruanas* (Asunción del Paraguay, 1950), 45.

36 For discussion of the impact of Inca conquest on community elites and local society, see R. T. Zuidema, "Algunos problemas etnohistóricos del Departamento de Ayacucho," *Wamani* 1 (Ayacucho, 1966), 68–75; John Earls and Irene Silverblatt, "Ayllus y etnías de la región Pampas-Qaracho. El impacto del imperio incaico" (paper delivered at the III Congreso Peruano del Hombre y la Cultura Andina, Lima, 1977); Spalding, *De indio a campesino,* 71–72.

37 BNP, Z313, 1616, ff. 164r–165r; ADA, PN, Romo 1577, ff. 202r–204r. For a contract from another region (Huánuco, north of Huamanga) which required the approval of sixteen chiefs, see BNP, A455, 1571; cf. BNP, A236, 1597, ff. 20r, 22r; Marx, *Pre-Capitalist Economic Formations,* 70.

38 Monzón et al. (1586), "Descripción . . . de Atunrucana y Laramati," 228; Monzón et al. (1586), "Descripción . . . de los Rucanas Antamarcas," 239. Cf. Murra, *Formaciones*, 30, 34–35.

39 Particularly fierce struggles between nearby communities of interspersed ethnic groups south of the Río Pampas, from the sixteenth century to the present, are documented in RPIA, tomo 5, partida VI, 18–21; tomo 8, partida XL, 132–34; tomo 10, partida CXXIII, 404–9; tomo 10, partida CXL, 468–69; tomo 13, partida LV, 328–34; tomo 14, partida VI, 39–60; tomo 21; partida XLVII, 457–69.

40 Monzón et al. (1586), "Descripción . . . de Atunsora," 221, 222; id. (1586), "Descripción . . . de Atunrucanas y Laramati," 228, 232; id. (1586), "Descripción . . . de los Rucanas Antamarcas," 239; Carabajal (1586), "Descripción . . . de Vilcas Guaman," 206.

41 On multiethnic outliers and struggles for strategic resources, see Carabajal (1586), "Descripción . . . de Vilcas Guaman," 208, 209, 214, 215; Ribera y Chaves (1586), "Relación de la ciudad," 194; RPIA, tomo 13, partida LV, 331; ADA, Corregimiento, Causas Ordinarias, [Leg. 2], 1678, f. 940v; AGN, Minería, Leg. 2, Ayacucho 1622, f. 79r; AGN, DI, Leg. 1, C. 9, 1567; Leg. 2, C. 17, 1573, f. 178r. See also Murra, *Formaciones*, 67–69, 79–80. The first AGN, DI document cited is discussed and reprinted in Waldemar Espinoza Soriano, "La coca de los mitmas cayampis en el reino de Ancara. Siglo XVI," *Anales científicos de la Universidad Nacional del Centro del Perú* 2 (Huancayo, 1973), 7–67.

42 Centro de Colaboración Pedagógica Provincial . . . de Parinacochas, *Monografía de la Provincia de Parinacochas* (2 vols., Lima, 1950), 1: 47.

43 For the explanatory power of non-Western thought systems, see Claude Lévi-Strauss, *The Savage Mind* (Chicago, 1966); E. E. Evans-Pritchard, *Witchcraft, Oracles and Magic among the Azande* (Oxford, 1937); R. Horton, "African Traditional Thought and Western Science," *Africa* 37 (1967), 50–71, 155–87.

44 For a definition of huacas, see Juan de Matienzo (1567), *Gobierno del Perú*, ed. Guillermo Lohmann Villena, in *Travaux de l'Institut Français d'Etudes Andines* 11 (Paris, 1967), 129.

45 Pablo Joseph de Arriaga (1621), *La extirpación de la idolatría en el Perú*, ed. Horacio H. Urteaga (Lima, 1920), 21; Albornoz (c. 1582), "Instrucción para descubrir," 25–35.

46 Arriaga (1621), *La extirpación*, 22, 25, 27. When quoting from Arriaga, I have consulted the translation published by L. Clark Keating (Lexington, 1968).

47 Cf. Meyer Fortes's analysis of Tale ancestor cults in *Oedipus and Job*, in *Folk Religion*, ed. Leslie, 47.

48 Arriaga (1621), *La extirpación*, 27, 74, 140 for all quotations.

49 Avila (c. 1598), *Dioses y hombres*, 21, 47, 99, 141, 77; Juan Polo de Ondegardo (1554), "De los errores y supersticiones de los indios . . . ," in *Colección de libros y documentos*, III, 38; John H. Rowe, "Inca Culture at the Time of the Spanish Conquest," in *Handbook*, ed. Steward, 2:280–81.

50 Avila (c. 1598), *Dioses y hombres*, 130–35.

51 My discussion of ritual has benefitted from Clifford Geertz's suggestion that the social function of ritual is to unify a people's ethos and world view through the use of sacred symbols. Geertz defines ethos as a style or quality of social rela-

tions which implicitly includes certain ideas and values. World view is a more conceptual and objective "picture" of the way the universe works. Geertz, *The Interpretation of Cultures* (New York, 1973), 90, 127.

52 Arriaga (1621), *La extirpación*, 49–50; cf. Avila (c. 1598), *Dioses y hombres*, 62–79.

53 Arriaga (1621), *La extirpación*, 50–51.

54 For confirmation of the importance of the juncture of two rivers in Andean purification, see Polo (1554), "De los errores," 35; Cristóbal de Molina (1574), *Relación de las fábulas y ritos de los incas*, in *Las crónicas de los Molinas*, ed. Francisco A. Loayza (Lima, 1943), 83.

55 Rowe, "Inca Culture," 265–66; Murra, "Economic Organization," 157–58; Sally Falk Moore, *Power and Property in Inca Peru* (New York, 1958), 133. On special homes for major huacas in Huamanga, see Bandera (1557), "Relación general," 176.

56 On the connection between everyday material welfare and relationships with the gods, see Polo (1554), "De los errores," 8, 13–15; Molina, *Relación de las fábulas*, 83.

57 Albornoz (c. 1582), "Instrucción para descubrir," 37.

58 See Avila (c. 1598), *Dioses y hombres*, 47, 49, 149, 151; Felipe Guaman Poma de Ayala (1615), *Nueva corónica y buen gobierno* (Paris, 1936), 109, 137, 158, 286.

59 Arriaga (1621), *La extirpación*, 52.

60 Avila (c. 1598), *Dioses y hombres*, 39. For examples of the connection between physiological health and social relationships, see Molina (1574), *Relación de las fábulas*, 13–15, 33.

61 Arriaga (1621), *La extirpación*, 33, 52.

62 Ibid., 32, 33.

63 Murra, *Formaciones*, 221; Pedro de Cieza de León (1553), *El señorío de los Incas (2a parte de la crónica del Perú)*, ed. Carlos Araníbar (Lima, 1967), ch. 13. For a description of the *mochar* motion, see Polo (1554), "De los errores," 6.

64 Cf. Fortes, *Oedipus and Job*, in *Folk Religion*, ed. Leslie, 47.

65 "Relación de Amancebados, Hechiceros y Huacas" (1584), in *Las informaciones de Cristóbal de Albornoz: documentos para el estudio del Taki Onqoy*, ed. Luis Millones (Cuernavaca, 1971), 4/11–4/16, 4/22–4/27, 4/33, 4/36–4/38.

66 Arriaga (1621), *La extirpación*, 36.

67 See Ibid.; Avila (c. 1598), *Dioses y hombres*, 113; Polo (1554), "De los errores," 31.

68 Avila (c. 1598), *Dioses y hombres*, 51.

69 For data on Andean societies, see Avila (c. 1598), *Dioses y hombres*, 65, 73, 140–47; Rowe, "Inca Culture," 263. For important theoretical contributions based on African societies, see Victor Turner, *The Forest of Symbols: Aspects of Ndembu Ritual* (Ithaca, 1967), esp. ch. 1; A. R. Radcliffe-Brown, *Structure and Function in Primitive Society* (New York: Free Press ed., 1965), 90–116.

70 For a succinct example, see Avila (c. 1598), *Dioses y hombres*, 52–55.

71 Ibid., 111.

72 Pedro de Cieza de León (1553), *Parte primera de la crónica del Perú*, in *Biblioteca de autores españoles*, vol. 26 (Madrid, 1853), ch. 88; Cieza (1553), *El señorío*, chs. 47–48; Marqués del Risco (1684), "Descripción de la provincia de los Angaraes,"

RGI 202 (quote). See also Alfredo Torero, *El quechua y la historia social andina* (Lima, 1974), 151.

73 Zuidema, "Algunos problemas etnohistóricos," 68–75; Risco (1684), "Descripción . . . de los Angaraes," 202; AGN, DI, Leg. 1, C. 9, 1567, f. 5r; Earls and Silverblatt, "Ayllus y etnías"; BNP, Z303, 1586, ff. 148r, 149r, 149v, 150v; Carabajal (1586), "Descripción . . . de Vilcas Guaman," 218–19; Ribera y Chaves (1586), "Relación de la ciudad," 181.

74 See Murra, *Formaciones,* 169; Albornoz (c. 1582), "Instrucción para descubrir," 17, 20–21, 25, 35; Murra, "Economic Organization," 170; Godelier, *Economía, fetichismo y religión,* 183, 191–94.

75 Murra, "Economic Organization," 126, 250–309; Godelier, *Economía, fetichismo y religión,* 176–84. Cf. Bandera (1557), "Relación general," 179–80.

76 Bandera (1557), "Relación general," 179.

77 Diego Avila Briceño (1586), "Descripción y relación . . . de los Yauyos . . . ," *RGI,* 164; AGN, DI, Leg. 1, C. 9, 1567, esp. ff. 3v, 5r.

78 See Murra, "Economic Organization," 250–309.

79 Cieza (1553), *Parte primera,* ch. 88; Cieza (1553), *El señorío,* chs. 47–48; Risco (1684), "Descripción . . . de los Angaraes," 202; Poma de Ayala (1615), *Nueva corónica,* sketch on 155.

80 AGN, DI, Leg. 1, C. 9, 1567, f. 5r; Poma de Ayala (1615), *Nueva corónica,* 113–14, 377–78, 397. See also John V. Murra, "La guerre et les rébellions dans l'expansion de l'état inka," *Annales. Économies, Sociétés, Civilisations* 33 (1978), 927–35.

81 Poma de Ayala (1615), *Nueva corónica,* sketch on 333; Monzón et al. (1586), "Descripción . . . de Atunrucana y Laramati," 231; Monzón et al. (1586), "Descripción . . . de Atunsora," 222.

82 Cf. Godelier, "Modo de producción asiático," 22–23, 55.

83 For population figures from c. 1572 and comparisons with pre-conquest demography among the large Lucanas and Soras groups, see Noble David Cook, ed., *Tasa de la visita general de Francisco de Toledo (1570–1575)* (Lima, 1975), 260–65; Monzón et al. (1586), "Decripción . . . de los Rucanas Antamarcas," 238; id. (1586), "Descripción . . . de Atunrucana y Laramati," 227; id. (1586), "Descripción . . . de Atunsora," 221. Note also the discussion above of strong local attachments to closer household and ayllu relatives.

84 Juan Polo de Ondegardo (1561), "Informe . . . al Licenciado Briviesca de Muñatones . . . ," *Revista Histórica* 13 (Lima, 1940), 176.

85 Domingo de Santo Tomás to Council of Indies, Lima, 1 July 1550, in José María Vargas, *Fray Domingo de Santo Tomás, defensor y apóstol de los indios del Perú: su vida y escritos* (Quito, 1937), "Escritos": 12.

86 See Frederick Engels, "Supplement," in Karl Marx, *Capital,* ed. Engels (3 vols., New York: New World Paperbacks ed., 1967), 896–99.

87 A forceful interpretation of slave society in the United States along these lines is Eugene D. Genovese, *The World the Slaveholders Made* (New York: Vintage Books ed., 1971), esp. 118–244; Genovese, *Roll, Jordan, Roll: The World the Slaves Made* (New York, 1974).

88 For examples, see BNP, A371, 1594; ADA, PN, Soria 1589, f. 67r–v. Cf. María

Rostworowski de Diez Canseco, "Succession, Coöption to Kingship, and Royal Incest among the Inca," *Southwestern Journal of Anthropology* 16 (Winter 1960), 417-27.

89 Avila (c. 1598), *Dioses y hombres*, 71.

CHAPTER 2: RISE AND DEMISE OF THE POST-INCAIC ALLIANCES

1 Poma de Ayala (1615), *Nueva corónica*, 369-70.

2 For the terms of Pizarro's early encomienda grants, see U.S. Library of Congress (Harkness Collection), *Documents from Early Peru. The Pizarros and the Almagros, 1531-1578*, ed. Stella R. Clemence (Washington, D.C., 1936), 154, 170. For discussion of the encomienda, see John H. Rowe, "The Incas Under Spanish Colonial Institutions," *HAHR* 37 (May 1957), 159-61; Enrique Torres Saldamando (1879-1880), *Apuntes históricos sobre las encomiendas en el Perú* (Lima, 1967); Manuel Belaúnde Guinassi, *La encomienda en el Perú* (Lima, 1945); Manuel Vicente Villarán, *Apuntes sobre la realidad social de los indígenas ante las leyes de Indias* (Lima, 1964), 25-100; James Lockhart, *Spanish Peru, 1532-1560. A Colonial Society* (Madison, 1968), 11-33 and passim.; Lockhart, "Encomienda and Hacienda: the Evolution of the Great Estate in the Spanish Indies," *HAHR* 49 (August, 1969), 411-29.

3 See Vasco de Guevara (1543), quoted by Marcos Jiménez de la Espada in *RGI*, 181-82, n. 2; Pedro de Cieza de León, "Guerra de las Salinas," in *CDIE*, LXVIII, Ch. 35; Bishop Vicente Valverde to the King, Cuzco, 20 March 1539, in *CDIAO*, III, 122; James Lockhart, *The Men of Cajamarca: A Social and Biographical Study of the First Conquerors of Peru* (Austin, 1972), 424. For a specific case of Inca mitmaq who fought against the Spanish, see AGN, DI, Leg. 1, C. 9, 1567, f. 5v.

4 *Los Mercedarios en el Perú en el siglo XVI. Documentos inéditos del Archivo General de Indias*, ed. Víctor M. Barriga (4 vols., Rome and Arequipa, 1933-53), 4: 90-94; *Libro del Cabildo de la Ciudad de San Juan de la Frontera de Huamanga, 1539-1547*, transcribed by Raúl Rivera Serna (Lima, 1966), 28-33, 140.

5 See *Libro del Cabildo*, 47, 64-65, 68, 71, 91, 95, 100, 121, 128-29, 137, 165, 194; and note 3 above.

6 See *Libro del Cabildo*, 21-22, 30, 31, 46-47, 54, 62, 64, 112, 189; HC, Doc. 985, 1571; BNP, A127, 1547, letter of Don Pedro de la Gasca, December 27, 1547.

7 *Libro del Cabildo*, 64.

8 Monzón et al. (1586), "Descripción . . . de los Rucanas Antamarcas," *RGI*, 238; id. (1586), "Descripción . . . de Atunrucana y Laramati," *RGI*, 226-27; *Gobernantes del Perú*, ed. Roberto Levillier (14 vols., Madrid, 1921-26), 2:103-4, 153, 183, 192; Pedro Pizarro (1571), "Relación del descubrimiento y conquista de los reinos del Perú . . . ," *CDIE*, V, 256.

9 *Libro del Cabildo*, 47, 69, 100; Juan Polo de Ondegardo (1561), "Informe . . . al Licenciado Briviesca de Muñatones," *Revista Histórica* 13 (Lima, 1940), 156; on the yanaconas as an auxiliary arm of conquest, see Nathan Wachtel, *Sociedad e ideología*, 149-58; John Hemming, *The Conquest of the Incas* (New York, 1970), 136, 171, 180, 184, 186, 305-6, 362. Some of the yanacona retainers of Europeans

may have been *yana* retainers alienated from ayllu society before Spanish conquest. On the pre-conquest yana, see Murra, *Formaciones,* 225-42.

10 *Libro del Cabildo,* 63.

11 For a concise history of the Spanish civil wars, see Lockhart, *Spanish Peru,* 3-5; for the role of Huamanga in colonial politics, see *Libro del Cabildo,* 71-72, 73-79, 85-88, 93-96, 98-99, 141, 142-45, 146-50, 152, 159-64, 168-74, 199; Domingo de Santo Tomás (1555), in *La iglesia de España en el Perú,* ed. Emilio Lissón Chaves (4 vols., Seville, 1943-46), 2:57; *Los Mercedarios,* ed. Barriga, 1:257-62.

12 See BNP, A127, 1547, p. 17; ADA, PN, Navarrete 1615-1618/*1627*/1630, ff. 473r-474r; AGN, DI, Leg. 6, C. 109, 1643, ff. 2r, 5v; Bandera (1557), "Relación general," 178; BNP, B44, 1612, f. 8r; *Libro del Cabildo,* 121, 142 for quotations; Poma de Ayala (1615), *Nueva corónica,* 431-33.

13 *Libro del Cabildo,* 45, 50-51, 130 (for other cases, 38, 45, 48, 61, 120, 124, 132).

14 Ibid., 61, 97, 100, 120; AGN, Tierras de Comunidades, Leg. 3, C. 19, 1806, ff. 40v, 42r; BNP, A203, 1557, f. 65v.

15 AGN, DI, Leg. 2, C. 17, 1573, ff. 195v, 226r-v.

16 HC, Doc. 1013, 1557. The Yauyos and Huancas mentioned in this document refer to those who lived in southern Huamanga (Chocorvos and Vilcashuamán) rather than their counterparts of the central sierra north of Huamanga.

17 AGN, DI, Leg. 2, C. 17, 1573, ff. 178r, 197r, 219v-220r.

18 Ibid., ff. 209r on resettlement; 191v, 208v on Inca lands and herds; 193r on compensation; 208r-v, 179r-v on tribute; 195v on gifts to the elite; 195r, 226r, 194v, 179r on food distribution and tribute relief; 194r on labor for the obraje; 209v for scissors and glasswares; 194v for cattle give-away; 192v on gifts to workers.

19 Ibid., ff. 195r, 208v, 215v; *Los Mercedarios,* ed. Barriga, 4:109; *Libro del Cabildo,* 121; BNP, A336, 1559, passim (trampling: entry of 4 November 1561); *Libro del Cabildo,* 122.

20 Encomenderos saw themselves as agents personally responsible for basic public tasks. To construct a church, they assessed themselves a labor draft of 510 Indian workers. Later, they assumed responsibility for supplying Indians to carry water to the city's households. *Libro del Cabildo,* 21-22, 112.

21 Ibid., 30, 31, 64; cf. Marie Helmer, "Notas sobre la encomienda peruana en el siglo XVI," *Revista del Instituto de Historia del Derecho* 10 (Buenos Aires, 1959), 124-43.

22 Domingo de Santo Tomás (1550), in Vargas, *Fray Domingo,* "Escritos": 10.

23 Polo (1561), "Informe . . . al Licenciado Briviesca de Muñatones," 157. Polo's observations were probably based upon patterns in Cuzco, but for similar data from Huamanga, see Monzón et al. (1586), "Descripción . . . de los Rucanas Antamarcas," 238.

24 Bandera (1557), "Relación general," 176; AGN, DI, Leg. 1, C. 9, 1567, ff. 20r-22v.

25 Poma de Ayala (1615), *Nueva corónica,* 559.

26 Monzón et al. (1586), "Descripción . . . de Atunrucana y Laramati," 227; AGN, TP, C. 747, 1625, ff. 4v (quotation), 16r-v.

27 *Libro del Cabildo,* 132 for whipping stock; 46–47, 126, 145, 184, 185, 196 for regulations; 21–22, 42–43, 54, 62, 112 for public works; 132 for deforestation.

28 Ibid., 35, 36, 38, 39–41, 43–46, 48, 51, 53, 54–59, 65, 72, 97, 121, 154.

29 Ibid., 40, 43, 46, 48, 52, 54, 56–61, 63, 73, 93, 120–22, 126–27, 130, 133, 153–55.

30 Ibid., 179 for quotation, 180–81, 182–83 for distribution.

31 BNP, A203, 1557, ff. 24v–25r.

32 For the stunning variety of items included in pre-1570 tribute lists, see AGN, DI, Leg. 1, C. 8, 1576, ff. 109v–112r; Leg. 2, C. 17, 1573, ff. 179v–180v, 184v–186r.

33 AGN, DI, Leg. 1, C. 8, 1576, f. 110v for prices in 1563.

34 In addition to the sources in notes 29–31 and 26, see *Libro del Cabildo,* 62; Cieza de León (1553), *Parte primera,* ch. 87; Juan López de Velasco (1571–1574), *Geografía y descripción universal de las Indias,* ed. Marcos Jiménez de la Espada (Madrid, 1971), 241; BNP, Z303, 1578; BNP, B75, 1626, ff. 23v, 46r; AGN, TP, Leg. 1, C. 8, 1568; ADA, Corregimiento, Causas Ordinarias, [Leg. 2], 1678, esp. f. 935r–v; RPIA, tomo 21, partida XXXIII, 330; BNP, A203, 1557, f. 33v.

35 On the distinction between industrial capital or capitalist production, and commercial capital in pre-capitalist settings, see Marx, *Capital,* esp. vol. 3, chs. 20, 36, 47. As Marx points out, it is important to distinguish between the dynamics of commercial capital within a capitalist economy, and the commercial capital which predates the dominance of capitalist production. In the text, I refer to the latter form of commercial capital.

36 ADA, PN, Ysidro 1577, ff. 248r–249v. For the widespread character of entrepreneurial activity in early colonial Peru, see Lockhart, *Spanish Peru,* passim.

37 *Libro del Cabildo,* 126.

38 Ibid., 50, 123, 142, 166; see *Gobernantes,* ed. Levillier, 1:190. On the social atmosphere of mining centers, see the fines collected in Atunsulla in the 1560s, as recorded in BNP, A336, 1559.

39 See AGN, Minería, Leg. 2, Ayacucho 1622, ff. 55r, 169r–172v, 192r–v; Fernando Montesinos (1642), *Anales del Perú,* ed. Víctor M. Maurtúa (2 vols., Madrid, 1906), 1:278; AGN, Minería, Leg. 13, Huancavelica 1585–1595, Exp. 1, f. 49r–v; Leg. 11, Huancavelica 1562–1572, ff. 254r–255v.

40 See BNP, Z313, 1616, ff. 164r–165r; ADA, PN, Romo 1577, ff. 202r–204r; BNP, B1485, 1600, ff. 62r, 247r; AGN, DI, Leg. 2, C. 17, 1573, ff. 193v–194r.

41 See Lockhart, *Spanish Peru,* 23; Lockhart, *The Men of Cajamarca,* 297; López de Velasco (1571–1574), *Geografía,* 241.

42 AGN, Minería, Leg. 2, Ayacucho 1622, f. 79r; AGI, V, Lima 313, Domingo de Santo Tomás to Royal Council of the Exchequer in Lima, Andahuaylas, 6 April 1562; AGI, VI, Lima 529A, f. 1335v; AGN, DI, Leg. 2, C. 17, 1573, ff. 192v–193r.

43 Bandera (1557), "Relación general," 177; AGN, DI, Leg. 1, C. 9, 1567, ff. 1r (for quotation), 3v.

44 AGN, DI, Leg. 2, C. 17, 1573, ff. 192v–193r, 193v–194r; cf. BNP, B1441, 1634, f. 102v.

45 *Libro del Cabildo,* 193, 112; AGN, DI, Leg. 2, C. 17, 1573, f. 192v; Polo (1561), "Informe . . . al Licenciado Briviesca de Muñatones," 189.

46 See HC, Doc. 983, 1571; Juan Polo de Ondegardo (1562), "Ordenanzas de las minas de Guamanga," in *Colección de libros y documentos referentes a la historia del Perú* (4 vols., Lima, 1916), 4:142; López de Velasco (1571–1574), *Geografía,* 241.

47 Bandera (1557), "Relación general," 177; BNP, Z306, 1592, ff. 490r, 491r; ADA, PN, Padilla *1602*/1613, f. 339v; HC, Doc. 1014, 1559; AGN, Minería, Leg. 11, Huancavelica 1562–1572, f. 258r–v.

48 ADA, PN, Peña 1596, f. 311r; AGN, DI, Leg. 2, C. 17, 1573, f. 193r.

49 Polo (1561), "Informe . . . al Licenciado Briviesca de Muñatones," 189.

50 Quotations ibid.; Bandera (1557), "Relación general," 180 (see also 177).

51 BNP, A336, 1559, entry for 13 October 1559.

52 See Matienzo (1567), *Gobierno,* 27–30; HC, Doc. 1015, 1557; Monzón et al. (1586), "Descripción . . . de Atunrucana y Laramati," 226 (quotation).

53 For examples, see Albornoz (c. 1582), "Instrucción para descubrir," 17, 18, 20, 35; Avila (c. 1598), *Dioses y hombres,* 130–35, 141. To be sure, Andean groups sometimes chose to defy enemy deities outright. See Hemming, *Conquest,* 240–41.

54 See HC, Doc. 1009, 1557; Bandera (1557), "Relación general," 176; Manuel J. Pozo, *Historia de Huamanga (época colonial)* (Ayacucho, 1924), 69–70. Cf. George Kubler, *Mexican Architecture of the Sixteenth Century* (2 vols., New Haven, 1948), 2:417.

55 The encomendero population was not completely stable in the first years after Huamanga's founding in 1539, but usually hovered around twenty-five.

56 For tribute lists in the 1550s and 1560s, see AGN, DI, Leg. 1, C. 8, 1576, ff. 109v–112r; Leg. 2, C. 17, 1573, ff. 184v–188v.

57 Bandera (1557), "Relación general," 179.

58 Polo (1561), "Informe . . . al Licenciado Briviesca de Muñatones," 169.

59 AGN, DI, Leg. 2, C. 17, 1573, f. 185r.

60 See Spalding, *De indio a campesino,* 31–60.

61 For clear examples from 1570–1572 in Andahuaylas and Parinacochas, see AGN, DI, Leg. 2, C. 17, 1573, ff. 181v–183v; YC, Vol. 5, f. 62v. Cf. BNP, A236, 1597, ff. 20r, 22r.

62 *Libro del Cabildo,* 40.

63 Bandera (1557), "Relación general," 180; ADA, PN, Romo 1577, ff. 331v–332v. Cf. three contracts recorded in Cuzco in 1560, in *Revista del Archivo Histórico* 4.4 (Cuzco, 1953), 25, 31, 32.

64 ADA, PN, Romo 1577, f. 332v.

65 See AGN, DI, Leg. 2, C. 17, 1573, ff. 179r–v, 186v–187r, 191r–192v, 207r–v, 213r, 216v–217r.

66 Guillermo Lohmann Villena, *Las minas de Huancavelica en los siglos XVI y XVII* (Seville, 1949), 28, 91–92; Polo (1562), "Ordenanzas de las minas de Guamanga," 139–51; Domingo de Santo Tomás (1562), in Vargas, *Fray Domingo,* "Escritos": 57–62; AGN, Minería, Leg. 11, Huancavelica 1562–1572, f. 62r; BNP, A603, 1568, f. 23v (quote). See also *Gobernantes,* ed. Levillier, 2:573, 578.

67 BNP, Z313, 1616, ff. 164r–165r; ADA, PN, Romo 1577, ff. 202r–204r, esp. 203r–v; BNP, A455, 1571; BNP, B1485, 1600, f. 61r; Miriam Salas de Coloma, *De los obrajes de Canaria y Chincheros a las comunidades indígenas de Vilcashuamán. Siglo XVI* (Lima, 1979), 99–100.

68   Santo Tomás, an opponent of the encomienda, was the more extreme propo-
nent of this view. On these two personalities, see Murra, *Formaciones,* 285–86,
306–11; Patricia J. Bard, "Domingo de Santo Tomás, a Spanish friar in 16th-
Century Peru" (M.A. thesis, Columbia University, 1967).

69   See Henry F. Dobyns, "An Outline of Andean Epidemic History to 1720," *Bulletin of the History of Medicine* 37 (1963), 494–97, 499–501; Monzón et al. (1586),
"Descripción . . . de los Rucanas Antamarcas," 238; id. (1586), "Descripción
. . . de Atunrucana y Laramati," 227.

70   See Noble David Cook, "The Indian Population of Peru, 1570–1620" (Ph.D.
diss., University of Texas at Austin, 1973), 238; John H. Rowe, "Inca Culture
at the Time of the Spanish Conquest," in *Handbook,* ed. Steward, 2:184. See also
the methodological discussion in Daniel E. Shea, "A Defense of Small Population Estimates for the Central Andes in 1520," in *The Native Population of the Americas in 1492,* ed. William M. Denevan (Madison, 1976), 157–80.

71   On the importance of herds as a kind of insurance resource against hardship in
agriculture in Huamanga and elsewhere, see Bandera (1557), "Relación general," 177; Murra, *Formaciones,* 202–3.

72   See "Relación de Amancebados, Hechiceros y Huacas" (1584), in *Las informaciones de Cristóbal de Albornoz: documentos para el estudio del Taki Onqoy,* ed. Luis Millones, (Cuernavaca, 1971); *Tasa de la visita general,* ed. Cook, 261; Hemming, *Conquest,* 386–87.

73   See HC, Doc. 1012, 1556; *Colección de documentos para la historia de la formación social
de Hispanoamérica,* ed. Richard Konetzke (2 vols. in 3 parts, Madrid, 1953,
1958), 1:452.

74   See Lockhart, *Spanish Peru,* 52–55, who coined the term "priest-entrepreneur."
See also Rubén Vargas Ugarte, *Historia de la iglesia en el Perú* (5 vols., Lima and
Buenos Aires, 1953–62), 1:126–28; 2:213–14.

75   HC, Doc. 1009, 1557; Bandera (1557), "Relación general," 176; HC, Doc. 1008,
1564.

76   HC, Doc. 1017, 1557.

77   For examples from the 1560s, see AGN, DI, Leg. 2, C. 17, 1573, f. 208r; Domingo de Santo Tomás (1562), in Vargas, *Fray Domingo,* "Escritos": 59.

78   Montesinos (1642), *Anales del Perú,* 1:243; 2:18; AGN, DI, Leg. 2, C. 17, 1573, ff.
194v, 209r.

79   See Polo (1562), "Ordenanzas de las minas de Guamanga," 139–51.

80   AGI, V, Lima 313, Santo Tomás to Don Alonso Manuel de Anaya, Huamanga,
23 March 1562; Santo Tomás to Royal Council of the Exchequer in Lima, Andahuaylas, 6 April 1562 (also available in Vargas, *Fray Domingo,* "Escritos": 55–
62).

81   BNP, A603, 1568, f. 23v.

82   AGI, V, Lima 300, Archbishop Gerónimo de Loayza to the King, Lima, 30
November 1562; Lima 313, Santo Tomás to Manuel de Anaya, Huamanga, 23
March 1562. See Hemming, *Conquest,* 385–90 for an overview of the encomi-
enda perpetuity issue.

83   All the evidence cited above is from the period 1563–1571. BNP, A336, 1559, entry for 3 May 1563; HC, Doc. 984, 1571; Lohmann, *Las minas,* 93, n. 3; AGN,

DI, Leg. 2, C. 17, 1573, f. 196r; Lohmann, *El corregidor de indios en el Perú bajo los Austrias* (Madrid, 1957), 28; Molina (1574), *Relación de las fábulas,* 79.

84 Molina (1574), *Relación de las fábulas,* 82; Albornoz (c. 1582), "Instrucción para descubrir," 36.

CHAPTER 3: A HISTORICAL WATERSHED

1 For accounts of the movement, see Luis Millones S. G., "Un movimiento nativista del siglo XVI: el Taki Onqoy," and "Nuevos aspectos del Taki Onqoy"; Nathan Wachtel, "Rebeliones y milenarismo"; all in *Ideología mesiánica del mundo andino,* ed. Juan M. Ossio A. (Lima, 1973), 85–94, 97–101, 105–42. Millones's essays originally appeared in *Revista peruana de cultura,* 3 (1964), and *Historia y Cultura,* 1 (1965). Wachtel's essay originally appeared in his important *La vision des vaincus: les indiens du Pérou devant la conquête espagnole, 1530–1570* (Paris, 1971), 225–82 (now available in English translation).

For perspectives on Taki Onqoy and on Indian nativism and idolatry, see Millones, "Introducción al estudio de las idolatrías," *Aportes* 4 (Paris, April 1967), 47–82; Pierre Duviols, *La lutte contre les religions autochtones dans le Pérou colonial: "L'extirpation de l'idolatrie" entre 1532 et 1660* (Lima and Paris, 1971); R. T. Zuidema, "Observaciones sobre el Taki Onqoy," *Historia y Cultura* 1 (Lima, 1965), 137; Franklin Pease G. Y., *El dios creador andino* (Lima, 1973).

Brief accounts by knowledgeable contemporaries are: Molina (1574), *Relación de las fábulas,* 78–84; Albornoz (c. 1582), "Instrucción para descubrir," 35–37.

2 Aside from the sources in note 1, Luis Millones has published testimonies by Spanish witnesses on behalf of Albornoz in 1570, 1577, and 1584, as well as administrative lists of the results of Albornoz's anti-idolatry inspection in Soras and Lucanas. *Las informaciones de Cristóbal de Albornoz: documentos para el estudio del Taki Onqoy,* ed. Millones (Cuernavaca, 1971). When citing or quoting from the testimonies, I will use witnesses with first-hand or special knowledge. The administrative lists were drawn up in 1584 as a "Relación de Amancebados, Hechiceros y Huacas."

3 Molina (1574), *Relación de las fabulas,* 80–81; *Las informaciones,* ed. Millones, 1/18.

4 *Las informaciones,* ed. Millones, 2/62, 2/110. "Dancing sickness" is, I think, the best of several possible meanings of "Taki Onqoy." For a discussion, see Duviols, *La lutte,* 113–14, n. 66.

5 *Las informaciones,* ed. Millones, 1/17, 2/109; Molina (1574), *Relación de las fábulas,* 79–80; Pease, *El dios,* 72–82; Wachtel, "Rebeliones y milenarismo," 118–19.

6 Molina (1574), *Relación de las fábulas,* 80.

7 Ibid.; *Las informaciones,* ed. Millones, 1/17, 2/109; Josep M. Barnadas, *Charcas: orígenes históricos de una sociedad colonial* (La Paz, 1973), 178, n. 152.

8 *Las informaciones,* ed. Millones, 2/109.

9 Ibid., 1/18.

10 Ibid., 1/18, 2/46, 2/52–2/53; Molina (1574), *Relación de las fábulas,* 80–81; Albornoz (c. 1582), "Instrucción para descubrir," 35–37.

11 Molina (1574), *Relación de las fábulas,* 81.

12 My calculations for about 500 taquiongos (not including leaders of the sect) among the Soras peoples indicate that some 55 percent were women. See "Rela-

ción de Amancebados" (1584), in *Las informaciones,* ed. Millones, 4/7-4/11, 4/18-4/22.

13 Ibid., 2/54. Several years later, Viceroy Toledo's inspection found a total native population in Huamanga of 122,160 (excluding Andahuaylas and Parinacochas). *Tasa de la visita general,* ed. Cook, xxviii-xxix.

14 *Las informaciones,* ed. Millones, 2/54.

15 Ibid., 2/62, 2/110, 3/30; Molina (1574), *Relación de las fábulas,* 82.

16 *Las informaciones,* ed. Millones, 1/17, 2/82, 2/101.

17 Ibid., 3/30.

18 Albornoz (c. 1582), "Instrucción para descubrir," 35; see also Molina (1574), *Relación de las fábulas,* 82.

19 See *Ideología mesiánica,* ed. Ossio; Zuidema, "Observaciones," 137; Pease, *El dios.*

20 For examples, see Molina (1574), *Relación de las fábulas,* 13-15, 33; Avila (c. 1598), *Dioses y hombres,* 39, 47, 49, 149, 151; Arriaga (1621) , *La extirpación,* 52; Poma de Ayala (1615), *Nueva corónica* 109, 137, 158, 286.

21 Cieza (1553), *Parte primera,* ch. 88.

22 See Pease, *El dios,* 51, 65-66; Avila (c. 1598), *Dioses y hombres,* 117-25; Albornoz (c. 1582), "Instrucción para descubrir," 21.

23 See Albornoz (c. 1582), "Instrucción para descubrir," 37; Cieza (1553), *Parte primera,* Chs. 72, 56. For a suggestive comparison, see Frances Fitzgerald, *Fire in the Lake: The Vietnamese and the Americans in Vietnam* (New York: Vintage Books ed., 1973), 17-18, 29.

24 For examples of this approach to foreign deities, see Albornoz (c. 1582), "Instrucción para descubrir," 17, 18, 20, 35; Avila (c. 1598), *Dioses y hombres,* 130-35, 141.

25 See the lists cited in "Relación de Amancebados" (1584), in *Las informaciones,* ed. Millones, 4/5-4/6, 4/11-4/16, 4/27, 4/41, 4/42-4/44, 4/36-4/38, 4/33.

26 Ibid., 2/52.

27 On the modified functions of traditional practices in colonial contexts, see Frantz Fanon, *A Dying Colonialism,* trans. Haakon Chevalier (New York, 1965).

28 For the previous two paragraphs, see Steve J. Stern, "Las ideologías nativistas, la aculturación y las clases sociales," *Churmichasun* 4-5 (Huancayo, June 1977), 25-32.

29 *Las informaciones,* ed. Millones, 2/53.

30 For a suggestive passage (albeit in the words of a knowledgeable Spanish observer) which pits "the huacas" and "the Indians" as unified categories opposite the Christian "God" and the "Spaniards," see Molina (1574), *Relación de las fábulas,* 80.

31 See *Las informaciones,* ed. Millones, 2/64; cf. AGN, JR, Leg. 23, C. 62, 1617, f. 113r.

32 Cf. Peter Worsley, *The Trumpet Shall Sound: A Study of 'Cargo' Cults in Melanesia* (2nd ed., New York, 1968), 236-38.

33 *Las informaciones,* ed. Millones, 1/17.

34 Molina (1574), *Relación de las fábulas,* 80 (emphasis mine). See also *Las informaciones,* ed. Millones, 1/17-1/18.

35 For a suggestive contrast along these lines, between colonizers and slaveholders, see Genovese, *Roll, Jordan, Roll,* 91.

36 See John Earls, "La organización del poder en la mitología quechua," in *Ideología mesiánica,* ed. Ossio, 395–414.

37 *Las informaciones,* ed. Millones, 1/22.

38 Ibid., 2/136.

39 On this kind of vision as a utopia of the native elite, see Emilio Choy, "La realidad y el utopismo en Guamán Poma," *Universidad,* no. 7 (Ayacucho, December 1966), 1–2.

40 For suggestive data on the usages of the "yanacona" term in the mining center of Potosí, see Helmer, "Notas sobre la encomienda," 124–43.

41 On the continuing appeal of the community environment for even the most deviant and marginalized members of Andean peasant communities, see López Albújar, "Ushanam-Jampi," in his *Cuentos andinos,* 43–56, esp. 49–50. Interesting data on Andean attempts to recreate community relationships for mitmaq colonizers in outlying pockets distant from their peoples' "core" area of settlement is given by Albornoz (c. 1582), "Instrucción para descubrir," 21. For comparative materials on the spiritual voids of Vietnamese individuals wrenched from the collective landscapes of community life, and their susceptibility to religious cults, see Fitzgerald, *Fire in the Lake,* 79, 239.

42 For examples, see *Las informaciones,* ed. Millones, 2/70, 2/44.

43 Ibid., 2/68, 4/15–4/16, 4/23, 4/3–4/5, 4/17–4/18; see also Albornoz (c. 1582), "Instrucción para descubrir," 38.

44 See *Las informaciones,* ed. Millones, 2/26, 2/36, 2/78, 2/89, 2/95, 2/104, 2/110, 1/22, 3/29.

45 The "Relación de Amancebados" (1584) contains useful though incomplete lists from Soras and Lucanas. See *Las informaciones,* ed. Millones, 4/6–4/11, 4/18–4/22, 4/41–4/42, 4/34–4/36, 4/31–4/32, upon which the analysis below is based.

46 *Las informaciones,* ed. Millones, 4/8.

47 Ibid., 1/22.

48 Some clear-cut contradictions, however, are provided by Francisco Chuqui Vilca, don Antonio Guaman Lauca, don Pedro Caxa, and Tomás Vázquez Tomay, in *Las informaciones,* ed. Millones, 4/34–4/36.

49 The data for Lucanas Laramati is in *Las informaciones,* ed. Millones, 4/31–4/39.

50 Ibid., 2/68, 2/64.

51 See the lists for Soras and Lucanas peoples in *Las informaciones,* ed. Millones, 4/16, 4/27–4/28, 4/38–4/39.

52 This distinction does not preclude the possibility that important leaders of the sect may have been lesser chiefs or close kin relatives of major kurakas. On intra-elite strife and divisions in Andean life, see María Rostworowski de Diez Canseco's *Curacas y sucesiones, costa norte* (Lima, 1961) and her "Succession," 417–27; BNP, A371, 1594.

   For a comparative example of lesser elites as a source of unrest in a lineage-based society, see E. R. Leach, *Political Systems of Highland Burma* (Boston: Beacon ed., 1965), 197–263.

53 *Las informaciones,* ed. Millones, 2/118.

54 See Albornoz (c. 1582), "Instrucción para descubrir," 22, 36.
55 Cf. Frantz Fanon, *The Wretched of the Earth,* trans. Constance Farrington (New York, 1968), 52-54.
56 See RPIA, tomo 5, partida VI, 19-20; tomo 8, partida XL, 132; tomo 10, partida CXXIII, 404-5; tomo 10, partida CXL, 468-69; tomo 14, partida VI, 42-43.
57 "Relación de Amancebados" (1584), in *Las informaciones,* ed. Millones, 4/44-4/45.
58 *Las informaciones,* ed. Millones, 2/69, 2/112, 2/90, 2/96, 2/22, 2/27, 2/33, 2/37, 2/54-2/55, 2/47, 4/33.
59 Ibid., 2/62, 2/46.
60 The characterization given above is an interpretation based on wide readings in the extensive literature on millenarianism. For some classic studies, see Kenelm Burridge, *New Heaven, New Earth: A Study of Millenarian Activities* (New York, 1969); Norman Cohn, *The Pursuit of the Millennium: Revolutionary Millenarians and Mystical Anarchists of the Middle Ages* (3rd ed., New York, 1970); E. J. Hobsbawm, *Primitive Rebels: Studies in Archaic Forms of Social Movements in the 19th and 20th Centuries* (New York, 1965); María Isaura Pereira de Queiroz, *Historia y etnología de los movimientos mesiánicos,* trans. Florentino M. Torner (Mexico, 1969); Anthony F. C. Wallace, "Revitalization Movements," *American Anthropologist* 58 (April 1956), 264-81; id., *The Death and Rebirth of the Seneca* (New York, 1969); Worsley, *The Trumpet.*
   I do not mean to imply that *all* millenarian movements involve an inability to launch a human politico-military attack against oppressors. Such a narrow and rigid approach overlooks cases in which millenarian ideologies have indeed inspired military assaults against the powers that be.
61 For examples of these two major approaches to millenarianism, see note 60. Wachtel, "Rebeliones y milenarismo," interprets Taki Onqoy in the context of "destructuration." For telling criticisms of both approaches, see Sylvia Thrupp, "Millennial Dreams in Action," in *Millennial Dreams in Action: Studies in Revolutionary Religious Movements,* ed. Thrupp (New York, 1970), 26-27.
62 On the neo-Incas, see George Kubler, "The Neo-Inca State (1537-1572)," *HAHR* 27 (May 1947), 189-203; Kubler, "The Quechua in the Colonial World," in *Handbook of South American Indians,* ed. Steward, 2:343-45; Hemming, *Conquest,* passim.
63 On the Huancas' history and post-conquest posture, see Waldemar Espinoza Soriano, *La destrucción del imperio de los Incas* (Lima, 1973); on their conspiracy in the 1560s, see Manuel de Odriozla, *Documentos históricos del Perú* (Lima, 1872), 3: 3-9; Wachtel, "Rebeliones y milenarismo," 113-15.
64 Wachtel, "Rebeliones y milenarismo," 119. See also Albornoz's suspicion that the neo-Incas instigated Taki Onqoy in order to stir up a rebellion. Albornoz (c. 1582), "Instrucción para descubrir," 35-37.
65 Molina (1574), *Relación de las fábulas,* 82.
66 On the crisis of the 1560s, and for the data above, see Guillermo Lohmann Villena, "Juan de Matienzo, autor del 'Gobierno del Perú' (su personalidad y su

obra)," *Anuario de Estudios Americanos* 22 (Seville, 1965), 767-886; John H. Rowe, "The Incas Under Spanish Colonial Institutions," *HAHR* 37 (May 1957), 184, 171; Lohmann, *El corregidor,* note on 28; Barnadas, *Charcas,* 283; Bard, "Domingo de Santo Tomás," 61; Hemming, *Conquest,* 304-7; Albornoz (c. 1582), "Instrucción para descubrir," 36.

67 *La iglesia,* ed. Lissón Chaves, 2:294.

68 Lohmann, "Juan de Matienzo," 767-99.

69 Ibid., 820-21.

70 Matienzo (1567), *Gobierno,* 98-100 (98 for quote). The landmark study of Matienzo, his treatise, and its historical significance is Lohmann, "Juan de Matienzo," 767-886.

71 Matienzo (1567), *Gobierno,* 189.

72 Ibid., 6-20, 43-44 (17 and 43 for quotes).

73 Ibid., 196.

74 Ibid., 313-15, 348, 273. On the idea of small proprietors as a stabilizing force, see also Robert G. Keith, *Conquest and Agrarian Change: The Emergence of the Hacienda System on the Peruvian Coast* (Cambridge, Mass., 1976), 81-84, 91-92.

75 Matienzo (1567), *Gobierno,* 48-59, 74, 77. On the revamped structure of authority in the native communities, see Karen Spalding, "Social Climbers: Changing Patterns of Mobility among the Indians of Colonial Peru," *HAHR* 50 (November 1970), 656-59; Spalding, "Indian Rural Society in Colonial Peru: The Example of Huarochirí" (Ph.D. diss., University of California, Berkeley, 1967), 209.

76 Matienzo (1567), *Gobierno,* 295.

77 On Matienzo, Titu Cusi, and the negotiations of the 1560s, see Matienzo (1567), *Gobierno,* 294-310; Guillermo Lohmann Villena, "El Inga Titu Cussi Yupangui y su entrevista con el oidor Matienzo, 1565," *Mercurio Peruano* 23, no. 167 (1941), 3-18; Hemming, *Conquest,* 299-339.

78 Matienzo (1567), *Gobierno,* 272-74, 348.

79 Ibid., 25-31, 273-74, 60-66 (esp. 60).

80 Ibid., 96-97, 162-63.

81 Ibid., 25-41, 48-77 (esp. 67), 82, 84-85, 90-91, 144-47, 180-89.

82 See, in addition to the discussion of punishment earlier in this chapter, Albornoz (c. 1582), "Instrucción para descubrir," 37-38; Poma de Ayala (1615), *Nueva corónica,* 676; *Las informaciones,* ed. Millones, 4/1-4/46, 2/110, 2/114, 2/49, 2/19, 2/150.

83 *La iglesia,* ed. Lissón Chaves, 2:296-97 (296 for quote); Hemming, *Conquest,* 379, 383-85. For an example of García de Castro's inability to put into effect a revival of the mercury mines at Huancavelica, see Lohmann, *Las minas,* 35.

84 On Toledo and his work, see Roberto Levillier, *Don Francisco de Toledo, supremo organizador del Perú, su vida, su obra (1515-1582)* (3 vols., Buenos Aires, 1935-42), esp. 1:73-138, 197-359; Hemming, *Conquest,* 392-456; Lohmann, *Las minas,* 37-137; *Tales of Potosí,* ed. R. C. Padden (Providence, 1975), xviii-xxiii; Arthur F. Zimmermann, *Francisco de Toledo, Fifth Viceroy of Peru, 1569-1581* (Caldwell, Idaho, 1938).

85 See *Las informaciones,* ed. Millones, 1/14–1/15, 1/23; Alejandro Málaga Medina, "Las reducciones en el Perú (1532–1600), " *Historia y Cultura* 8 (1974), 162; *Gobernantes,* ed. Levillier, 2:589.

86 Poma de Ayala (1615), *Nueva corónica,* 445.

87 See above, note 84.

88 Rowe, "The Incas," 156; Monzón et al. (1586), "Descripción . . . de Atunrucana y Laramati," 227. See also Málaga, "Las reducciones," 165.

89 For a good description of Tupac Amaru's execution, see Hemming, *Conquest,* 447–49.

90 See Worsley, *The Trumpet,* 193, 231–32; George Shepperson, "The Comparative Study of Millennial Movements," in *Millennial Dreams,* ed. Thrupp, 44–52; Burridge, *New Heaven,* 112.

91 Fanon, *The Wretched of the Earth,* 52–54.

92 Levillier, *Don Francisco de Toledo,* 1:267–68. See also *Gobernantes,* ed. Levillier, 5: 315.

93 For examples, see Rostworowski, "Succession," 417–27; BNP, A371, 1594.

94 See the suggestive comment of Matienzo, writing in 1567: "they amuse themselves by changing chiefs, even if they would be better off with the old than the new." Matienzo (1567), *Gobierno,* 17. See also AGN, DI, Leg. 2, C. 17, 1573, f. 208r.

95 ADA, PN, Soria 1589, f. 67r (emphasis added).

96 RPIA, tomo 14, partida VI, 42–43; tomo 10, partida CXXIII, 405. Cf. tomo 5, partida VI, 19.

97 Compare the impact of the great eighteenth-century rebellions on the behavior of the Peruvian elite during the Wars of Independence. Heraclio Bonilla and Karen Spalding, "La independencia en el Perú: las palabras y los hechos," in Bonilla et al., *La independencia en el Perú* (Lima, 1972), 15–64.

CHAPTER 4: THE POLITICAL ECONOMY OF COLONIALISM

1 For a perceptive analysis of colonial social structure in terms of estates and corporations, see Lyle N. McAlister, "Social Structure and Social Change in New Spain," *HAHR* 43 (August 1963), 349–70.

2 For the results of Toledo's visita in Huamanga, see *Tasa de la visita general,* ed. Cook, 260–80. The tributary figure I cite excludes 179 kurakas exempted from tribute and mita liability. The boundaries of the Huamanga district changed somewhat during the entire colonial period. The figures cited for twenty-three core repartimientos exclude the Jauja repartimientos to the north, five small groups of mitmaq whose colonies lay in the Chocorvos district, and several peripheral repartimientos (ibid., 257–60, 282–84, 275–76, 280–82).

3 See Murra, *Formaciones,* 30–31, 33–34.

4 On the establishment of the colonial mita and its rules, in Huamanga and elsewhere, see AGN, Minería, Leg. 2, Ayacucho 1622, f. 82r–v; Lohmann, *Las minas,* 93–99; Luis J. Basto Girón, *Las mitas de Huamanga y Huancavelica* (Lima, 1954); Málaga "Las reducciones," 159; Rowe, "The Incas," 170–79; Jorge Basadre, "El régimen de la mita," in *El virreinato del Perú,* ed. José Manuel Valega (Lima, 1939), 187–203; Villarán, *Apuntes,* 101–45.

5 See Polo (1571), "Relación de los fundamentos," 60, 66-67, 70-73; Murra, *Formaciones,* 30-34, 146, 154-57, 251.

6 See Bandera (1557), "Relación general," 179; AGI, V, Lima 308, Report of the inspection by Bishop Verdugo, 1625, p. 10 (microfilm copy); AGN, JR, Leg. 23, C. 62, 1617, ff. 174r, 176r-v, 179v-180r, 182v, 202v, 204r-v, 211r, esp. 202v; Basto Girón, *Las mitas,* 10.

7 See especially BNP, B1505, 1644, ff. 24v-25r. See also ibid., ff. 3v, 24v-25r; AGN, JR, Leg. 24, C. 65, 1618, ff. 252r-295v; BNP, A236, 1597, ff. 18r, 20r.

8 On the fate of mitayo relatives in various Huamanga mitas, see BNP, Z436, 1595, ff. 226v, 230r; Poma de Ayala (1615), *Nueva corónica,* 521, 532; AGN, Minería, Leg. 13, Huancavelica 1585-1591, Exp. 2, f. 14v; BNP, B1485, 1600, f. 49v; Salas, *De los obrajes,* 71, 79-80; BNP, A18, 1599, f. 4r.

9 On conditions in the mines, the "mercury sickness," and the latter's widespread incidence and impact, see Antonio Vázquez de Espinosa (1629), *Compendio y descripción de las Indias occidentales,* ed. Charles Upson Clark (Washington, D.C., 1948), 504; Juan de Aponte Figueroa (1622), "Memorial que trata de la reformación del reino del Pirú . . . ," *CDIE,* LI, 528-29; Lohmann, *Las minas,* 50, 170-74; Poma de Ayala (1615), *Nueva corónica,* 527; Arthur Preston Whitaker, *The Huancavelica Mercury Mine. A Contribution to the History of the Bourbon Renaissance in the Spanish Empire* (Cambridge, 1941), 18-19; BNP, B1079, 1629, ff. 16v, 17r, 17v, 20r-v, 24v, 26r, 28r, 31r, 32r, 35r, 42r, 45v, 52v, 53r, 54v, 82r-85r; BNP, B856, 1616, f. 2v; B876, 1629, f. 13v; B1159, 1629, ff. 11r-12r; B1505, 1644, f. 10v. There may have been some improvement in the physiological conditions of work during the course of the seventeenth century, especially for hired free laborers. See Lohmann, *Las minas,* 310-12.

10 The figure is calculated from records available for 1,724 mitayos sent from the Lucanas provinces (Lucanas Laramati, Lucanas Andamarcas, and Soras) to Castrovirreyna during 1597-1603. The records have the following identifications in the BNP: A233, 1598; A230, [1598]; B968, 1602; B971, 1603; B895, 1603; B806, 1604.

11 See BNP, A18, 1599, f. 5r; Carabajal (1586), "Descripción . . . de Vilcas Guaman," 205; BNP, Z436, 1595, ff. 222v, 225r, 226v.

12 For food purchases in the mines and elsewhere, see AGN, JR, Leg. 11, C. 29, 1593, f. 266r; AGN, Minería, Leg. 13, Huancavelica 1585-1591, Exp. 2, ff. 7v-8r, 9v, 14v; BNP, Z436, 1595, f. 225r; A230 [1598], f. 9r-v (debts of Pedro Quispe and Alonso Chipana); B1485, 1600, ff. 55v, 56r, 214r, 250v, 314r; Aponte (1622), "Memorial . . . de la reformación," 533.

13 Food prices varied according to harvests and place of marketing, but around 1590, suppliers of corn and wheat to Huamanga preferred to send the grains to mining markets such as Huancavelica or Castrovirreyna rather than sell them at 20 reales in Huamanga. HC, Doc. 975, 1591. See also AGN, JR, Leg. 11, C. 29, 1593, f. 266r. In July, 1602, at a time of year when maize was abundant, the tribute maize of a group of Papres Indians brought 18 reales per fanega in Huamanga. ADA, PN, Padilla *1602*/1613, f. 334v.

14 For the coca market in mining centers and elsewhere, see Matienzo (1567), *Gobierno,* 97, 161-66; BNP, B1485, 1600, ff. 62v, 250v, 314r.

15 Poma de Ayala (1615), *Nueva corónica*, 528, 530; Aponte (1622), "Memorial . . . de la reformación," 533; AGI, VI, Lima 1189, Sentence against Francisco Venturo de Belalcázar (1648), charges against Vidaya, Mexia y Gonzales.

16 For delays and difficulties in collecting wages, and the need to purchase foodstuffs while waiting, see the mita records cited in note 10; and BNP, A18, 1599, f. 3r; B875, 1628; AGN, Minería, Leg. 13, Huancavelica 1585-1591, Exp. 2, accounts on ff. 26v-27r, and comments on 7v-8r, 9v, 14v; BNP, Z436, 1595, f. 226v.

17 On attempts by entrepreneurs to expand and control their workers' market consumption, by distributing needed and unneeded goods at inflated prices, see BNP, B1485, 1600, ff. 2r, 50v, 52r, 55v, 58v, 61r, 62v, 70r; Poma de Ayala (1615), *Nueva corónica*, 526; Aponte (1622), "Memorial . . . de la reformación," 533.

18 The mita records cited in note 10 above fully bear out this kind of reputation, which was recorded by an Indian chronicler from Huamanga. See Poma de Ayala (1615), *Nueva corónica*, 734; [Anonymous] (1607), "Memorial y relación de las minas de azogue del Pirú," *CDIAO*, VIII, 438-39. Both sources also discuss Juan García de la Vega, a mestizo miner with a benevolent reputation.

19 For evidence that tribute was often deducted at the time of mita wage payment, see BNP, B875, 1628.

20 See BNP, A218, 1591, f. 1v; A18, 1599, f. 4r.

21 For a path-breaking analysis of the logic of pre-capitalist enterprise in feudal Poland, which shows that the large profits of grain-exporting estates depended directly upon their ability to avoid paying out in monies the full costs (from a capitalist point of view) of production, see Witold Kula, *Teoría económica del sistema feudal,* trans. Estanislow J. Zembrzuski (Mexico, 1974), 30-34. The original Polish version was published in 1962.

22 See Chapter 6 for a discussion of the "monetization" of mita obligations, which in practice shifted a disproportionate burden on poorer peasants. Cf. the evidence from seventeenth-century Bolivia, in Nicolás Sánchez-Albornoz, *Indios y tributos en el Alto Perú* (Lima, 1978), 107.

23 See BNP, B1079, 1629, f. 80v; AGN, Minería, Leg. 13, Huancavelica 1585-1591, Exp. 2, f. 8r; BNP, Z436, 1595, f. 226v; B1485, 1600, ff. 49v, 337r.

24 For accounting records which document the delays in Huancavelica and Castrovirreyna, see AGN, Minería, Leg. 13, Huancavelica 1585-1591, Exp. 2, ff. 26v-27r; BNP, A342, 1592; A233, 1598; A230, [1598]; B968, 1602; B971, 1603; B895, 1603; B806, 1604.

25 Poma de Ayala (1615), *Nueva corónica*, 1164; BNP, Z436, 1595, f. 225r.

26 The major exception was the Castrovirreyna mita, which lasted four months.

27 BNP, B28, 1607, f. 2v.

28 The net attrition rate would exclude those who fled the mines, but returned to their home communities. The calculation for Andahuaylas assumes an otherwise stable total tributary mass, in which new eighteen-year old males would cancel out declines due to old age, sickness, and death.

29 See the sources in note 23. On the importance of complex coordination of various agricultural and herding cycles in traditional Andean society, see Jürgen Golte, *La racionalidad de la organización andina* (Lima, 1980), esp. 25-33.

30 The important study by Lorenzo Huertas Vallejos, "Historia de las luchas sociales de Ayacucho, 1700-1940" (unpub. ms., 1974), points out the basic contrast between sixteenth and eighteenth century communities, and the resulting differences in the nature of their struggles.

31 Ribera y Chaves (1586), "Relación . . . de Guamanga," 185.

32 See HC, Doc, 1010, 1587; BNP, B75, 1626, ff. 51r-53r, 53r-54v; Z304, 1591, f. 1r-v; ADA, PN, Romo 1577, ff. 186r-188v, 91r-94v, 89r-90v, 86r-87v, 20v-24v; AGN, DI, Leg. 2, C. 25, 1578; AGN, TP, C. 380, C. 665 (ff. 42v-44r), C. 174, C. 8.

33 AGI, VI, Lima 529A, Residencia of Don Juan Manuel de Anaya, f. 1335v; AGI, V, Lima 313, Domingo de Santo Tomás to Royal Exchequer, Andahuaylas, 6 April 1562.

34 HC, Doc. 1010, 1587; Monzón et al. (1586), "Descripción . . . de Atunsora," 224; id. (1586), "Descripción . . . de Atunrucana y Laramati," 235; id. (1586), "Descripción . . . de los Rucanas Antamarcas," 247; Carabajal (1586), "Descripción . . . de Vilcas Guaman," 211, 212, 213, 214, 215, 216, 217 for modest production of European crops; Salas, De los obrajes, 86-89; AGN, JR, Leg. 24, C. 65, 1618, f. 404r-v; Juan López de Velasco (1571-1574), Geografía y descripción universal de las Indias, ed. Marcos Jiménez de la Espada (Madrid, 1971), 241.

35 The wealth represented by the herding economies in the south of Huamanga was obvious to the Europeans. Examples from the Lucanas repartimientos (Lucanas Laramati, Lucanas Andamarcas, Soras) are in AGI, VI, Lima 529A, ff. 1330v-1331r, 1342v, 1345r. Toledo was so impressed with the wealth of Lucanas Laramati that he nearly tripled their tribute assessment. Tasa de la visita general, ed. Cook, 261. The Soras encomienda of the powerful Palomino family enjoyed a reputation as Huamanga's richest. Lockhart, The Men of Cajamarca, 340. The natural abundance of pastures among the Chocorvos of Castrovirreyna, and the convertibility of herds into liquid wealth is indicated in the permission they received to commute tribute assessments — including money tributes in one case — to tributes in animals. AGN, JR, Leg. 24, C. 65, 1618, ff. 252r-295v. See also Poma de Ayala (1615), Nueva corónica, 559.

36 YC, Vol. 3, ff. 93r, 94r.

37 See HC, Doc. 1010, 1587; BNP, A314, 1588, ff. 1r-9r; AGI, VI, Lima 529A, ff. 1332r-v, 1330r, 1335r, 1342r, 1358r-v, 1369r, 1385v-1394r, 1406v-1407r; BNP, A236, 1597, f. 3r; A364, 1596; Z306, 1592, ff. 479v-480r; ADA, PN, Navarrete 1615-1618/1627/1630, ff. 605v-610v; AGN, Superior Gobierno, Leg. 2, C. 38, 1618, f. 33r.

38 Contrast the evidence given in the judicial reviews (residencias) of two corregidores of Lucanas, one in 1578-1580, and the other in 1633-1636. AGI, VI, Lima 529A; BNP, B1441, 1634; B1505, 1644. The surpluses available in the tributes extracted from relatively wealthy, dynamic local economies in Huamanga during the sixteenth century are highlighted in HC, Doc. 1004, 1581.

39 See Marx, Capital, 3:790-91.

40 Lockhart, Spanish Peru, 206-7.

41 With the establishment of a special corregidor for Castrovirreyna later in the

sixteenth century, the Indians of the province of Chocorvos fell under the juris-diction of the governor-corregidor of the city of Castrovirreyna.

42 For an excellent, detailed history of the corregidores de indios, which bears comparing with the data from Huamanga, see Lohmann, *El corregidor.*

43 See Spalding, "Social Climbers," 655–58, 661–62.

44 For a bitter denunciation of the power group by a remarkable Indian chronicler from Huamanga, see Poma de Ayala (1615), *Nueva corónica,* 489–95, 662–63, sketch on 596. For an important article discussing similar dynamics in Brazil, see Stuart B. Schwartz, "Magistracy and Society in Colonial Brazil," *HAHR* 50 (November 1970), 715–30. For a discussion of internal contradictions within the power structure, see Chapter 5 below.

45 AGI, VI, Lima 529A, f. 1344r; BNP, Z306, 1592, ff. 490r, 491r (silversmiths); ADA, PN, Soria 1598, f. 668r (central plaza); ADA, Corregimiento, Causas Ordinarias, [Leg. 2], 1678, f. 935r–v (lands); BNP, Z1421, 1634, ff. 211r–216v (lands, loans); RPIA, tomo 21, partida XXXIII, 338–39, 326 (lands); ADA, PN, Palma 1619, ff. 441r, 384r–385r (lands); AAA, Siglo XVII, Estante 3, Exp. 7 (lands); AGN, JR, Leg. 11, C. 29, 1593, item 14, ff. 123r–159v (lands, herds, meat supplier "by custom"); ADA, PN, Navarrete *1615–1618*/1627/1630, f. 69v (mines in Parinacochas); Palma 1619, ff. 310r–314r (loans); Palma 1625, ff. 262v–263v, 266r–267r, 808v–809v, 434v–435v, 452r–453v (loans); Morales 1630, ff. 310r–311r (loans); Palma 1609, ff. 248r–250v (patron of Santo Domingo).

46 AGI, VI, Lima 529A, ff. 1330v, 1335v; ADA, PN, Ysidro 1577, ff. 190r–201v.

47 AGI, VI, Lima 529A, f. 1345v. Cf. Poma de Ayala (1615), *Nueva corónica,* 809.

48 AGN, JR, Leg. 24, C. 65, 1618, f. 407r. Cf. Poma de Ayala (1615), *Nueva corónica,* 489.

49 For specific examples, see ADA, PN, Cárdenas 1585, ff. 173v–174v, 198v–199v (fianzas by two high elites and encomenderos); AGN, TP, C. 388, 1636, f. 30r; JR, Leg. 23, C. 62, 1617, ff. 184r, 187r, 219r (local hacendados as lieutenants of corregidor). Cf. AGI, VI, Lima 1188, Sentence against Mateo de Cáceres y So-tomayor (1636), item 4.

50 For particularly vivid accounts with Spanish as well as Indian victims, see AGI, VI, Lima 532A, Residencia of Don Esteban López de Silves, esp. ff. 1r, 6v, 21r–23r, 26r; AGN, JR, Leg. 24, C. 65, 1618, f. 139v; BNP, B28, 1607, esp. f. 6v.

51 This is precisely what happened to Anaya in Lucanas (see AGI, VI, Lima 529A), whose cruel reputation was recorded in Poma de Ayala (1615), *Nueva co-rónica,* 607. For another corregidor who overreached himself by expropriating animals, leathers, and other goods from Spaniards as well as Indians, see ADA, PN, Cárdenas 1585, ff. 198v–199v. Similar cases involving priests are in AAA, Siglo XVII, Estante 3, Exp. 28 and Exp. 51. On the residencia as a bureau-cratic institution, see John Leddy Phelan, *The Kingdom of Quito in the Seventeenth Century: Bureaucratic Politics in the Spanish Empire* (Madison, 1967), 216–17.

52 AGN, JR, Leg. 11, C. 29, 1593, ff. 68v–69r; BNP, Z1124, 1631, f. 489r. For the conversion of sugar loaves into arrobas, and the judgment that an arroba was "worth" five pesos corrientes (8–9 reales each), see BNP, Z1124, 1631, ff. 542r, 519v. The five pesos figure is conservative, and well below prices in decent mar-ket years. (For sale of the hacienda's sugar at eight pesos per arroba some twelve

years earlier, in 1618, see ADA, PN. Navarrete *1615-1618*/1627/1630, f. 243r.) For a contract with a modestly prosperous Indian muledriver, which includes a (generous) two reales per day for food expenses, see ADA, PN, Morales 1630, f. 290r. At that rate, nine arrobas of sugar, worth about forty-five pesos corrientes, would have easily fed the muledriver six months or more.

53 See ADA, PN, Soria 1593/*1601,* f. 105v; Ysidro 1577, ff. 188r-189r. The latter documents Anaya's shipment of fourteen ingots and a plate of silver, worth 4,700 pesos ensayados, from Huamanga to Lima in 1577.

54 AGI, VI, Lima 529A, ff. 1344r, 1345v for labor and textiles; 1330v-1331r, 1342v-1343r for forced sale of animals; 1326v-1327r, 1329v-1330r, 1341v-1342r for arrangement with Troncoso.

55 Ibid., ff. 1332r-v, 1335v, 1342r, 1329v, 1330r, 1328v, 1341v, 1406v-1407r.

56 ADA, PN, Cárdenas 1585, ff. 198v-199v; HC, Doc. 1010, 1587; BNP, A236, 1597, f. 3r; A314, 1588, f. 2r; A364, 1596; Poma de Ayala (1615), *Nueva corónica,* 489. Cf. Lohmann, *El corregidor,* 293-306.

57 See, for examples and complaints, BNP, B57, 1616; B59, 1618; AGN, JR, Leg. 23, C. 62, 1617, f. 142r-v; BNP, Z37, 1640, ff. 387v-389v.

58 See AGN, JR, Leg. 11, C. 29, 1593, ff. 61v, 67v, 166r; Leg. 23, C. 62, 1617, ff. 142r, 184r, 187v; Leg. 24, C. 65, 1618, ff. 57v, 65v, 107v.

59 AGN, JR, Leg. 24, C. 65, 1618, ff. 57v-58r, 59r, 65v, 67r, 108r, 258r-v, 404r-v; ADA, PN, Cárdenas 1585, f. 198v; BNP, A239, 1587, f. 1r. (The latter document concerns confiscation of coca in the Cuzco part of the montaña which stretched from Huamanga to Cuzco, but there is every reason to believe that similar practices abounded in Huamanga's portion of the montaña.)

60 AGN, JR, Leg. 24, C. 65, 1618, ff. 404v, 259v, 57r, 62v-63r, 65r, 66r, 107v (quotation), 108r, 404r-407v; Leg. 23, C. 62, 1617, ff. 199v, 120r; BNP, B1485, 1600, f. 70r. Cf. Lohmann, *El corregidor,* 424.

61 For examples in cases other than corregidores and their lieutenants, see AGN, JR, Leg. 11, C. 29, 1593, f. 68v; AAA, Siglo XVII, Estante 3, Exp. 51, ff. 25v-26r, 27v, 68r-89v, 168v-169r; AGI, VI, Lima 1189, Sentence against Gregorio Fernández de Castro (1647), penalty against Alonso de Sotomayor, protector de naturales. See also Aponte (1622), "Memorial . . . de la reformación," 527.

62 For a single repartimiento with dozens of lay assistants who thereby claimed mita exemptions, see BNP, B28, 1607, f. 2r-v. Cf. Spalding, "Social Climbers," 657-58; Pablo Macera, "Feudalismo colonial americano: el caso de las haciendas peruanas," in Macera, *Trabajos de historia* (4 vols., Lima, 1977), 3:170-71.

63 Poma de Ayala (1615), *Nueva corónica,* 1101; AAA, Siglo XVII, Estante 3, Exp. 51, f. 133r.

64 See AAA, Siglo XVII, Estante 3, Exp. 51, esp. ff. 25v-26r, 27v-30v, 69v, 89r-90r, 133r-v, 168v-169v for particularly concrete data on relations with a rural priest. For evidence that a rural parish offered a good base for extensive commercial interests, see ADA, PN, Ysidro 1577, ff. 190r-201v, 205v-206v; Soria 1593/*1601,* f. 206r. On the priest in the mines, AAA, Siglo XVII, Estante 3, Exp. 28, f. lv (quote).

65 On the censos and the cajas de comunidad as a source of capital or revenue, see

HC, Doc. 1010, 1587; BNP, A314, 1588, ff. 1r-9r; Z306, 1592, ff. 479v-480r; B865, 1634, ff. 1r-2v; Z323, 1616, f. 19v; A364, 1596, f. 1r; ADA, PN, Navarrete 1615-1618/*1627*/1630, ff. 605v-610v; BNP, B1505, 1644, ff. 37v-39r; AGI, VI, Lima 529A, ff. 1358r-1406v. Cf. Vilma Cevallo López, "La caja de censos de indios y su aporte a la economía colonial, 1565-1613," *Revista del Archivo Nacional del Perú* 26, entrega 2 (Lima, 1962), 269-352.

66 Lohmann, *Las minas,* 59-89, 101-22; BNP, B1042, 1627, f. 4r; B846, 1618, f. 3r.

67 Data on the composiciones de tierras in Huamanga abounds in the documents cited in Appendix B, "Guide to Colonial Land Tenure Documents for Huamanga." For a general overview, see Rowe, "The Incas," 181-82; Rolando Mellafe, "Frontera agraria: el caso del virreinato peruano en el siglo XVI," in *Tierras nuevas,* ed. Alvaro Jara (Guanajuato, 1969), 37-42; Saldamando (1879-1880), *Apuntes,* 97-102.

68 The list of mitayos and beneficiaries, in BNP, A18, 1599, accounts for 761 of the 778 mita natives. The calculations which follow exclude 80 natives distributed to ten corporate institutions such as the public jail, Dominican convent, etc.

69 In two cases, the "citizen" actually denotes a group of heirs.

70 The ten are Antonio de Mañueco, heirs of Jerónimo de Oré, Melchor de Cárdenas, Doña Ynés de Villalobos (widow of Amador de Cabrera), Hernando Palomino, Pedro Díaz de Rojas, Pedro de Rivera, Diego Gavilán, Hernán Guillén de Mendoza, heirs of Leonor de Valenzuela.

71 The calculation includes the siblings, spouses, and children of the people cited in note 70. Because Hernando Palomino and Doña Leonor de Valenzuela were brother and sister, we are dealing with nine rather than ten elite families.

72 The examples are from a loose folio in BNP, A18, 1599, which records the changing mita obligations of six repartimientos.

73 Salas, *De los obrajes,* 61-64; AGN, DI, Leg. 6, C. 113, 1646, ff. 1r-2r; BNP, Z351, 1616, f. 663r; Z441, 1633, f. 2r; B28, 1607.

74 See the documents cited in note 10; Poma de Ayala (1615), *Nueva corónica,* 734; Lohmann, *Las minas,* 24, 26, 50, 72, 103-6, 120-21, 124.

75 For examples, see ADA, PN, Soria 1598, f. 248v (Juan de Sotomayor); AGN, TP, C. 682, 1602 (Julián de Bastida).

76 See Lohmann, *Las minas,* 59-89, 126-28, 142-43; BNP, B934, 1616, f. 6r-v; AGN, Superior Gobierno, Leg. 2, C. 38, 1618, f. 33r-v.

77 Poma de Ayala (1615), *Nueva corónica,* 489, 763; AGN, JR, Leg. 24, C. 65, 1618, f. 407r; TP, Leg. 18, C. 370, 1607-1688, f. 11r; DI, Leg. 6, C. 108, 1643, ff. 8r-9v; ADA, PN, Peña 1596, ff. 171v-176r; Navarrete 1615-1618/*1627*/1630, ff. 420r-424v; Ysidro 1577, ff. 229r-230r, 256r-257r. Cf. Mellafe, "Frontera agraria," 33-34.

78 For the cabildo and its composition, see AGN, JR, Leg. 11, C. 29, 1593, f. 344r; Leg. 16, C. 44, 1599, ff. 3v-4r. Cf. John Preston Moore, *The Cabildo in Peru under the Hapsburgs* (Durham, N.C., 1954). For six examples of rural priests from prestigious families, see AGN, JR, Leg. 23, C. 62, 1617, f. 35r-v; BNP, B1505, 1644, ff. 6v, 7r-v. For examples of Huamanga elites as collector of church taxes, rural corregidor, and inspector of land titles, see BNP, Z351, 1616, f. 664v; AAA, Siglo XVII, Estante 3, Exp. 28, f. 8r; BNP, B820, 1643, f. 19r.

79 ADA, PN, Navarrete *1615–1618*/1627/1630, f. 130r; AGN, TP, C. 10, 1576, f. lv; BNP, Z306, 1592, ff. 472r–473v for the specific cases mentioned. (The documents for Huamanga are filled with further examples.)

80 BNP, Z313, 1616, ff. 184r–188r for dowry; Frederick P. Bowser, *The African Slave in Colonial Peru, 1524–1650* (Stanford, 1974), Appendix B, for slave prices.

81 BNP, A236, 1597, ff. 51v–52r, 106r–110v; AGN, JR, Leg. 23, C. 62, 1617, ff. 142r–v, 66v–67r, 79v, 92v–93r, 124r, 144r–v, 145r–v, 171r–198v, and the comment in Chapter 5, note 24.

82 See AAA, Siglo XVII, Estante 3, Exp. 51, esp. ff. 25r–27v, 31v, 37v–39v, 73r–75r, 80r–83v, 133r–v. Note the signatures by the *kuraka principal* on a document against the priest in 1630, and on a supportive document in 1631. Ibid., ff. 80v, 133v.

83 On this murky event, which gained notoriety in Huamanga, see Rubén Vargas Ugarte, *Historia general del Perú* (10 vols., Lima, 1966–71), 3:20–21; Fidel Olivas Escudero, *Apuntes para la historia de Huamanga ó Ayacucho* (Ayacucho, 1924), 15–16.

84 According to a chronicler from the Huamanga region, encomenderos and their wives had themselves carried on litters as part of a festive procession when visiting their Indians. Poma de Ayala (1615), *Nueva corónica,* 554–55.

85 See AGN, JR, Leg. 23, C. 62, 1617, ff. 46v, 73r–v (for Vilcashuamán quotation), 66v–67r, 79v, 92v–93r, 124r, 142r–v, 145r–159v, 204r; BNP, B1505, 1644, f. 24r–v; DI, Leg. 3, C. 50, 1606, f. 103r (Andahuaylas quotation).

86 For the last two paragraphs, see Lohmann, *Las minas,* 93, esp. note 3; HC, Doc. 984, 1571; BNP, B1441, 1634, ff. 79r, 80r–v, 83v, 85v–86r, 88r, 89r, 90v, 93r, 103r; B28, 1607; Z313, 1616, f. 196r–v; B57, 1616, ff. 2v, 4v, 5v; B1079, 1629, f. 76v; AGN, DI, Leg. 4, C. 65, 1619, f. lv; JR, Leg. 11, C. 29, 1593, f. 69r; Poma de Ayala (1615), *Nueva corónica,* 520; Aponte (1622), "Memorial . . . de la reformación," 534–35.

87 BNP, A6, 1599.

88 This was the standard notation for deficits among Lucanas mitayos sent to Castrovirreyna, as recorded in the sources cited in note 10. For six mitas between 1597–1603, the percentages of no-shows were 9.7, 8.9, 0.0, 0.7, 0.3, and 2.7 percent. For the increasing severity of the problem in the seventeenth century, see Chapter 5.

89 Lohmann, *Las minas,* 251–52. For possible evidence of another such case, see BNP, A6, 1599, and A18, 1599, f. 4v.

90 BNP, B28, 1607, esp. f. 6v; Poma de Ayala (1615), *Nueva corónica,* 520. Cf. BNP, B1079, 1629, f. 76v.

91 AGN, JR. Leg. 24, C. 65, 1618, f. 139v. For other examples of punishment ranging from physical confinement to outright hangings, see AGI, VI, Lima 529A, f. 1345r; Poma de Ayala (1615), *Nueva corónica,* 494–97, 525–26, 557–58.

92 Poma de Ayala (1615), *Nueva corónica,* 529–30; Ribera y Chaves (1586), "Relación . . . de Guamanga," 186, for quotations.

93 See AAA, Siglo XVII, Estante 3, Exp. 28, f. lv; Estante 3, Exp. 51, ff. 31r, 169r. For vivid examples of violent fighting and gang-style rampages which plagued social life in Huamanga, see AGI, VI, Lima 532A, Residencia of Don Esteban

López de Silves, corregidor of Huamanga (1637), ff. 1r, 8v, 9r, 21r–23r, 26r, 45v, 46r.

94 AGN, DI, Leg. 1, C. 8, 1576, f. 28v.

95 Bernabé Cobo (1653), *Historia del nuevo mundo,* in *Biblioteca de Autores Españoles,* vols. 91–92 (Madrid, 1956), bk. 12, ch. 37; Lohmann, *Las minas,* 137. For an early seventeenth-century example of fears of potential violence or rebellion, see Vargas Ugarte, *Historia general,* 3:173–74.

96 See BNP, B1441, 1634, ff. 27v, 28v; Z1124, 1631, ff. 481v, 518v, 543r for mention of fires; AGN, JR, Leg. 23, C. 62, 1617, f. 13v for precautions against fire; Leg. 24, C. 65, 1618, f. 175r for sabotage in putting-out systems; Minería, Leg. 13, Huancavelica 1585–1591, Exp. 2, f. 8r for quotation.

97 AGN, JR, Leg. 23, C. 62, 1617, ff. 174r, 176r–v, 179v–180r, 182v, 202v, 204r–v, 211r.

98 See Lohmann, *Las Minas,* 31 (n. 65), 34, 452–53 (production figures in Column I). Lohmann's figures correspond well to those recorded for 1586–1588 in a contemporary document about royal finances, except in 1586, when Lohmann's figure seems 2100 quintales too low. See ff. 5r–8r of a 154-folio document included within AGN, Minería, Leg. 13, Huancavelica 1585–1591, Exp. 2.

99 For official production figures and prices paid to the Crown treasury for mercury in 1587, see AGN, Minería, Leg. 13, Huancavelica 1585–1591, Exp. 2, ff. 5r–8r (of extra 154-folio document included within Exp. 2). On contraband as a high share, perhaps 40 percent, of total production, see ibid., ff. 10v–11r, 15v, 40r–50r (of main document); Lohmann, *Las minas,* 445; Vázquez (1629), *Compendio,* 502. For a 15:1 ratio of ore to refined mercury in 1569, see AGN, Minería, Leg. 11, Huancavelica 1562–1572, ff. 256v–257r. Even after allowing for substantial technical improvements, the ratio was no better than 10:1. Cf. Lohmann, *Las minas,* 130. On corregidor salaries (I used an average figure of 1,700 pesos corrientes, or c. 1,200 pesos ensayados), see Lohmann, *El corregidor,* 182–83, 595–600.

100 BNP, A218, 1591, f. 1r; Vázquez (1629), *Compendio,* 493–94, for production of 36,000–40,000 marks of silver (c. 5 pesos ensayados, or 7 pesos corrientes, each) a year.

101 In Huancavelica, the royal "quinto," or the Crown's right to a fifth of registered mercury provided the royal treasury about 1,940 quintales, or 182,360 pesos corrientes at 94 pesos per quintal. On the remaining 7,760 quintales, the Crown made 51 pesos per quintal by paying miners low prices for mercury resold to merchants at the official price. The mark-up totalled 395,760 pesos. The combined revenues totalled 578,120 pesos, or 47.3 percent of total production, estimated at 13,000 quintales (1,222,000 pesos).

At Castrovirreyna, the Crown's revenues were estimated at about 45,000 pesos corrientes (c. 32,000 pesos ensayados) around 1610, when total production was 250,000–275,000 pesos. Vázquez (1629), *Compendio,* 495.

102 Merchants paid 94 pesos (of nine reales) per quintal to the Crown for mercury in 1587. By paying about 39 pesos less for contraband mercury, they made 128,700 pesos on a conservative estimate of 3,300 quintales of contraband.

103 See especially AGN, Minería, Leg. 13, 1585–1591, Exp. 2, ff. 7v–8r, 10v–11r, 15v,

18r, 20r, 21r, 22v, 44r–50r, 54r–v; ADA, Corregimiento, Causas Ordinarias, Leg. 1, C. 14, 1650, f. 2r; cf. AGN, Superior Gobierno, Leg. 2, C. 38, 1618, ff. 31v–32r, 33r–v, 34v–35r, 37r, 38v–39r. For the proliferation of small to medium miners, see a partial list of twenty-three miners (or mining partnerships), including five Indians, for 1577, in BMA, Libro 1.31, ff. 48r–71v.

104 AGN, Minería, Leg. 13, Huancavelica 1585–1591, Exp. 2, ff. 26r–27r.

105 For calculations of official mita wages at 67.1 percent of total cost of production for a Huancavelica miner with rights to 100 mitayos, see Lohmann, *Las minas,* 443–44. At this rate, costs of production beyond mita wages would have come to 109,631 pesos.

106 On Eastern Europe, see note 21. For examples of attempts to hold down the "monetarization" of expenses in an obraje-hacienda complex of Huamanga, even when the accumulated debt of the owner to Indian workers could total thousands of pesos (e.g., the equivalent of more than an entire year's profits), see BNP, B1485, 1600, ff. 13v–45r; Salas, *De los obrajes,* 72–79, 83–85, 124, 162–63. On the mines, see the discussion which follows in the text, and the sources in notes 107 and 109.

107 In addition to the discussion of the mita earlier in this chapter, see HC, Doc. 981, 1578; AGN, Minería, Leg. 13, Huancavelica 1585–1591, Exp. 2, f. 7v.

108 For estimates of 1587 costs and revenues, see the discussion in the text above. For a contemporary calculation of expenses for a mine with 100 mitayos which shows that savings on nominal wage costs could increase profits handsomely, see Lohmann, *Las minas,* 443–45.

109 For the specific examples of Juan de Sotomayor, Pedro de Contreras, and Amador de Cabrera, all of them leading miners, see the sources in note 10; Poma de Ayala (1615), *Nueva corónica,* 734; AGN, Minería, Leg. 11, Huancavelica 1562–1572, f. 681r–v; JR, Leg. 11, C. 29, 1593, f. 274r; BNP, Z532, 1624, f. 557r–v.

110 The standard calculation of official productivity was normally three quintales per mitayo. See AGN, Minería, Leg. 14, Huancavelica 1592–1594, f. 33r. After deducting the royal fifth (60 of 300 quintales), the Crown would have paid the miner for 240 quintales. Prices fluctuated, but at a low price of 50 pesos corrientes per quintal, Crown payments would total 12,000 pesos. If we assume a conservative 25-percent contraband rate, total production would have been 400 quintales. At 55 pesos corrientes, merchants would have paid 5,500 pesos for contraband. Gross revenues would have totalled 17,500 pesos.

111 BNP, B846, 1618, esp. ff. 1r–3r.

112 The importance of Huancavelica, Castrovirreyna, and Huamanga as commercial and economic "poles" attracting a flow of commodities in human beings (slaves), labor-power (rental of mitayos and hired laborers), agricultural and animal products, and artisanal and manufactured goods was well known to contemporaries and is obvious in the notarial records of the late sixteenth and early seventeenth centuries deposited at the ADA. On the role of mines and cities as economic "poles," see Gwendoline B. Cobb, "Supply and Transportation for the Potosí Mines, 1545–1640," *HAHR* 29 (February 1949), 25–45; Carlos Sempat Assadourian, "Integración y desintegración regional en el espacio colonial: un enfoque histórico," *EURE. Revista Latinoamericana de Estudios Urbanos Regionales* 4

(1972), 11–23; Assadourian et al., *Minería y espacio económico en los andes. Siglos XVI–XX* (Lima, 1980), 20–33.

113 BNP, Z1124, 1631, f. 544r; Salas, *De los obrajes,* 100.

114 See Salas, *De los obrajes,* 57, 115–18; Poma de Ayala (1615), *Nueva corónica,* 489; BNP, A236, 1597, f. 106r.

115 Fray Luis Jerónimo de Oré, *Symbolo Catholico Indiano* (Lima, 1598), 31 (copy in BNP, Sala de Investigaciones); HC, Doc. 975, 1591.

116 This level of production applied to irrigated fields, which later lost waters diverted to the city of Huamanga. AGN, JR, Leg. 11, C. 29, 1593, f. 274r; BNP, A203, 1557, ff. 24v–25r.

117 Marcos Jiménez de Espada, ed., note in Ribera y Chaves y de Guevara (1586), "Relación . . . de Guamanga," 187–88; Rodrigo de Cantos de Andrada (1586), "Relación de la Villa Rica de Oropesa y minas de Guancavelica," *RGI,* 304; Lohmann, *Las minas,* 47–50, 113–14, 128–31; Vázquez (1629), *Compendio,* 493–94; D. A. Brading and Harry E. Cross, "Colonial Silver Mining: Mexico and Peru," *HAHR* 52 (November 1972), 551–52, 555–56.

118 Patterns of enterprise and land tenure emerged from examination of hundreds of documents. For a partial guide to documents related to land tenure in Huamanga, see Appendix B.

119 This was the case of Antonio de Oré. Salas, *De los obrajes,* 44–46. For a comparable portfolio of diversified economic interests, see the sources on Hernando Palomino cited in note 45 above.

120 Evidence for these patterns is extensive in the land tenure documents cited in Appendix B, and in the notarial books deposited in ADA. A few specific examples are cited in note 121. On the technology of colonial mining and manufactures, which meant that initial capital costs were considerable, see Lohmann, *Las minas,* passim; "Tecnología indígena: el obraje de Cacamarca," ed. Carlos A. Romero, *Inca* 1 (1923), 624–50.

121 BNP, B75, 1626, ff. 1r, 7r–8v, 11r–14v, 49v–50r, 56r; Z1124, 1631, f. 515v; A473, 1597, ff. 1r–5r.

122 For an inventory of the estate of a deceased Castrovirreyna miner who left behind 54 bars of silver valued at 25,000 pesos corrientes (19,355 pesos ensayados), see AGN, TP, C. 682, 1602, ff. 21v–27v.

123 See E. J. Hobsbawm, "The Crisis of the Seventeenth Century," in *Crisis in Europe, 1560–1660,* ed. Trevor Aston (New York, 1967), 5–62; Pío Max Medina, *Monumentos coloniales de Huamanga (Ayacucho)* (Ayacucho, 1942).

CHAPTER 5: THE INDIANS AND SPANISH JUSTICE

1 AGN, DI, Leg. 39, C. 798, 1624, f. 3r for quotations. La Merced, the church mentioned above, is on the street from the plaza to the house of a descendant of the family in contemporary Ayacucho.

2 Mario Góngora, *El estado en el derecho indiano. Época de fundación (1492–1570)* (Santiago de Chile, 1951), 29–35, 196, 308–9; Phelan, *The Kingdom of Quito,* 38.

3 HC, Doc. 1012, 1556; *Gobernantes,* ed. Levillier, 8:257–60, 263–72.

4 Land pressure became more common in the late colonial period. The investiga-

tions of Lorenzo Huertas Vallejos show that Indian struggles for land held a prominent place in Ayacucho's eighteenth-century history, but not earlier.

5 On the composición de tierras, see Rowe, "The Incas," 181-82; Mellafe, "Frontera agraria," 36-40.

6 The composiciones for lands without legal title always included statements testifying to their unused state, but for evidence that fallow lands were subject to usurpation even by other Indians, see AGN, DI, Leg. 6, C. 107, 1642, f. 27v.

7 Rowe, "The Incas," 191.

8 See BNP, A393, 1594, ff. 47v-48r; Z1067, 1685, ff. 237r-238v.

9 AGN, DI, Leg. 6, C. 107, 1642, ff. 5r-v, 10r-11v, 14r-v, 82r-v; RPIA, tomo 5, partida LXI, 176; ADA, PN, Navarrete 1615-1618/1627/*1630,* ff. 712v-718r, 711v-712r, 720r-725v. See also BNP, Z1067, 1685, ff. 205r-206r, 237r-238v, for another payoff to get Indian litigants to withdraw a suit.

10 ADA, PN, Peña 1596, f. 82r.

11 AGN, DI, Leg. 6, C. 113, 1646, ff. 1r-2v; BNP, B1370, 1625, f. 1r.

12 See Appendix C; BNP, A18, 1599. For evidence of even earlier inspections, see BNP, Z436, 1595, f. 222r.

13 BNP, B934, 1616.

14 On the widespread character of such attempts to "stretch" exemptions, see Pablo Macera, "Feudalismo colonial," in Macera, *Trabajos,* 3:170-71.

15 BNP, B28, 1607, passim. (f. 6v for quote).

16 BNP, Z313, 1616, ff. 196r-206r; Z351, 1616, f. 661v.

17 See AGI, VI, Lima 529A, Residencia of Don Juan Manuel de Anaya, esp. ff. 1332v, 1406v-1407r, and Anaya's comeback as royal treasurer in 1601, in ADA, PN, Soria 1593/*1601,* f. 105v; AGN, JR, Leg. 11, C. 29, 1593, f. 350r-v; Leg. 24, C. 65, 1618, ff. 1r-2v, 193r-194v, 202r-203r.

18 Salas, *De los obrajes,* 163-69.

19 BNP, B1485, 1600, ff. 62r, 247r, 49r.

20 See BNP, Z1067, 1685, ff. 206r-238v; A393, 1594, ff. 36r-v, 47v-48v, 50r, 51v-52r; B1525, 1647, ff. 2r-3v; ADA, Corregimiento, Causas Ordinarias, Leg. 1, C. 2, 1599, f. 4r-v; [Leg. 2], 1678, f. 935r.

21 BNP, Z304, 1591, ff. 2v-3r. See also AGN, TP, Leg. 18, C. 370, 1607, f. 15r.

22 See AAA, Siglo XVII, Estante 3, Exp. 28, 1626.

23 BNP, Z436, 1595, ff. 222r-223r, 225v-227r, 229v-230v, 231r-v.

24 For widespread suspicions and evidence that many were well founded, see BNP, B57, 1616; B59, 1618; B1505, 1644, ff. 24v-25r; Z37, 1640, ff. 387v-389v, 398v-401r; A236, 1597, ff. 51v-52r, 106r-110v; B1485, 1600, f. 59v; AGN, JR, Leg. 23, C. 62, 1617, ff. 66v-67r, 79v, 92v-93r, 124r, 142r-v, 144r-v, 145r-v, 171r-198v. The latter citation documents favorable opinions of a corregidor by Indians whom he supposedly abused in a vain attempt to collect tributes, and the encomenderos' contention that the tribute collection attempts were perfunctory cover-ups of an unofficial extractive system managed by corregidor and kurakas.

25 On the protector de indios, in Huamanga and more generally, see Constantino Bayle, *El protector de indios* (Seville, 1945); Lohmann, *El corregidor,* 333-34; AGI,

VI, Lima 1189, Sentence against Gregorio Fernández de Castro (1647), charges against Alonso de Sotomayor; Aponte (1622), "Memorial . . . de la reformación," 526-27.

26 AGI, VI, Lima 1189, Sentence against Gregorio Fernández de Castro (1647), charges against Sotomayor.

27 ADA, PN, Cárdenas 1585, ff. 178v-180r; Soria 1589, ff. 140r-141r, 207r-v, 208r-v, 269v-270v.

28 ADA, PN, Peña 1596, ff. 237v-238v (237v for quote).

29 See AGN, DI, Leg. 39, C. 798, 1624, ff. 2v-3v; Leg. 24, C. 686, 1601, f. 1r-v.

30 In particular, see the record in BNP, B1079, 1629, passim. See also AGN, DI, Leg. 4, C. 73, 1622, esp. ff. 311r, 316r; Leg. 3, C. 50, 1606, ff. 88r, 106v.

31 BNP, B1079, 1629, ff. 86r-93r.

32 Ibid., ff. 68r-80r.

33 AGN, DI, Leg. 6, C. 109, 1643, f. 5r.

34 BNP, B856, 1616; B876, 1629, f. 13v; B1079, 1629, ff. 68r-80r, 82r-85r, 86r-93r; B1159, 1629, ff. 7r-32v; B1505, 1644, ff. 13v-17r; AGN, DI, Leg. 4, C. 73, 1622.

35 AGN, DI, Leg. 39, C. 798, 1624, f. 3r; BNP, B1505, 1644, ff. 13v-17r; B1159, 1629, ff. 3r-v, 4r.

36 BNP, B1505, 1644, ff. 24v-25r (emphasis added).

37 BNP, B1079, 1629, f. 10v.

38 AGN, DI, Leg. 3, C. 50, 1606, ff. 64r, 110v-111r.

39 For a day-by-day summary account of a revisita which took nearly five months and produced a written record of 740 folio pages, see ibid., ff. 101r-107v.

40 AGN, DI, Leg. 4, C. 65, 1619, f. 2v; Leg. 4, C. 73, 1622, ff. 311r, 316r.

41 BNP, B1505, 1644, ff. 24r-31r, esp. 26r-27v. Cf. the case of Lucanas Laramati on ff. 13v-16r. On epidemic disease in the 1580s, see Dobyns, "An Outline," 501-8.

42 See AGN, DI, Leg. 3, C. 50, 1606, ff. 81r-v, 65r-66v, 86r-89r (86v for quote).

43 BNP, B54, 1609, f. 21v. The idolatry investigation recorded in this document was transcribed, with some errors, as "Idolatrías de los indios Huachos y Yauyos," *Revista Histórica* 6 (1918), 180-97. On the use of terrain and elusive settlement patterns to hide natives during the seventeenth century, see the perceptive comments of Franklin Pease G. Y., *Del Tawantinsuyu a la historia del Perú* (Lima, 1978), 199-200.

44 AGI, V, Lima 308, Report of the inspection by Bishop Verdugo, 1625, pp. 3, 9 (of microfilm copy).

45 For evidence of the significance of forasteros in a revisita before 1650 (despite the group's unimportance for inspection purposes at the time), see AGN, DI, Leg. 6, C. 119, 1648, ff. 109r, 111v, 113r, 114r, 116v. See also ADA, Cabildo, Causas Civiles, Leg. 1, C. 6, 1676, f. 5r; AGI, V, Lima 308, Description of the Bishopric of Huamanga, 1624-1625, notations for Tambo, Mayoc, Pampas, Huambalpa, Gerónimo; Report of the inspection by Verdugo, pp. 2-3.

46 AGI, V, Lima 308, Report of the inspection by Verdugo, p. 8.

47 Lorenzo Huertas Vallejos et al., *La revisita de los Chocorbos de 1683* (Ayacucho, 1976), 55, 61-70, 145, 150. These figures exclude forasteros attached to European lands, but include three adult sons of community forasteros. For back-

ground on the forasteros and data that supports their statistical importance, see Sánchez-Albornoz, *Indios y tributos*; Oscar Cornblit, "Society and Mass Rebellion in Eighteenth-Century Peru and Bolivia," in *Latin American Affairs,* ed. Raymond Carr (St. Anthony's Papers, No. 22, London, 1970), 24-27. The forthcoming dissertation of Ann Wightman, Yale University, on forasteros in Cuzco will do much to enlighten our understanding of this group.

48 See Basto, *Las mitas,* 5-6, 10-11; AGI, V, Lima 308, Report of the inspection by Verdugo, p. 3; ADA, PN, Palma 1609, ff. 82v, 207v; AGN, DI, Leg. 6, C. 109, 1643, f. 3r; BNP, B1079, 1629, ff. 73v, 75r, 76v, 79r. Note also the discussion of accumulations by Indians, and the dynamic role of native women, in Chapter 7 below.

49 For a discussion of birth rates and population fluctuations in preindustrial societies, see E. A. Wrigley, *Population and History* (New York, 1969), 62-106. For eighteenth-century evidence that an ethnic group could double a reduced population in thirty years, see Whitaker, *The Huancavelica Mercury Mine,* 49.

50 For the colonial history of Huancavelica, see Lohmann, *Las minas*; Brading and Cross, "Colonial Silver Mining," 545-79; Whitaker, *The Huancavelica Mercury Mine*; Gwendoline Ballantine Cobb, "Potosí and Huancavelica: Economic Bases of Peru, 1545 to 1640" (Ph.D. diss., Univ. of California, Berkeley, 1947).

51 BNP, A18, 1599 passim.; B462, 1601, f. 1r (Hernández quote); Z436, 1595, ff. 222r-v, 224r-v, 226r, 229v (222r for Castañeda quote). See also BNP, B740, 1610.

52 ADA, Cabildo, Asuntos Administrativos, Leg. 64, Exp. 2, 1645, ff. 3r-4r, 5r-v, 1r-v.

53 AGN, Minería, Leg. 2, Ayacucho 1622, ff. 16v-17v, 58r-v, 76r-v, 78r; see also Ribera y Chaves, "Relación . . . de Guamanga," 193.

54 See Lohmann, *Las minas,* 103, 107, 120, 144-45, 160-61, 178, 185-86, 222, 242-43, 251-60, 266, 284-85, n. 31 on 285; cf. Vargas, *Historia general,* 2:333-34 and 3:27, 180-83.

55 See AGN, DI, Leg. 4, C. 65, 1619, ff. 1r-4r (2v for quote); Lohmann, *Las minas,* 251-60; Vargas, *Historia general,* 3:181.

56 See, in addition to the sources in note 55, AGN, DI, Leg. 4, C. 65, 1619, ff. 4v-9v, 10r-12v (10r for quote), 15r-20r, 21v-22r; *Memorias de los virreyes que han gobernado el Perú* (6 vols., Lima, 1859), 1:85-88.

57 The Crown and the Marqués de Oropesa held tribute rights in fifteen of thirty-eight rural parishes toured by the Bishop of Huamanga. This figure excludes Parinacochas and Andahuaylas, where the two claimants held rights in fifteen of twenty-three rural parishes. See AGI, V, Lima 308, Description of the Bishopric of Huamanga, passim. On absenteeism among Huamanga's pensioners, see Fred Bronner, "Peruvian Encomenderos in 1630: Elite Circulation and Consolidation," *HAHR* 57 (November 1977), 653. On the Marqués de Oropesa, see Vargas, *Historia general,* 3:173-74. For a detailed history of the changing administration of Indian tribute, see Ronald Escobedo, *El tributo indígena en el Perú (siglos XVI-XVII)* (Pamplona, 1979).

58 See *Tasa de la visita general,* ed. Cook, 260-64, 276-80, xxviii-xxix, xvii; BNP, B1441, 1634, ff. 78v, 81r-v, 86v, 91r, 101r, 28r, 29r, 34r-35r, 46r-47r; B1505, 1644,

f. 4r–v, 14v–16r, 36v; AGN, JR. Leg. 23, C. 62, 1617, ff. 66v–67r, 79v, 92v–93r, 124r, 142r–v.

59 BNP, B1505, 1644, f. 24r.

60 The data above can be gleaned from BNP, B1370, 1625, f. 1r; Z313, 1616, ff. 164v–165v; Z351, 1616, ff. 662r–v, 663r, 668v; AGN, DI, Leg. 6, C. 113, 1646; BNP, B450, 1643, ff. 2r–4r; B164, 1640.

61 For a revealing set of documents on land histories of rival communities, see the community registries of lands in RPIA, tomo 5, partida VI, 18–21; tomo 8, partida XL, 132–34; tomo 10, partida CXXIII, 404–9; tomo 10, partida CXL, 468–69; tomo 13, partida LV, 328–34; tomo 14, partida VI, 39–60; tomo 21, partida XLVII, 457–69. See also AGN, DI, Leg. 6, C. 107, 1642, ff. 16r–v, 32r; Tierras de Comunidades, Leg. 3, C. 19, 1806, ff. 40r–43r, 46r–47v; ADA, PN, Soria 1589, f. 65v.

     We still await a historical study of the conditions which tended to favor or undermine a more or less stable *modus vivendi* in ethnically variegated areas. The investigations of John Earls south of the Río Pampas will represent an important contribution to this difficult topic.

62 See Rostworowski, "Succession," 417–27; Rostworowski, *Curacas y sucesiones*; and the sources in notes 64–65 below.

63 Murra, *Formaciones,* 193–223, esp. 221, 223; BNP, A387, 1594, f. 2r; YC, Vol. 5, ff. 62v, 63r (tribute payments by ayllu and ethnic lord).

64 ADA, PN, Peña 1596, f. 137r. Cf. Soria 1589, f. 67r.

65 BNP, A371, 1594; ADA, PN, Soria 1589, ff. 67r–71r (67r for Llanto quotes); Peña 1596, f. 137r. Cf. Cárdenas 1585, f. 144v.

66 Poma de Ayala (1615), *Nueva corónica,* 974. The example is from Sancos, south of the Río Pampas. Whatever the problems with Poma's general characterizations, my research tends to support Poma's veracity when he cites specific people or events in Huamanga.

67 See "Información presentada . . . en nombre de Juan Mocante," included in BNP, B856, 1616; AGN, DI, Leg. 6, C. 107, 1642, ff. 8r–v, 16r–v, 27v–28r; Leg. 6, C. 109, 1643, ff. 1r–4v, 3r for quote (cf. Leg. 6, C. 108, 1643, f. 1r).

68 See Spalding, *De indio a campesino,* 72–85, esp. 77, 82–83.

69 See ibid., 77–79; and note 24 above.

70 BNP, A387, 1594, f. 2r–v (2v for quote). The sites totalled some 1650 topos, an Andean measure which varied depending upon ecological conditions affecting productivity. One sale of twenty-seven topos by the same chief was, according to Spanish measure, thirty fanegadas (nearly ninety hectares). At that rate, the chief's total holdings would have amounted to some 5,000 hectares. Ibid., f. 4r–v. See also AGN, DI, Leg. 6, C. 107, 1642, ff. 16v–20r, 25v, 27r–v.

71 AGN, DI, Leg. 6, C. 107, 1642, f. 14r.

72 ADA, PN, Cárdenas 1585, ff. 110r–112v; Soria 1598, ff. 302r–303v.

73 AGN, DI, Leg. 3, C. 50, 1606, ff. 86v ("discord among the caciques"), 90v–91r (ranked hierarchy). My comments on the techniques of judge-investigators are speculation based on descriptions of the methods used by investigators of early seventeenth-century idolatry. For a revealing glimpse, albeit one from outside

the Huamanga region, see Arriaga (1621), *La extirpación,* esp. 133, 138. See also, from Huamanga, Albornoz (c. 1582), "Instrucción para descubrir, 38.

74 This process was partial and contradictory, in part because class and racial bonds sometimes worked at cross-purposes. But it was nonetheless very real, and served to integrate native elites more effectively into the world of Hispanic power. See Chapter 7 below, and for a more general discussion, Spalding, *De indio a campesino,* 31–87, 147–93.

75 See Ribera y Chaves (1586), "Relacion . . . de Guamanga," 185–86 for a common characterization; BNP, Z1124, 1631, ff. 472r–485r for records of missed workdays at an hacienda "because there were no people"; Poma de Ayala (1615), *Nueva corónica,* 529–30, for a revealing anecdote about a timid Spaniard unable to get the Indians to serve him.

76 On fires, BNP, B1441, 1634, ff. 27v, 28v; Z1124, 1631, ff. 481v, 518v, 543r. For an important treatment of anonymous or covert forms of protest as the normal outgrowth of an outwardly deferential society, see E. P. Thompson, "The Crime of Anonymity," in Douglas Hay et al., *Albion's Fatal Tree: Crime and Society in Eighteenth-Century England* (New York, 1975), 255–308.

77 BNP, B54, 1609, f. 26r; Stern, "Las ideologías nativistas," 26.

78 Any understanding of legality and ethics as an instrument of the hegemony of a ruling class benefits from the pioneering work of Antonio Gramsci. See especially "State and Civil Society," in Gramsci, *Selections from the Prison Notebooks,* eds. Quintin Hoare and Geoffrey Nowell Smith (New York, 1971), 206–76. It should be noted, however, that Gramsci developed the concept of hegemony with reference to modern capitalist societies. For important treatments of the social significance of "justice" or law in other kinds of societies, see Douglas Hay, "Property, Authority and the Criminal Law," in Hay et al., *Albion's Fatal Tree,* 17–63; Genovese, *Roll, Jordan, Roll,* 25–49.

Recent work illuminating patterns of governance and "legitimacy" in peasant-state relations include James C. Scott, *The Moral Economy of the Peasant: Rebellion and Subsistence in Southeast Asia* (New Haven, 1976), and for Spanish America, William B. Taylor, *Drinking, Homicide and Rebellion in Colonial Mexican Villages* (Stanford, 1979), esp. 128–45, 168–70; John Leddy Phelan, *The People and the King: The Comunero Revolution in Colombia, 1781* (Madison, 1978).

CHAPTER 6: THE POLITICAL ECONOMY OF DEPENDENCE

1 For reports on the Spanish and mestizo populations, and their concentration in the dynamic zones of Huamanga, see AGI, V, Lima 308, Description of the Bishopric of Huamanga, 1624–25; Vázquez (1629), *Compendio,* 486, 491, 503. See also Vargas, *Historia general,* 3:116–17.

2 BNP, A18, 1599, for the mitayo distribution.

3 I prefer to call many exactions "extra-legal" rather than illegal, since their formally illegal status was tempered by tacit acceptance, on all levels of lawful authority, of a certain amount of profiteering by officeholders. See Lohmann, *El corregidor,* 293–306; Phelan, *The Kingdom of Quito,* 145, 320–37.

4 For the early development and evolution of slavery, yanaconaje, and certain

forms of "wage labor" in Huamanga and elsewhere, see Chapter 2 above; Lockhart, *Spanish Peru,* esp. 171–205, 219–20; Bowser, *The African Slave;* Villarán, *Apuntes,* esp. chs. 2–5; Rolando Mellafe, "Evolución del salario en el virreinato peruano," *Ibero-Americana Pragensia* 1 (Prague, 1967), 91–107.

5 On the use of skilled blacks for a few special positions in the mines, and for household service, see AGN, Minería, Leg. 11, Huancavelica 1562–1572, ff. 258r–v, 635r–v; cf. Rolando Mellafe, *Breve historia de la esclavitud en América Latina* (Mexico, 1973), 94–96. On the advantages of ethnically isolated Africans, see Lockhart, *Spanish Peru,* 181; Bowser, *The African Slave,* 79. On the costs of blacks, Bowser, *The African Slave,* 11, and Appendix B.

6 See the discussion below and the sources in note 12.

7 On the link between the scale of profits and access to cheap mita labor, and the continuing desirability of mitayos even when voluntary laborers assumed a greater role in production, see the discussion of the mita and of profitability in Chapter 4 above; Lohmann, *Las minas,* 286, 405. Cf. Brading and Cross, "Colonial Silver Mining," 559–60.

8 Bowser, *The African Slave,* 94, n. 87 on 410; BNP, B890, 1616, ff. 1r–2v. For the notable presence of blacks and mulattoes at Castrovirreyna, see AGI, V, Lima 308, Description of the Bishopric, p. 29 (of microfilm copy). A brisk slave trade for the late sixteenth and early seventeenth centuries has been documented by Lorenzo Huertas Vallejos in his studies of Huamanga's notarial registers (personal communication).

9 For lands of "yanacona" field workers, house servants, and skilled workers (silversmiths), specifically protected in land rental contracts made by the Indians' masters, see ADA, PN, Padilla *1602*/1613, ff. 339v–340r; Palma 1619, f. 441r. On wage credits, see note 11 below. For a revealing overview of the rights and obligations of yanaconaje in Huamanga, see AGN, DI, Leg. 4, C. 65, 1619, ff. 20r–24r.

10 ADA, PN, Navarrete *1615–1618*/1627/1630, ff. 17r–18v for numerous examples of neglect or sabotage by dependent workers on an hacienda (f. 18v for quote).

11 On commercialized accounts with yanaconas or long-term Indian dependents, based on wage credits versus debits, and the need to impose debts and distribute goods to avoid excessive disbursement of money, see BNP, Z323, 1616, f. 16v; AGN, TP, C. 311, 1636, f. 8v; ADA, PN, Palma 1609, f. 170v; Navarrete *1615–1618*/1627/1630, ff. 17r–19r.

12 ADA, PN, Romo 1577, ff. 331v–332v; Soria 1593/*1601,* ff. 259r–262v; BNP, A18, 1599, entries for Alonso Gallardo (f. 2r and loose folio numbered 127v); ADA, PN, Palma 1609, ff. 170v–171v.

13 AGN, DI, Leg. 4, C. 65, 1619, ff. 18r–20r. I have considered children ten years of age or older as capable of performing significant work.

14 ADA, PN, Navarrette *1615–1618*/1627/1630, ff. 17r–19r.

15 For a well-documented case of such an adaptation, see the data on the Cacamarca obraje of Vilcashuamán, in BNP, B1370, 1625, f. 1r; Z313, 1616, ff. 164v–165v; Z351, 1616, ff. 662r–v, 663r, 668v; AGN, DI, Leg. 6, C. 113, 1646; BNP, B450, 1643, ff. 2r–4r; B164, 1640. For a similar tendency to assimilate ayllu In-

dians to a yanacona-like position in the case of another Huamanga obraje with a history of labor troubles, see BNP, B1485, 1600, ff. 338r–v, 340v, 341r, 343v.

16 Villarán, *Apuntes,* 162–63.

17 AGN, DI, Leg. 4, C. 65, 1619, ff. 1r–18r (f. 10r for "great harm" quote); AGI, V, Lima 308, Report of the inspection by Bishop Verdugo, 1625, p. 2 (of microfilm copy).

18 The scarcity of yanaconas, relative to demand, is indicated by payment of thousands of pesos to protect retainers on a sugar hacienda against claims by Huancavelica miners. BNP, Z1124, 1631, ff. 488v, 496v, 497r. Consider also the comment that Spaniards "promise the moon" ("les prometen montes de oro") to secure retainers. AGI, V, Lima 308, Report of the inspection by Bishop Verdugo, 1625, p. 2 (of microfilm copy).

19 BNP, Z1124, 1631, ff. 486r–502r; Salas, *De los obrajes,* 67–68; BNP, B1485, 1600, ff. 13v–45r; note 15 above; Lohmann, *Las minas,* 286, 357–58.

20 These contracts are listed in Appendix D, "Asientos of Indians in the City of Huamanga, 1570–1640," under three categories: asientos with European masters for "unskilled" work (Table D.1); asientos with European masters for "skilled" work (Table D.2); asientos with Indian masters (Table D.3). A discussion of these contracts and some of their implications is in Steve J. Stern, "Nuevos aspectos sobre la mano de obra indígena: el caso de los 'asientos' de Huamanga, 1570–1640," *Revista del Archivo Departamental de Ayacucho* 1 (1977), 26–37.

21 For apprenticeships, Appendix D, Table D.1, Contracts 2, 6, 17, 19, 27, 50; Table D.3, Contracts 2, 3, 8. For protection against mita, tribute, and debt claims, Table D.1, Contracts 9, 27, 31, 36, 38, 43.

22 Apprenticeships with no monetary compensation: Appendix D, Table D.1, Contracts 6, 17, 27, 50; Table D.3, Contracts 3, 8. Apprenticeships with monetary rewards: Table D.1, Contracts 2, 19; Table D.3, Contract 2.

23 Appendix D, Table D.2, Contract 2. Cf. Contracts 1, 4, 6, 9, 11, 14, 16, 19.

24 For asientos which probably formalized coercive relations exercised by a local encomendero-hacendado over Indian dependents, and where the wages promised seem suspiciously low for the times, Appendix D, Table D.1, Contracts 44, 47, 48, 49; for debt relationships which opened the way to coercions, note 27 below; for difficulty collecting wages, BNP, B1485, 1600, ff. 2r, 7r, 13v–45r, 49r–v, 50v–51r, 52r–v, 55v, 58v, 62v. The six-month wage interval was a standard feature of many asientos.

25 For organization of agricultural and putting-out work according to ayllu structures, BNP, Z313, 1616, ff. 200r–206r; ADA, PN, Palma 1619, ff. 234v–235v; AAA, Siglo XVII, Estante 3, Exp. 51, ff. 89r–90r.

26 BNP, Z1124, 1631, ff. 486r–502r for expenses on a sugar hacienda; Salas, *De los obrajes,* 67–68, and BNP, B1485, 1600, ff. 13r–45r for evidence of short-term labor associated with obraje production; BNP, B1485, 1600, ff. 55v, 58v for evidence of change in actual wage disbursements, change which implies that certain administrators had to pay a higher proportion of salaries in money; Lohmann, *Las minas,* 210–11, 286, 357–58, and ADA, PN, Palma 1609, f. 352r for the role of wage laborers in mining.

27 One out of six asientos in Huamanga linked the contract to a prior debt or
    money advance. Appendix D, Table D.1, Contracts 7, 8, 9, 13, 23, 24, 31, 35,
    46; Table D.2, Contract 17; Table D.3, Contracts 1, 4, 6. See also AGN, Regis-
    tro Notarial Ica, Siglo XVI, Protocolo 1 (Carbajo 1597-98), f. 327r–v; ADA,
    PN, Palma 1619, f. 660v; Navarrete *1615–1618*/1627/1630, ff. 17r–18v for the role
    of debits. For specific cases in which debts led to long-term dependence, Appen-
    dix D, Table D.1, Contracts 9, 24; Table D.3, Contracts 1, 6; ADA, PN, Palma
    1609, ff. 110r–112r. For the resemblance to yanacona relationships, ADA, PN,
    Palma 1609, ff. 441v–442v, esp. 442r.
28 ADA, PN, Palma 1609, f. 152r.
29 The limited scope of "free labor" is suggested by the fact that even a major mine
    center like Huancavelica needed no more than several thousand laborers at any
    given time. See also the discussion in the text below (and note 76) on the ability
    of Indians to maintain or recreate a subsistence economy. For suggestions that
    "free laborers" were irregular in their willingness to work, and subject to round-
    ups, see Lohmann, *Las minas,* 410–12, including n. 3. For further evidence of
    the coercive dimensions of contracted labor, see notes 24 and 27 above. Some
    evidence of seasonal fluctuation in the supply of available Indians is suggested
    by the distribution of dates on asiento contracts listed in Appendix D. The sup-
    ply apparently shot up after the May-June harvests; June-July accounted for
    nearly a third (29.5 percent) of all the contracts. A second "bulge" occurred in
    October (12.8 percent), probably after fields were sown for the coming agricul-
    tural season.
        These limitations do not necessarily deny the reality of an emerging market
    for labor, despite its narrow, "impure" character. Even in North Atlantic areas
    which experienced capitalist revolutions of economy and society, the rise of a la-
    bor market was a historical process characterized by uneven rates of develop-
    ment, and the application of numerous coercive sanctions to counteract the
    "scarcity" or "indolence" of laborers. See Maurice Dobb, *Studies in the Development
    of Capitalism* (rev. ed., New York, 1963), Ch. 6, esp. 231–35, and n. 1 on 266.
30 This is the strong impression I received from a rapid look at AGN, Registro No-
    tarial Ica. The range of wages promised an adult Indian in Ica asientos in 1597–
    98 was about 20–30 pesos. Ibid., Siglo XVI, Protocolo 1, ff. 63r–v, 264r–v, 274r,
    327r–v (excludes apprenticeship contracts). In Huamanga, the range for 1596–
    98 was about 12–15 pesos, and the average was only about 15 pesos. Appendix
    D, Table D.1, Contracts 7–14, 16, 20–23 (excludes apprentice contracts).
31 The data is for adult men who were not apprentices or skilled laborers (artisans,
    arrieros, or the like), and who hired themselves out to Europeans. (Three pesos
    normally sufficed to purchase a two-month supply of corn for an adult male.)
    All the contracts are in Appendix D, Table D.1. For 1596–1602, Contracts 7–14,
    16, 20–25, 28; for 1609, Contracts 31–34, 36–39; for 1619–1625, Contracts 40–49.
    The average given for 1619–1625 is probably an underestimate because Con-
    tracts 44, 47, 48, and 49 involve coercive relationships and comparatively paltry
    wages.
32 Lohmann, *Las minas,* 286, 357. Inflation of the price of necessities may have
    played a role in rising nominal wages (ibid., 405, n. 18), especially if Indians re-

fused to work for a declining share of "subsistence." But such a pattern would confirm the existence of a primitive labor market mechanism.

33 AGI, V, Lima 308, Report of the inspection, p. 2 ("les prometen montes de oro").

34 An alternative explanation of wage fluctuations by time and space is that from time to time government regulations provided for a "just" wage for Indians based on the specific conditions, including price levels, of various regions and kinds of work. But Lima did not establish a systematic policy on wages for "free" and un-free labor until 1687. Even then, the regulations seemed to be modeled greatly on the historical experience of various regions. See "Arancel de los jornales del Perú, 1687," in Pablo Macera, *Mapas Coloniales de Haciendas Cuzqueñas* (Lima, 1968), 132–55. See also ibid., lxxiii–lxxiv; Lohmann, *Las minas,* 393–408.

35 This statement is relative rather than absolute. It is possible that Indians had "known" prospective employers, or other Indians who lived with them, but few employers coincided with the specific families and individuals, most of them descendants of encomendero families, who dominated the particular rural district of contracted natives. It is worth recalling (see note 27) that only one of six contracts recorded a prior debt or money advance — that is, a prior obligation which already bound Indian to employer.

36 See notes 24, 27, 28 above; cf. Macera, *Mapas,* cix.

37 Escape even under the extremely coercive conditions of the mita is documented in Chapter 4. On the difficulty of controlling physical mobility, consider the complaint of a European about a troublesome dependent: "he left for his pueblo without my knowing. . . ." ADA, PN, Navarrete *1615–1618*/1627/1630, f. 18r. Consider also the casual statement of a native cowboy working on a Spanish ranch: "he lives *at present* [my emphasis] in . . . " AGI, VI, Lima 532A, Resi-dencia of Don Esteban López de Silves, corregidor of Huamanga (1637), f. 33r. On the alternatives available to escapees, see notes 18 and 71; Lohmann, *Las minas,* 412. One of the chief asiento obligations was a promise of the Indian to stay with the master throughout the contractual period.

38 For temporary work and collection of wages, AGI, VI, Lima 532A, ff. 9r, 22r; BNP, Z1124, 1631, ff. 486r–502r, 544r, 581r, 585v; Salas, *De los obrajes,* 67–68; Lohmann, *Las minas,* 210–11, 286, 357–58; ADA, PN, Palma 1609, f. 352r; AGN, Superior Gobierno, Leg. 2, C. 38, 1618, f. 33v. For complaints of cheat-ing on wage payments which show that some wages were indeed paid, BNP, B1485, 1600, ff. 58v, 55v; HC, Doc. 981, 1578; AGN, JR, Leg. 24, C. 65, 1618, ff. 57v, 65v, 107v. Cf. Poma de Ayala (1615), *Nueva corónica,* 892.

It is suggestive to contrast labor asientos in Chile with those of Huamanga. In Santiago, nine of ten (88.8 percent) asientos promised no monetary remu-neration whatsoever. In Huamanga, a more dynamic commercial region which included rich mines, the corresponding ratio is only one in ten (10.3 percent). Alvaro Jara, *Los asientos de trabajo y la provisión de mano de obra para los no-encomenderos en la ciudad de Santiago, 1586–1600* (Santiago de Chile, 1959), 77; Ap-pendix D, Tables D.1, D.2, D.3.

39 BNP, Z1124, 1631, occasional notations on ff. 472r–485r.

40 See AAA, Siglo XVII, Est. 3, Exp. 51, ff. 69v, 88r–89v; AGN, JR, Leg. 23, C. 62, 1617, ff. 174r, 182v, 202v, 204r–v, 211r; Leg. 24, C. 65, 1618, ff. 57v, 65v, 107v.

It is also noteworthy that in the latter document (ff. 57v–58r, 65v, 108r, 258r–v, 59r, 67r, 404r–v), Indians did not oppose the sale of goods to Europeans, but rather the unfair prices they had received. Lucanas during the 1570s offers a suggestive contrast: AGI, VI, Lima 529A, Residencia of Don Juan Manuel de Anaya, ff. 1330v–1331r, 1342v–1343r.

41 David Brading and Harry Cross have pointed out the critical importance of analyzing the causes and consequences of "free" labor in colonial mining. "Colonial Silver Mining," 557–60.

42 The use of political clout for economic gain is analyzed in Chapter 4; on the fees collected by itinerant judges, AGN, DI, Leg. 3, C. 50, 1606, passim.; for payment of salaries to schoolteachers and other Indian officials, AGN, JR, Leg. 24, C. 65, 1618, f. 260r, and Spalding, "Social Climbers," 658.

43 On the conversion of specific obligations such as mita service into monetary equivalents, see Basto, *Las mitas,* 5–6, 10–13; AGN, DI, Leg. 6, C. 109, 1643, f. 3r. For debts incurred by Indians accused of neglecting or losing animals, see ADA, PN, Soria 1593/*1601,* f. 46v; Palma 1619, f. 20v; Palma 1625, f. 558r–v.

44 On the voluntary monetization of tributes in kind, see the sources in Chapter 4, note 7; cf. AGN, JR, Leg. 8, C. 20, 1590–1595, ff. 4r, 5v, 7r.

45 For ayllus protecting people from the mita, see Basto, *Las mitas,* 5–6, 10–13; BNP, B1079, 1629, ff. 73v, 75r, 76v; Poma de Ayala (1615), *Nueva corónica,* sketch on 531. For payoffs to chiefs and notables, see AGN, DI, Leg. 4, C. 65, 1619, f. 2v; Poma de Ayala (1615), *Nueva corónica,* 532. For designated mitayos hiring other Indians, see ADA, PN, Palma 1609, ff. 82v, 207r–v; AGN, DI, Leg. 6, C. 109, 1643, f. 3r.

46 For evidence of the heavy economic burden imposed by judicial activity, see BNP, A393, 1594, ff. 47v–48r; Z1067, 1685, ff. 237r–238v; ADA, PN, Peña 1596, f. 137r; AGN, DI, Leg. 3, C. 50, 1606, ff. 64r–66r, 110v–111r.

47 AGN, JR, Leg. 24, C. 65, 1618, ff. 259v, 275r–v for purchases of shears and knives by communities with substantial herds; BNP, B1485, 1600, f. 249r for evidence of knickknack items sold by itinerant peddlers.

48 AGN, Registro Notarial Ica, Siglo XVII, Protocolo 127 (Velasco 1605), f. 326r. On the symbolic importance of Hispanic attire, see Chapter 7 below, and Stern, "Las ideologías nativistas," 28–29.

49 See AGN, JR, Leg. 24, C. 65, 1618, ff. 259v, 260r; ADA, Corregimiento, Causas Ordinarias, Leg. 1, C. 1, 1595, ff. 21r–22r, 25r–26v; Stern, "Las ideologías nativistas," 28–29; José María Arguedas, "Notas elementales sobre el arte popular religioso y la cultura mestiza de Huamanga," *Churmichasun* 4–5 (Huancayo, June 1977), 3–16. See also the suggestive comments on Indian churches in Risco (1684), "Descripción . . . de los Angaraes," 203.

50 See, in addition to the discussion of mita life and labor in Chapter 4, Poma de Ayala (1615), *Nueva corónica,* 67, 259; ADA, PN, Peña 1596, f. 183v; Mesagil 1637–1639, ff. 186r, 919v–920v.

51 The accumulation of cash reserves is discussed in Chapter 4. In the highly commercialized Huancavelica-Huanta zone, there is mention of Indian craftsmen of Spanish furniture, and evidence that traditional *queros* (wooden cups) had be-

come commodities valued not only for local use, but also to earn exchange. George Kubler, "The Quechua in the Colonial World," in *Handbook,* ed. Steward, 2:364; AGN, DI, Leg. 6, C. 107, 1642, f. 22r.

On marketing a surplus versus selling labor-power as a means by which to earn tribute money, compare the comments in: Monzón et al. (1586), "Descripción . . . de Atunsora," 224, and Carabajal (1586), "Descripción . . . de Vilcas Guaman," 208. See also the attempt, in 1607–1608, of Indians of Ongoy to save their coca fields in Mayomarca, from which they claimed to earn funds which paid their tributes. ADA, Cabildo, Causas Civiles, Leg. 2, C. 16, 1699, f. 6r-v. Twenty-five years later Indians from Ongoy were listed among the natives who paid tributes by earning wages on a nearby sugar hacienda. BNP, Z1124, 1631, f. 498v.

52   Evidence on patterns of expropriation and conflicts over "strategic" resources, including lands, is given in Chapters 4–5. For revenues available to seventeenth-century corregidores by collecting interest owed Indians on long-term "loans" initiated in the sixteenth century, see BNP, B1505, 1644, ff. 37v–38v. For evidence that Indian entrepreneurs laid claim to valuable lands, see the payment of nearly 500 pesos by Indians who sought to claim legal title to coca fields in Mayomarca through the composiciones de tierras. ADA, PN, Soria 1598, f. 677v. See also Chapter 7. For evidence that Lucanas peoples who had once held abundant herds paid money equivalents to protect dwindling llama flocks from tribute in the seventeenth century, see BNP, B1505, 1644, f. 3v. A similar economic decline afflicted the Chocorvos peoples, whose subsistence was threatened by a composición de tierras in the 1640s. BNP, B1525, 1647, esp. ff. 1r–3v; also BNP, B685, 1634. Fifty years earlier, when Poma de Ayala was drafting his *Nueva corónica,,* the Chocorvos were noted for their wealth and vast herds (p. 728).

53   For examples, see BNP, Z88, 1646, ff. 548r–549r, 551v–554r, 554v–559r; AGN, TP, C. 370, 1607–1688, subcuaderno number 9, passim.; C. 354, 1632; BNP, A473, 1597, f. 4r–v; Z312, 1594, ff. 283r–284r; AGN, DI, Leg. 6, C. 118, 1648; ADA, PN, Navarrete 1615–1618/*1627/1630,*ff. 346r–347v, 637r–639v, 811v–813v; Mesagil 1637–1639, ff. 636r–640v, 652v–654r.

54   The effect of the colonial regime on local expectations and reciprocities is discussed in Chapter 4. John V. Murra has emphasized the importance of local preservation and storage skills, but much archaeological work remains to be done. *La organización,* 181–82, 190–97, 37. See also Murra, "The Conquest and Annexation of Qollasuyu by the Inka State" (paper delivered at the Fortieth Annual Meeting of the Society for American Archaeology, Dallas, May 1975).

55   For suggestions that Indians could no longer draw on reserves for food during hard times, see BNP, B1485, 1600, ff. 250v, 314r, 316r, 53r, 55v, 56r. In this document, an obraje administrator defended himself against charges of forced distribution of goods by arguing that natives asked for them because of a disastrous agricultural season. Even if he lied, the statement was plausible. The Indians themselves complained of a declining subsistence economy, food deficits, and lack of funds with which to buy food. Their complaints seemed directed as

much against "unfair" prices as against the distribution per se, and they made reference to the prevailing market price of coca in their province. Ibid., esp. ff. 49v, 50v–51r, 52r, 53r, 55v, 56r, 61r, 62v.

56 For coca, note 55; Ribera y Chaves (1586), "Relación . . . de Guamanga, 196. For salt, Carabajal (1586), "Descripción . . . de Vilcas Guaman," 210, 212, 213, 216, 218; contrast the groups which still produced salt independently: 208, 209, 214, 215. For maize and ají, note 55 above; ADA, PN, Mesagil 1637–1639, ff. 184r–186r, 918r–922r. For coarse cloth, ADA, PN, Mesagil 1637–1639, f. 920v; Silvera/*Mesagil* 1636–1639, f. 389r–v; AGN, JR, Leg. 24, C. 65, 1618, f. 404r–v; Salas, *De los obrajes,* 90, and Cuadro 5 (between 118–19), entry on 20 September 1598.

57 See Spalding, "Social Climbers," 658, 661–63; Stern, "Las ideologías nativistas," 28; and Chapter 7 below.

58 On the importance of money for avoiding mita, note 45; on the differentiated pattern of wages and debts among mitayos, Chapter 4 above. Cf. Nicolás Sánchez-Albornoz, *El indio en el Alto Perú* (Lima, 1973), 45–46.

59 Revisitas document widespread access to land despite a certain process of differentiation. AGN, DI, Leg. 4, C. 61, 1646; BNP, B876, 1629; B1079, 1629 esp. ff. 13r–60r; AGN, DI, Leg. 6, C. 119, 1648. The responsibility of chiefs for the collective tributes and mitas of kinfolk, if enforced, also limited internal accumulation. See BNP, B1079, 1629, ff. 75r, 76v–77r, 78r–79r. But note also differentiation of tribute burdens among ayllus: BNP, A236, 1597, f. 22r.

60 Such patterns led to an ironic land history. In the 1630s, the Quiguares of Acocro, southeast of the city of Huamanga, spent 420 pesos to buy valuable lands held by the poorer Indians of Guaychao. Twenty years later, the Quiguares had fallen on hard times and had to sell the same lands to an outsider, a rich Hanan Acos Indian from Quinua. ADA, Corregimiento, Causas Ordinarias, Leg. 1, C. 13, 1647, ff. 1r, 12v. For more extensive documentation of the circulation of lands as Indian commodities, see Chapter 7 below.

61 For commodities and personal effects left in the care of rural Indians by Spanish merchants and peddlers, ADA, PN, Ysidro 1577, f. 199v; Padilla *1602*/1613, f. 443r–v. For matter-of-fact mention of a storekeeper ("pulpera") and innkeeper ("tambero") in Quinua and Huachos, AGN, TP, C. 645, 1637, f. 1r; JR, Leg. 24, C. 65, 1618, f. 139v.

62 The liability of ayllu peasants for the monetary transactions of elites is illustrated by a kuraka of Canaria (Vilcashuamán) who "repaid" a loan of sixty pesos by sending ten Indians to work on haciendas. ADA, PN, Palma 1619, f. 234v–235v.

63 ADA, PN, Navarrette 1615–1618/*1627*/1630, f. 301r; Mesagil 1637–1639, ff. 185r–186r, 918v–920v (chuño mentioned on ff. 919v, 920r). See also Peña 1596, f. 252v; Palma 1609, ff. 82v–83r, 268r–269r, 269v–270r; Palma 1625, ff. 707r–708r.

64 ADA, PN, Peña 1596, ff. 25v, 266r–v; Palma 1609, f. 82v; Palma 1619, f. 20r–v; Cabildo, Asuntos Administrativos, Leg. 64, Exp. 1, 1625, f. 1v.

65 Appendix D. Table D.1, Contracts 7, 8, 9, 13, 23, 24, 31, 35, 46; Table D.2, Contract 17; Table D.3, Contracts 1, 4, 6. The quote is from ADA, PN, Palma

1609, f. 177r (a contract which appears incomplete in the notary book and is therefore not listed in Tables D.1–D.3).

On the very limited power of money advances to secure the labor of natives as individuals in the early post-conquest period, see the comments of Karen Spalding, "*Kurakas* and Commerce: A Chapter in the Evolution of Andean Society," *HAHR* 53 (November 1970), 588–89; and the patterns of labor described in Chapter 2 above.

66   For the earlier corregidor, see the description of Don Juan Manuel de Anaya in Chapter 4; for the role of money and commerce, and apparently a somewhat more successful relationship with kurakas, by his later counterpart, see BNP, B1441, 1634, ff. 79r, 80r–v, 83v, 85r–86r, 88r, 89v–90r, 90v, 92v, 93r, 96v, 103r.

67   The fear of isolation is especially understandable in a society where economic welfare was closely associated with kinship ties. In Quechua, *wak'cha* means both "poor" and "orphan." For an extremely perceptive discussion of the trauma of "civil death," or the loss of social bonds, see López Albújar, "Ushanan-Jampi," in *Cuentos andinos*.

68   For evidence from the late seventeenth century that forasteros varied in their linkage to original homelands, see Huertas et al., *La revisita de los Chocorbos,* 61–150. See also note 75 below.

69   See Chapter 4 above on flight by mitayos. For Indians who left Huancavelica and ended up in Andahuaylas, hundreds of kilometers away, see BNP, Z1124, 1631, ff. 496v, 497r.

70   BNP, B1079, 1629, esp. ff. 68v–69r. Cf. José Miranda, *El tributo indígena en la Nueva España durante el siglo XVI* (Mexico, 1952), 249–50. In a survey of Indians living in the city of Lima in 1613, I found 123 from Huamanga. Five of six (103) were males, and of these over three-fourths (79) were single. Among the married males, only one in six (4 of 24) had wives from Huamanga. Miguel de Contreras (1613), *Padrón de los indios de Lima en 1613,* ed. Noble David Cook (Lima, 1968).

71   On flight to the montaña or jungle, BNP, B1477, 1626, ff. 1r–3r; Poma de Ayala (1615), *Nueva corónica,* 581; *Colección,* ed. Konetzke, 2:191. Forastero Indians who developed relationships with communities are discussed in Chapters 5 and 7. For obvious reasons I have not encountered documentation on vagabonds, but the recorded Indian population of Lima included a notable group from Huamanga (note 70 above). The case of Alonso Coro of Lucanas, listed as a "journeyman" (*jornalero*), is particularly suggestive. He "came to this city, where he wanders for his livelihood, bringing firewood, and working wherever there might be something." Contreras (1613), *Padrón,* 11. Cf. Bernabé Cobo (1629), *Historia de la fundación de Lima,* ed. M. González de la Rosa (Lima, 1882), 51.

72   On the forasteros' integration into the monetary economy, and tensions with originarios, see Chapter 7. On the hunt for runaways, BNP, B1079, 1629, ff. 68r, 76r–v, 78r; Z1124, 1631, ff. 496v, 497r. Cf. Sánchez-Albornoz, *El indio en el Alto Perú,* 27–31.

73   ADA, PN, Palma 1609, f. 316v.

74   BNP, B450, 1643, esp. f. 2v; B164, 1640.

75   Ambiguous situations might include a phenomenon discussed earlier in this

chapter: ayllu Indians who lived and worked with Spanish masters under conditions which tended to approximate yanaconaje. We know also of "yanaconas" who lived near homelands and had not lost ayllu identities, and of minor chiefs who doubled as majordomos on nearby haciendas. BNP, Z313, 1616, ff. 200r–206r, 247r. Consider also the case of ayllu Indians who served asientos which tied them to Spanish masters for six months, a year, or longer. In one case, the native was contracted "in the presence of his cacique Don Felipe Astocavana," who signed the document. ADA, PN, Palma 1619, f. 621r–v.

76 The pattern of irregularity by "voluntary laborers" may explain why Huancavelica miners sought to stabilize their access to labor by acquiring haciendas whose peons could be sent to the mines. Henri Favre, "Evolución y situación de la hacienda tradicional de la región de Huancavelica," in *Hacienda, comunidad y campesinado en el Perú,* ed. José Matos Mar (2nd ed., Lima, 1976), 109; see also Lohmann, *Las minas,* 410–12, incl. n. 3.

77 BNP, B1485, 1600, esp. ff. 55v, 59v, 49r–v; Salas, *De los obrajes,* 57.

78 ADA, PN, Palma 1609, f. 152r; Navarrete *1615–1618*/1627/1630, ff. 17r–19r; BNP, Z323, 1616, ff. 16v, 20r; Z313, 1616, ff. 170r, 239r, 244v, 245r–v, 251r, 278r–v; Z351, 1616, ff. 664v, 665v, 673r; B1485, 1600, ff. 13v–45r.

79 This complex pattern of labor, clearly in evidence in Huamanga by the 1600s, has already been observed for late colonial haciendas. Macera, *Trabajos,* 3:171–204; Jorge Polo y la Borda G., *La hacienda Pachachaca: autobastecimiento y comercialización (segunda mitad del siglo XVIII)* (Lima, 1976), 50–69.

80 For "generosity," mostly in the wills of dying Europeans, to dependents who included ayllu Indians and yanaconas as well as mestizos and mulattoes, see ADA, PN, Padilla 1602/*1613,* ff. 102r–104r; Cabildo, Causas Civiles, Leg. 1, C. 4, 1671, esp. ff. 71v–73r; BNP, Z1268, 1590, f. 4r; Z351, 1616, f. 665r–v; Z313, 1616, ff. 239r, 245r–v, 251r; Z323, ff. 15v–16r, 16v, 17r; ADA, PN, Navarrete *1615–1618*/1627/1630, f. 199r; Corregimiento, Asuntos Administrativos, Leg. 31, C. 4, 1617, f. 43r–v; C. 5, 1621, ff. 1r–11r; BNP, B820, 1643, ff. 36v–37r; ADA, PN, Navarrete 1615–1618/1627/*1630,* f. 699r–v; AGN, TP, C. 370, 1607–1688, sub-cuaderno 6, ff. 2v–3r.

CHAPTER 7: THE TRAGEDY OF SUCCESS

1 ADA, PN, Pēna 1596, ff. 184v–186r, for purchase of the outfit described, except for the hat and shoes; see also Poma de Ayala (1615), *Nueva corónica,* sketches on 366, 739, 741.

2 The transactions are dated 1585–1639, but all except three are from the 1601–39 period. Six of the transactions are rentals, half of them for 85 pesos a year or more. The distribution of purchase prices is weighted more heavily toward large amounts for suburban and rural lands (32.0 percent over 100 pesos) than for city lots and homes (23.8 percent over 100 pesos).

   In chronological order, the sources of the transactions are: ADA, PN, Cárdenas 1585, ff. 98r–v, 99r–v; Peña 1596, ff. 134v–136v; Soria 1593/*1601,* ff. 28r–v, 150r–v, 185v, 193v–194v, 220v–221v; Palma 1609, ff. 71r–72r, 99v–101v, 180v–183v, 203r–204v, 237v–238v, 244r–v, 245r–v, 278v–280r; Corregimiento, Causas Ordinarias, Leg. 1, C. 5, 1617, ff. 17r–19v (sale dated 1613); PN, Padilla 1602/*1613,* ff. 156v–157v; Navarrete *1615–1618*/1627/1630, ff. 88r–89v; Palma 1619, ff. 226r–228r, 259v–260r; Palma 1625, ff. 36r–37r, 145v–147r, 397v–398v, 632v–634v, 879r–880v; Navarrete 1615–1618/*1627/1630,* ff. 346–347v, 466r–467r, 570r–571r, 637r–639v, 651r–v, 758r–v, 811v–813v, 828v–829v, 838r–839r; Morales, 1630, ff. 22r–v, 320r–v, 446r–447v; AGN, TP, C. 354, 1632; ADA, PN, Silvera/Mesagil 1636–1637, ff. 4r–v, 90v–91v, 97r–98v, 625r–v; Mesagil 1637–1639, ff. 141r–142v, 236r–237r, 242r–243v, 324r–325r, 471v–472r, 480r–481v, 633r–v, 636r–640v, 652v–654r; Corregimiento, Causas Ordinarias, Leg. 2, C. 18, 1676, ff. 2r–4v (sale dated 1639).

3 The legal state tribute amounted to just over six pesos of eight reales (i.e., four pesos ensayados, of 12.5 reales). Even if doubled, the tribute burden was only twelve or thirteen pesos. For unskilled asiento wage credits, see Appendix D, Table D.1. For mitayo rentals, see ADA, PN, Palma 1609, ff. 82v, 207r–v; AGN, DI, Leg. 6, C. 109, 1643, f. 3r.

4 ADA, Corregimiento, Causas Ordinarias, Leg. 1, C. 5, 1617, ff. 17r–19v; PN, Navarrete 1615–1618/*1627*/1630, ff. 637r–639v, 811v–813v; Palma 1619, ff. 259v–260r for the individual cases. On rental of slave artisans, and purchase prices of slaves, see Bowser, *The African Slave,* 138, Appendix B, Table B.4.

5 AGN, DI, Leg. 4, C. 71, 1622, ff. 12r–14v; ADA, PN, Navarrete 1615–1618/*1627*/1630, ff. 300v–302v, 519r–520v; Mesagil 1637–1639, ff. 184r–186r, 918r–922r.

6 ADA, PN, Palma 1609, ff. 13v–14r, 268r–269r, 269v–270r; Palma 1619, ff. 20r–21r.

7 ADA, PN, Silvera/Mesagil 1636–1637, ff. 542v, 515r–516v; Padilla 1602/*1613,* ff. 1r–2r; Palma 1609, f. 390r–v; Soria 1598, ff. 308r–310v; Peña 1596, f. 311v.

8 The wages of mine laborers rose from seven to twelve reales by the mid-seventeenth century (Chapter 6). At nine reales a day, twenty-five working days per month, and expenses of four reales a day (for thirty days), a mine laborer might save some thirteen pesos (of eight reales) a month. It is worth recalling (Chapter 4) that a certain fraction of mitayos, even, earned significant net wages. For sale of contraband mercury by Indians working in the mines, AGN, Minería, Leg. 13, Huancavelica 1585–1591, Exp. 2, f. 8r.

9 ADA, PN, Ysidro 1577, ff. 162r–164r; Peña 1596, f. 180v; Navarrete *1615–1618*/1627/1630, f. 254r; Palma 1619, ff. 372r–373r; Palma 1625, ff. 292r–v, 837r–838r; BNP, Z317, 1586, f. 3r; AGN, JR, Leg. 23, C. 62, 1617, f. 120r; Leg. 24, C. 65, 1618, f. 260r; Appendix D, Table D.2, Contracts 4, 6, 7, 16; Table D.3, Contracts 2, 3, 4, 7, 8. See also the sources in note 10 below.

10 ADA, PN, Palma 1609, ff. 248r–250v, 252v–253r, 315r–316r; Navarrete *1615–1618*/1627/1630, ff. 84r–85r; Soria 1598, f. 623r.

11 For asiento and wage levels, see Appendix D. For the semifinished hides, Table D.2, Contract 6. For extra cloth to arrieros, Table D.2, Contracts 8, 10, 11, 12, 15, 18, 19, 20; Table D.3, Contract 5. For the quotation, Table D.2, Contract 2.

12 See ADA, PN, Palma 1619, ff. 298r–299r; Silvera/Mesagil 1636–1637, f. 389r–v; AGN, JR, Leg. 11, C. 29, 1593, f. 69r; DI, Leg. 4, C. 71, 1622, ff. 11r–14v.

13 Evidence on Indian accumulation of private property is very extensive. In addition to note 2 above, see AGN, TP, C. 370, 1607–1688, sub-cuaderno 9; C. 42,

1595; DI, Leg. 6, C. 107, 1642, esp. ff. 16v–27v; C. 108, 1643; ADA, Corregimiento, Causas Ordinarias, Leg. 1, C. 1, 1595, ff. 21r–22r; C. 8, 1637, f. 1211r–v;
PN, Soria 1589, ff. 111r–115r; Soria 1598, ff. 539v, 677v; Palma 1619, ff. 174r–
176r; Navarrete 1615–1618/*1627*/1630, ff. 300v–302v; Silvera/Mesagil 1636–1637,
ff. 25r–v, 515r–516v; Mesagil 1637–1639, ff. 560r–562r, 930v–932r; BNP, A387,
1594, ff. 2r–3r; B769, 1650, ff. 1v–2r; B820, 1643; B1525, 1647, ff. 9v–12r, esp.
11r; Z888, 1646; RPIA, tomo 16, partida XLI, 313; Monzón et al. (1586), "Descripción . . . de los Rucanas Antamarcas," 246; Centro de Colaboración
Pedagógica Provincial . . . de Parinacochas, *Monografía de la Provincia de Parinacochas* (2 vols., Lima, 1950), 1:120–25.

14 See esp. BNP, B1079, 1629, ff. 75r, 76v–77r, 78v–79r; B28, 1607, f. 6v.

15 See the discussion of forasteros in Chapter 5 above, and also below in this chapter's discussion of "Strife, Tension, and Purification."

16 BNP, A387, 1594, esp. ff. 2r–3r, 4r–v; AGN, DI, Leg. 6, C. 107, 1642, ff. 16r–
27v; also Chapter 5 above.

17 For evidence of accumulation and circulation of private property among Indians, see notes 2, 13, and 16 above. For sale or rental of private Indian lands to
Europeans or mestizos, see ADA, PN, Navarrete *1615–1618/1627*/1630, ff.
35r–36r, 215r–216v, 538r–539v; Mesagil 1637–1639, ff. 86r–87v; AGN, TP, C.
645, 1637, ff. 18v–19r, 20r. See also C. 370, 1607–1688, sub-cauderno 9, passim.

18 Independent women heads of household would include single adults, widows,
and women married to forasteros. The percentage of women purchasers and
renters is based on the transactions cited in note 2 above. On the prominence of
women merchants and forastero producers in commercial agriculture for the
city market of Huamanga, see AGN, JR, Leg. 11, C. 29, 1593, f. 69r. Forasteros
and artisans, though not always identified as such, are prominent in rural as
well as urban accumulations in the sources cited in notes 2 and 13 above.

19 See Spalding, "Social Climbers," 658, 661–63.

20 Note the different payments by tributaries of different ayllus, and apparent collection of double the legal tribute, in BNP, A236, 1597, f. 22r–v; ADA, PN,
Palma 1609, ff. 441v–442v. Cf. Poma de Ayala (1615), *Nueva corónica,* 974.

21 See Spalding, "Social Climbers," 661; AGN, DI, Leg. 6, C. 119, 1648, f. 111v. For
two cases of women occupying chieftainships normally reserved for men, ADA,
PN, Mesagil 1637–1639, ff. 636r–640v; BNP, Z888, 1646, f. 551v.

22 See the sources cited in Chapter 5, note 24.

23 See Appendix D, Table D.1, Contracts 2, 6, 17, 19, 27, 50; Table D.3, Contracts
2, 3, 8.

24 See AGN, DI, Leg. 6, C. 107, 1642, ff. 10r, 14r; BNP, B1079, 1629, f. 79r.

25 This statement applies not only to Indians bound to the ayllus into which they
were born, but also to forasteros who acquired property by marrying into foreign Indian communities.

26 See ADA, PN, Peña 1596, f. 312r; Mesagil 1637–1639, f. 920r; AGN, DI, Leg.
6, C. 108, 1643, f. 15r; BNP, B820, 1643, ff. 36v–37r, 35r; Poma de Ayala (1615),
Nueva corónica, 892; Lohmann, *Las Minas,* 27. Note also the inclusion of five Indians in a 1577 list of twenty-four Huancavelica mining entrepreneurs, in
BMA, Libro 1.31, ff. 48r–71v.

27 Lohmann, *Las minas,* 163, 27. For another grant of mitayos to an Indian woman, Doña Leonor Pilcosisa Coya, see BNP, A18, 1599, loose folio.

28 See Appendix D (Table D.3 for asientos with Indian masters). The specific cases cited are Table D.3, Contracts 5, 6.

29 ADA, PN, Navarrete 1615-1618/1627/*1630,* ff. 811v-813v, 758r-v, 300v-302v. See also the notation of a small debt by three ayllus of Pausa (Parinacochas) to Juana de Araneda, an itinerant Indian merchant from Pausa. ADA, PN, Mesagil 1637-1639, f. 185v.

30 ADA, PN, Peña 1596, f. 266r-v (Appendix D, Table D.3, Contract 1).

31 See, for examples, BNP, B1079, 1629, passim.; B769, 1650, f. 1v; ADA, PN, Padilla *1602*/1613, f. 339r; Mesagil 1637-1639, ff. 560v, 919r-v; AGI, VI, Lima 532A, Residencia of Don Esteban López de Silves, corregidor of Huamanga (1637), ff. 23r, 26r; AGN, DI, Leg. 6, C. 119, 1648, f. 108r; JR, Leg. 23, C. 62, 1617, f. 153r. On Indian incorporation of selective elements of Hispanic material culture, and on the complexities of Hispanization, see George Kubler, "The Quechua," in *Handbook,* ed. Steward, 2:354-59; Erwin P. Grieshaber, "Hacienda-Community Relations and Indian Acculturation: An Historiographical Essay," *Latin American Research Review* 14 (1979), 107-28.

32 See ADA, PN, Peña 1596, ff. 183r-186r; Padilla *1602*/1613, f. 338v; Mesagil 1637-1639, ff. 185r, 186r, 560v-561v; AGN, DI, Leg. 4, C. 71, 1622, ff. 13r-14v; Leg. 6, C. 109, 1643, f. 13r; BNP, A236, 1597, f. 88r. One should note that the acquisition of fine European articles by no means excluded collection of prized Indian articles, including luxury cloth.

33 For revealing examples, see ADA, PN, Navarrete *1615-1618*/1627/1630, ff. 164r-165r; Palma 1619, f. 259v; Mesagil 1637-1639, ff. 184v, 185v; Corregimiento, Causas Ordinarias, Leg. 2, C. 18, 1676, f. 2r-v (sale dated 1639).

34 For petitions written by Indians of Huamanga, AGN, DI, Leg. 6, C. 107, 1642, f. 10r; C. 108, 1643, f. 15r. Less refined but nonetheless remarkable is a 1,200 page "letter" to the King of Spain: Poma de Ayala (1615), *Nueva corónica.*

35 See Luis Martín and Jo Ann Geurin Pettus, *Scholars and Schools in Colonial Peru* (Dallas, 1973), 18-19, 126-38; Virgilio Galdo Gutiérrez, *Educación de los curacas: una forma de dominación colonial* (Ayacucho, 1970); Poma de Ayala (1615), *Nueva corónica,* 493, 741-56 (a ranked Indian hierarchy with varying degrees of Hispanic dress), 786-87.

36 BNP, B769, 1650, ff. 1v-2r (2r for quote); ADA, PN, Peña 1596, f. 185r (price of clothes); Mesagil 1637-1639, f. 561v (price of gun); AGN, DI, Leg. 6, C. 109, 1643, ff. 2r, 13r (Inca gun collector); C. 108, 1643, ff. 9r, 15r (kin to Spaniards, irrigated lands); ADA, PN, Silvera/Mesagil 1636-1637, f. 625r-v (urban property).

37 On the spotty, superficial character of the Christian overlay, see Poma de Ayala (1615), *Nueva corónica,* 296, 601, 682, 781; AGI, V, Lima 308, Report of the inspection by Bishop Verdugo, 1625, pp. 2-3, 5-7 (of microfilm copy); AGI, V, Lima 308, Fray Agustín de Carvajal to His Majesty, 25 March 1616. See also Duviols, *La lutte.*

38 On the possible usefulness of Indian cofradías (ritual lay associations) as a social welfare institution among city Indians, see ADA, PN, Palma 1619, f. 355r-v.

Cf. BNP, B54, 1609, ff. 5r, 15v, 18v; and the purchase of an image worth 1000 pesos by the Indian cofradías of Huamanga in 1620, in "Letras Annuas de la Provincia del Perú de la Compañía de Jesús, 1620–1724," *Revista de Archivos y Bibliotecas Nacionales* 5 (Lima, 1900), 71 (courtesy of the Monastery of San Francisco de Asís, Ayacucho).

For suggestions, however, of the limits of Indian "Christianization" even in cities, see Arriaga (1621), *La extirpación,* 83; AGN, JR, Leg. 11, C. 29, 1593, f. 67v.

39 See AGN, DI, Leg. 6, C. 109, 1643, ff. 27r–v, 29r; Leg. 4, C. 71, 1622, ff. 11v–12v, (12v for quote), 14r–v; Leg. 6, C. 107, 1642, ff. 20r–22v; TP, C. 246, 1651; ADA, PN, Peña 1596, ff. 311r–312r; Padilla *1602*/1613, ff. 337v–338v; Navarrete 1615–1618/*1627*/1630, ff. 300v–301r, 302r, 519r–v; Mesagil 1637–1639, ff. 897r, 918v, 919r, 930v; ADA, Corregimiento, Causas Ordinarias, Leg. 1, C. 1, 1595, ff. 21r–22r; Spalding, "Social Climbers," 656–59; note 40 below.

40 ADA, Corregimiento, Causas Ordinarias, Leg. 1, C. 1, 1595, ff. 21v, 25r–v (25v for quote of Pata's son); PN, Mesagil 1637–1639, ff. 560r–562r (561v for quote of Quino). The lands of the benefice amounted to nine or ten "topos"; a topo is an Andean measure which signifies an amount needed to support a household, and therefore varies in size according to ecological conditions affecting productivity.

41 On Andean views of cloth and religion, see Chapter 1 above, and John V. Murra, "Cloth and Its Functions in the Inca State," *American Anthropologist* 64 (August, 1962), 710–28.

42 ADA, Corregimiento, Causas Ordinarias, Leg. 1, C. 1, 1595, ff. 25r–26r; C. 8, 1637, f. 1211r; PN, Soria 1593/*1601,* f. 97v; Navarrete *1615–1618/1627*/1630, ff. 36v, 302v; Silvera/*Mesagil* 1636–1637, ff. 477v–478r; Mesagil 1637–1639, ff. 460v, 561r, 897r, 931v; AGN, DI, Leg. 6, C. 107, 1642, ff. 20r, 22r–v; TP, C. 246, 1651.

43 ADA, PN, Navarrete 1615–1618/*1627*/1630, f. 420r; BNP, Z329, 1611; Z330, 1612; Z328, 1613.

44 AGN, JR, Leg. 23, C. 62, 1617, ff. 184r, 187v; TP, C. 311, 1636, f. 6r (Ramírez quote); RPIA, tomo 21, partida XXXIII, 335–36 (335 for quote of Vischongo kuraka); AGN, TP, C. 370, 1607–88, sub-cuaderno 9, f. 11r; sub-cuaderno 6, ff. 3r–4v for the specific cases cited. For other cases, see AGN, DI, Leg. 6, C. 108, 1643, ff. 8r–9v, 3r–v; TP, C. 663, 1618.

45 López received usufruct rights during her lifetime, and their son received title to the property. López herself donated city property to the upkeep of their son. ADA, PN, Peña 1596, ff. 171v–176r (175r for quote). On Arriola's status as a "citizen," see Palma 1619, f. 631v. For the respectability of López's first husband, Alonso Padillo, see BNP, A18, 1599, f. 2v (mitayo assigned to heirs of Padillo).

46 ADA, PN, Navarrete *1615–1618*/1627/1630, ff. 215r–216v, 60r–61v. See also Ibid., f. 346r–v; Romo 1577, f. 108r–v. For suggestive examples of Indian women buying Indian lands on behalf of European men with whom they were not married, see Silvera/Mesagil 1636–1637, ff. 477v–478r; Mesagil 1637–1639, f. 460v.

47 Poma de Ayala (1615), *Nueva corónica,* 539 (cf. ibid., 514, 510). Poma does admit the role of violence elsewhere in his chronicle. For specific examples of assaults

by Spanish men against Indian women, see BNP, A336, 1559, passim; BNP, B54, f. 30v.

48 In some areas of the countryside, as mestizo heirs claimed important properties and social positions, racial inheritance itself would reinforce the Hispanic-mestizo character of the upper strata in Indian society. It is well-known that mestizos occupied leadership positions in many Indian communities in the eighteenth century.

49 Poma de Ayala (1615), *Nueva corónica*, 775 (quote), 768.

50 See ADA, PN, Navarrete 1615-1618/*1627*/1630, ff. 300v-302v (302v for quote). On traditional Andean inheritance patterns, see Diez de San Miguel (1567), *Visita . . . de Chucuito*, 35.

51 See BNP, B820, 1643, esp. ff. 2r-4v, 7v, 19r, 21r-v ("Indian hacendada"), 30r, 37r (Indian identity of Puscotilla's husband). Puscotilla came from Guayllay (some thirty kilometers west of Espíritu Santo) and was probably a Chanca by ethnic origin. See Risco (1684), "Descripción . . . de los Angaraes," 203.

52 See ADA, PN, Morales 1630, f. 446r ("master shoemaker"); Silvera/*Mesagil* 1636-1637, ff. 515r-516v.

53 ADA, Cabildo, Causas Civiles, Leg. 1, C. 6, 1673, ff. 5r-6v (f. 5r for quote). Cf. AGN, DI, Leg. 6, C. 109, 1643, f. 35r-v.

54 AGN, DI, Leg. 6, C. 119, 1648, ff. 111v-112r.

55 ADA, PN, Silvera/*Mesagil* 1636-1637, f. 542v; cf. BNP, B820, 1643, f. 35r.

56 See AGN, JR, Leg. 23, C. 62, 1617, ff. 174r, 176r-v, 179v-180r, 182v, 202v, 204r-v, 211r.

57 For discussion of threats to the authority of chiefs, see Chapter 5 above (esp. "The Impact of Judicial Politics: Native Society"). See also BNP, Z37, 1640, f. 385r. For evidence that by the late seventeenth and eighteenth centuries, a number of kurakas in Huamanga and elsewhere were viewed by natives as not only rich, but also abusive, see note 73 below. An extended and comparative discussion of this complex topic will appear in my "The Struggle for Solidarity: Class, Culture, and Community in Highland Indian America" (in progress).

58 To stabilize their tenure, forasteros who acquired "private" property by right of purchase from ayllu Indians sometimes sought the formal approval of local kurakas. ADA, PN, Palma 1619, ff. 174r-176r; Silvera/Mesagil 1636-1637, f. 25r-v. It is noteworthy, too, that Indians expected chiefs to assert a prior, community right over apparently "private" property if necessary to protect them against dispossession. AAA, Siglo XVII, Est. 1, Exp. 5, f. 1r-v; see also ADA, Cabildo, Causas Civiles, Leg. 1, C. 4, 1671, ff. 1r-2v.

59 See AGN, DI, Leg. 6, C. 107, 1642, ff. 10r, 14r, 27v; C. 108, 1643, ff. 1r-15r. In both cases, the dispossessed were literate in Spanish, and the litigation includes petitions in their own handwriting. Recall also the expropriation of revenues by chiefs to pay for tributes or mitas, discussed in Chapter 5 above.

60 One should note that Hispanism was not a *sure* path to success, and its lure left broken lives in its wake. Moreover, "success" in Indian society was often petty by Hispanic standards, and in these cases especially, respectability in Spanish-mestizo society was fragile or nonexistent.

61 Excellent testimony on the religious dimension of this crisis of confidence is given in BNP, B54, 1609, ff. 19r–30r, 36v–37r.

62 The Jesuit record is in BNP, B54, 1609, ff. 20r–27r, from which the following four paragraphs (and their quotations) are drawn. A transcription of the document—with some errors—was published in Lima as "Idolatrías de los indios Huachos y Yauyos," *Revista Histórica* 6 (1918), 180–97. Sr. Alfredo R. Alberdi Vallejo has told me that he has discovered documentation of nativism related to Taki Onqoy for the late sixteenth or early seventeenth centuries. A discussion of the common dimensions of Taki Onqoy and the nativist movement of 1613 is in my "Las ideologías nativistas," 25–32.

63 Poma de Ayala (1615), *Nueva corónica*, 863. On the persistence of idolatry, see note 37 above, and AAA, Siglo XVII, Estante 3, Exp. 28, ff. 8r–v, 9v–10r; BNP, B54, 1609, ff. 20v–21r; "Letras Annuas . . . de la Compañía de Jesús, 1620–1724," 72–75.

64 For elite participation and leadership of "traditional" paganisms, the latter's inclusion of some anti-Christian sentiment, and syncretic interpenetrations, see "Letras Annuas . . . de la Compañía de Jesús, 1620–1724," 74–75; Poma de Ayala (1615), *Nueva corónica*, 773–74, 781, 861; AAA, Siglo XVII, Estante 3, Exp. 28, ff. 9v–10r. Cf. Millones, "Introducción," 81–82; Spalding, "Social Climbers," 660–61.

65 It should be noted that the huacas could not command absolute "purity," since they recognized the fact of Spanish dominance. Despite their anti-Christian preachings, they also ordered that three major fiestas be celebrated under cover of Spanish festivals. BNP, B54, 1609, f. 26r.

66 Ibid., f. 20r.

67 Given the attempts of elites to earn prestige by participating in—and even leading—"tamer" forms of idolatry which included nativist undercurrents, they could not easily back off from community religion when anti-Hispanic nativist currents assumed greater prominence. See ibid., ff. 20v, 21r; note also the discussion of elite "vulnerability" below in this chapter.

68 Recall the individual cases and conflicts already cited in this chapter. It should be noted also that many successful Indians were forasteros anyway; that is, their important socioeconomic relationships with Indians tended not to be with traditional ayllu relatives.

69 For racial ideology in colonial Huamanga and greater Peru, see Ribera y Chaves (1586), "Relación de . . . Guamanga," 185–187; Carabajal (1586), "Descripción . . . de Vilcas Guaman," 206; Basto, *Las mitas*, 4, 24; and the discussion of Juan de Matienzo in Chapter 3. For European hostility toward ladinos, see Poma de Ayala (1615), *Nueva corónica*, 493, 605.

For suggestive discussions of the psychology of colonial situations, and the ambivalences created by oppressive relationships, see Albert Memmi, *The Colonizer and the Colonized*, trans. Howard Greenfeld (Boston, 1965); Frantz Fanon, *Black Skin, White Masks*, trans. Charles Lam Markmann (New York, 1967); id., *A Dying Colonialism*, esp. 35–67, 121–45; O. Mannoni, *Prospero and Caliban: The Psychology of Colonization*, trans. Pamela Powesland (2nd ed., New York, 1964).

70 The discussion in the previous paragraph and the one that follows should be compared with Richard Price, "Introduction," in *Maroon Societies: Rebel Slave Communities in the Americas,* ed. Price (Garden City, N.Y., 1973), 19–21; Fanon, *A Dying Colonialism,* 131–32. For two cases of women serving as chiefs of local society, ADA, PN, Mesagil 1637–1639, ff. 636r–640v; BNP, Z888, 1646, f. 551v.

71 See BNP, B54, 1609, ff. 19r, 24v–25r; "Letras Annuas . . . de la Compañía de Jesús, 1620–1724," 72–73. I lack "hard" data documenting the socioeconomic status of Indians who experienced dreams and visions in Huamanga, but believe they included elites (as well as commoners). It is noteworthy that extremely acculturated Indians unleashed "pagan" impulses by getting drunk. See Poma de Ayala (1615), *Nueva corónica,* 863, 495. For a clear case of an Indian elite torn by conflicts between Andean huacas and Christian religion, in the province of Huarochirí northeast of Lima, see Avila (c. 1598), *Dioses y hombres,* chs. 20–21.

72 Poma de Ayala (1615), *Nueva corónica,* 494–98 (see also 557–58).

73 Various historians and sources have documented the existence of a wealthy Indian elite (in part composed of forasteros and urban Indians) for the late colonial period, and the emergence of strained relationships between kurakas and ayllu peasants. See Spalding, *De indio a campesino,* 31–60, 147–93; Sánchez-Albornoz, *Indios y tributos,* esp. 99–110, 113–49; Brooke Larson, "Caciques, Class Structure and the Colonial State in Bolivia," *Nova Americana* 2 (Turin, 1979), 197–235, esp. 202–4. For Huamanga, see BNP, B670, 1690.

74 This inability to excape one's racial identification had an important impact on the ideology of future generations of successful Indians. See esp. John Rowe, "El movimiento nacional inca del siglo XVIII," *Revista universitaria* 43 (Cuzco, 1954), 17–47; Spalding, *De indio a campesino,* 147–93.

CHAPTER 8: HUAMANGA'S COLONIAL HERITAGE

1 For an introduction to nineteenth and twentieth century Ayacucho, see Lorenzo Huertas Vallejos, "Prólogo" (to "Revisita de la Doctrina de Santa María Magdalena . . . de Huamanga"), *Revista del Archivo Departamental de Ayacucho* 1 (Ayacucho, 1977), 52–56; José María Arguedas, *Yawar fiesta* (Lima, 1940); Arguedas, "Puquio: una cultura en proceso de cambio," in *Estudios sobre la cultura actual en el Perú,* ed. Universidad Nacional Mayor de San Marcos (Lima, 1964), 221–72; Antonio Díaz Martínez, *Ayacucho: hambre y esperanza* (Ayacucho, 1969); Billie Jean Isbell, *To Defend Ourselves: Ecology and Ritual in an Andean Village* (Austin, 1978), 41–46 and passim.

  For a comparative introduction to conquest folklore in Latin America, see Nathan Wachtel, *La vision des vaincus: les indiens du Pérou devant la conquête espagnole* (Paris, 1971), 21–98.

2 There is a sense in which generally depressed wage levels and employment render the distinction between "underemployed" and "employed" problematic, especially since many "employed" cannot subsist on their wages alone. Even if we set aside this problem, official statistics for Peru estimate "underemployment" alone at 44–48 percent of the economically active population during the years 1976–1979. *Latin America Economic Report,* 7:6 (9 February 1979), 48.

3 In addition to Chapter 2 above, see the revealing comments by Matienzo (1567), *Gobierno,* 133, 162–64.

4 For an introduction to Inkarrí and the timing of the myth's emergence, see Pease, *El dios,* 69–93 (esp. 80), 139–40; *Ideología mesiánica del mundo andino,* ed. Juan M. Ossio (Lima, 1973), esp. 219–25, 379–91; Alejandro Ortiz Rescaniere, *De Adaneva a Inkarrí* (Lima, 1973).

5 The Indians' very success at judicial politics, for example, eventually undermined the effectiveness of legal strategies of resistance, especially after colonials developed alternative forms of extraction to replace official mitas and tributes. This tendency could not help but change the nature of the Indians' relationship to the Hispanic power structure and its representatives (indeed, many corregidores were killed by Indians in the eighteenth century). Similarly, the profound political disaffection of a segment of the Indian elite in the late colonial period had roots in the contradictions of race and class discussed in Ch. 7, and the barriers to the more complete merger of wealthy, acculturated Indians into white Hispanic society.

6 For more detail on each of these "paths" to exploitable labor and tributes, see Chapters 2, 4, and 6. When distinguishing the three modes of exploitation, I do not mean to deny that kurakas could play a significant role in the state and private forms. But in these cases, the kurakas' role was that of subordinated functionaries who complied (willingly or by force) with the rules of a colonial society. In the case of the indigenous form, the kurakas' role was that of more autonomous allies who mediated Indian-white relations, and managed production and labor relationships on the basis of the "traditional" prestige, norms, and reciprocities binding chiefs and peoples.

7 The meaning of the term "yanacona" was probably broader in the pre-Toledan period than later, and may have included fairly independent "retainers" who worked for wages or a share of the commodities they produced.

8 The political and economic problems which emerged in Jauja (heartland of the Huancas) and in Cuzco (center of Inca tradition and influence) are discussed briefly in Chapter 3 ("Millenarianism as Social Crisis"). For the colonials' economic dependence on indigenous tradition in early Potosí, and the handicaps it implied, see Carlos Sempat Assadourian, "La producción de la mercancía dinero en la formación del mercado interno colonial," in *Ensayos sobre el desarrollo económico de México y América Latina,* ed. Enrique Florescano (Mexico, 1979), 223–92; *Tales of Potosí,* ed. Padden, xiv–xviii.

9 See Basto, *Las mitas,* 5–6, 10–12; Enrique Tandeter, "Rent as a Relation of Production and as a Relation of Distribution in Late Colonial Potosí," Paper presented at Latin American Studies Association Meetings, Pittsburgh, Pa., 5–7 April 1979.

10 It is worth recalling that in the context of a labor shortage, considerable geographical mobility, and a prosperous commercial economy, "voluntary" laborers were in a position to command wages and work conditions which lessened their attractiveness to entrepreneurs.

11 Such actions represented *both* an attempt to maintain standing among kin, as well as to enhance the specific interests of chiefs (which might diverge, in part, from those of peasants).

Glossary

ají. hot peppers

alcalde. mayor; judge on the municipal council (cabildo)

alguacil mayor. policeman and official of the municipal council (cabildo)

arriero. muleteer; driver of animal train

arroba. Spanish measure of weight, approximately twenty-five pounds (11.5 kilograms, or 25.3 pounds)

asiento. labor contract in which the hired party agrees to settle with and serve a master and employer for a specified length of time

audiencia. viceregal court and governing body (located in Lima in the case of the Peruvian viceroyalty)

ayllu. the basic kin unit of Andean social structure, formally an endogamous lineage claiming descent from a common ancestor

ayni. Andean root word, in both Quechua and Aymara languages, for measured reciprocity relationships

cabildo. municipal council

cacicazgo. Spanish term for chieftainship, or kuraka jurisdiction

cacique. Spanish term for Andean ethnic lord (kuraka)

cacique principal. Spanish term for chief kuraka representing a community or ethnic group as a whole, and associated in particular with the group's "upper half" or moiety, as distinguished from the *segunda persona* ("second person") representing the group as a whole, and associated in particular with its "lower half"

caja de comunidad. community box established in the Indian repartimientos to hold cash and documents

cantor. church choir leader

censo. long-term loan, whose interest provided an annuity to the lender, and whose principal was paid back at the option of the borrower

chácara. modest farm

chicha. Andean alcoholic beverage, often corn beer, but also made from other fermented plant bases

261

chuño. freeze-dried potatoes, made in high and dry zones experiencing large daily fluctuations of temperature, whose long-term preservation capacity makes them a valuable storage food for emergencies

cofradía. ritual lay association of the Catholic Church

compadre. cogodparent; cogodfather (cogodmother: *comadre*)

composición de tierras. inspection and legalization of land titles

conopa. Andean household god, commonly a stone, serving as a guardian of a family, its crops, and so forth

corregidor. chief Spanish magistrate, or judge-administrator, of a district

corregidor de españoles. a corregidor in charge of a Spanish municipality

corregidor de indios. a corregidor in charge of a rural Indian district

corregimiento. the district of jurisdiction of a corregidor, normally combining several repartimientos into one larger district in the case of the corregidor de indios

cumbi. Andean "luxury cloth," distinguished from everyday textiles by its beauty and quality

doctrinero. Catholic priest responsible for religious indoctrination of Indians

encomendero. Spanish colonizer in whose charge the Crown "entrusted" Indians, from whom the encomendero could collect tribute and labor services in exchange, presumably, for tending to the natives' spiritual and material welfare

encomienda. the grant of Indian peoples held by an encomendero

estancia. ranch or grazing site

extirpador. Catholic priest charged with "extirpating" native religion

fanega. Spanish measure of volume, about 1.5 bushels

fanegada. Spanish measure of area, about 2.9 hectares as used in Huamanga

fianza. a surety, often posted to guarantee the accounts of incoming colonial officials

forastero. immigrant Indian no longer living with original kin group or community, as contrasted with *originario* Indians

gobernador. governor

hacendado. hacienda owner

hacienda. sizable landed estate, normally mixing farming and ranching

hanan. Andean term for the "upper" half or moiety of a group

hatun runa. Andean term, literally "big man," denoting a male head of household

huaca. a native Andean god; a sacred being or spirit, often thought of as an ancestor, and materialized in the form of hills, waters, caves, stones, or ancestor mummies

huacacamayoc. Andean priest, literally a caretaker of a huaca

hurin. Andean term for the "lower" half or moiety of a group

ichu. a bunch grass common on the puna

kuraka. Andean ethnic lord

kurakazgo. Andean chieftainship, institution of kuraka authority

ladino. Indian of relatively Hispanized culture, demeanor, and trappings

malqui. ancestor mummy

manta. Andean cloak, often used for carrying items or babies on one's back

merced. grant, usually a land grant

mestizo. descendant of mixed Indian-white parentage

mit'a. literally "turn," more broadly the pre-Columbian Andean system of rotating "turns" of service in the performance of community labor, as distinguished from the colonial mita, or forced labor draft

mita. colonial forced labor draft institution providing rotations of native laborers to selected beneficiaries of the state, as distinguished from its indigenous antecedent, the mit'a

mita de plaza. mita labor draft sending natives to the plaza of a Spanish municipality to serve its citizens and respectable residents in farms, ranches, and household duties, as distinguished from mitas sending natives to work in mining or obraje manufactures

mitayo. an Indian laborer serving on a mita draft

mitmaq. Indian colonizers, whether representatives of a community or ethnic group sent to exploit a special ecological zone, or peoples transferred by the Incas to ethnically foreign settings for political or economic reasons

montaña. relatively warm and wet ecological zones of the eastern Andean slopes, a transition area to tropical Amazonian rainforests

obraje. primitive textile factory or workshop

originario. ayllu Indian still living among original kin groups descended from common ancestor-gods, as distinguished from forastero Indians

pacarícuc. all-night vigil important in major Andean religious festivals

pacarina. hills or waters venerated by Andean peoples as mythological places of origin

peso. monetary unit whose value varied according to the number of *reales* contained

peso corriente. a peso of nine reales (singular: real)

peso ensayado. a peso of 12.5 reales (singular: real)

puna. high, cold Andean plains, important habitat of llamas and alpacas

quero. traditional Andean wooden cup

quintal. Spanish weight measure of four arrobas, or about one hundred pounds

real. basic measuring unit of Spanish pesos (equivalent to 34 *maravedís*, or to 0.6 grams of silver)

reducciones. resettlement program to cluster scattered native peoples into Hispanic-style towns; the resettled villages

regidor. alderman of a cabildo, administrative aide of its alcalde

repartimiento. encomienda district or jurisdiction (the only meaning, of several possible ones, used in this book)

residencia. judicial review taken by incoming official of an outgoing functionary's conduct in office

revisita. a reinspection to revise the findings of earlier tours of inspection

sacristán. church sexton

selva. tropical jungle lowlands, distinguished ecologically and as a culture zone from the highlands

solar. town lot

Taki Onqoy. literally "dancing sickness," the name of an anti-Christian millenarian movement

tambo. lodging site for travellers

taquiongo. "possessed" messenger of the Andean gods in the Taki Onqoy movement

tincu. Andean term and concept denoting perfection, balance, justice

visita. tour of inspection

visitador. the judge-inspector of a colonial visita

waranqa. Andean measure of 1,000 units

yana. as used in this book, pre-Columbian retainers alienated from ayllu life to serve other natives for life-long duty, as distinguished from colonial yanaconas

yanacona. a native retainer or serf bound to a colonial overlord

yanaconaje. institution of long-term personal bondage attaching yanaconas to masters

yunga. Andean term referring to warm-weather people or lands of low altitudes

Bibliography

The materials used to reconstruct the social history of Huamanga's native peoples were mainly unpublished manuscript sources, supplemented by published documents and by secondary works of analytical or empirical importance. It would be impractical to list all materials consulted during research, but I can present a partial selection of unpublished and published sources for those who wish to pursue research leads, to check titles and references of documents, books, and articles cited in the notes, or to read further on Huamanga and on colonial Andean history.

ARCHIVES

Huamanga's history has generated vast and diverse sets of manuscript materials. These include administrative records, among them population counts, cabildo proceedings, and reports to political and religious authorities; juridical materials ranging from simple petitions and legal decrees to complicated litigation that dragged on for decades; land titles and account records of proprietors (or their managers); notarial records tracing all kinds of transactions (sales, rentals, donations, dowries, wills, inventories, labor contracts, partnerships, powers of attorney, formal declarations or agreements); reports on idolatry and religious affairs. Often, the formal date of a document is misleading because litigants and officials frequently had good reason to include copies of earlier documents or transactions to justify their claims or rulings. Thus a proceeding dated in the 1650s might include transcriptions of materials from the sixteenth century.

The manuscript documents cited in this book are housed in the following archives: Archivo Arzobispal de Ayacucho (AAA); Archivo Departamental de Ayacucho (ADA); Archivo General de Indias, Seville (AGI); Archivo General de la Nación, Lima (AGN); Biblioteca Municipal de Ayacucho (BMA); Biblioteca Nacional del Perú, Sala de Investigaciones, Lima (BNP); Harkness Collection, U.S. Library of Congress, Washington, D.C. (HC); Registro de Propiedad Inmueble de Ayacucho (RPIA); Latin American Collection, Yale University, Sterling Library, Department of Manuscripts and Archives, New Haven, Ct. (YC).

The AGI, AGN, and BNP house enormous quantities of administrative and judicial material, and the data for Huamanga is very rich. The HC is valuable for its collection of early (pre-Toledan) viceregal decrees directed specifically to conditions in Huamanga, and for early cabildo records, since published as *Libro del Cabildo de la Ciudad de San Juan de la Frontera de Huamanga, 1539–1547,* transcribed by Raúl Rivera Serna (Lima, 1966). The BMA has a fine set of cabildo records from the late colonial period, but has few manuscripts relevant to the sixteenth and early seventeenth centuries. The BMA does hold, however, some early production records from Huancavelica (Libro 1.31). The ADA has, under the direction of Dr. Lorenzo Huertas, become a superb regional archive whose collection extends from the sixteenth century to the present. Administrative and judicial records are thin for the early colonial period, but a fine collection of "Protocolos Notariales" (PN) begins in the 1570s. This rich notarial collection complements the AGN and BNP documents nicely, and Indians are surprisingly active in the transactions. Some Indian communities joined private proprietors in registering their land titles with the RPIA in the twentieth century, and supported their claims with community land tenure documents ranging as far back as the sixteenth century. RPIA data on ethnic conflict is especially good for the present-day province of Víctor Fajardo (south of the Río Pampas). The AAA has a large collection of church-related documents, but there, as elsewhere, materials on idolatry for Huamanga are either scarce or inaccessible. More plentiful is data on church properties and taxes, and civil or criminal suits involving priests. The YC collection on Peru includes some early colonial records from Parinacochas and Andahuaylas, which border the "core" region of Huamanga.

The following list offers short titles of specific documents *cited* in the notes of this book. The list will be useful to scholars interested in identifying the titles, contexts, or issues dealt with in specific documents mentioned in the notes. The list excludes AGI documents (they are fully identified in the notes), and excludes HC documents, which were all viceregal decrees. For summaries of specific HC sources, see the U.S. Library of Congress publication cited in this Bibliography. The list also excludes identification of individual notarial transactions, which constituted the overwhelming majority of sources used from the ADA. The notes specify the notary(ies) and year(s) of the register book, and the folio(s) where the transaction is located. Further identification of each transaction would use excessive space. The AGN title list is complete except that it excludes the "Títulos de propiedad" (TP) section (land titles). The BNP list, similarly, presents all cited BNP sources *except* those cited only in Appendix B (land tenure documents). In the case of the AAA, "Estante" represents the shelf number counting from the top down, and "Exp." marks the place of the document on a given shelf, counting from left to right. (There is no formal catalogue or order, except by centuries, of AAA documents). The reader should note also that Legajo and Expediente numbers of ADA documents were still tentative at the time of my research in Ayacucho.

To save space, the AGN's "Juicios de Residencias" (JR) section simply identifies the ex-official who was the object of the judicial review (*residencia*), and the district where he served. The RPIA list gives simply the registrant, and year of land registration.

ARCHIVO ARZOBISPAL DE AYACUCHO (AAA)

Siglo XVII, Estante 1, Exp. 5. Untitled, defends right of Miguel Mayo (Indian) to lands near Guamanguilla (1645).

Siglo XVII, Estante 3, Exp. 28. "Causa de capitulos Puestos . . . a El Padre Andres gomez . . . en las minas de guayllay [1626]."

Siglo XVII, Estante 3, Exp. 51. Untitled, criminal charges by Don Carlos Quinto, kuraka, against the priest Blas Jacinto Baca de Otel, Parinacochas (1630–1631).

ARCHIVO DEPARTAMENTAL DE AYACUCHO (ADA)

Cabildo, Asuntos Adminstrativos, Leg. 64, Exp. 2, 1645. "Prouiciones sobre el entero de la mita de la plassa [de Huamanga]."

Cabildo, Causas Civiles, Leg. 1, C. 4, 1671. "Causa que sigue Luisa Bernarda . . . por un alfalfar y tierras ubicadas en el valle de la Totora."

Cabildo, Causas Civiles, Leg. 1, C. 6, 1673. Untitled, concerns Huanta lands of Clemente de Chaves, Indian of city of Huamanga.

Cabildo, Causas Civiles, Leg. 2, C. 16, 1699. Untitled, concerns Mayomarca lands of Indians of Ongoy.

Corregimiento, Asuntos Administrativos, Leg. 31, C. 4, 1617. Untitled, concerns capellanía founded by Don Sancho de Córdova.

Corregimiento, Asuntos Administrativos, Leg. 31, C. 5, 1621. Untitled, will of Antonio de Chaves, citizen of Huamanga.

Corregimiento, Causas Ordinarias, Leg. 1, C. 1, 1595. Untitled, includes composición of montaña lands of Cintiguayllas (Huanta), and will of Catalina Pata, Indian.

Corregimiento, Causas Ordinarias, Leg. 1, C. 2, 1599. Untitled, concerns lands of Cañares Indians.

Corregimiento, Causas Ordinarias, Leg. 1, C. 8, 1637. Untitled, land donation of Ysabel de Chaves, Indian of Guanta.

Corregimiento, Causas Ordinarias, Leg. 1, C. 13, 1647. Untitled, concerns lands sold by Guaychao Indians in 1630s.

Corregimiento, Causas Ordinarias, Leg. 1, C. 14, 1650. Untitled, concerns relations of silver miners and merchants.

Corregimiento, Causas Ordinarias, [Leg. 2], 1678. Untitled, concerns history of lands in Huanta, disputed among various Europeans (including Hernando Palomino) and Indians (including the Caviñas, Angaraes, and Quiguares, and community of Motoy).

ARCHIVO GENERAL DE LA NACIÓN (AGN)

DI (Derecho Indígena), Leg. 1, C. 8, 1576. "Testimonio de los autos que siguió doña María Carrillo . . . sobre . . . la mitad del Repartimiento de ANDAMARCA . . . de Lucanas."

DI, Leg. 1, C. 9, 1567. "Autos criminales que siguieron Juan Tucabamba y Pedro Cachi, indios . . . de Matibamba . . . sobre ciertas chacaras de coca."

DI, Leg. 2, C. 17, 1573. "Autos . . . contra Juan Arias Maldonado . . . heredero del Capitán Diego Maldonado, encomendero . . . de Andahuaylas."

DI, Leg. 2, C. 25, 1578. "Testimonio . . . en nombre de don Lázaro y de don Andres Guacras, Caciques . . . de TANQUIGUA."

DI, Leg. 3, C. 50, 1606. "Autos que siguió Agustín Arce de Quirós, Juez . . . de la revisita . . . de Andahuaylas."

DI, Leg. 4, C. 61, 1616. "Revisita y padrón de los indios de Parinacochas."

DI, Leg. 4, C. 62, 1616. "Padroncillo y Tasa . . . de los Quiguares orejones, provincia de Angaraes."

DI, Leg. 4, C. 65, 1619. "Testimonio de . . . documentos relativos a la visita y reducción de don Alonso de Mendoza Ponce de León."

DI, Leg. 4, C. 71, 1622. "Autos que siguió Isabel Ñusta Yaro Chumbi . . . sobre un sitio y solar en . . . Huancavelica."

DI, Leg. 4, C. 73, 1622. "Autos que siguieron don Juan Guarcaya y don Alonso Choquiguacra, Curacas . . . de Lucanas . . . sobre acreditar el fallecimiento del indio tributario Juan Sulma."

DI, Leg. 6, C. 107, 1642. "Autos seguidos por doña Catalina y doña Luisa Cucichimbo, indias . . . de Socos . . . sobre propiedad de unas tierras."

DI, Leg. 6, C. 108, 1643. "Autos seguidos por don Fernando y don Melchor Ataorimachi, indios principales . . de Huamanguilla . . . contra don Juan Huamanhuaraca, Cacique . . . de los huantacochas . . . de Huanta."

DI, Leg. 6, C. 109, 1643. "Autos que siguieron don Melchor y don Salvador Ataurimachi . . . sobre . . . los privilegios y excepciones á que tenían derecho."

DI, Leg. 6, C. 113, 1646. "Real provisión . . . a favor del tesorero D. Juan de la Maza . . . renovando . . . las mercedes de indios de mita."

DI, Leg. 6, C. 118, 1648. "Testimonio . . . de compraventa de un solar . . . de Huanta que Pedro Guacachi, indio . . . otorgó a favor de Juan Bautista Ramos."

DI, Leg. 6, C. 119, 1648. "Revisita y padrón . . . de SAN JUAN DE LOS SANCOS . . . de Lucanas."

DI, Leg. 24, C. 686, 1601. "Auto . . . nombrando Don Juan Lopez Tinoco, para que termine la revisita de los indios . . . ANANCHILQUES."

DI, Leg. 39, C. 794, 1600. "Provisión . . . para que revisite a los indios . . . de Urinchilques y Ananchilques."

DI, Leg. 39, C. 798, 1624. "Provisión . . . librada a Dn. Juan Ramirez Romero, Corregidor . . . de Vilcashuamán, para que visite a los indios . . . encomendados en Dn. Miguel de Bendezú."

JR (Juicios de Residencias), Leg. 8, C. 20, 1590–1595, of Don Francisco de Cepeda, corregidor of Parinacochas.

JR, Leg. 11, C. 29, 1593, of Don Alonso de Herrera Padilla and Don Francisco Guerra y de Céspedes, corregidores of Huancavelica and Huamanga.

JR, Leg. 16, C. 44, 1599, of García Solís de Portocarrero, corregidor of Huamanga.

JR, Leg. 23, C. 62, 1617, of Don Perefan de Rivera, corregidor of Vilcashuamán.

JR, Leg. 24, C. 65, 1618, of Don Cristóbal de Ulloa y Mercado, corregidor of Castrovirreyna.

Minería, Leg. 2, Ayacucho 1622. "Don Diego de Salazar pide que se le ampare . . . en la posesion de unas minas . . . en el cerro de Tunsulla."

Minería, Leg. 11, Huancavelica 1562–1572. Untitled, concerns property and debts of Amador de Cabrera.

Minería, Leg. 13, Huancavelica 1585–1595, Exp. 2. Untitled, concerns cargos against Juan Pérez, the royal factor of Huancavelica.

Minería, Leg. 14, Huancavelica 1592–1594, Exp. 1. "Expediente seguidos por los acreedores de Juan de Raya."

Superior Gobierno, Leg. 2, C. 38, 1618. "Autos promovidos por Dn. Juan Enciso Navarrete, vecino y hacendado . . . de Huamanga."

Tierras de Comunidades, Leg. 3, C. 19, 1806. "Autos que sigue el Común de Indios de Pueblo de Chiara . . . sobre . . . las tierras nombradas Uchuymarca y Ataquisuar."

BIBLIOTECA NACIONAL DEL PERÚ (BNP)

A6, 1599. "Auto . . . sobre la inasistencia de indios a una reunión ordenada por el Corregidor."

A18, 1599. "Repartición de los indios de plaza . . . entre los vecinos y moradores de [Huamanga]."

A127, 1547. "Copia de la correspondencia de D. Pedro de La Gasca."

A203, 1557. "Libro de Cabildo . . . de Huamanga."

A218, 1591. "Título de Protector de los Naturales de las minas de Urcococha y Choclococha."

A230, [1598]. "Pago de los indio lucanas, soras y andamarcas."

A233, 1598. "Pago de los indios lucanas, soras y andamarcas."

A236, 1597. "En la residencia secreta que se le tomó a Dn. Francisco de Cepeda, Corregidor . . . de Parinacochas."

A314, 1588. "Testimonio de un censo que se paga . . . a los indios del pueblo del Espíritu Santo."

A329, 1587. "Expediente . . . seguida por Juan y Miguel Bermeo contra Pablo Bamboa, Corregidor . . . de los Andes."

A336, 1559. "Libro de penas de Cámara y gastos de justicia de la ciudad de Huamanga."

A364, 1596. "Juro en la real caja . . . de los indios Chocorvos."

A371, 1594. "Don Pedro Quispillamoca, contra Dn. Pedro Vilcanacari, sobre el cacicazgo de la segunda persona . . . de los Soras."

A387, 1594. "Expediente . . . presentada por Lázaro Yupa Inca Vacachi, Gobernador y Cacique Principal . . . de Pampas, para que se le expida título de amparo y posesión."

A390, 1592. "Cabeza de proceso contra Luis de Revolledo."

A393, 1594. "Expediente . . . presentada por Domingo de Villamonte, para que se le admita a la composición de unas tierras."

A455, 1571. "Concierto en el asiento de Colcabamba por el Lic. Diego Alvarez, con los caciques principales."

A473, 1597. "Razón de los títulos de la estancia nombrada Pauranga y sus sitios anexos . . . en la provincia de Castrovirreyna."

A603, 1568. "Libro 5° del Cabildo . . . de Huamanga."

B28, 1607. "Relación de la visita . . . al repartimiento de los indios de Andahuaylas."

B44, 1612. "Provisión de los indios Cañaris de Vilcas. Ordenanzas para no pagar mitas ni tributos."

B54, 1609. "Letras annuas de este colegio [de Jesús] de Huamanga."

B57, 1616. "V. E. confirme . . . las provisiones . . . acerca de que la mita de Choclococha se entere cumplidamente."

B59, 1618. "Provisión . . . para que el corregidor de los Chocorbos envíe a la villa de Huancavelica la cantidad de indios necesarios para el laboreo de las minas."

B75, 1626. "Testimonios de los títulos . . . de los molinos de Guatata, Churucana y Pacuaro."

B164, 1640. "Provisión . . . por la cual se mandan a los corregidores de Vilcashuamán, no impidan a los indios que voluntariamente quisieran trabajar en el obraje de Cacamarca."

B450, 1643. "Para que el corregidor . . . de Vilcasguamán guarde y execute la provisión . . . a pedimiento de los caciques . . . de Anan Chilques."

B462, 1601. "Para que el corregidor . . . en la rebaja . . . de los indios Tanquihuas."

B620, 1636. "Para que los indios . . . de Quinua cumplan con dar para . . . las minas de Huancavelica y otras mitas."

B670, 1690. "Expediente . . . entre el común de indios de Huancavelica y su Curaca Francisco Rodriguez."

B685, 1634. "Expediente . . . presentada por el Protector de Naturales de Castrovirreyna para que se cumpla."

B740, 1601. "Para que habiéndose rebajado a Dña. Teresa de Castañeda el número de los indios que le estaban repartidos."

B769, 1650. "Contra Juana Fernández, india . . . por 200 ps. de a 8 reales . . . procedido de la composición."

B806, 1604. "Pago de los indios lucanas, soras y andamarcas."

B820, 1643. "Expediente . . . en nombre de Catalina Pucotilla, india, para que se le de posesión de unas tierras."

B846, 1618. "Expediente . . . de una escritura de arrendamiento . . . por unos ingenios y haciendas [de Castrovirreyna]."

B856, 1616. "Memoria de los indios muertos . . . de los Andamarcas."

B875, 1628. "Cuentas que se han tomado a Andrés de Santo Domingo cobrador de tasas de los indios . . . que mitan a . . . Castrovirreyna."

B876, 1629. "Revisita de los indios . . . de Aspite y Vilcanchos de los Chocorvos."

B890, 1616. "V. E. confirma la cuenta . . . en favor de Domingo Grisoli de la mitad de los ingenios . . . en Castrovirreyna."

B895, 1603. "Pago de los indios lucanas, soras y andamarcas."

B934, 1616. "Expediente . . . presentada por el Cacique Principal del pueblo de Luricocha para que se le exima del envio de indios para . . . las minas de Huancavelica."

B968, 1602. "Pago de los indios lucanas, soras y andamarcas."

B971, 1603. "Pago de los indios lucanas, soras y andamarcas."

B1042, 1627. "Autos . . . por los oficiales reales . . . [de Castrovirreyna] y pregones para el arrendamiento de las haciendas, minas e ingenio que quedo por fin y muerte del Presidente."

B1079, 1629. "Expediente . . . en nombre de Diego Cuma, Miguel Cañana y Juan Huamanpusa, caciques de Huaros para que se envíe revisitadores."

B1159, 1629. "Sobre el empadronamiento de los indios tributarios de la villa de Huancavelica."

B1370, 1625. "Despacho . . . a pedimiento de Hernán Guillén de Mendoza confirmando la posesión en . . . el obraje."

B1441, 1634. "Expediente sobre el juicio de residencia . . . al Corregidor . . . de Andamarcas, Andrés de Paredes."

B1477, 1626. "Expediente . . . para que se le reciba información sobre la ausencia de mitayos."

B1485, 1600. "Para que el corregidor . . . de Vilcashuamán . . . [haga] averiguaciones de los agravios . . . [que reciben los indios Chilques en el obraje a cargo de Gaspar de Marquina]."

B1505, 1644. "Expediente . . . en nombre del Cap. Juan de Arriaga y de la Rosa, Corregidor de Lucanas."

B1525, 1647. "Expediente . . . en nombre de Dn. Sebastián Antonio de Contreras para que se restituya a los indios Chocorbos las tierras."

Z37, 1640. "Instrucción que . . . ha de guardar y cumplir . . . en el juicio de residencia que ha de tomar el Corregidor . . . de Vilcashuamán."

Z301, 1578. "Testimonio . . . presentada por Leonor de Valenzuela, para que se le de título de posesión de unas tierras."

Z303, 1586. "De las cuadras y tierras de Vilcas, molino y obraje."

Z304, 1591. "Escritura de venta de las tierras de Huancapuquio."

Z306, 1592. "Registro de escrituras públicas . . . ante el escribano Gaspar Antonio de Soria."

Z313, 1616. "Causa de cuentas dada por Dn. Diego Guillén de Mendoza."

Z317, 1586. "Carta de concierto. Diego Guillén de Mendoza, Lázaro Huaman Pujaico y Francisco Asto Hanampa, para construir un molino."

Z323, 1616. "Expediente sobre la petición presentada por el Lic. Pedro Guillén de Mendoza y Dn. Hernán Guillén de Mendoza."

Z351, 1616. "Sobre la causa seguida entre Gabriel Bautista de Saravia en nombre de Diego Guillén de Mendoza, y Lorenzo de Aliaga."

Z436, 1595. "Información de las haciendas y ganados y de los indios, que son necesarios."

Z441, 1633. "Expediente . . . presentada por Dña. Inés Hurtado de Mendoza para que se le continúe asignando los indios ananchilques fijados a su marido."

Z888, 1646. "Testimonio y composición de la Hacienda de Conoc."

Z1067, 1685. "Título de la Hda. de Sillco y Guallacha, situadas en la doctrina de los Angaraes."

Z1124, 1631. "Expediente . . . en nombre de los hijos legítimos y herederos de Dña. Bernardina de Romaní, para que se procedan al nombramiento de un tasador de unos bienes."

Z1268, 1590. "Testamento, inventario y almoneda de Dña. Elvira Gallardo, difunta."

Z1421, 1634. "Testamento cerrado de Fernando Palomino."

REGISTRO DE PROPIEDAD INMUEBLE DE AYACUCHO (RPIA)
Tomo 5, partida VI. Community of San Juan de Sarhua, 1905.
Tomo 5, partida LXI. Community of Tiquihua, 1906.
Tomo 5, partida CL. Convent of Santo Domingo of Lima, 1909.
Tomo 8, partida XL. Community of San Gerónimo de Yaulli, 1916.

Tomo 10, partida CXXIII. Community of Lucanamarca, 1921.
Tomo 10, partida CXL. Community of San Yldefonzo de Chuquihuarcaya, 1921.
Tomo 13, partida LV. Community of Saccsamarca, 1928.
Tomo 14, partida VI. Community of HuancaSancos, 1928.
Tomo 16, partida XLI. Community of Ccarampa, 1933.
Tomo 21, partida XXXIII. Monastery of Santa Clara, 1942.
Tomo 21, partida XLVII. Community of Carapo. 1943.

YALE UNIVERSITY, LATIN AMERICAN COLLECTION (YC)

Vol. 3. "Libro de los remates de tributos de los repartimientos que se cobran en esta caja. Cuzco, 1575–1582."
Vol. 5. "Libro común de sumas . . . por el tesorero Miguel Sánchez. Cuzco, 1572–1573."

PUBLISHED DOCUMENTS

The historian of colonial Andean life enjoys a large collection of published primary sources. Here I have listed only documentary sources cited in the notes. Readers interested in a more comprehensive list may consult the bibliographies of the books by Josep Barnadas and John Hemming cited in this Bibliography. The reader is cautioned that some publications combine scholarly articles with transcription of one or several documents. Occasionally, therefore, a publication listed among this Bibliography's secondary sources includes primary source material. A list of abbreviations used here appears at the beginning of the Notes.

Albornoz, Cristóbal de. c. 1582. "Instrucción para descubrir todas las guacas del Pirú y sus camayos y haciendas." Edited by Pierre Duviols. In *Journal de la Société des Américanistes* 56, no. 1 (1967), 17–39.
Aponte Figueroa, Juan de. 1622. "Memorial que trata de la reformación del reino del Pirú. . . ." *CDIE,* LI, 521–62.
Arriaga, Pablo Joseph de. 1621. *La extirpación de la idolatría en el Perú.* Edited by Horacio H. Urteaga. Lima, 1920.
Avila, Francisco de. c. 1598. *Dioses y hombres de Huarochirí.* Translated by José María Arguedas. Lima, 1966.
Avila Briceño, Diego, 1586. "Descripción y relación . . . de los Yauyos." *RGI,* 155–65.
Bandera, Damián de la. 1557. "Relación general de la disposición y calidad de la provincia de Guamanga." *RGI,* 176–80.
Bertonio, Ludovico. 1612. *Vocabulario de la lengua Aymara.* Edited by Julio Platzmann. 2 vols. Leipzig, 1879.
Cantos de Andrada, Rodrigo de. 1586. "Relación de la Villa Rica de Oropesa y minas de Guancavelica." *RGI,* 303–9.
Carabajal, Pedro de. 1586. "Descripción fecha de la provincia de Vilcas Guaman." *RGI,* 205–19.

Cieza de León, Pedro de. 1553. *El señorío de los Incas (2a parte de la crónica del Perú)*. Edited by Carlos Araníbar. Lima, 1967.

Cieza de León, Pedro de. "Guerra de las Salinas." *CDIE,* LXVIII, 1-451.

Cieza de León, Pedro de. 1553. *Parte primera de la crónica del Perú.* In *Biblioteca de Autores Españoles,* 26: 349-458. Madrid, 1853.

Cobo, Bernabé. 1629. *Historia de la fundación de Lima.* Edited by M. González de la Rosa. Lima, 1882.

Cobo, Bernabé. 1653. *Historia del nuevo mundo.* In *Biblioteca de Autores Españoles.* Vols. 91-92. Madrid, 1956.

Colección de documentos inéditos para la historia de España. 113 vols. Madrid, 1842-1945. Abbreviated as CDIE.

Colección de documentos inéditos relativos al descubrimiento, conquista, y organización de las antiguas posesiones españolas de América y Oceania. 42 vols. Madrid, 1864-1884. Abbreviated as *CDIAO.*

Contreras, Miguel de. *Padrón de los indios de Lima en 1613.* Edited by Noble David Cook. Lima, 1968.

Diez de San Miguel, Garci. 1567. *Visita hecha a la provincia de Chucuito. . . .* Transcribed by Waldemar Espinoza Soriano. Lima, 1964.

Documentos históricos del Perú. Edited by Manuel de Odriozla. Lima, 1872.

González Holguín, Diego. 1608. *Vocabulario de la lengua general de todo el Perú llamada qquichua o del Inca.* Edited by Juan G. N. Lobato. Lima, 1901.

Huertas Vallejos, Lorenzo, et al. *La revisita de los Chocorbos de 1683.* Ayacucho, 1976.

La iglesia de España en el Perú. 4 vols. Edited by Emilio Lissón Chaves. Seville, 1943-46.

Las informaciones de Cristóbal de Albornoz: documentos para el estudio del Taki Onqoy. Edited by Luis Millones. Cuernavaca, 1971.

Konetzke, Richard, ed. *Colección de documentos para la historia de la formación social de Hispanoamérica.* 2 vols. in 3 parts. Madrid, 1953, 1958.

"Letras Annuas de la Provincia del Perú de la Compañía de Jesús, 1620-1724," *Revista de Archivos y Bibliotecas Nacionales* 5 (Lima, 1900), 35-140.

Levillier, Roberto. *Don Francisco de Toledo, supremo organizador del Perú, su vida, su obra (1515-1582).* 3 vols. Buenos Aires, 1935-42.

Levillier, Roberto, ed. *Gobernantes del Perú. Cartas y papeles, siglo XVI.* 14 vols. Madrid, 1921-26.

Libro del Cabildo de la Ciudad de San Juan de la Frontera de Huamanga, 1539-1547. Transcribed by Raúl Rivera Serna. Lima, 1966.

López de Velasco, Juan. 1571-74. *Geografía y descripción universal de las Indias.* Edited by Marcos Jiménez de la Espada. Madrid, 1971.

Matienzo, Juan de. 1567. *Gobierno del Perú.* Edited by Guillermo Lohmann Villena. In *Travaux de l'Institut Français d'Études Andines* 11. Paris, 1967.

"Memorial y relación de las minas de azogue del Pirú" (1607). *CDIAO,* VIII, 422-29.

Memorias de los virreyes que han gobernado en el Perú. 6 vols. Lima, 1859.

Los Mercedarios en el Perú en el siglo XVI. Documentos inéditos del Archivo General de Indias. Edited by Víctor M. Barriga. 4 vols. Rome and Arequipa, 1933-53.

Molina, Cristóbal de. 1574. *Relación de las fábulas y ritos de los incas.* In *Las crónicas de los Molinas.* Edited by Francisco A. Loayza. Lima, 1943.

Montesinos, Fernando de. 1642. *Anales del Perú.* Edited by Víctor M. Maurtúa. 2 vols. Madrid, 1906.

Monzón, Luis de, et al. 1586. "Descripción de la tierra del repartimiento de Atunrucana y Laramati." *RGI,* 226–36.

Monzón, Luis de, et al. 1586. "Descripción de la tierra del repartimiento de Atunsora." *RGI,* 220–25.

Monzón, Luis de, et al. 1586. "Descripción de la tierra del repartimiento de los Rucanas Antamarcas." *RGI,* 237–48.

Oré, Luis Jerónimo de. *Symbolo Catholico Indiano.* Lima, 1598.

Pizarro, Pedro. 1571. "Relación del descubrimiento y conquista de los reinos del Perú. . . ." *CDIE,* V, 201–388.

Polo de Ondegardo, Juan. 1554. "De los errores y supersticiones de los indios. . . ." In *Colección de libros y documentos referentes a la historia del Perú* 3:3–43. 4 vols. Lima, 1916.

Polo de Ondegardo, Juan. 1561. "Informe . . . al Licenciado Briviesca de Muñatones. . . ." *Revista Histórica* 13 (Lima, 1940), 125–96.

Polo de Ondegardo, Juan. 1562. "Ordenanzas de las minas de Guamanga." In *Colección de libros y documentos referentes a la historia del Perú* 4:139–51. 4 vols. Lima, 1916.

Polo de Ondegardo, Juan. 1571. "Relación de los fundamentos acerca del notable daño que resulta de no guardar a los indios sus fueros," in *Colección de libros y documentos referentes a la historia del Perú* 3:45–188. 4 vols. Lima, 1916.

Poma de Ayala, Felipe Guaman. 1615. *Nueva corónica y buen gobierno.* Paris, 1936.

Relaciones geográficas de Indias — Perú, vols. 1–2. Edited by Marcos Jiménez de la Espada. Reprinted in *Biblioteca de Autores Españoles,* vol. 183. Madrid, 1965. Abbreviated as *RGI.*

Ribera, Pedro de, and Chaves y de Guevara, Antonio de. 1586. "Relación de la ciudad de Guamanga y sus términos." *RGI,* 181–201.

Risco, Marqués del. 1684. "Descripción de la provincia de los Angaraes." *RGI,* 201–4.

Santillán, Fernando de. 1563. "Relacion del origen, descendencia, política y gobierno de los Incas." In *Tres relaciones de antigüedades peruanas* (Asunción del Paraguay, 1950), 33–131.

Tales of Potosi. Edited by R. C. Padden. Providence, 1975.

Tasa de la visita general de Francisco de Toledo (1570–1575). Edited by Noble David Cook. Lima, 1975.

"Tecnología indígena: el obraje de Cacamarca." Edited by Carlos A. Romero. *Inca* 1 (1923), 624–50.

Tiruel, Luis de. 1613. "Idolatrías de los indios Huachos y Yauyos," *Revista Histórica* 6 (1918), 180–97.

U.S. Library of Congress (Harkness Collection). *Documents from Early Peru. The Pizarros and the Almagros, 1531–1578,* Edited by Stella R. Clemence. Washington, D.C., 1936.

Vázquez de Espinosa, Antonio. 1629. *Compendio y descripción de las Indias Occidentales.* Edited by Charles Upson Clark. Washington D.C., 1948.

SECONDARY SOURCES

The corpus of secondary literature for the Andean region is huge. I have, by and large, avoided the temptation to expand this list beyond the publications cited in the notes. The few exceptions are additions of particular interest to specialists on early colonial Andean history. Most of the sources listed below refer specifically to the Andean region, but some are studies which were cited in the notes for theoretical or comparative purposes.

Adorno, Rolena. "Las otras fuentes de Guaman Poma: sus lecturas castellanas." *Histórica* 2 (December 1978), 137–58.

Arguedas, José María. "Notas elementales sobre el arte popular religioso y la cultura mestiza de Huamanga." *Churmichasun* 4–5 (Huancayo, June 1977), 3–16.

Arguedas, José María. "Puquio: una cultura en proceso de cambio." In *Estudios sobre la cultura actual en el Perú*, 221–72. Edited by Universidad Nacional Mayor de San Marcos. Lima, 1964.

Arguedas, José María. *Yawar Fiesta*. Lima, 1940.

Armas Medina, Fernando de. *Cristianización del Perú (1532–1600)*. Seville, 1953.

Assadourian, Carlos Sempat. "Integración y desintegración regional en el espacio colonial: un enfoque histórico." *EURE. Revista Latinoamericana de Estudios Urbanos Regionales* 4 (1972), 11–23.

Assadourian, Carlos Sempat. "La producción de la mercancía dinero en la formación del mercado interno colonial." In *Ensayos sobre el desarrollo de México y América Latina*, 223–92. Edited by Enrique Florescano. Mexico, 1979.

Assadourian, Carlos Sempat, et al. *Minería y espacio económico en los andes. Siglos XVI–XX*. Lima, 1980.

Bard, Patricia J. "Domingo de Santo Tomás, a Spanish friar in 16th Century Peru." M. A. thesis, Columbia University, 1967.

Barnadas, Josep M. *Charcas: orígenes históricos de una sociedad colonial*. La Paz, 1973.

Basadre, Jorge. "El régimen de la mita." In *El virreinato del Perú*, 187–203. Edited by José Manuel Valega. Lima, 1939.

Basto Girón, Luis J. *Las mitas de Huamanga y Huancavelica*. Lima, 1954. Includes document.

Bayle, Constantino. *El protector de indios*. Seville, 1945.

Belaúnde Guinassi, Manuel. *La encomienda en el Perú*. Lima, 1945.

Bennet, Wendell C. "The Andean Highlands: An Introduction." In *Handbook of South American Indians* 2:1–60. Edited by Julian H. Steward. 7 vols. Washington, D.C., 1946–59.

Bohannan, Paul. *Justice and Judgment among the Tiv*. Oxford, 1957.

Bonilla, Heraclio, and Spalding, Karen. "La independencia en el Perú: las palabras y los hechos." In Bonilla et al., *La independencia en el Peru*, 15–64. Lima, 1972.

Bowser, Frederick P. *The African Slave in Colonial Peru, 1524–1650*. Stanford, 1974.

Brading, D. A., and Cross, Harry E. "Colonial Silver Mining: Mexico and Peru." *HAHR* 52 (November 1972), 545–79.

Bronner, Fred. "Peruvian Encomenderos in 1630: Elite Circulation and Consolidation." *HAHR* 57 (November 1977), 633–59.

Burga, Manuel. *De la encomienda a la hacienda capitalista. El valle de Jequetepeque del siglo XVI al XX.* Lima, 1976.

Burkett, Elinor C. "Early Colonial Peru: The Urban Female Experience." Ph.D. diss., Univ. of Pittsburgh, 1975.

Burkett, Elinor C. "Indian Women and White Society: The Case of Sixteenth-Century Peru." In *Latin American Women: Historical Perspectives,* 101–28. Edited by Asunción Lavrin. Westport, Ct., 1978.

Burridge, Kenelm. *New Heaven, New Earth: A Study of Millenarian Activities.* New York, 1969.

Cavero, Luis E. *Monografía de la Provincia de Huanta.* 2 vols. Lima, 1950.

Centro de Colaboración Pedagógica Provincial . . . de Parinacochas. *Monografía de la Provincia de Parinacochas.* 2 vols. Lima, 1950.

Cevallo López, Vilma. "La caja de censos de indios y su aporte a la economía colonial, 1565–1613." *Revista del Archivo Nacional del Perú* 26, entrega II (Lima, 1962), 269–352.

Choy, Emilio. "La realidad y el utopismo en Guamán Poma." *Universidad,* no. 7 (Ayacucho, December 1966), 1–2.

Cobb, Gwendoline Ballantine. "Potosí and Huancavelica: Economic Bases of Peru, 1545 to 1640." Ph.D. diss., Univ. of California, Berkeley, 1947. Also available as *Potosí y Huancavelica: Bases económicas del Perú, 1545—1640.* Translated by Jorge Muñoz Reyes. La Paz, 1977.

Cobb, Gwendoline Ballantine. "Supply and Transportation for the Potosí Mines, 1545–1640." *HAHR* 29 (February 1949), 25–45.

Cohn, Norman. *The Pursuit of the Millennium: Revolutionary Millenarians and Mystical Anarchists of the Middle Ages.* 3rd ed. New York, 1970.

Cook, Noble David. "The Indian Population of Peru, 1570–1620." Ph.D. diss., University of Texas, Austin, 1973.

Cornblit, Oscar. "Society and Mass Rebellion in Eighteenth-Century Peru and Bolivia." In *Latin American Affairs.* Edited by Raymond Carr. St. Anthony's Papers, no. 22 (London, 1970), 9–44.

Davies, Keith Arfon. "The Rural Domain of the City of Arequipa, 1540–1645." Ph.D. diss., Univ. of Connecticut, 1974.

Díaz Martínez, Antonio. *Ayacucho: hambre y esperanza.* Ayacucho, 1969.

Dobb, Maurice. *Studies in the Development of Capitalism.* Rev. ed. New York, 1963.

Dobyns, Henry F. "An Outline of Andean Epidemic History to 1720." *Bulletin of the History of Medicine* 37 (1963), 493–515.

Duviols, Pierre. *La lutte contre les religions autochtones dans le Pérou colonial: "L'extirpation de l'idolatrie" entre 1532 et 1660.* Lima and Paris, 1971.

Earls, John. "La organización del poder en la mitología quechua." In Ossio, ed., *Ideología mesiánica,* 393–414.

Earls, John, and Silverblatt, Irene. "Ayllus y etnías de la región Pampas-Qaracho. El impacto del imperio incaico." Paper delivered at the III Congreso Peruano del Hombre y la Cultura Andina, Lima, 1977.

Escobedo, Ronald. *El tributo indígena en el Perú (siglos XVI-XVII).* Pamplona, 1979.

Espinoza Soriano, Waldemar. "El alcalde mayor indígena en el virreinato del Perú." *Anuario de Estudios Americanos* 17 (1960), 183-300.

Espinoza Soriano, Waldemar. "La coca de los mitmas cayampis en el reino de Ancara. Siglo XVI." *Anales científicos de la Universidad Nacional del Centro del Perú* 2 (Huancayo, 1973), 7-67.

Espinoza Soriano, Waldemar. *La destrucción del imperio de los Incas*. Lima, 1973.

Evans-Pritchard, E. E. *Witchcraft, Oracles and Magic among the Azande*. Oxford, 1937.

Fanon, Frantz. *A Dying Colonialism*. Translated by Haakon Chevalier. New York, 1965.

Fanon, Frantz. *Black Skin, White Masks*. Translated by Charles Lam Markmann. New York, 1967.

Fanon, Frantz. *The Wretched of the Earth*. Translated by Constance Farrington. New York, 1968.

Favre, Henri. "Evolución y situación de la hacienda tradicional de la región de Huancavelica." In *Hacienda, comunidad y campesinado en el Perú*, 105-38. Edited by José Matos Mar. 2nd ed., Lima, 1976.

Fitzgerald, Frances. *Fire in the Lake: The Vietnamese and the Americans in Vietnam*. New York: Vintage Books ed., 1973.

Fortes, Meyer. *Oedipus and Job in West African Religion*. Cambridge, 1959. Reprinted in *The Anthropology of Folk Religion*. Edited by Charles Leslie. New York, 1960.

Galdo Gutiérrez, Virgilio. *Educación de los curacas: una forma de dominación colonial*. Ayacucho, 1970.

Geertz, Clifford. *The Interpretation of Cultures*. New York, 1973.

Genovese, Eugene D. *Roll, Jordan, Roll: The World the Slaves Made*. New York, 1974.

Genovese, Eugene D. *The World the Slaveholders Made*. New York: Vintage Books ed., 1971.

Godelier, Maurice. *Economía, fetichismo y religión en las sociedades primitivas*. Madrid, 1974.

Godelier, Maurice. "Modo de producción asiático y los esquemas marxistas de evolución de las sociedades." In Godelier et al., *Sobre el modo de producción asiático*, 13-67. Barcelona, 1969.

Golte, Jürgen. *La racionalidad de la organización andina*. Lima, 1980.

Góngora, Mario. *El estado en el derecho indiano. Época de fundación (1492-1570)*. Santiago de Chile, 1951.

Gramsci, Antonio. *Selections from the Prison Notebooks*. Edited by Quintin Hoare and Geoffrey Nowell Smith. New York, 1971.

Grieshaber, Erwin P. "Hacienda-Community Relations and Indian Acculturation: An Historiographical Essay." *Latin American Research Review* 14 (1979), 107-28.

Guillén Guillén, Edmundo. "El cronista don Felipe Guaman Poma y los manuscritos hallados en el pueblo de Chiara." *Amaru* 10 (Lima, 1969), 89-92.

Harth-terré, Emilio. *Negros e indios: un estamento social ignorado del Perú colonial*. Lima, 1973.

Hay, Douglas. "Property, Authority and the Criminal Law." In Hay et al., *Albion's Fatal Tree: Crime and Society in Eighteenth-Century England*, 17-63. New York, 1975.

Helmer, Marie. "Notas sobre la encomienda peruana en el siglo XVI." *Revista del Instituto de Historia del Derecho* 10 (Buenos Aires, 1959), 124-43.

Hemming, John. *The Conquest of the Incas*. New York, 1970.

Hobsbawm, E. J. *Primitive Rebels: Studies in Archaic Forms of Social Movements in the 19th and 20th Centuries.* New York, 1965.

Hobsbawm, E. J. "The Crisis of the Seventeenth Century." In *Crisis in Europe, 1560–1660,* 5–62. Edited by Trevor Aston. New York, 1967.

Horton, R. "African Traditional Thought and Western Science." *Africa* 37 (1967), 50–71 and 155–87.

Huertas Vallejos, Lorenzo. "Historia de las luchas sociales de Ayacucho, 1700–1940." Unpub. ms., 1974.

Huertas Vallejos, Lorenzo. "Prólogo" (to "Revisita de la Doctrina de Santa María Magdalena . . . de Huamanga"). *Revista del Archivo Departamental de Ayacucho* 1 (Ayacucho, 1977), 52–56.

Isbell, Billie Jean. "Parentesco andino y reciprocidad." In *Reciprocidad e intercambio en los andes peruanos,* 110–52. Edited by Giorgio Alberti and Enrique Mayer. Lima, 1974.

Isbell, Billie Jean. *To Defend Ourselves: Ecology and Ritual in an Andean Village.* Austin, 1978.

Jara, Alvaro. *Los asientos de trabajo y la provisión de mano de obra para los no-encomenderos en la ciudad de Santiago, 1586–1600.* Santiago de Chile, 1959.

Keith, Robert G. *Conquest and Agrarian Change: The Emergence of the Hacienda System on the Peruvian Coast.* Cambridge, Mass., 1976.

Kubler, George. *Mexican Architecture of the Sixteenth Century.* 2 vols. New Haven, 1948.

Kubler, George. "The Neo-Inca State (1537–1572)." *HAHR* 27 (May, 1947), 189–203.

Kubler, George. "The Quechua in the Colonial World." In *Handbook of South American Indians* 2:331–410. Edited by Julian H. Steward. 7 vols. Washington, D.C., 1946–59.

Kula, Witold. *Teoría económica del sistema feudal.* Translated by Estanislow J. Zembrzuski. Mexico, 1974.

Larson, Brooke. "Caciques, Class Structure and the Colonial State in Bolivia." *Nova Americana* 2 (Turin, 1979), 197–235.

Leach, E. R. *Political Systems of Highland Burma.* Boston: Beacon ed., 1965.

Lévi-Strauss, Claude. *The Savage Mind.* Chicago, 1966.

Lockhart, James. "Encomienda and Hacienda: the Evolution of the Great Estate in the Spanish Indies." *HAHR* 49 (August 1969), 411–29.

Lockhart, James. *Spanish Peru, 1532–1560. A Colonial Society.* Madison, 1968.

Lockhart, James. *The Men of Cajamarca: A Social and Biographical Study of the First Conquerors of Peru.* Austin, 1972.

Lohmann Villena, Guillermo. *El corregidor de indios en el Perú bajo los Austrias.* Madrid, 1957.

Lohmann Villena, Guillermo. "El Inga Titu Cussi Yupangui y su entrevista con el oidor Matienzo, 1565." *Mercurio Peruano* 23, no. 167 (1941), 3–18.

Lohmann Villena, Guillermo. "Juan de Matienzo, autor del 'Gobierno del Perú' (su personalidad y su obra)." *Anuario de Estudios Americanos* 22 (Seville, 1965), 767–886.

Lohmann Villena, Guillermo. *Las minas de Huancavelica en los siglos XVI y XVII.* Seville, 1949.

López Albújar, Enrique. *Cuentos andinos.* Lima, 1920.

Lumbreras, Luis Guillermo. *Las fundaciones de Huamanga. Hacia un prehistoria de Ayacucho.* Lima, 1974.

Macera, Pablo. *Mapas coloniales de haciendas cuzqueñas.* Lima, 1968.

Macera, Pablo. *Trabajos de historia.* 4 vols. Lima, 1977.

Málaga Medina, Alejandro. "Las reducciones en el Perú (1532-1600)." *Historia y Cultura* 8 (1974), 141-72.

Mannoni, O. *Prospero and Caliban: The Psychology of Colonization.* Translated by Pamela Powesland. 2nd ed. New York, 1964.

Martín, Luis, and Pettus, Jo Ann Geurin. *Scholars and Schools in Colonial Peru.* Dallas, 1973.

Marx, Karl. *Capital.* Edited by Frederick Engels. 3 vols. New York: New World Paperbacks ed., 1967.

Marx, Karl. *Pre-Capitalist Economic Formations.* Translated by Jack Cohen. Edited by E. J. Hobsbawm. New York, 1965.

Mayer, Enrique. "Las reglas de juego en la reciprocidad andina." In *Reciprocidad e intercambio en los andes peruanos,* 45-62. Edited by Giorgio Alberti and Enrique Mayer. Lima, 1974.

McAlister, Lyle N. "Social Structure and Social Change in New Spain." *HAHR* 43 (August 1963), 349-70.

Medina, Pío Max. *Monumentos coloniales de Huamanga (Ayacucho).* Ayacucho, 1942.

Mellafe, Rolando. *Breve historia de la esclavitud en América Latina.* Mexico, 1973.

Mellafe, Rolando. "Evolución del salario en el virreinato peruano." *Ibero-Americana Pragensia* 1 (Prague, 1967), 91-107.

Mellafe, Rolando. "Frontera agraria: el caso del virreinato peruano en el siglo XVI." In *Tierras nuevas,* 11-42. Edited by Alvaro Jara. Guanajuato, 1969.

Memmi, Albert. *The Colonizer and the Colonized.* Translated by Howard Greenfeld. Boston, 1965.

Millones S. G., Luis. "Introducción al estudio de las idolatrías." *Aportes* 4 (Paris, April 1967), 47-82.

Millones, S. G., Luis. "Nuevos aspectos del Taki Onqoy." In Ossio, ed., *Ideología mesiánica,* 95-101. Lima, 1973.

Millones S. G., Luis. "Un movimiento nativista del siglo XVI: el Taki Onqoy." In Ossio, ed., *Ideología mesiánica,* 83-94.

Miranda, José. *El tributo indígena en la Nueva España durante el siglo XVI.* Mexico, 1952.

Moore, John Preston. *The Cabildo in Peru under the Hapsburgs.* Durham, N.C., 1954.

Moore, Sally Falk. *Power and Property in Inca Peru.* New York, 1958.

Murra, John V. "Aymara Lords and their European Agents at Potosí," *Nova Americana* 1 (Turin, 1978), 231-43.

Murra, John V. "Cloth and Its Functions in the Inca State." *American Anthropologist* 64 (August 1962), 710-28. Also available in Murra, *Formaciones,* 145-70.

Murra, John V. *Formaciones económicas y políticas del mundo andino.* Lima, 1975.

Murra, John V. "La guerre et les rébellions dans l'expansion de l'état inka." *Annales. Économies, Sociétés, Civilisations* 33 (September-December 1978), 927-35.

Murra, John V. "The Conquest and Annexation of Qollasuyu by the Inka State." Paper delivered at the Fortieth Annual Meeting of the Society for American Archaeology, Dallas, May 1975.

Murra, John V. "The Economic Organization of the Inca State." Ph. D. diss., University of Chicago, 1956. Also available as *La organización económica del estado Inca.* Mexico, 1978.

Olivas Escudero, Fidel. *Apuntes para la historia de Huamanga ó Ayacucho.* Ayacucho, 1924.

Ortiz Rescaniere, Alejandro. *De Adaneva a Inkarrí.* Lima, 1973.

Ossio A., Juan M., ed. *Ideología mesiánica del mundo andino.* Lima, 1973.

Pease G. Y., Franklin. *Del Tawantinsuyu a la historia del Perú.* Lima, 1978.

Pease G. Y., Franklin. *El dios creador andino.* Lima, 1973.

Pereira de Queiroz, María Isaura. *Historia y etnología de los movimientos mesiánicos.* Translated by Florentino M. Torner. Mexico, 1969.

Phelan, John Leddy. *The Kingdom of Quito in the Seventeenth Century: Bureaucratic Politics in the Spanish Empire.* Madison, 1967.

Phelan, John Leddy. *The People and the King: The Comunero Revolution in Colombia, 1781.* Madison, 1978.

Platt, Tristan. "Acerca del sistema tributario pre-Toledano en el Alto Perú." *Avances* 1 (February 1978), 33–46.

Platt, Tristan. "Symétries en miroir. Le concept de *yanantin* chez les Macha de Bolivie." *Annales. Économies, Sociétés, Civilisations* 33 (September–December 1978), 1081–1107.

Polo y la Borda G., Jorge. *La hacienda Pachachaca: autobastecimiento y comercialización (segunda mitad del siglo XVIII).* Lima, 1976.

Pozo, Manuel J. *Historia de Huamanga (época colonial).* Ayacucho, 1924.

Price, Richard, ed. *Maroon Societies: Rebel Slave Communities in the Americas.* Garden City, N.Y., 1973.

Pulgar Vidal, Javier. *Las ocho regiones naturales del Perú.* Lima, 1946.

Purizaga Vega, Medardo. *El estado regional en Ayacucho (período intermedio tardío, 1200–1470).* Huancayo, 1972.

Radcliffe-Brown, A. R. *Structure and Function in Primitive Society.* New York: Free Press ed., 1965.

Rivera Palomino, Jaime. *Geografía general de Ayacucho.* Ayacucho, 1971.

Rostworowski de Diez Canseco, María. *Curacas y sucesiones, costa norte.* Lima, 1961.

Rostworowski de Diez Canseco, María. *Etnía y sociedad: costa peruana prehispánica.* Lima, 1977.

Rostworowski de Diez Canseco, María. "Succession, Coöption to Kingship, and Royal Incest among the Inca." *Southwestern Journal of Anthropology* 16 (Winter 1960), 417–27.

Rowe, John H. "El movimiento nacional inca del siglo XVIII." *Revista universitaria* 43 (Cuzco, 1954), 17–47.

Rowe, John H. "Inca Culture at the Time of the Spanish Conquest." In *Handbook of South American Indians,* 2:183–330. Edited by Julian H. Steward. 7 vols. Washington, D.C., 1946–59.

Rowe, John H. "The Incas Under Spanish Colonial Institutions." *HAHR* 37 (May, 1957), 155–99.

Ruiz Fowler, José R. *Monografía histórico-geográfico del Departamento de Ayacucho.* Lima, 1924.

Salas de Coloma, Miriam. *De los obrajes de Canaria y Chincheros a las comunidades indígenas de Vilcashuamán. Siglo XVI.* Lima, 1979.

Salomon, Frank. "Don Pedro de Zambiza, un varáyuj del siglo XVI." *Cuadernos de Historia y Arqueología* 42 (Guayaquil, 1975 [1980]), 285-315.

Sánchez-Albornoz, Nicolás. *Indios y tributos en el Alto Perú.* Lima, 1978.

Schwartz, Stuart B. "Magistracy and Society in Colonial Brazil." *HAHR* 50 (November 1970), 715-30.

Scott, James C. *The Moral Economy of the Peasant: Rebellion and Subsistence in Southeast Asia.* New Haven, 1976.

Shea, Daniel E. "A Defense of Small Population Estimates for the Central Andes in 1520." In *The Native Population of the Americas in 1492,* 157-80. Edited by William M. Denevan. Madison, 1976.

Shepperson, George. "The Comparative Study of Millennial Movements." In *Millennial Dreams in Action: Studies in Revolutionary Religious Movements,* 44-52. Edited by Sylvia Thrupp. New York, 1970.

Silva Santisteban, Fernando. *Los obrajes en el Virreinato del Perú.* Lima, 1964.

Silverblatt, Irene. "Andean Women in the Inca Empire." *Feminist Studies* 4, No. 3 (1978), 37-59.

Silverblatt, Irene. "Andean Women Under Spanish Rule." In *Women and Colonization: Anthropological Perspectives,* 149-85. Edited by Mona Etienne and Eleanor Leacock. New York, 1980.

Smith, C. T. "Despoblación de los andes centrales en el siglo XVI." *Revista del Museo Nacional* 35 (1967-68), 77-91.

Spalding, Karen. *De indio a campesino: cambios en la estructura social del Perú colonial.* Lima, 1974.

Spalding, Karen. "Indian Rural Society in Colonial Peru: The Example of Huarochirí." Ph.D. diss., Univ. of California, Berkeley, 1967.

Spalding, Karen. "*Kurakas* and Commerce: A Chapter in the Evolution of Andean Society." *HAHR* 53 (November 1973), 581-99. Also available in Spalding, *De indio a campesino,* 31-60.

Spalding, Karen. "Social Climbers: Changing Patterns of Mobility among the Indians of Colonial Peru." *HAHR* 50 (November 1970), 645-64. Also available in Spalding, *De indio a campesino,* 61-87.

Stern, Steve J. "Las ideologías nativistas, la aculturación y las clases sociales." *Churmichasun* 4-5 (Huancayo, June 1977), 25-32.

Stern, Steve J. "Nuevos aspectos sobre la mano de obra indígena: el caso de los 'asientos' de Huamanga, 1570-1640." *Revista del Archivo Departamental de Ayacucho* 1 (1977), 26-37.

Taylor, William B. *Drinking, Homicide and Rebellion in Colonial Mexican Villages.* Stanford, 1979.

Thompson, E. P. "The Crime of Anonymity." In Douglas Hay et al., *Albion's Fatal Tree: Crime and Society in Eighteenth-Century England,* 255-308. New York, 1975.

Thrupp, Sylvia. "Millennial Dreams in Action." In *Millennial Dreams in Action: Studies in Revolutionary Religious Movements,* 11-27. Edited by Thrupp. New York, 1970.

Torero, Alfredo. *El quechua y la historia social andina.* Lima, 1974.

Torres Saldamando, Enrique. 1879–80. *Apuntes históricos sobre las encomiendas en el Perú*. Lima, 1967.

Troll, Carl. *Structure Soils, Solifluction, and Frost Climates of the Earth*. Wilmette, Ill., 1958.

Turner, Victor. *The Forest of Symbols: Aspects of Ndembu Ritual*. Ithaca, 1967.

Vargas, José María. *Fray Domingo de Santo Tomás, defensor y apóstol de los indios del Perú: su vida y escritos*. Quito, 1937.

Vargas Ugarte, Rubén. *Historia de la iglesia en el Perú*. 5 vols. Lima and Buenos Aires, 1953–62.

Vargas Ugarte, Rubén. *Historia general de Perú*. 10 vols. Lima, 1966–71.

Villarán, Manuel Vicente. *Apuntes sobre la realidad social de los indígenas ante las leyes de Indias*. Lima, 1964.

Wachtel, Nathan. "Rebeliones y milenarismo." In Ossio, ed., *Ideología mesiánica*, 103–42.

Wachtel, Nathan. *La vision des vaincus: les indiens du Pérou devant la conquête espagnole*. Paris, 1971.

Wachtel, Nathan. *Sociedad e ideología: ensayos de historia y antropología andinas*. Lima, 1973.

Wallace, Anthony F. C. "Revitalization Movements." *American Anthropologist* 58 (April 1956), 264–81.

Wallace, Anthony F. C. *The Death and Rebirth of the Seneca*. New York, 1969.

Whitaker, Arthur Preston. *The Huancavelica Mercury Mine. A Contribution to the History of the Bourbon Renaissance in the Spanish Empire*. Cambridge, 1941.

Worsley, Peter. *The Trumpet Shall Sound: A Study of 'Cargo' Cults in Melanesia*. 2nd ed. New York, 1968.

Wrigley, E. A. *Population and History*. New York, 1969.

Zimmerman, Arthur F. *Francisco de Toledo, Fifth Viceroy of Peru, 1569–1581*. Caldwell, Idaho, 1938.

Zuidema, R. T. "Algunos problemas etnohistóricos del Departamento de Ayacucho." *Wamani* 1 (Ayacucho, 1966), 68–75.

Zuidema, R. T. "Observaciones sobre el Taki Onqoy." *Historia y Cultura* 1 (Lima, 1965), 137.

Zuidema, R. T. *The Ceque System of Cuzco*. Leiden, 1964.

Index

JACKET DESIGNED BY IRA NEWMAN
COMPOSED BY METRICOMP, GRUNDY CENTER, IOWA
MANUFACTURED BY MALLOY LITHOGRAPHING, INC.,
ANN ARBOR, MICHIGAN
TEXT AND DISPLAY LINES ARE SET IN BASKERVILLE

Library of Congress Cataloging in Publication Data
Stern, Steve J., 1951–
Peru's Indian peoples and the challenge of
Spanish conquest.
Bibliography: pp. 265–282
Includes index.
1. Indians of South America—Peru—Ayacucho
(Dept.)—History. 2. Indians of South America—
Peru—Ayacucho (Dept.)—Economic conditions.
3. Ayacucho (Peru : Dept.)—History. 4. Ayacucho
(Peru : Dept.)—Economic conditions. I. Title.
F3429.1.A9S75   985'.29200498   81-70017
ISBN 0-299-08900-2   AACR2